Developmental Education for Young Children

International Perspectives on Early Childhood Education and Development

Volume 7

Series Editors

Professor Marilyn Fleer, *Monash University, Australia*
Professor Ingrid Pramling-Samuelsson, *Gothenburg University, Sweden*

Editorial Board

Early childhood education in many countries has been built upon a strong tradition of a materially rich and active play-based pedagogy and environment. Yet what has become visible within the profession, is essentially a Western view of childhood preschool education and school education.

It is timely that a series of books be published which present a broader view of early childhood education. This series, seeks to provide an international perspective on early childhood education. In particular, the books published in this series will:

- Examine how learning is organized across a range of cultures, particularly Indigenous communities
- Make visible a range of ways in which early childhood pedagogy is framed and enacted across countries, including the majority poor countries
- Critique how particular forms of knowledge are constructed in curriculum within and across countries
- Explore policy imperatives which shape and have shaped how early childhood education is enacted across countries
- Examine how early childhood education is researched locally and globally
- Examine the theoretical informants driving pedagogy and practice, and seek to find alternative perspectives from those that dominate many Western heritage countries
- Critique assessment practices and consider a broader set of ways of measuring children's learning
- Examine concept formation from within the context of country-specific pedagogy and learning outcomes

The series will cover theoretical works, evidence-based pedagogical research, and international research studies. The series will also cover a broad range of countries, including poor majority countries. Classical areas of interest, such as play, the images of childhood, and family studies will also be examined. However the focus will be critical and international (not Western-centric).

Bert van Oers
Editor

Developmental Education for Young Children

Concept, Practice and Implementation

 Springer

Editor
Dr. Bert van Oers
Department of Theory and Research
 in Education
VU University
Van der Boechorststraat 1
Amsterdam
Netherlands

ISBN 978-94-007-4616-9   ISBN 978-94-007-4617-6 (eBook)
DOI 10.1007/978-94-007-4617-6
Springer Dordrecht Heidelberg New York London

Library of Congress Control Number: 2012940733

Printed on acid-free paper

Springer is part of Springer Science+Business Media (www.springer.com)

Preface

Like many other countries all over the world, the Dutch government struggles to maintain high quality in Dutch schools. However, policy makers often do not shine in their educational imagination and seem to believe that direct instruction and norm-referenced standardised measurements of learning outcomes will finally provide the solution to the problem of achieving academic excellence in all pupils. Apparently they seem to hope that this will subsequently guarantee a good position in the international competitions of the knowledge economy.

In the past decades, however, a number of educators have been deeply worried about this exclusively economy-based approach to the education of the upcoming generation. Of course, they agreed that it is important that schools contribute to the formation of well-informed citizens, but they also saw that much more is required (at the level of loyalty to the community, fairness, personal sense, creativity, moral position, democratic attitude, etc.) to face the future problems of our world community and our planet. Schools also have duties in fostering what Hannah Arendt has called *amor mundi*. It is this critical "love for the world" that enables future generations to live their lives as morally and intellectually responsible citizens, and to see life – using Vygotskij's words – as an essentially creative endeavour.

In the Netherlands, a small community of educationalists addressed the problem described above as an essentially *pedagogical problem* and as an issue of meaningful learning. From a Vygotskian perspective they developed both theory and examples of good practice for promoting cultural learning in play contexts within the school. This resulted in an approach embodied in an evolving play-based curriculum for the primary school. A large number of highly engaged teachers, teacher trainers, curriculum innovators, and academics succeeded in turning this ideal into an effective interdisciplinary collaboration for the realisation of innovated classroom practices. Our presentations of this approach and its outcomes for young children, both at international conferences and in journals, sparked much interest among many colleagues, especially with respect to how we implement this approach in the context of everyday classrooms. This interest led to the conception of this book *Developmental Education for Young Children*. We are grateful to the series editor Marilyn Fleer who encouraged us to embark on this ambitious enterprise. We hope that this book can satisfy for the moment the interest that has been expressed in the approach, even though it remains one that is ever-evolving.

Composing and editing a book like this, with the collaboration of so many over-committed people, is no small thing. The engagement of everybody to contribute and make time for this project is in itself a sign of the deep personal engagement of the members of this interdisciplinary community. For the fact that the book could finally be published I must thank all contributors and especially two persons who have patiently and effectively supported me in the final stage of the project: Frea Janssen-Vos and the publisher's agent Astrid Noordermeer.

Amsterdam   Bert van Oers

Acknowledgements

Pictures in the book were taken by:
Anneke Hoogenberg: 4.7a, b; 4.8a, b
Ester van Oers: 4.6a, b
Hanneke Verkley: 4.1.a–e; 4.3, 4.4, 4.5a, b; 4.9a, b
Lieke Roof: 9.1, 9.2, 9.3
All photographers have given their written permission for publication.
All photographed persons have given their consent for publication.

Contents

List of Figures

Figures/Photos 4.1a-e; 4.3, 4.4, 4.5a, b; 4.9a, b are made by
         Photography Hanneke Verkleij
Figure/Photo 4.6a, b are made by Ester van Oers
Figures/Photos 4.7a, b; 4.8a, b are from Anneke Hoogenberg

Pictures in this chapter were taken by the author.

List of Tables

About the Contributors

Renata Adan-Dirks (M.Sc. in Education), has taught at various Dutch primary schools in the area of Amsterdam and is currently a pre-kindergarten teacher at Amsterdam International Community School (www.aics.eu).

Hans Bakker (M.Sc. in Education), teacher and teacher trainer, Christian University of Professional Studies, Ede (CHE), the Netherlands. Faculty of Education (Teacher Training College). Additionally teacher/tutor in the Master training "Educational Leadership" and the Master training "Education and Innovation".

Dorian de Haan (Ph.D.), professor in Developmental Education, Inholland University of Applied Sciences, Haarlem, Faculty of Learning, Education and Philosophy of Life. Assistant Professor in Developmental Psychology, Utrecht University.

Lorien de Koning (M.Sc. in Education), works as an educational developer and teacher trainer at "De Activiteit," National Centre for Developmental Education. Additionally, she also works as a primary school teacher.

Niko Fijma (M.Sc. in Education), educated as a primary school teacher and educationalist. Currently, teacher trainer and managing director of "De Activiteit," National Centre for Developmental Education (Alkmaar). Expert in early childhood education, particularly mathematics in primary school.

Frea Janssen-Vos started as a kindergarten teacher. After studying educational theory she dedicated her work to improving curricula and practice in early childhood education in several institutes. Since 1990 she and her project group in the APS (Dutch institute for educational innovation) are broadly acknowledged as the founders of the approach *Basisontwikkeling*, based on the cultural-historical activity theory.

Barbara Nellesteijn (M.Sc. in Education), editor-in-chief of *Zone*, a journal for Developmental Education, De Activiteit, Alkmaar, The Netherlands.

Isabel Peters (M.Sc. in Education), Researcher, "De Activiteit Alkmaar.".

Mariëlle Poland (Ph.D.), educational and pedagogical consultancy, Wieringerwerf, the Netherlands. Main function is coaching of high-sensitive children and their parents/teachers, in educational institutions and at home.

Bea Pompert (M.Sc. in Education), educated as a primary school teacher and educationalist. Currently, teacher trainer and managing director of "De Activiteit," (Alkmaar). Chair of the "Academie voor Ontwikkelingsgericht Onderwijs" (the Dutch association for Developmental Education). Expert in early childhood education, literacy, and language in primary school. For many years she has been involved in the nation-wide implementation of Developmental Education through a joint activity of teachers, trainers, and researchers in the direction of sustainably transformed classrooms.

Lieke Roof (M.Sc. in Education), teacher at the primary school "De Groote Wielen" in Rosmalen, The Netherlands.

Chiel van der Veen (M.Sc. in Education), lecturer and Ph.D. candidate in the Department of Theory and Research in Education, VU University, Amsterdam. Teacher trainer at "De Activiteit.".

Bert van Oers (Ph.D.), professor in VU University, Amsterdam, Faculty of Psychology and Education, Department Theory and Research in Education.

Ester van Oers (M.Sc. in Education), teacher coach at the primary school "De Archipel" in Amsterdam and member of the editorial board of *Zone*, a journal for Developmental Education.

Willem Wardekker (Ph.D.), professor of Quality of Education (retired), Windesheim University of Professional Studies, Zwolle, Netherlands, and assistant professor of Education, VU University, Amsterdam, Netherlands.

André Weijers, primary school teacher. Currently working as educational developer and teacher trainer at "De Activiteit," National Centre for Developmental Education. He also works as teacher trainer at "Bureau Inzet," an organisation for starting teachers.

About the Editor

Bert van Oers (1951) is professor in *Cultural-Historical Theory of Education* at the Department of Theory and Research in Education in the Faculty of Psychology and Education of the VU University Amsterdam. He was trained as a psychologist, specialising in the theory of learning and developmental psychology at Utrecht University in the Netherlands. Since the mid-1970s he has been engaged with Vygotskij's cultural-historical theory and defended his dissertation "Activity and Concept" (in Dutch) in 1987 at the VU University Amsterdam. In the 1980s, he focused his research activities on early childhood education from a Vygotskian point of view and contributed to the elaboration of the concept *Ontwikkelingsgericht Onderwijs* ("Developmental Education"). In conjunction with many teachers, curriculum innovators, teacher trainers, and academics he collaborated in the nation-wide implementation of Developmental Education in the Netherlands. For his work on early childhood education he received an honorary doctorate from the University of Jyväskylä in Finland.

His research interests are in play as a context for learning in the primary school (all grades), concentrating particularly on the development of mathematical thinking, literacy, and aesthetic thinking. Some of his English book publications are: *The transformation of learning. Advances in cultural-historical activity theory* (co-edited with Wardekker, Elbers and van der Veer; Cambridge University Press, 2008), *Narratives of childhood* (Amsterdam: VU Press, 2003), and *Symbolizing, Modeling and Tool Use in Mathematics Education* (co-edited work: Gravemeijer, Lehrer, van Oers, and Verschaffel; Dordrecht: Kluwer, 2003). He is a member of several editorial boards of journals on early childhood education. See: www.bertvanoers.nl.

Chapter 1
Introduction

Bert van Oers

This book describes an approach for the education of 3–8 year-old children in primary school, which was developed in the Netherlands on the basis of Vygot-skij's[1] cultural-historical theory of human development. The purpose of the book is to clarify the views and concepts underlying this approach, to present illustrative practices, and to explain the strategies for the implementation of the approach in the lower grades of Dutch primary school classrooms (grades 1 through 4). Given the theoretical tenets of the approach and the strongly theory-driven applications and implementation strategies, it doesn't seem unreasonable to assume that most of the understandings described here may be applicable under appropriate circumstances beyond the borders of the Netherlands.

In Dutch the approach is named *Ontwikkelingsgericht Onderwijs*, which can be literally translated as "development-oriented schooling". In order to avoid cumbersome terminology, in international communications the approach is usually called *Developmental Education*. However, both in Dutch and in English, this term

---

[1] A note on the transliteration of Russian names must be given. Although we have striven to be consistent in the transliteration of Russian names into the Roman alphabet, some inconsistency is unavoidable due to the worldwide mixture of different transliteration systems in use, and the necessary acknowledgement of current customs in the spelling of frequently used names. Basically, this book will employ the United Nations system UN87 as a method of transliteration which does more justice to the actual spelling of the Russian names than the current American transliteration customs. As a result, some names may appear in different form than the ones the reader may be familiar with (like for example Vygotskij vs. Vygotsky, Lurija vs. Luria; Bachtin vs. Bakhtin etc.). In cases of renowned publications (like for example Vygotsky 1978) we did not, however, change the spelling of the names. Care has been taken to avoid ambiguity.

B. van Oers, Ph.D. (✉)
Department Theory and Research in Education, Faculty of Psychology and Education,
VU University Amsterdam, Amsterdam, The Netherlands
e-mail: bert.van.oers@vu.nl

B. van Oers (ed.), *Developmental Education for Young Children*, International
Perspectives on Early Childhood Education and Development 7,
DOI 10.1007/978-94-007-4617-6_1,
© Springer Science+Business Media Dordrecht 2012

1

has turned out to be ambiguous and maybe even misleading. Therefore, a brief note on its historical background and a preliminary explanation of the intended meaning of the term may be in order.

A Historical Note

The first steps in the elaboration of the concept of "Developmental Education" (DE) date back to the 1980s in the Netherlands, when two different groups of people started thinking, relatively independently from one another, about innovations of school learning and teaching which go beyond the deterministic, cognitivist solutions that had become popular during that period (based on the works of Thorndike, Ausubel, Gagné, Reigeluth, Taba, for example). Some educationalists by this time had serious doubts about the deterministic assumptions with respect to the regulation of human learning and development, and emphasised the importance of acknowledging cultural impact on the developmental process of children. In their view, the course of human development is an open process that depends to some extent on cultural (pedagogical) choices in the ways a society tries to promote the development of its members. Grave misgivings emerged regarding the then current conception of educational theory as a kind of applied psychology. Although detailed theories about alternatives were not yet available, people were looking for ways to conceive of a more *pedagogically oriented educational approach* that could account both for the modern psychological understandings of learning and development, and at the same time do justice to the individuality of the pupils and to the normative and critical choices educators make in their goal-oriented interactions with the pupils.

One of the centres involved in this endeavour to find a new approach to education, schooling and development was the department of educational psychology of Utrecht University. Two scholars from this department, Carel van Parreren and Jacques Carpay, became deeply involved in the study of cultural-historical theory. In 1972 they published a monograph, called "Sovjetpsychologen aan het woord" (Soviet psychologists speaking), that introduced Vygotskij's cultural-historical theory into the discussions of Dutch education. In those days students in this department were trained as educational psychologists, socialised in cultural-historical thinking about learning, development, and schooling. The editor of this book was one of them.

In the late 1970s Carpay and van Oers moved to the Vrije Universiteit (VU University) in Amsterdam, where Wim Wardekker (with a background in pedagogy) came to join them in the early 1980s. A number of significant developments took place during these years (1980s–1990s). First, as a research group we were deeply involved in discussions about the characteristics and possibilities of the school that intended to promote human development deliberately, and aimed to contribute to the formation of critical agency and emancipation of developing pupils. We called this type of education "Developmental Education". This approach was often articulated by contrasting it with "*Following* Education" which suggested in a

Piagetian sense that schooling should follow behind development (see Vygotsky 1978, p. 80). Examples of such education can also be found in progressive movement schools that adjusted pedagogical interactions strictly to the natural developmental rhythm of the child, like Montessori-schools, or Fröbel-schools (see Chap. 3 on Progressive Education). Secondly, in the wake of these discussions on Developmental Education, we also started working on problems of implementation of cultural-historical theory in real classroom practices (see for example Roegholt et al. 1998).

In the 1980s, some members of the group began to address problems in the early grades of primary education (4–8 year-olds). There were several reasons for this. In our research with older pupils we saw that our ambitions to create an emancipatory and development-promoting education could only be realised when we were able to influence children's development from an early age.

The re-orientation on younger children was further stimulated by political discussions about Dutch schools. In the mid 1980s significant political decisions were made in the Netherlands with regard to the institutional education of 4 and 5 year-olds. In 1985 these children were integrated into the regular primary school system and many people were deeply concerned that this would lead to a programme-based form of direct teaching for these young children. We thought this trend could be countered with the help of Vygotskij's ideas about play as a leading activity for young children.

In this same period, another group in the Netherlands was also concerned with the innovation of educational practices in early years classrooms. Since the early 1980s Frea Janssen-Vos and her colleagues (including Bea Pompert) at an educational institute (APS) in Utrecht had been working on the innovation of early childhood education practices. Her engagement with early childhood practices drew from different theoretical sources (like social pedagogy, experiential learning). She developed a strategy that could be used by teachers in classrooms to organise rich and stimulating interactions with young children. This approach acknowledged both the *children's own experiences*, the *adults' responsibilities* in their work with young children, and the importance of a *broad conception of developmental goals* that go beyond narrow cognitive achievements. Janssen-Vos deliberately didn't want her approach to be seen as a fixed curriculum that imposes rigid structures and tasks upon young children. She passionately argued for an approach to early childhood education that would aim to stimulate children's development through rich and meaningful interactions between children and adults in the context of children's play. Her approach was called *Basisontwikkeling* (translated as: Basic Development) and is still known by this name (Janssen-Vos 1990, see also Chap. 4 of this book). In her view "Basic Development" is an educational strategy for working with 4–8 year-old children that aims to lay a broad and firm foundation ("a basis") for children's development as cultural agents.

The refusal to design a strict school curriculum for early childhood education that prescribes teachers' actions on a day-to-day basis had an important consequence: teachers were given substantial responsibility for children's learning and therefore they had to learn themselves how to work with children in this new way. A logical consequence of the approach was that much attention had to be given to the implementation of "Basic Development" into everyday school practices. To support this implementation process, different practice-oriented books have been published since the 1990s, including publications in the domains of literacy and mathematical thinking (Knijpstra et al. 1997; Fijma and Vink 1998).

In the early 1990s the two lines described above crossed and discovered a good deal of similarity in the missions of these academic and practical approaches. In fact, Basic Development could be interpreted as a practical elaboration of the concept of Developmental Education for the early grades of primary school. Several collaborative works have been published since then (van Oers and Janssen-Vos 1992; van Oers et al. 2003). Developmental Education also has been elaborated for preschool children (see Janssen-Vos 2008; Janssen-Vos and Pompert 2001) and is currently being elaborated for the higher grades of primary school as well (see for example van Oers 2009a). A current state of the art, including a description of its nation-wide infrastructure is described in van Oers (2009b).

Implementing Developmental Education

An assumption underpinning the process of implementation of Developmental Education in classroom practices is that it essentially boils down to questions of professionalisation and learning to teach in the type of play-based curriculum outlined in this book. The principles for development-promoting learning that are assumed for pupils are taken to be valid for the learning of teachers as well. The learning of teachers who want to improve their ability to act as agents in Developmental Education practices is also based on assisted forms of participation in these practices, and appropriation of the relevant tools in meaningful ways. In one way, however, the situation of teachers is fundamentally different from that of pupils. Teachers do not just carry out their job of promoting cultural development in pupils and looking for ways to improve that work on a day-to-day basis. For the benefit of the pupils and their developmental potentials, teachers must also think about permanently and critically *improving* their own work conditions so that they can maintain the optimal and ever-changing standards for learning and development. Hence, Developmental Education not only entails the realisation of optimal classroom conditions for developmental learning, but it also requires permanently optimising the conditions that make the whole system an optimal learning context for both pupils and teachers.

A consequence of this conception of the role of teachers is that they need to be seen as classroom researchers as well, examining the classroom processes and looking for ways of improving and testing them. Hence teachers have always played an important role in the construction of the Developmental Education approach. In collaboration with teacher trainers and academic researchers the DE-approach has been built up as a kind of *design research* in which teachers, teacher trainers and researchers have often worked closely together in order to set up practices, make them work, and examine their consequences for both pupils and teachers. At some moments in the whole process academic research often takes a more distanced view (with case-studies, observational studies, ethnographic studies and quasi-experimental studies) in order to gauge the quality of the approach, to collect supporting empirical evidence, and find moments for further critique and innovation. This book is not meant as a scientific justification of the evidence and underlying methodology, but these studies are available for inspection (see for example van Oers 2003, 2009b, 2010a, b, 2012; Poland et al. 2009; Wardekker 2000). Consequently, they will not be further discussed here.

Overview of the Book

In the present book we focus on Developmental Education for young children (4–8 year olds). We will focus on the elaboration of the general approach, and describe a number of selected examples of practical work and some implementation strategies. It must be emphasised, however, that the approach for young children described here is driven by a general theory on education and cannot be appropriately understood without some awareness of broader theoretical and practical issues. Therefore some of the chapters address broader issues that do not specifically refer to young children (see Chaps. 3 and 17), but the ideas presented in these chapters are definitely essential for the understanding and improvement of education for young children.

The general structure of the book reflects three aspects that we consider important for a good understanding of Dutch Developmental Education practices in schools. The first part (Chaps. 2,3, 4) addresses *fundamental conceptual issues* that constitute the theoretical framework underpinning the reasoning in both the elaboration of good practices and their implementation in real classrooms. Part II (Chaps. 5, 6, 7, 8, 9, 10, 11) presents a number of core issues, and describes how they have been leading the development of *good practices*. Although the book is not meant as a presentation of the underlying research and attempts at verification, some of the chapters in this section do refer to research in order to sketch some of the empirical evidence that supported the ongoing construction of the described practical issues. No deep methodological justification is given, however, as this would require another type of discourse that goes beyond the intentions of this book, which basically focuses on Developmental Education practices and how they are implemented in everyday classrooms. The *implementation problems and strategies* are described in Part III (Chaps. 12, 13, 14, 15, 16, 17).

All of the chapters look at Developmental Education and its implementation in real classroom practices from a coherent theoretical point of view. Chapters 3 and 4 will elaborate the general approach in greater detail. Chapter 3 analyses the important notion of responsible teaching and demonstrates how Developmental Education attempts to realise responsible teaching in the classroom, what it requires from teachers with regard to their view of development and aims of development.

Building pupils' and teachers' identity as responsible citizens turns out to be a major aim of Developmental Education. This includes the education of the youngest pupils in school.

Chapter 4 concentrates on the general picture of Developmental Education for young children from the perspective of classroom practice. This practical approach is called Basic Development. Focusing on the early years classrooms, the authors point out how the broad development of pupils can be accomplished through getting children meaningfully involved in playfully formatted cultural practices and encouraging them to use cultural tools of literacy, mathematics, construction etc., for the improvement of their abilities to participate in real-life cultural practices. The chapter also describes a number of tools that teachers need for promoting and assessing broad development in pupils.

After this general introduction of basic concepts, a number of good practices of the Developmental Education early years curriculum will be described in Part II. Each of Chaps. 5, 6, 7, 8, 9, 10, 11 starts out from a short Vygotskian interpretation of a specific element of the Developmental Education curriculum. Chapter 5 focuses on ways to stimulate the communicative development of young children, following the reasoning of Vygotskij combined with a functional linguistic approach (like Halliday's). Communicative development is basically a process of learning how to *mean* and as such it is basic to all processes of cultural learning across the curriculum. The chapter reveals some of the roles that teachers must learn to play in cooperation with pupils in order to support their development in communicative activities. All chapters of the book in some way acknowledge the communicative dimensions in cultural learning processes. The differences between the various areas of the curriculum depend on the differences in objects and perspectives of communication. Examples of these can be found in Chaps. 8 and 9, where it is demonstrated that both abstract and aesthetic thinking depend on taking specific points of view of the world and communicating about these with different tools and rules that are taken as valid in distinct practices and communities.

It goes without saying that teaching in Developmental Education classrooms is a goal-directed process and that it also requires careful sensitive assessment. Assessment is a core issue in Developmental Education, and Chaps. 6 and 7 give examples of how this is conceived in the domains of vocabulary development and narrative competence. Both examples of assessment are elaborations of Vygotskij's approach to assessment rooted in his view of the zone of proximal development. These chapters give illustrations of *dynamic assessment* that focuses on what children can learn rather than on what they have learned. The chapters serve as descriptions of alternatives for standardised testing that tend to underestimate children's real developmental potentials in a certain area.

It is important for teachers in Developmental Education to be able to fine-tune the help they give, and their interactions with, children. As a result, each child is considered a special child, and this is basically the starting point for the interactions with children who seem to have problems with learning in everyday classroom environments, both those who are generally called "special needs children", as well as highly gifted children. Chapter 10 provides lively descriptions of how

Developmental Education teachers cope with differences among children, in order to stimulate the development of all children and at the same time to maintain inclusiveness, keeping all children together as a group (including the children-at-risk). This chapter nicely demonstrates how Developmental Education truly is a *caring* curriculum, not just by applying a general ethical rule of providing help, but by acting out a deep engagement with individual needs, rooted in a sense of responsibility to guide each child towards the perfection of its personal version of cultural identity.

Fine-tuning is also an important quality of teachers' interactions with parents. Chapter 11 addresses the idea of educative partnership between parents and teachers for the benefit of children. Developmental Education schools take a very specific position towards the role of parents in the educational process. Parents are seen as partners in education, and teachers carefully try to get them engaged in a process of mutual border-crossing where parents and teachers take part (really or virtually) in each others' daily educational practices.

Part III of the book concentrates on questions of how Developmental Education should be implemented in real classroom practices, what it demands of teachers, and of the coaches who assist teachers in this innovation process. The Developmental Education movement in the Netherlands is associated with a broad network of schools, teachers, teacher trainers, educational innovators, and researchers, which brings together and distributes the expertise that has been gathered over more than two decades. With particular regard to the implementation process of Developmental Education in schools and classrooms, teachers' learning has been an area of growing understanding. On the basis of many experiences with schools that wanted to innovate their teaching along the lines of Developmental Education, it has become clear that the initial stage of the process is very important and requires serious attention in order to make a start that fits in with the school's and teachers' needs (see Chap. 12). After the initial stage it is important to continue coaching the teachers in their classrooms, and to set up collaborative teaching activities. Chapter 13 demonstrates that this enterprise often requires a fundamental innovation of teachers' basic educational assumptions, which often go beyond mere cosmetic practical adjustments. The chapter points out how this can be accomplished, especially how teachers can learn to view children's play in a new way, participate in children's play and give impulses to children's learning through embedded teaching without disturbing the play format of these activities. As described above, a key instrument in Developmental Education is the assessment (evaluation, registration, and planning) of children's learning. Chapter 14 reveals in great detail what this entails, and how teachers can appropriate the evaluation strategy of Developmental Education.

Due to the play-based and caring nature of the Developmental Education curriculum, beginning teachers (but parents and inspectors too) sometimes doubt whether pupils will indeed master enough of the basics of cultural learning goals. Chapters 15 and 16 demonstrate how learning to read and learning to mathematise can successfully take place in a play-based curriculum without making concessions to the acquired contents, and to the level and quality of learning achievements.

Both examples elegantly show the heart of cultural learning on a Vygotskian basis. In both areas (literacy and mathematics) children are invited to take part in well-known cultural practices and experience new emerging needs for cultural tools that may enhance their abilities to participate. The chapters demonstrate how this can be managed in heterogeneous classrooms by assisting pupils to improve their communicative activities (see also Chap. 5) in the areas of literacy and numbers.

One of the things we have learned over the years is that implementation of Developmental Education in a school may vary from one school to the next. Most of the time, the character of the implementation depends to a great extent on the institutionalised conditions for innovation that are constituted in these schools. Chapter 17 discusses a number of conditions that have turned out to be important for successful broad implementation of Developmental Education in classrooms. It is important that a school conceives of itself as a learning organisation that keeps encouraging teachers, coaches and principals to strive for ongoing professional development and create a culture for critical learning in the school that permanently optimises the social situation of development of pupils and teachers, and gives pupils a firm basis for participation and critical learning in the context of cultural practices. This is essentially what we mean by Developmental Education as responsible teaching, and although it is not explicitly elucidated in Chap. 17 for young children, it is valid for teachers of young children as well.

This book is an attempt to demonstrate how these principles can be elaborated for different domains of the child's cultural life in the context of education in (pre) school settings, and to demonstrate how this works out for the implementation process and the professionalisation of teachers.

The book ends with a brief concluding reflection on the core ideas and potentials of Developmental Education for the present and for the future (Chap. 18).

References

Fijma, N., & Vink, H. (1998). *Op jou kan ik rekenen* [I can count on you]. Assen: van Gorcum.

Janssen-Vos, F. (1990). *Basisontwikkeling* [Basic Development]. Assen: van Gorcum.

Janssen-Vos, F. (1997). *Basisontwikkeling in de onderbouw* [Basic Development in the early grades of primary school]. Assen: van Gorcum.

Janssen-Vos, F. (2008). *Basisontwikkeling voor peuters en kleuters* [Basic Development for preschool and early grades]. Assen: van Gorcum.

Janssen-Vos, F., & Pompert, B. (2001). *Startblokken van Basisontwikkeling* [Starting Blocks of Basic Development]. Assen: van Gorcum.

Knijpstra, H., Pompert, B., & Schiferli, T. (1997). *Met jou kan ik lezen en schrijven* [With you I can read and write]. Assen: van Gorcum.

Poland, M., van Oers, B., & Terwel, J. (2009). Schematising activities in early childhood education. *Educational Research and Evaluation, 15*(3), 305–321.

Roegholt, S., Wardekker, W., & van Oers, B. (1998). Teachers and pluralistic education. *Journal of Curriculum Studies, 30*(2), 125–141.

van Oers, B. (2003). Learning resources in the context of play. Promoting effective learning in early childhood. *European Early Childhood Education Journal, 11*(1), 7–26.

van Oers, B. (2009a). *Ontwikkelingsgericht werken in de bovenbouw van de basisschool. Een theoretische verkenning met het oog op de praktijk* [Working in the upper grades of primary school according to the Developmental Education approach]. Alkmaar: De Activiteit.

van Oers, B. (2009b). Developmental education: Improving participation in cultural practices. In M. Fleer, M. Hedegaard, & J. Tudge (Eds.), *Childhood studies and the impact of globalisation: Policies and practices at global and local levels – World yearbook of education 2009* (pp. 293–317). New York: Routledge.

van Oers, B. (2010a). The emergence of mathematical thinking in the context of play. *Educational Studies in Mathematics, 74*(1), 23–37. doi:10.1007/s10649-009-9225-x.

van Oers, B. (2010b). Implementing a play-based curriculum in primary school: An attempt at sustainable innovation. In A. Tuna & J. Hayden (Eds.), *Early childhood programs as the doorway to social cohesion. Application of Vygotsky's ideas from an East-West perspective* (pp. 145–158). Cambridge: Cambridge Scholars Publishing.

van Oers, B., & Duijkers, D. (2012). Teaching in a play-based curriculum: Theory, practice and evidence of developmental education for young children. *Journal of Curriculum Studies, 44*(1), 1–24.

van Oers, B., & Janssen-Vos, F. (Eds.). (1992). *Visies op onderwijs aan jonge kinderen.* [Visions on early childhood education]. Assen: van Gorcum.

van Oers, B., Janssen-Vos, F., Pompert, B., & Schiferli, T. (2003). Teaching as a joint activity. In B. van Oers (Ed.), *Narratives of childhood. Theoretical and practical explorations for the innovation of early childhood education* (pp. 110–126). Amsterdam: VU University Press.

Vygotsky, L. S. (1978). *Mind in society. The development of higher psychological processes.* Cambridge: Harvard University Press.

Wardekker, W. L. (2000). Criteria for the quality of inquiry. *Mind, Culture and Activity, 7*(4), 259–272.

Part I
Developmental Education: Core Issues

Chapter 2
Developmental Education: Foundations of a Play-Based Curriculum

Bert van Oers

A Vygotskian Approach to Cultural Development

In the past decades many people (teachers, innovators, academics) in the Netherlands have been involved in elaborating an approach to the education of primary school children on the basis of Vygotskij's cultural-historical theory of human development and learning. In Dutch the approach was named *Ontwikkelingsgericht Onderwijs*. In international discussions this approach came to be called "Developmental Education". The mission of the approach was the development of a theoretically well-grounded practice for the education of (young) children that would be inherently pedagogical, that is to say an approach that aims to deliberately promote the cultural development of children, acknowledging the responsibilities and normative choices that educators have to make (and want to make) in helping children to become autonomous and critical agents in society.

In recent years we have noticed, however, that both the Dutch and English names for the approach have been used by several others in ways that do not cover the Vygotskian intention that was initially invested in the Developmental Education approach. Obviously, most modern approaches to schooling will claim that they are oriented to children's development, and that they stimulate this development in appropriate ways. We must bear in mind, however, that some of these approaches start out from a theoretical point of view that conceives of schooling as a process of cultural transmission on the basis of fixed and scientifically approved methods (curricula), imposing culture upon pupils; others reason from a strictly child-centred position, claiming that schooling must take into account the inherent psychological characteristics of individual children's development and organise the teaching

B. van Oers, Ph.D. (✉)
Department Theory and Research in Education, Faculty of Psychology and Education,
VU University Amsterdam, Amsterdam, The Netherlands
e-mail: bert.van.oers@vu.nl

B. van Oers (ed.), *Developmental Education for Young Children*, International
Perspectives on Early Childhood Education and Development 7,
DOI 10.1007/978-94-007-4617-6_2,

process accordingly. This latter approach is sometimes called "developmentally appropriate education" or "adaptive education". These approaches are often close to a type of *following* education, which were actually rejected by Vygotskij as a type of teaching that does not foster children's full potential (see Vygotsky 1978). Both the transmission and the following approaches seem premised on the image of the individual child with characteristic personal potentials that should be taken into account for the realisation of appropriate education. However, Developmental Education, as we conceive it following Vygotskij, is based on an image of the child as an inherently socio-cultural being whose agency and developmental potentials depend essentially on the interaction between inherited bioneurological character- istics, acquired psychological personal qualities, and on the quality of the child's environment (including socio-cultural interactions). A child's potentials depend to a great extent on the expectations of its educators and the quality of the interactive support it receives (or has received in the past). Therefore, Developmental Education is committed to *innovating* children's social-cultural development that goes beyond the child's personal imaginations, capacities, or wishes. Of course, Developmental Education takes account of the child's actual levels of achievement, but it also intentionally seeks to expand the child's repertoire of participation in cultural practices by permanently and deliberately constructing new zones of proximal development in interaction with the children.

One distinctive subtlety must be mentioned here. Developmental Education should not be identified with Davydov's educational approach of "developmental teaching". Although both approaches share the same theoretical framework, they are different in their answers to the question of how developmental trajectories of pupils should be organised. In Davydov's view the course of school learning ("curriculum") is dominated by *cultural contents* and a conception of a (dialectically organised) *structure* of subject matter, starting out from a so-called "germ cell" that leads systematically to new steps in the pupils' appropriation of subject matter (see for example Davydov 1972, 1986). In contrast, Developmental Education, as envisioned in the present book, does not pre-organise developmental trajectories of pupils on the basis of subject matter structures, but builds developmental trajectories on *a collaborative process of structuring* current activities, based on negotiations between teacher and pupils. In these negotiations the educator's pedagogical responsibilities (including the provision of cultural tools), the personal queries of the pupils, and the resulting need for new cultural tools for the solution of their (communicative) problems are brought together. Davydov has been rather reluctant to acknowledge the pupils' agency as a determining factor in the progress of understanding (see Carpay and van Oers 1993), but he finally shifted to a position that accepted the importance of discursive learning in which pupils play a significant role in order to achieve personalisation in pupils' understanding (see for example Davydov 1996, pp. 226–228). Nevertheless, he sticks to his starting point that gives prevalence to cultural contents as represented by experts in a logical order in the organisation of developmental trajectories, thus limiting the pupils' contributions to co-structuring this process. In brief, we can summarise the different positions as follows: Davydov's concept of developmental teaching proposes to organise developmental trajectories on the basis of *cultural meanings* that should be given personal sense in the teaching/learning process, while Developmental Education articulates *personal sense* as a starting point for collaborative structuring of current cultural activities that should be further enriched with cultural meanings in the interactive process between pupils and teachers.

Our view of Developmental Education essentially emphasises education as a critical and collaborative process, in which cultural values, personal values and responsibility are combined in the interactions with (young) pupils in order to help them become autonomous agents in a wide range of cultural practices. In the next sections of this chapter the Vygotskian conceptual framework underpinning this ambition will be outlined by focusing on some core concepts that back up Developmental Education and its implementation in the classroom.

The Relationship Between Learning and Development

From the Vygotskian perspective, a mutual (dialectical) relationship between learning and development is assumed (Vygotsky 1978, chapter 6). Vygotskij summarises his point of view as follows:

> *Learning is not development; however, properly organised learning results in mental development and sets in motion a variety of developmental processes that would be impossible apart from learning. Thus, learning is a necessary and universal aspect of the process of developing culturally organised, specifically human, psychological functions* (Vygotsky 1978, p. 90).

A number of conclusions can be drawn from this statement. First of all, for Vygotskij human development is synonymous with cultural development and – consequently – dependent on interactions with other cultural beings who can instigate and assist the processes of learning required for cultural development. Therefore, in the same chapter Vygotskij also writes:

> *Human learning presupposes a specific social nature and a process by which children grow into the intellectual life of those around them* (p. 88).

Without exaggeration this can be seen as one of the fundamental insights of Vygotskij, and he sometimes formulates it even more prominently as the general genetic law of cultural development:

> *Every psychological function in the child appears twice, on two planes: first on the social and later on the psychological plane, that is to say: first as a function between people (as an interpsychological category), later as a function within the child (as a psychological category)* (Vygotskij 1983, p. 145).

It is obvious that human learning for Vygotskij is embedded in socio-cultural processes, and to be more precise even *presupposes* a socio-cultural context. In our modern jargon we can interpret these statements as an endorsement of the close relationship between participation in cultural practices and learning. It is evident, however, that learning cannot be interpreted *as* social participation (as some authors today seem to think, referring to Wenger 1998, p. 4). Learning is not identical to social participation, but needs a social environment for its content and course.

Vygotskij was never very specific about his definition of learning. Indirectly we can infer that for Vygotskij learning was an explanation for the fact that people can acquire the ability to use cultural tools independently in future situations. "Learning" refers to the process of building psychological processes and functions with the help of tools that progressively facilitate future actions. This view of learning was developed further by Leont'ev (1975b), Galperin (1969) and Davydov (1972).

New steps in development follow from structural innovations in the cognitive system (consciousness), which emerge as a result of learned actions and sometimes even go beyond these actions themselves. In his study of the historical development of higher psychological functions Vygotskij (1983) points out that by learning an action properly, a person not only acquires the possibility to execute that specific action structure, but also appropriates an activity of structuring reality in a variety of ways that are consistent with the originally learned action. As a result, the person appropriates new action potency that stimulates new needs and interacts in new ways with already available needs and functions. Imagine, as an example, a child who has learned to make his first steps. The child, however, has not only learned to make these steps, but has made a start too on developing the new action potency of walking around, opening up new ways of interacting with the world and exploring its opportunities.

Until now I have only focused on the possible contribution of learning to development. It is important to clarify the reverse relationship as well.

According to El'konin (1972) newly learned actions and needs may rouse tensions with already available actions that can only be solved by new developmental formations that will become manifest as new stages in development (see also Chaiklin 2003). This new stage in development characteristically opens up new ways of relating to reality, new ways of acting, and new ways of learning. An important consequence of this is that learning itself qualitatively changes with new stages in development. Young children's learning is basically different from the learning of older children or adolescents. According to El'konin, young children's learning (2–8 year-olds) is inherently related to their playful relation to the world. For the elaboration of the Developmental Education approach this was also an important starting point, which finally led to the idea of a play-based curriculum.

In a later section I will address some of these issues in greater conceptual detail. First it is necessary to briefly reflect on the aim of development from a cultural-historical point of view.

Aim of Development: Agency in Cultural Practices

Although Vygotskij and his colleagues did not explicitly develop a philosophy of education, formulating general or specific aims of education, inferences about such issues can be made from their works. For Vygotskij (see Vygotsky 1997), education and a theory of development would be impossible without a theory of what he called "social ethics", which could help to decide on the aims of development. From his work on pedagogy and from biographical sketches (for example Vygodskaja and Lifanova 1996; Yaroshevski 1989; Leont'ev 1990) we can infer that Vygotskij saw a broad developmental perspective in his educational theorising. In his view, education should help children to become cultural beings that join in the intellectual, moral, social, aesthetic, expressive and technical areas of cultural heritage. Vygotskij rejected the idea of schooling as an educational technique that transmits only cognitive pieces of knowledge and information. In his view, *living is creating* (Vygotsky 1997, p. 346), and education should help children to take part creatively in social-cultural life and should therefore focus on broadly defined cultural aims, that make personal sense for the children. Fostering creativity is one of the aims of Developmental Education.

In later elaborations of the cultural-historical theory this dimension is picked up as a focus on personality development (see for example Leont'ev 1975a; Petrovskij 1984). Petrovskij took pains to explain that the influence of a community on the development of its members should not be taken as an argument for unification in education. According to Petrovskij, educators should encourage *personalisation* of cultural heritage, meaning that every member of a community should be enabled and allowed to make a personal version of a cultural act. In his later works Leont'ev emphasised the importance of the role of a world view ("obraz mira") in the educational process and particularly pointed out that the role of education was to support the development of a personal world view in children. In fact, he says (Leont'ev 1983a, b), that the basis of humanity is its *moral relationship* to the world. This moral relationship finds its expression in what Leont'ev calls *a deed* ("postupok"). In his deeds the person expresses his convictions, affects, world view, engagement with and understanding of the world. The main goal of education, then, should be to help children develop such a moral relationship to the world and participate in cultural activities as an agent who takes responsibility for his actions in cultural activities.[1]

From the works of cultural-historical scholars, it is possible to summarise the view of the aims of education in modern educational jargon as the development of *agency* in the context of cultural practices. Recent analyses of the notion of agency have revealed that it takes form through critical participation in cultural practices, and that it depends on the values accepted in the community, and on the capacity to recognise and use the support of others (see Edwards and D'Arcy 2004; Holland et al. 1998). Agency manifests itself in critical involvement, sometimes

---

[1] In fact a similar position is taken by Bachtin. For him "postupok" (deed) is an essentially ethical act, an enactment of personalised values. According to him the deed is intrinsically related to "answerability" (i.e. taking responsibility), and is the basic expression of personality (see Bachtin 1986; p. 7–8). Further analysis of the notion of the deed would be interesting, but it is beyond the scope of this chapter.

expressing itself in a person's ability to act self-dependently and reflectively in a cultural practice, to take responsibility for their actions. Sometimes it shows itself in resistance to parts of the practice and in the wish to change some of its basic assumptions (Podd'jakov 2003). Such critical agency is a core issue in the development of responsible citizenship.

Taking "critical agency in cultural practices" as the main aim of Developmental Education implies that we need to ask ourselves how to start this process in early childhood education. Rainio (2010) has studied the development of agency in young children in the context of a play world, and was able to demonstrate that young children can indeed develop such critical positions in a meaningful, shared activity with others, and invent different strategies for maintaining and expressing their identity even in less favourable (oppressive) conditions. She acknowledged that the acceptance of the notion of agency as a goal of education implies that teachers sometimes have to deal with children who resist the educational objectives. She concludes: "The challenge for teachers is how to best mobilise the creativity of pupil resistance without totally giving up curricular goals and developmental needs" (Rainio 2010, p. 120).

One of the assumptions behind the notion of Developmental Education is that teachers can learn to deal with these challenges in their work of promoting agency in pupils. A good understanding of the conceptual basis of Developmental Education practices is an important tool for the teachers' own agency. The next section will present some of the underpinning concepts.

Some Conceptual Tenets of Developmental Education

For the practical application of Vygotskij's cultural-historical theory in classrooms a number of concepts needed further specification. Although the concepts described below in our view remain faithful to the basic mission of Vygotskij's cultural-historical theory, some of the explanations go beyond the texts of Vygotskij and his close colleagues (like Leont'ev and El'konin), due to our increased understandings in the course of implementing and researching the approach.

Social Situation of Development

In his book *Pedagogical Psychology* (1991/1926), Vygotskij is unambiguous about what he sees as a starting point for meaningful learning. In his view the teacher should add quality to the pupils' own actions, and therefore the basis of the learning process should always be in the pupil's own actions. Through interactions with others in the context of social activities the child acquires the cultural tools that are going to mediate his goal-directed actions and give these actions cultural meaning. However, Vygotskij is aware that a person's actual behaviour is always an amalgam of cultural influences and the creative and emotional assimilations of these influences by the person.

In a very important article on the role of the environment for the cultural development of children Vygotskij further specifies the dynamics of the development of a child's activity in his socio-cultural environment by claiming that:

> the environment's role in the development of higher, specifically human characteristics and forms of activity is a source of development, i.e. that it is just this interaction with the environment which becomes the source of these features in children (Vygotsky 1994, p. 351).

For him, an environment is not just a setting for human activity. Referring to interaction with the environment as the *source* of cultural development, Vygotskij basically points out that it is the interpersonal *activity* that should be seen as the context for development. This situated and shared cultural activity influences a child's development in two fundamental ways: first it creates the conditions for the emergence of cultural actions in the child, and, secondly, it presents the ideal (cultural) forms of that practice through the activities of the participating adults, and gives the child an idea of what it is supposed to learn. Or to use Michael Cole's (1996, pp. 183–186) expression: cultural activities bring the future into the child's present.

The dynamic relationship between the child and the cultural practice ("environment") in which he or she is involved, produces a unique and significant circumstance for the child, which is called the child's *social situation development* (Vygotskij 1984, pp. 258–260). This social situation is the basic starting point for a child's cultural development. However, this situation is not a uniform entity, but one that changes with the child's age and with the characteristics of the participants. Hence, this environment can never be defined in purely objective terms, but depends on how the child emotionally relates to the environment, perceives and interprets his/her social situation, and psychologically represents this situation in his mind. In every developmental period, the child's social situation is unique, and dependent on a number of psychological processes (see also Vygotsky 1994, p. 346), which will be connected here to five core concepts of the cultural-historical theory of development that play a pivotal role in the elaboration of the Developmental Education: meaningful learning, leading activity, zone of proximal development, involvement, and play.

Meaningful Learning

From a Vygotskian perspective, meaningful learning is fundamental for learning that aims to promote broad cultural development and agency. However, it is essential to bear in mind that for him learning could only be meaningful when it makes sense for the pupil and actually contributes to his or her potency for action. Meaningful learning in this perspective always and necessarily covers two dimensions: it should be focused on the appropriation of *cultural meanings* ("značenie"), which results in learning outcomes that have exchange value in the community (knowledge, abilities and personal qualities that have societal significance), while it should also be related to the learner's own value system (motives, interests, convictions) and be imbued with *personal meaning* ("smysl"), which adds personal value to the appropriated cultural meanings.

The assignment of personal meanings ("sense") to the process of cultural transactions is essential in cultural-historical thinking about development-promoting learning. Leont'ev (1964, p. 327/1973, p. 242) argued that without sense human action and learning causes alienation, and this blocks the development of responsible agency. Likewise, Menčinskaja (1989/1968) has argued that developmental education essentially acknowledges the subjectivity of the pupils and should take their interests and personal characteristics into account. According to Menčinskaja, the progress of development is regulated at every moment both from within and from without.

This twofold conception of meaningfulness in learning is an essential starting point in Developmental Education. We have to recognise pupils as individual subjects who bring their own voices and histories into the process of participating and learning. However, as Leont'ev (1975b, p. 286) has pointed out, sense cannot be taught by direct instruction, but must be formed in the interaction process between a person and the social environment, on the basis of experiences and valorisation. In our view of Developmental Education, the conditions for the development of sense in the appropriation of cultural meanings are assumed to be warranted by starting from cultural practices that make sense for the pupils and in which the pupils are taken seriously, can participate, want to participate, and build up confidence that they will get help when needed.

Leading Activity

An important tenet of cultural-historical theory is that people's ways of acting (and hence their ways of participating in cultural practices) depend on how they relate to the environment. One of the dimensions that characterise human ontogenesis is related to changes in ways of relating to the environment. In his article on the role of play in development (Vygotskij 1966, 1978) Vygotskij points out that at an early stage of development children relate to their environment in a playful way. He introduced the term "leading activity" to refer to the characteristic way of accomplishing activities depending on this relation to the environment. Leont'ev (1964) picked up this notion and related it to children's developing motives for dealing with reality. El'konin (1972) further elaborated this concept of leading activities and defined it as the specifically motivated ways of acting at certain moments of development. Such activities can promote ("lead") development as they constitute activity contexts that prompt new needs in children which can only be met by appropriating new tools and qualities (see Karpov (2005) for further detailed explanations of this developmental theory).

According to El'konin, the child's relation to the activities in which he is involved alternates between two forms: in some periods the child is focused on the material part of reality and wants to explore, use and know objects and tools; in other periods the child is focused on the social relations in his cultural environment and wants to explore, use, and master the social and moral rules for interacting with other people. The course of human development can be characterised, according to this view, as a permanent alternation of these orientations to the cultural environment. Each period characterised by a specific relation to the cultural environment is called a leading activity.

From this point of view, El'konin describes human ontogenetic development as a process that consists of a series of different leading activities. At the beginning of life, activities are focused on seeking *social contact*, followed in the second year by a period in which the child concentrates on the manipulation of (cultural) objects. This latter period of *manipulative play* is followed by a period of *role-playing* (in 4–7/8 year-olds) which concentrates once more on social relations. After the age of 8 the child becomes focused again on cultural objects and ways of dealing with them. In this period, dominated by *learning activity*, children want to build up their understanding of cultural objects and tools, and acquire conceptual knowledge that helps them to improve their participation in the cultural practices of the community. After the age of 12, new activities continue to concentrate alternately on social relationships or understanding and mastery of cultural objects and tools.

In our elaborations of Developmental Education this conception of development has played a crucial role (see van Oers 2009b, 2010). Following El'konin, we must add two specifications with respect to the early stages of school development (see also van Oers 2012):

1. the leading activity of young children aged between 2 and 8 is *play* (although within this age group the way of playing can be seen to evolve into different forms);
2. the appearance of play as a leading activity during this developmental period is not a natural event, but depends on cultural-historical conditions, specifically the dominating views in a certain culture or cultural period on children's possibilities to participate in cultural activities.

These starting points lay the foundation for the characterisation of Developmental Education as a play-based approach to school learning in the early years (3–8 year-olds).

Zone of Proximal Development

The zone of proximal development is generally seen as the core concept of Vygotskij's view of development-promoting learning. As Vygotskij (see Vygotsky 1978, p. 89) pointed out, learning that promotes development should be ahead of the children's actual level of performance. Hence, the educator should deliberately introduce new tools and ways of acting into children's activities and help them to appropriate these. Unfortunately, however, the most quoted definition of the zone of proximal development refers exclusively to the *discrepancy between what the child can do independently and what he can do with appropriate help from adults or more knowledgeable peers* (Vygotsky 1978, p. 86). Actually, this is a dangerous definition as it opens the way for all kinds of learning that can be triggered in the child, including training and direct instruction, *regardless of the sense this learning has for the child* itself. The problem with this definition is that it misrepresents Vygotskij's idea about developmental learning which – as we have seen – necessarily needs to make sense for the child as well. For Vygotskij, the zone of proximal development is intrinsically related to imitation (see Vygotskij 1982, p. 250), and *imitative participation in cultural practices* (van Oers 2009a, 2010). This means that the promotion of children's development should take place within the context of cultural practices in which the child wants to participate (given its orientation to reality), can participate (given its actual level of development and its personal interpretation of that practice), and in which it learns new actions with the help of others, in accordance with the emerging needs of that child in the current cultural practice. Within the imitative participation in cultural practices, zones of proximal development can be constructed in the interaction between child and adult which become valuable contexts for developmental learning, when the child gets appropriate help.

Involvement

As we have seen, an important dimension of the social situation of development is the emotional relationship an actor establishes with a particular situation (cultural activity). It refers to the extent to which a person feels deeply involved in (and not alienated from) the activity he is taking part in. That means that he or she feels accepted in the activity and plays his or her part in a personally meaningful way. Vygotskij referred to this emotional involvement in the situation as *pereživanie*. "Pereživanie" is not easy to translate into an English equivalent. It refers to intensely experiencing an activity when one is immersed in that activity. As such it refers to a condition of authentic and emotional involvement. This involvement (pereživanie) is, according to Vygotskij, essential for building up a meaningful and functional social situation for cultural development. Explaining the concept in terms of activity-theory, we can say that this involvement manifests itself when an actor is taking *a role* in an activity he feels emotionally related to, a role which is supported by a personal imagination of what it means to act out this role.

Interestingly, this same notion of pereživanie is used by a contemporary of Vygotskij, the world famous stage director Stanislavskij (see for example Stanislavsky 1989). Stanislavskij's use of the concept "pereživanie" may be helpful here in understanding the relevance of this concept for education. In his approach to mastering a role for a stage play, he tries to avoid mechanical enactments of a role.

Instead, he encourages the player to profoundly live "into" the role so that the part can be played as momentarily *being* (and not just pretending to be) the character that figures in the scene. In terms of the previously introduced terminology we can rephrase this last sentence as "avoiding alienation and promoting genuine agency".

Involvement is also taken as an essential element of Developmental Education. It is only through such involvement in cultural practices that actors can learn to become agents in that activity, i.e. become engaged in learning processes that potentially promote broad development. Teachers in Developmental Education schools involve children in cultural practices that make sense to them and encourage children from an early age to take a role in cultural practices and act out this role ("imitating it") in a personal way.

Play

Drawing together the different concepts elaborated above towards a concept of activity-based learning in early childhood, I have come to a new conception of play, which rejects the idea of play as a distinct phenomenon *sui generis*, apart from other types of human enterprises like work or learning. Instead, I have argued in several places (see for example van Oers 2009a, b, 2010, 2012) that play basically refers to the way an activity is carried out, i.e. to the *format of cultural activities* (practices). Formats of activity can be characterised by the values of three parameters: the type of *rules* that constitute the activity, the level of *involvement*, and the *degrees of freedom* that the cultural community allows to the player.

Characterising Developmental Education as an approach that advocates a play-based curriculum, means that learning is embedded in meaningful practices (practices that make both cultural and personal sense) that follow a play format, in which:

1. the cultural status of the activity, especially the rules that constitute it, are taken seriously and are maintained, if necessary through educational support systems ("help") that facilitate the enactment of the activity without simplifying it;
2. the pupils and the teacher take up roles that make sense to them and that they may enact voluntarily (to an extent that is culturally, ethically, and systematically permitted), with authentic involvement, and in personally meaningful ways;
3. the teacher encourages the pupils to develop their ability to participate in that practice as self-dependent, critical, and responsible agents by deliberately stimulating pupils to appropriate the tools and rules that go with the impersonated role. In this process pupils have some degrees of freedom to explore and experiment with the tools and meanings.

Permanent monitoring of this process and taking advantage of meaningful teaching opportunities in the context of play are fundamental professional abilities of teachers in a play-based curriculum.

An important and distinctive characteristic of this approach must be briefly emphasised here. In this view, a play-based curriculum is *not* just a curriculum that allows children to play at some moments (in addition to learning and work). In the play-based curriculum of Developmental Education playfulness is an essential characteristic of all children's activities, and opportunities for teaching may be embedded in these activities at moments that make sense for the pupils. A play-based curriculum is not to be conceived as a curriculum that allows children to play now and then, but as a curriculum that basically takes playfully formatted cultural activities as contexts for learning.

References

Bachtin, M. M. (1986). Iskusstvo i otvetstvennost' [Art and answerability]. In M. M. Bachtin (Ed.), *Estetika slovesnogo tvorčestva*. Moscow: Iskusstvo.

Carpay, J. A. M., & van Oers, B. (1993). Didaktičeskie modeli i problema obučajuščej diskussii [Didactical models and the problem of instructional conversations]. *Voprosy Psichologii, 4*, 20–26.

Chaiklin, S. (2003). The zone of proximal development in Vygotsky's theory of learning and school instruction. In A. Kozulin, B. Gindis, V. S. Ageyev, & S. M. Miller (Eds.), *Vygotsky's educational theory in cultural context* (pp. 39–64). Cambridge: Cambridge University Press.

Cole, M. (1996). *Cultural psychology. A once and future discipline*. Cambridge: Belknap/Harvard.

Davydov, V. V. (1972). *Vidy obobščennie v obučenii* [Types of generalisation in education]. Moscow: Pedagogika.

Davydov, V. V. (1986). *Problemy razvivajuščego obučenija: Opyt teoretičeskogo i eksperimental'nogo issledovanija* [Problems of developmental teaching: Outcomes of theoretical and experimental research]. Moscow: Pedagogika.

Davydov, V. V. (1996). *Teorija razvivajuščego obučenija* [Theory of developmental teaching]. Moscow: Intor.

Edwards, A., & D'Arcy, C. (2004). Relational agency and disposition in sociocultural accounts of learning to teach. *Educational Review, 56*(2), 147–156.

El'konin, D. B. (1972). Toward the problem of stages in the mental development of the child. *Soviet Psychology, 10*(3), 225–251.

Galperin, P. Ja. (1969). Stages in the development of mental acts. In M. Cole & I. Maltzman (Eds.), *A handbook of contemporary Soviet psychology* (pp. 249–273). London: Basic Books.

Holland, D., Lachicotte, W., Skinner, D., & Cain, C. (1998). *Identity and agency in cultural worlds*. Cambridge, MA: Harvard University Press.

Karpov, Y. Y. (2005). *The neo-Vygotskian approach to child development*. Cambridge: Cambridge University Press.

Leont'ev, A. N. (1964/1973). *Problemy razvitija psichiki* [Problems of the psychological development]. Moscow: Isd-vo Moskovskogo Universiteta. Translated in German as: Probleme der Entwicklung des psychischen. Berlin: Fischer, 1973.

Leont'ev, A. N. (1975a). *Dejatel'nost', soznanie, ličnost'* [Activity, consciousness, personality]. Moscow: Politisdat.

Leont'ev, A. N. (1975b). Psichologičeskie voprosy soznatel'nosti učenija [Psychological problems of conscious learning]. In: A. N. Leont'ev (Ed.), *Dejatel'nost', soznanie, ličnost'. Priloženie* [Appendix to: Activity, consciousness, personality]. Moscow: Politisdat.

Leont'ev, A. N. (1983a). Obraz mira [Image of the world]. In A. N. Leont'ev (Ed.), *Isbrannye psichologičeskie proisvedenija, T. II* (pp. 251–261). Moscow: Pedagogika.

Leont'ev, A. N. (1983b). Načalo ličnosti – postupok [The basis of personality: The deed]. In A. N. Leont'ev (Ed.), *Isbrannye psichologičeskie proizvedenija, T. I* (pp. 381–385). Moscow: Pedagogika.

Leont'ev, A. A. (1990). *L.S. Vygotskij.* Moscow: Proveščenie.

Menčinskaja, N. A. (1989). Psichologičeskie voprosy razvivajuščego obučenija i novye programmy [Psychological problems of developmental education and the new programmes]. In N. A. Menčinskaja (Ed.), *Problemy učenija i umstvennogo razvitija škol'nika* (pp. 32–43). Moscow: Pedagogika (Originally published in Sovetskaja Pedagogika, 1968, 21–39).

Petrovskij, A. V. (1984). Formirovanie psichologičeskoj teorii kollektiva i ličnosti [The construction of a psychological theory of the collective and personality]. In A. V. Petrovskij (Ed.), *Voprosy istorii i teorii psichologii. Isbrannye trudy. Čast' 2* [Historical and theoretical problems of psychology, part 2] (pp. 139–258). Moscow: Pedagogika.

Podd'jakov, A. N. (2003). Obraz mira i voprosy soznatel'nosti učenija: sovremennij kontekst [World view and the problems of conscious learning: The modern context]. *Voprosy psichologii, 2,* 122–132.

Rainio, A. P. (2010). *Lionhearts of the playworld. An ethnographic study of the development of agency in play pedagogy.* Doctoral dissertation, Helsinki University, Helsinki.

Stanislavsky, K. (1989). *An actor prepares.* New York: Routledge.

van Oers, B. (2009a). *Ontwikkelingsgericht werken in de bovenbouw van de basisschool. Een theoretische verkenning met het oog op de praktijk* [Working in the upper grades of primary school according to the Developmental Education approach]. Alkmaar: De Activiteit.

van Oers, B. (2009b). Developmental education: Improving participation in cultural practices. In M. Fleer, M. Hedegaard, & J. Tudge (Eds.), *Childhood studies and the impact of globalisation: Policies and practices at global and local levels – World yearbook of education 2009* (pp. 293–317). New York: Routledge.

van Oers, B. (2010). Children's Enculturation through play. In L. Brooker & S. Edwards (Eds.), *Engaging play* (pp. 195–209). Maidenhead: McGraw Hill.

van Oers, B. (2012). Culture in play. In J. Valsiner (Ed.), *The Oxford handbook of culture and psychology.* New York: Oxford University Press.

Vygodskaja, G. L., & Lifanova, T. M. (1996). *Lev Semënovič Vygotskij. Žisn', dejatel'nost', štrichi k portretu* [Lev Semënovič Vygotskij. Leven, activiteit, biographical sketch]. Moscow: Smysl.

Vygotskij, L. S. (1966). Igra i eë rol' v psichičeskom razvitii rebënka. *Voprosy psichologii, 6,* 62–76. (Translated as The role of play in development. In: L. S. Vygotsky, Mind in society (pp. 92–104). Cambridge: Harvard University Press).

Vygotskij, L. S. (1982). Myšlenie i reč [Thinking and speech]. In L. S. Vygotskij (Ed.), *Sobranie sočinenij* (Vol. II, pp. 5–361). Moscow: Pedagogika.

Vygotskij, L. S. (1983). Istorija razvitija vysšich psichičeskich funkcij [The history of the development of higher psychological functions]. In L. S. Vygotskij (Ed.), *Sobranie sočinenij. III* (pp. 6–328). Moscow: Pedagogika.

Vygotskij, L. S. (1984). Problema vozrasta [The problem of age]. In L. S. Vygotskij (Ed.), *Sobranye sočinenij, Tom IV* (pp. 244–268). Moscow: Pedagogika (L. S. Vygotsky, Trans., *Collected Works*, Vol. 5, chapter 6. Ney York: Plenum).

Vygotskij, L. S. (1991/1926). *Pedagogičeskaja Psichologija* [Pedagogical Psychology]. Moscow: Pedagogika. (L. S. Vygotsky, Trans., *Educational psychology.* Boca Raton: St. Lucie Press, 1997).

Vygotsky, L. S. (1978). *Mind in society. The development of higher psychological processes.* Cambridge: Harvard University Press.

Vygotsky, L. S. (1994). The problem of the environment. In R. van der Veer & J. Valsiner (Eds.), *The Vygotsky reader* (pp. 338–354). Oxford: Blackwell.

Vygotsky, L. S. (1997). *Educational psychology.* Boca Raton: St Lucie Press. (Translation of Vygotskij (1991/1926)).

Wenger, E. (1998). *Communities of practice. Learning, meaning and identity.* Cambridge: Cambridge University Press.

Yaroshevski, M. (1989). *Lev Vygotsky.* Moscow: Progress.

Chapter 3
Responsible Teaching

Willem Wardekker

Introduction

Teachers have a responsibility for the learning and for the well-being of the pupils entrusted to them. But to whom, exactly, are they responsible – to parents, to the inspectorate and other authorities, to society in general, to the pupils themselves? And for what, exactly, are they responsible – for high test scores, for happy pupils, for the continuation and development of society, or for all of these, and then with what priorities? Opinions differ, even when sometimes the same words are used. What, for instance, does it mean when a teacher says she is intent on "getting everything out of a pupil that is in him"? Does she interpret "everything" solely as high SAT scores, or aim at multi-faceted development? Does she have fixed ideas of what is "in" that pupil, or does she see his possibilities of development as flexible and at least partially dependent on the way she establishes a relationship with him? Yes, opinions differ, but they do not differ randomly. Views of what teachers' responsibility entails are related to views of how children develop, what learning is and how it is related to development, and of what the aims of education are and how teaching and learning can reach those aims. In fact, Developmental Education as we understand it rests on specific choices from the available alternative answers to these questions, and in those choices it differs from other ideas about education, leading to a different view of what responsible teaching is. In this chapter, I will compare some of these choices with those made in other more or less popular traditions in educational thinking, and inquire into the consequences for the topic of responsible teaching of the choices made by Developmental Education. Specifically, as this book is about education for young children, the comparison will be with other rather popular views

W. Wardekker, Ph.D. (✉)
Department of Education, VU University, Amsterdam, The Netherlands
e-mail: w.l.wardekker@vu.nl

B. van Oers (ed.), *Developmental Education for Young Children*, International
Perspectives on Early Childhood Education and Development 7,
DOI 10.1007/978-94-007-4617-6_3,
© Springer Science+Business Media Dordrecht 2012

of primary and pre-primary education. I will confine myself to two of these: the urge toward "effective education" which is now reaching the early years scene, and a generalised concept of "progressive education", in which admittedly Developmental Education has found inspiration for some of its practical ideas about teaching.

Effective Education

There is a strong tendency at the moment, much favoured by politics, to emphasise the cost-effectiveness of education. No doubt, this is related to the current economic problems in the Western world, but also to the rising number of pupils with different languages and different background cultures. This tendency implies that schools should not devote much time to matters that are considered of secondary importance, like play, social competence, or the emotional well-being of pupils. Instead, for primary education, language and arithmetic skills are considered of primary importance, sometimes next to the induction of "shared values" of the community.

Although maybe not all of its proponents are aware of this, the idea of effective education is in many ways a return to the "academic" variant of the traditional transmission paradigm of education. This variant rests on the presupposition that people ideally act in rational ways, guided by the best knowledge available, so that they are able to make the best possible action choices. In this context, "rational" is to be understood in a technical sense, as "goal oriented rationality" in the schema of Habermas (1968). In other words, education should provide people with certainties that their rational actions will result in the desired effects, so that, at least in the technical sense, one will know what to do in as many situations as possible. Therefore, it is important to make as much valid knowledge available for pupils as possible. Also, education should induce people to act rationally, that is, not to act on intuition, on superstition or false beliefs, or on unchecked desires. In that sense, education has an emancipatory function: it enables people to act in more effective ways, so that on the one hand society is rationalised, and on the other hand, educated people are at an advantage over the uneducated – their possibilities for agency are improved.

This interpretation of the main aim of education rests on a specific view of what knowledge is and how it functions in human acting. Knowledge can be seen as a "mirror of the world"; ideally, it is an objective description of how the world really is, a description independent of the knowing person. It can be "possessed" in the sense that one can "have" knowledge of some aspect of the world. For that to be true, the knowledge a person "has" must be exactly the same as that which is held in some store of knowledge that is independent of that, or any, person – that is, in what Karl Popper once described as the "third world" of knowledge. A person acting on that knowledge can be relatively sure that the intended results will be reached. Relatively sure, because the knowledge in question may not be an ideal mirror of reality (knowledge is fallible) and the situation in which that person acts may be more complicated, or more opaque, than the actor realises. Of course, the more knowledge that actor has, the less is the danger of not understanding the situation correctly. And it is important that the sciences keep perfecting the available mirrors (which largely explains the structure of the curriculum in secondary schools: it is derived from the structure of scientific disciplines). The implication is that "the world" can be understood as largely deterministic in nature: it is to a large extent predictable on the basis of our knowledge of causal relationships.

From this it follows that the first task of education, and thus the first responsibility of the teacher, is to equip pupils with as much relevant knowledge as possible. And this implies starting at an early age, preferably with literacy and numeracy, because these form the basis of many of the other elements of knowledge. As there is only one way to interpret the world correctly, there is no room for a pupil's own ideas: these are considered potentially false judgments, to be replaced by the right ones. Whether the pupil has acquired these correctly can be objectively tested: there is only one right answer to every problem.

According to Egan (1997), this way of thinking was already propagated by Plato, who considered the mind "primarily an epistemological organ" – or in modern terms, an organ for the processing of information. But Plato also understood that having the right information does not automatically imply acting on it. Acting also requires understanding and the will to act in a specific way. These aspects, however, do not seem to be a prominent concern in modern education that follows this paradigm.

Of course, teachers know that pupils are not merely information-processing machines. They also feel responsible for the well-being of pupils. However, as the paradigm is oriented exclusively to the future intellectual well-being of the pupils, their actual well-being is seen largely in function of their future (they have to work and obey now in order to ensure a good future – never mind that they themselves cannot see the connection, and teachers often have trouble seeing the relevance of curricular content too). And thus, when responsibility for the curriculum and responsibility for the current well-being here and now of the pupils come into conflict, as they must do at some time, a "responsible" teacher cannot but choose the curriculum. The content and pace of curriculum "delivery" become the norm for measuring the "quality" of pupils.

Something along the same lines is true for the ethical implications of the curriculum. Of course, teachers feel a responsibility to educate their pupils to become "good" persons, responsible citizens who feel responsible for the well-being of others. However, the knowledge taught in schools is largely abstract, that is, not related to concrete situations in which action decisions are required. This is knowledge stripped of any ethical relations, as ethics is always related to concrete situations. Therefore, becoming a "good person" is an "extra" goal for education, not contained in the core of the curriculum but relegated to separate subjects that are considered relatively marginal. This remains true even where transmitting "generally accepted values" is an explicit goal of the curriculum. Moreover, it is questionable whether such a goal contributes to the pupils gaining agency to autonomously participate in societal practices.

It is thus difficult for teachers to live up to the responsibility they feel for their pupils, other than in helping them get high SAT scores. And they are not helped by politicians, and parents, who think that those high SAT scores are exactly what education should be about. The way of thinking behind this paradigm, that values the acquisition of knowledge above becoming somebody who knows what to do (and what not to do) with that knowledge, is pervasive in our culture. And indeed, we do not wish to suggest that acquiring knowledge is unimportant. However, as many thinkers about education have pointed out, it is a one-sided way of thinking that reduces pupils to reservoirs of knowledge, reduces development to intellectual learning, and ignores the importance of emotion, creativity and imagination, and ethics. In that sense, one can understand Vygotskij's dictum that in this paradigm, development equals learning. One relatively recent insight that figures prominently in the work of Vygotskij and others is that the human mind does not work like a computer, that is, purely as an organ for the processing of discrete and abstract information. Vygotskij emphasised the importance of the connection between cognitions and emotions in the concept of *pereživanie* (see also Chap. 2 of this volume). Egan (1992) points out that imagination and narrative are crucial in making sense of information. And the implication is that development cannot be equated with purely intellectual development. It has to be understood as a process in which many aspects and faculties develop together and in interaction. Here lies a problem with what is often called "adaptive" education. As not all pupils have the same intellectual capabilities or "talents", effectiveness includes differentiation as to the amount of knowledge a pupil is capable of acquiring, and as to the time in which this can be done. "Adaptive" teaching means just that within this paradigm: adapting to the intellectual possibilities of pupils.

In the Netherlands, and probably in other countries too, "effective education" is now being propagated by the government, partly in reaction to perceived problems with forms of education that were (more or less loosely) based on constructivist ideas. This is something of an about-turn, for in the 1990s, the government actively induced secondary schools to introduce forms of education in which pupils were activated, because being active is seen in constructivist theory as a condition for learning. Pupils were no longer to be told the desired content, but had to find the knowledge for themselves, working together on teacher-defined problems. It was sometimes supposed that this form of constructivism constituted an implementation of Vygotskian ideas. However, the theory of knowledge and knowledge acquisition behind this innovation was Piagetian rather than Vygotskian in nature. Problems to be studied were normally not negotiated with pupils. Pupils were supposed to motivate themselves to study any problem regardless of whether this made sense to them or was related to a cultural practice, and the knowledge they obtained was still evaluated on the basis of objective criteria. Fundamentally, it does not matter in this respect whether this acquisition is thought of as "passive" (the filling of an empty bucket) or "active", as in constructivist theories of learning. Of course, this does make a lot of difference in what a teacher does, and thus in what is considered "responsible" teaching within this paradigm: "responsible" is what is most effective given our ideas about how learning works. It is, thus, a responsibility toward the future possibilities of pupils, and in that sense remains squarely within the paradigm of effective education. On the other hand, constructivism is based on a theory of development in which development no longer equals learning, but where experience and growth together create the conditions under which further learning becomes possible. This Piagetian view of development is now also being advocated by those who embrace a neurological approach to development and learning. It is, however, exactly on this point that Vygotskij strongly differed with Piaget, even though in other respects he agreed with Piaget on the insufficiency of the development models behind both traditional and progressive education.

A related innovation, especially implemented in vocational and pre-vocational education (which in the Netherlands is organised in separate schools), is called competence oriented education. This tries to do away with "irrelevant" and abstract knowledge, combining theory and practice in projects derived from the future occupations of pupils. Here, there is a clear relation to societal practices, which might be interpreted as a Vygotskian principle. However, actually it seems more like an unconscious return to ideas already propagated in the 1920s by Bobbitt (1918) on the basis of a Taylorian analysis of occupational practices. This is especially the case where broad competences are being broken down into sometimes very small parts.

Progressive Education

Where traditional education expects the emancipation of mankind on the basis of knowledge produced by the sciences, progressive education expects it from the liberation of the child's development from societal constraints. It is optimistic about the possibilities of human nature, and relatively pessimistic about culture and the influence of society on development. Just as in effective education, an important aim is to provide pupils with certainties for life in an uncertain world; but these certainties do not rest on knowledge of that world in itself. Rather, education should allow pupils to build a strong personality, so that they can find that certainty within themselves. Following their own, uncorrupted nature provides better guidance in life than using abstract principles and knowledge.

This implies that "development" means something completely different in this tradition. Just like plants, the body and the mind develop spontaneously, according to an inborn programme and inborn possibilities. Development is determined by these programmes, although it can be stunted by unfavourable circumstances. Each child is unique, in that he/she has different possibilities from every other child; and it is the task of educators to ensure that they recognise these possibilities and create the best possible environment for them to develop. These possibilities are not just cognitive in nature; children may have all kinds of combinations of "intelligences" (Gardner 1983). As an acorn may grow into an oak given the right conditions, but never into a buttercup, so it is useless and even harmful to try and guide development in a direction that is not within the natural possibilities of the child – which is precisely what, in the eyes of progressive educators, traditional education tries to do by prescribing a common curriculum for all. In fact, in an ideal form of progressive education, not only is there no set or common curriculum, but also the curriculum is not intended in the first place to be "learned" as knowledge about the world; it is seen as an environment and means for stimulating development of both body and mind.

This view of development implies that teachers have a totally different kind of responsibility than in traditional education, including its more "modern" forms based on constructivism. Their primary responsibility is for the *actual*, not the future, well-being of the child, because that is the condition under which development can run an optimal course. And in that course, the child's curiosity about the world will awaken, so that a condition for learning in the usual sense is created. Thus, in the words of Vygotskij, in this paradigm learning is considered to follow development. But once again, this learning about the world is not the primary aim of education; its aim is the development of all capacities of the child, so that the child can also develop a strong sense of its own capabilities, enabling it to act in the world from a sense of security and certainty founded in its own inner life. Teachers need to understand the "laws" of development, so that they can help and stimulate each unique child to develop optimally; part of that development is related to the acquisition of knowledge, but this is not a main task for education. Indeed, this orientation, which also leads sometimes to a neglect of knowledge, has been a source of criticism in the past. As elements of progressive education become adopted in many schools, and are now not only found in schools explicitly designated as progressive, this criticism has also become more widespread, for instance in the form of a critique of the "therapeutisation" of education (Ecclestone and Hayes 2009).

Of course, this is a rather one-sided and idealistic view of progressive education. Most teachers and schools are aware that children need to grow up in society, and that this requires learning and development in certain directions. In progressive education, there is the same conflict between curriculum and well-being as in traditional education, but with a different emphasis. Teachers struggle to handle this conflict, but in reality it is caused not by society but by an interpretation of the relationships between learning and development, and between individual and society, that is inadequate. Children do not learn solely as a result of an inner urge arising from autonomous development; they are not pure individuals that must learn to adapt to an impure society. Although the attention to the development of the "whole child" is commendable, and gives rise to many superficial similarities between progressive and Developmental Education, these differences in theoretical background imply that Developmental Education cannot be understood as just another form of progressive education. In fact, thinking in a dichotomy of "traditional" versus "progressive" forms of education misinterprets the fundamental properties of Developmental Education.

Developmental Education

As may now be clear, Developmental Education is not just an amalgam of, or a "golden middle road" between, traditional and progressive forms of education.

Instead, its background theory of development and learning brings thinking about such issues to a higher level.

In Developmental Education, we see people as fundamentally social and cultural beings. This implies much more than that they (have to) live in a social and cultural world and participate in socially and culturally structured activities. For their development and well-being, children are dependent on participation in culturally structured activities, entailing both social contacts and being introduced into culture. The development of the "higher mental functions" is intimately connected with language use, and thus with being and becoming a participant in culture. Thus, development is not a matter of acquiring "technical" knowledge about how to behave in an acceptable way and about how one's actions can effectively lead to desired results. Neither is it a question of adapting one's inner self to having to live in a world with others. The "inner self" only comes into being through contact with others while participating in practices: development is not to be understood as socialisation, but rather as individualisation, as a gradual development of specific characteristics and competences. These characteristics are amalgams of culturally available possibilities and potentialities already present in the child, while their development is driven and sustained by the participation of the child in social and cultural activities. Thus, "culture" is not a bag of instruments to be used at will; culture defines the individual's essence. There is no culture-free "inner being".

This does not mean, however, that individuals are totally determined by the culture they live in and by which they are formed. The "social situation of development", as Vygotskij called it, is always a situation as *perceived* by the child in the context of its "leading activity". As a consequence, culturally available elements are never adopted "as such"; they are transformed by the mental work of that individual, combining them with previously learned elements, but above all coloured with emotions, to "make sense" of them. In that process, both the cultural elements and the person are transformed. Each developing individual thus develops a unique interpretation of, and a unique stance towards, the culture that it grows up in. It is this process of transformation that ensures the possibility of cultural change.

And change is necessary for any culture. No culture has adequate and everlasting answers to each and every problem that the world poses. The quicker a culture and the world it exists in change, the less one can rely on answers developed in that culture over the ages. Also, different cultures have different ways of seeing the world and human existence within it, and in a multicultural society one is confronted with citizens who do not have the same ways of understanding the world and relations with others. Any interaction with others (and maybe even with oneself) is fraught with uncertainties, as every human being has at least partly a different interpretation of the culture they live in, and culture does not determine our behaviour anyway but just provides guidelines. In our view, a consequence for education is that it should not try to equip pupils with so-called certainties, whether based in knowledge or in the "inner being". Instead, it should teach pupils to handle uncertainties in a positive way. Learning to cope with living in an uncertain world is maybe one of the most pressing "developmental tasks", and the school can and should play a role in this learning process.

Here is, first of all, how proponents of Developmental Education see the role of knowledge. Children make sense of the world and of their own existence within it by experiencing how others make sense of it, and education introduces them to ways of sense-making that are relatively new to them. Or, in different terms, they are inducted into "communities of discourse" that "make sense of the world" in specific ways, ways that are valued in the community. Again, this does not mean that these "ways of understanding the world" determine their thinking and actions; they act as "guidelines" for, rather than as determinants of actions. New ways of interpreting the world and oneself may be co-constructed in such communities of discourse. The important point, however, is that acquiring such ways of sense-making is different from acquiring "objective" knowledge: "sense" as it is used here denotes an integration of knowledge with affect, with previous experiences and with projections of one's future existence: which is to say that learning to make sense of the world in specific ways transforms one's outlook on the world and oneself, one's self-concept or personality. Learning leads to personality development. Teaching means offering pupils access to the solutions, the ideas, theories, ways of understanding, and schemas, which were developed by previous generations when they were confronted with problems. The knowledge we have was generated within human practices, related to human problems, and in that sense it is not "objective", immutable or beyond doubt, especially since the problems we are confronted with now may not be exactly the same. However, this wealth of culturally and historically produced knowledge can help us to see the world and ourselves differently, and often more usefully, than we would if left to our own individual devices. Probably this is true more for schemas, models and procedures than for separate facts about the world: schemas and models allow us to reduce complexity and thereby get a grasp on the world and on our actions within it. Pupils need to learn how to use them – but also in what situations *not* to use them, and to realise that there are situations where they do not suffice, which implies that creativity is as important as knowledge. Or to put this more precisely, creativity is not the opposite of knowledge; knowledge is a condition for creativity to be used adequately in a situation that is not entirely covered by available knowledge and procedures. New knowledge does not appear out of the blue, but is built creatively on existing knowledge. Agency in social activities requires this form of creativity and the production of new forms of action. An important goal for education is to make pupils realise that they, too, can be not only users of knowledge, but should become authors of knowledge as well – in co-operation with others. Agency and authorship are intrinsically related. Creativity and imagination should not be thought of as the unique capacity of gifted individuals. Creativity too is a social phenomenon, arising in participation in cultural activities. Thus, to teach children to use available cultural resources in adequate and creative ways, to become authors of knowledge and of their own existence, it is essential to allow them to participate, in a developmentally adequate way, in such activities. This, and not just its positive effects on children's involvement in learning, is the primary reason for Developmental Education to introduce (simulated) cultural activities in the school as learning environments (cf. Wardekker et al. 2012). It is also an important reason not to follow the ideas of Davydov that focus on the teaching of basic concepts of scientific disciplines (see Chap. 2 in this volume).

Responsible Developmental Teaching

This brings us to the question of what "responsible teaching" is within the paradigm of Developmental Education. Developmental Education invites the introduction of children to the wealth of culturally available concepts, schemas and procedures. It takes care that these become meaningful for the pupils – that is, they do not just understand them or can apply them in school situations, but these cultural instruments transform the way they understand the world and their own position and possibilities within it. In this respect, Developmental Education resembles some of the ideas behind the European neo-humanist educational concept of "Bildung", which is also behind some interpretations of "liberal education" in the Anglo-Saxon world. Vygotskij knew this concept well and certainly built on it. In its basic beliefs, Developmental Education is probably closer to this concept than it is to either traditional or progressive education. However, there are also important differences. In the Bildung paradigm, the educational subject matter is thought to possess in itself the power to engage and educate pupils both in the technical and in the moral sense, once they have been introduced to this subject matter by the teacher. It relies on finding cultural products that have high educational power, and this often results not only in a culturally biased selection but also in the idea that it is a concept best suited for older pupils who can study and appreciate literature and other forms of art individually. Developmental Education, on the other hand, finds this power to engage and educate in pupils' co-operative participation in cultural practices introduced (in some adequate form) in the school. This participation may indeed, as Bert van Oers shows, be understood as playfulness, especially for younger children: play is not a category of actions separate from "work", but a form that participation can take. It is a form that allows for creativity and for the potential of authorship to emerge.

In Developmental Education, the teacher's responsibility relates both to the child and its development, and to the preservation of the cultural inheritance, exactly because development is dependent on that inheritance. The teacher is not, however, as in the Bildung paradigm, seen as a representative of the best that civilization has to offer, an example to be emulated by the pupils. A responsible teacher helps children to develop their personality, to acquire agency in culturally structured activities, by assuming the role of a more experienced participant in such activities. She challenges children to become more central, more competent participants, even taking over part of her teaching role. She takes over those parts of their roles that they are as yet unable to fulfil, provides them with the cultural instruments (especially, in primary education, words and reading and writing skills) that are needed in the context, and follows and stimulates each child's development. In this way, responsible teaching is also responsive teaching: responsive also in the sense that the teacher does not carry out a pre-programmed script. In that respect the teacher herself also needs to be able to handle uncertainty.

At the same time, responsible teaching implies that the teacher does have a long-term view of the possible and desirable development of her pupils. Activities cannot be chosen and filled with cultural instruments in a haphazard way. On the one hand, there are goals and other prescriptions that have been prescribed on a national level; and even though these were probably constructed with a different theory of education and development in mind, they need to be observed, if only because children may migrate to a different school. On the other hand, each child has its own possibilities and optimal pace of development. Thus, ideally the teacher should have in mind a hypothetical long-term trajectory of development for every child: hypothetical in the sense that it rests on the teacher's own judgment of the child's possibilities, a judgment that needs to be constantly checked and revised on the basis of actual development. And needless to say, this hypothetical trajectory concerns not only the child's cognitive development, but tries to understand development in a holistic or multifaceted way – exactly because, as Vygotskij already pointed out, cognitive development is not separate from other aspects of development, and is especially related to emotion (see also Chap. 10 of this volume).

Teacher Competence

Responsiveness to the development and the immediate needs of pupils, of course, is not the only characteristic of a responsible teacher. She is also responsive to her colleagues, to parents, and to other persons who play a role in the development of her pupils. To be more precise, we regard teaching as a distributed activity. It does not take place in an isolated classroom, because learning does not only take place in that classroom: children are learning all the time, and bring what they have learned elsewhere into the classroom. But the same goes for the teacher. She will not have learned all she has to know and be able to do in a pre-service education, and indeed she learns from her pupils as well as from her colleagues in the school and in other places. This, of course, requires a school organisation and climate where learning from other teachers and discussions of teaching and the development of actual pupils are valued.

We have already mentioned one other important teacher competence: being able to handle uncertainty in a positive and creative way. Where other paradigms of education try to reduce uncertainty, for instance by prescribing precisely detailed lesson plans and syllabi, and by constraining the possible contributions of the pupils, Developmental Education encourages teachers to use informed creativity to structure learning situations and activities in a responsive way. This does not mean that all teaching is made dependent on the wishes and actual needs of pupils. As will be elaborated in subsequent chapters, schemas and suggestions are available to teachers, and they largely know what pupils should have mastered at the end of each term; but they can never just follow a syllabus, let alone that there could be precise protocols for teaching and for handling "problem" pupils, as is now being advocated by the Evidence Based Teaching movement. In this respect, Developmental Education can be quite taxing for teachers, and this too requires a school climate where they are supported by colleagues. There is also an important role here for school based teacher advisors and for external advisory services specialising in Developmental Education.

Finally, we need to point out that responsible teaching involves constant innovation. Partly, this is a consequence of the fact that the paradigm itself is, and always will remain, "under construction". It is also a consequence of the importance of placing education squarely within a living and changing cultural and social world. For this implies not only that the practices represented in the school need to change, but also that the "social situation of development" of the children, inasmuch as it is also situated outside the school, is changing, and thus in fact the children themselves are not the same now as they were yesterday, or as they will be tomorrow (figuratively speaking). Schools and teachers, however, do not just respond to changing circumstances. They are, or at least should be, themselves agents in such change, and thus are at least partly responsible for a constant amelioration of the children's social situation of development. This dialectical relation between school and society requires that teachers and schools take responsibility for their own development in the sense of constantly enhancing their professionalism (see also Chap. 13 of this volume).

In the Netherlands, a set of seven "teacher competences" has been formulated that is being used by teacher training centres and by the inspectorate. The original formulation of these competences does not adequately reflect the specific competences of a teacher in Developmental Education. As an aid to teachers and to teacher trainers, they have been re-specified for Developmental Education as they appear in the appendix to this chapter. Of course, these formulations are also subject to the need for constant innovation and revision.

This brings us to the question of how to prepare prospective teachers for teaching on the basis of the Developmental Education paradigm. Several teacher training centres in the Netherlands offer student teachers the opportunity to specialise in this paradigm. This, however, is fraught with difficulties. Teaching Developmental Education requires teacher trainers who themselves have adequate knowledge of, and experience with, the paradigm, and these are few. The centres are trying to adapt the way they teach themselves, using principles derived from the paradigm, but as it has been elaborated mainly for use in primary education, the transition to what is in effect adult education is not easy. Also, the opportunities for student teachers to actually experience, and teach in, a school that has adopted Developmental Education, are not easily found in the present situation. And finally, the centres have to fight against the suspicions of the higher education inspectorate, of other centres, and often also of those teacher trainers within the centre who do not subscribe to the paradigm. Nevertheless, the interest of student teachers and the number of centres that offer courses are growing, so that we can hold out hope for a developmentally oriented future, and for responsible teaching in an increasing number of everyday classrooms for (young) children.

Appendix: Teacher Competences for Developmental Education

The generally accepted framework for teacher competence in the Netherlands recognises seven fields of competence:

– interpersonal competence
– competence in group processes
– competence in content knowledge and teaching procedures
– competence in organising
– competence in co-operating with colleagues
– competence in co-operating with the school environment
– competence in reflection

All of these have been specified for DE teachers in an (as yet unofficial) document. The text is too long to quote here in full. As examples, we translate the text for "interpersonal competence" and for "competence in reflection".

Interpersonal competence

A DE teacher recognises her specific pedagogical task in a changing and sometimes insecure society. Pupils come to school to develop their personalities in a broad sense. Knowledge and skills are of importance in this process. Kids in a DE classroom relate to what they are learning. The teacher strives for the pupils to build attachment to her, to each other, and to the content and aims of education.

Characteristic for the climate in a DE classroom is that everything that is treated will be meaningful for every individual and relevant for the whole group.

Interpersonal relationships in a DE classroom are built up in joint activities and conversations, where the contribution of everybody is sought and valued.

A DE teacher always pronounces high expectations of the possibilities of her pupils. Nothing is too difficult in advance and if you want to participate you are never too young.

Together with the pupils, the teacher builds learning environments in which children can explore safely and are challenged to redefine their limits.

How does the teacher do this?

– making contact: she takes time to come into real (verbal and nonverbal) contact with her pupils and to understand their actual interests and skills. She helps them to reflect on their actions
– relating pupils to each other: she organises individual and collective activities in which the children have mutual contacts and learn to take responsibility for themselves and for the group
– taking part: she takes part in the pupils' activities aiming at the construction of a zone of proximal development, and provides positive feedback on participation rather than achievement
– building a learning environment: continually, together with the group, she engages in designing a rich learning environment relevant to the development of the learning theme. An environment that encourages learning together.

Competence in reflection and development

Reflection is very important in DE: both reflection on what happens with the pupils in the group and reflection on the teacher's own actions.

How does the teacher do this?

- reflection in the group: daily she reflects on the primary process in the classroom, aided by the DE reflection instruments (HOREB). Together with the pupils, she daily organises evaluative moments in which she reflects together with them on what has been worked on, what progress has been made, and what activities could come next. Also, she evaluates the pupils' development together with them
- Reflection on her own development: periodically she reflects her skills in DE. She is able to sketch an image of herself as a DE teacher and to mention points for further development. Working on these points, she is able to use available DE materials.

References

Bobbitt, F. (1918). *The curriculum.* Cambridge, MA: Riverside Press.

Ecclestone, K., & Hayes, D. (2009). *The dangerous rise of therapeutic education.* London: Routledge.

Egan, K. (1992). *Imagination in teaching and learning.* Chicago: University of Chicago Press.

Egan, K. (1997). *The educated mind. How cognitive tools shape our understanding.* Chicago: University of Chicago Press.

Gardner, H. (1983). *Frames of mind. The theory of multiple intelligences.* New York: Basic Books.

Habermas, J. (1968/1978). *Knowledge and interest.* Cambridge: Polity Press.

Wardekker, W., Boersma, A., Ten Dam, G., & Volman, M. (2012). Motivation for school learning. In M. Hedegaard, A. Edwards, & M. Fleer (Eds.), *Motives, emotions and values in the development of children and young people* (pp. 153–169). Cambridge: Cambridge University Press.

Chapter 4
Developmental Education for Young Children: Basic Development

Frea Janssen-Vos and Bea Pompert

Introduction

For more than 35 years, members of a Dutch institute for educational innovation (APS) have been concerned with the quality of early education in the Dutch "kleuterscholen" (preschools) for 4–6 year-old children. The Dutch national school reform in 1985 – aiming at an integrated primary school for 4–12 year-olds – was a new challenge in our work. This national reform was meant to promote continuity in development and education so that the start of cultural learning processes would no longer be fixed at a particular moment in the academic year. Instead, education should harmonise with children's actual developmental levels. However, the innovation attempts were not very successful and many preschool teachers feared that they would be forced into the traditional "classical teaching" of primary schools. In 1988 APS took the initiative to make an alternative contribution to the innovation processes.[1] A project group was invited to design a practice-theory to answer the question of how schools can realise continuity and cohesion in the early years education of children from 4 to 8 years of age. At this time Bert van Oers introduced us to the Vygotskian approach which proved to be a perfect source and guide in designing the desired curriculum!

---

[1]Members of the project group are Bea Pompert (by that time Hogeschool Alkmaar), Trudy Schiferli (School Advisory Institute) Henk Vink and Frea Janssen-Vos (APS Amsterdam). Bert van Oers is the group's external adviser.

F. Janssen-Vos
e-mail: janssen-vos@planet.nl

B. Pompert, M.Sc. (✉)
De Activiteit National Centre for Developmental Education, Alkmaar, The Netherlands
e-mail: b.pompert@de-activiteit.nl

B. van Oers (ed.), *Developmental Education for Young Children*, International
Perspectives on Early Childhood Education and Development 7,
DOI 10.1007/978-94-007-4617-6_4,
© Springer Science+Business Media Dordrecht 2012

The challenge was to propose a practical, relevant, theory-driven curriculum in which playing and learning are not seen as two different moments, but as basically related requirements for identity development: a curriculum that transcends the gap between a focus on individual development and a focus on cultural equipment. In Dutch we named this *Basisontwikkeling*, which literally translates as "Basic Development", referring to an approach to the education of young children that aims to lay a firm foundation ("basis") for children's future cultural participation (Janssen-Vos 2008). In this chapter we present the characteristics of this Basic Development "curriculum", based upon the Vygotskian foundations that Bert van Oers describes in Chap. 2.

The curriculum consists of several elements by which teachers can build up their own developmental practice while working with the children in their classrooms (Pinar and Pinar 1995).

In 2000 the government instigated projects to stimulate early education for 2–6 year-old children (from social-economically deprived and immigrant families), and to encourage the implementation of developmental programmes in preschool centres and in the first years of primary schools. By that time, Basic Development had been gradually adopted by school management and teachers of many preschool-groups (4–6 year-olds). Later we developed an extension of this play-based curriculum for teachers working with 2–4 year-old children. We named this new programme *Startblokken van Basisontwikkeling* ("Starting Blocks of Basic Development"). Nowadays, Basic Development is the curriculum for children aged from 3 to about 7 years old and the name "Starting Blocks" is reserved for special provisions for children under the age of 4.

Aiming at Broad Development in Young Children

We start with a description of activities in a kindergarten group of 4–6 year-olds. These children play, work and learn in the context of the theme "Airplanes".

High Flight, an Example of Good Practice

The environment presents elements of an airport and of an airplane: we see the check-in zone, with labels on the suitcases and documents that are needed to check-in. There is a cabin built with windows, seats, and facilities to distribute snacks and drinks. A cockpit with realistic instrument panels (from old devices) and instruments, and materials such as clothing buttons for the control buttons. All this makes it seem quite real and is attractive for the children to play with. Watching these scenes one recognises that the children are involved in several role-

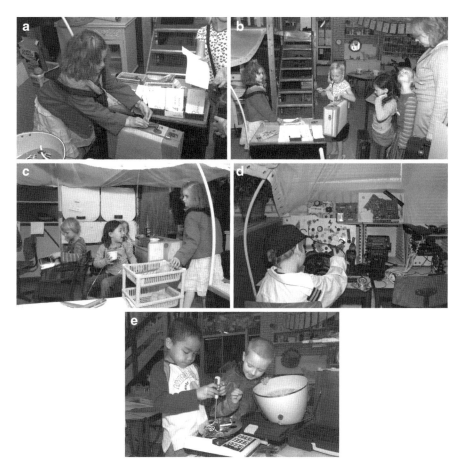

Fig. 4.1 (**a**) In the check-in zone self made labels are attached to the luggage. (**b**) The passengers (children and teacher) hand over their documents to be checked. (**c**) In the cabin the stewardess is serving snacks and drinks. (**d**) In the cockpit the pilot is checking the instrument panels. (**e**) Mechanics are trying to repair the engine

play and construction activities. It is easy to imagine that they pretend to be flight attendants, passengers, pilots and mechanics. There is much interaction and the children communicate with each other a lot, often even in the air flight jargon, using words and phrases such as "cockpit", "fasten your seatbelt", "trolley", "departure" and "arrival". If one looks closely at the photos one sees a lot of texts that are written or stamped by the children themselves. You may wonder: why all this? (Fig. 4.1).

What are the aims of such practice? Developmental Education envisions education as a process that should focus first of all on a broad development of children's identity. Children need more in their personal lives and for their future place in society than just knowledge and skills. Instead of focusing on short-term objectives

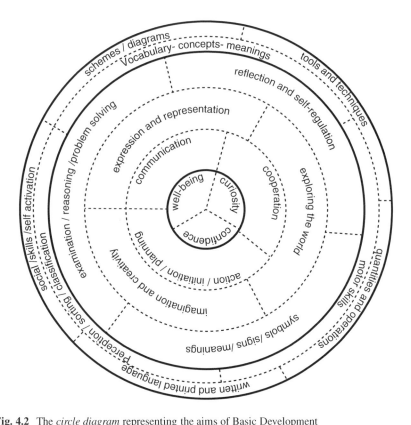

Fig. 4.2 The *circle diagram* representing the aims of Basic Development

in the domain of language and intellectual skills, we chose three kinds of connected objectives. First, the affective dimension: well-being, self-confidence and curiosity. Secondly, (meta-) cognitive elements of a broad development, like communication, expression of thoughts and feelings, making plans, exploring the social, cultural and physical world, and problem solving. And thirdly, the specific skills that also need to be acquired for a broad personality development. All aspects are represented in a circle diagram for the aims of "Basic Development" (Fig. 4.2).

These goals are addressed through activities which stimulate cooperation, and generate both personal sense and cultural meaning, as we can see in the airplane theme. Specific knowledge and skills become necessary and useful in children's ongoing activities and as such they become objectives for meaningful learning. When these objectives are achieved they can expand children's broad development. For instance, in small groups children develop the need to find solutions for problems they encounter in joint activities, like how to make instruments for the plane's cockpit. When they play at being flight attendants and passengers in the check-in zone, they learn to communicate and negotiate with their playmates about the kind of papers passengers need to show, or about what a boarding pass looks like. This classroom example also shows that different scholarly target areas come into sight in all kinds of inter-related play activities.

Here we see a basic principle of the Developmental Education approach: the need for knowledge and skills arises in activities that make sense for the children, and become useful, functional, necessary or simply convenient within their current activities. This principle calls for initiatives on the part of teachers. They observe the children and record their activities, needs and learning; on that basis, objectives and new actions are planned in order to contribute to the development of children in the group. The teacher's particular intentions with the airplane theme are, for instance, to promote experiences with symbols and signs and with self-direction and reflection. She also plans for specific skills and techniques that go along with these intentions, like making plans and performing numeric operations. The teacher takes care to include the children's interests in her own plans for the theme.

How to Support Development?

The Vygotskian theory provides many suggestions about how teachers can support children's development. The following are particularly key notions in Developmental Education and in Basic Development:

- *Meaningful learning* is essential for a broad cultural development: meaningful for the children themselves and for their cultural development as stated in the official curriculum goals. This process of dual meaning-making starts with children's engagement in cultural activities which make personal sense to them, which they like and in which they want to participate. In such activities they can count on help from the teacher and other children.
- The theory of the *leading activities* introduced by El'konin (1972) clarifies which types of activities are meaningful at a given point in development. El'konin notes that children display a particular preference for a certain type of activity depending on their stage of development: activities that are in line with their actual interests, on the one hand, and that appear to play a special role in their total developmental process, on the other hand. From birth onwards manipulative play and role-play are the most frequent and leading in the developmental process. This play activity gradually progresses into a conscious (productive) learning activity that is going to dominate during the ages of approximately 7–12 years old.
- The third key concept is the *zone of proximal development*. This concept does not refer to an abstract potential to learn new things with the help of others, but to the ability of children to participate in socio-cultural activities and improve their ability to participate with the help of others (see Chap. 1). Adults can facilitate children's participation in such activities by inviting them to take part in specially organised activities that match their needs and capabilities. Educators should

organise joint activities with groups of children and interact with them (Kravtsova 2007). The groups are preferably not too big and mixed with regard to age and development levels. The teacher is also a participant in the group's activity. This requires taking into account what the children's levels of development are, their interests, and how well they interact with others.

These concepts have led to the development of a range of meaningful and development-promoting activities, in which the teacher plays an important role. These activities will be described in more detail in the following sections.

Meaningful and Development-Promoting Activities and Contents

Educational activities are the most conducive to development, if they are embedded in the leading activity that characterises the child at that particular point in time (El'konin 1972). As previously stated, for young children, play is the most frequent and leading activity in the development process. All social and intellectual activities start in play. In fact, all intellectual learning activities during primary education exhibit a play character (van Oers 2010; see also Chap. 2 of this volume). It is this theory of emerging stages in development which clarifies the idea of continuity in education. The old border between play during the first years at school and learning to read and write in the following years, can now change into an early childhood period (3–7 years of age) where play continues to be the leading activity for all developmental aspects, gradually followed up by formal education in play contexts.

Today many people are calling for a revaluation of play as a development-promoting activity (Goorhuis-Brouwer 2008). Often they have only the spontaneous play of children in mind, without mentioning the adults' contribution or seriously considering the adults' influences. However, in the Developmental Education approach play is more than an attractive, free and non-committal activity of children. Van Oers (2010) defines play as a format of cultural activities that are characterised by *rules* that constitute the activity, by the level of *involvement*, and by the *degrees of freedom* that the cultural community allows to the player. If play is to become a truly important development promoter, then this is only feasible when the environment, and especially adults, play a supporting and stimulating role (Pompert 2010).

Although we will not elaborate on productive learning here, it is important to note that in Developmental Education learning activity remains formatted like play with explicit rules, a high level of engagement and some degrees of freedom for the learner. Play is a major dimension in the play-based curriculum in Developmental Education. The foundations of playing are laid in the early years "Basic Development" curriculum.

Core Activities

With these Vygotskian notions in mind, we developed five cultural core activities with a play character which are considered essential for all 3–7 year-old children:

- Object play and role-play.
- Construction play: making products with creative materials, construction and building materials and techniques.
- Conversation activities: interactions and conversations between teacher and children in small and larger groups, and in other activities in circle-time.
- Literacy activities: initial literacy in play, book reading, functional reading and writing with children's own narratives and texts.
- Mathematical activities: mathematical actions in play, schematising and mathematical cognitive operations in social-cultural contexts.

In our view, elements of conscious learning activity are already manifested in embryonic form in the play of young children. Play brings forth the motivation and capacity for formal learning. Thus, not only typical kindergarten activities such as manipulative play and role-play but also academic activities and skills in the field of literacy and numeracy deserve a place in a play-based curriculum, particularly when children are given the appropriate support. These activities too start in young children's play when, for example, they pretend to read a book, write a letter, count money, or use maps and construction plans.

Contents

The core activities are imbued with socio-cultural contents representing interesting situations and experiences that children can encounter in their everyday environments. In the airplane scenario (described above) we can recognise the meaningful contents and all five of the core activities. For example, we witness role-play as the children pretend to be pilots and flight attendants, and constructive play when they create the cockpit and when the mechanics do their repair work. The players are also involved in literacy activities when they make and use signs, labels for the suitcases or documents for the passengers. In this airplane play the construction of the instrument panel in the cockpit requires a lot of math and schematising. The related conversational activities take place throughout the whole day, when the children are talking and discussing in airplane-related activities, in small groups and in the large group.

Teachers select social-cultural themes, which are (or can become) both interesting for the children involved, and important from an educational point of view. Activities are taken from several sources, such as:

- themes concerning children's concrete life situations, like going to the supermarket or the post office, a visit to the doctor, a baby being born, moving to a new house, and going on a holiday trip;

- themes representing the wider cultural and physical world such as visual arts, sports, fashion, a school garden, celestial bodies and the oceans;
- themes connected with current events like a sudden winter storm, Christmas and a traffic accident.

The teacher takes care of selecting a wide range of interesting themes from these sources.

Developmental Perspectives of Core Activities

We elaborated El'konin's theory further, into what we call, "perspectives" of play activities that reveal stages in play development in a more detailed way.

Developmental Perspectives in Young Children's Play[2]

Developmental perspectives refer to the types of play that young children are engaged in successively. We identify object play, role-bound play, thematic role-play, and learning activity.

Object Play

Young children like to play with all kinds of objects. In this manipulative play they explore their environment and link words to objects (ball, brick, shoe, car, etc.) and to their own actions (walk, wash, make dinner, and play outside). Playing with concrete materials also encourages social contact with other children and stimulates them to be more considerate of others. Object play needs a rich environment with interesting materials and the presence of other children to interact and play with.

Young children love to mess about with sand and water, and with almost everything else the environment offers. A bucket of water and all kinds of instruments makes the sand extra interesting to experiment with. And the objects in the doctor's corner invite them to manipulate, to try out and to explore the characteristics, although it may seem sometimes as if the children are just running around to touch and replace every object that triggers their interest (Figs. 4.3 and 4.4).

---

[2] In this section we will concentrate on the development perspectives of role-play and constructive play. Some of the other core activities will be addressed in a number of the following chapters of this book.

Fig. 4.3 Two boys are delightfully messing about with sand balls

Fig. 4.4 In the doctor's corner nurses and doctors are exploring all kinds of interesting objects

Fig. 4.5 (**a**) After the teachers' reading a story about a sick bear, all children want to play doctor. (**b**) The (play) plasters and needles make them feel, act and talk like real doctors

Role Bound Play

Role bound play marks a certain moment in play development when 2 and 3 year-olds start expanding their object play towards giving objects a meaning, like using a straw as a spoon to feed the baby with or a barrel by way of a pram. They imagine object situations or actions that do not exist in reality and use these as substitutes. Soon, they take a role in the play themselves, initially without having to name this role (the mother, the baker, etc.). Language now expands beyond using words for objects, towards expressing relations between objects and roles. From that point on, children talk about events as well and refer to the roles of other participants: "My baby is going to the doctor"; "I'm baking a cake to take to my granny." Actions are put into words in the right sequence: "I will wrap the present for you and put it in a plastic bag." Actions are gradually extended because children imitate each other and because the teacher gives new impulses. El'konin states that the transition to the performance of actions with meanings detached from objects prepares the development of symbolic thought (see Karpov 2005).

An example: in the home corner of the classroom, a play is taking place about celebrating the birth of a new baby. The children collect materials which can be used to make sand cakes for guests. They assume for themselves the role of cake bakers, perform role bound play and use the language that comes with it: "I'm baking a cake"; "I'll decorate the cake"; "This cake is ready so I will put it on the shelf". Another teacher reads a book with the children about a sick bear and disposes all kinds of doctor's instruments and props in one of the play corners. She proposes making beds for the class' bears, using two small chairs. Some children are happy to just explore the objects; others, inspired by the picture book, like to play doctor and examine and nurse the sick bears (Fig. 4.5a, b).

Thematic Role-Play

Most 4 year-olds are engaged in more extensive role-play with more complex actions and connections with other children's roles in the play. Their play also becomes more directed by a common theme as children now have many experiences with a shared world and are able to imagine situations (like visiting the post office). This achievement enables them to form a joint play script. Playing roles and taking relations between different roles into account mark this stage. Language that suits the situation is employed, for instance concepts like "expensive", "change", or "a pound" are used. Actions and language are directed by imagination, that is to say, by thinking the play over in advance. Now, making plans and discussing how the play is to be set up, becomes common in play activities. In this stage literacy and mathematical activities are also part of the play settings.

In the theme "Babies" we see more and more thematic role-play in which children play out a story together, with roles, actions and events appropriate to the theme. In the home corner the maternity nurse takes care of the baby while the mother takes a nap. Grandpa and grandma come to visit and bring a present with them. There is a shop where one can buy baby supplies, where customers buy presents and salesmen give them advice. There are conversations going on about purchases and gifts are wrapped and paid for. The children make the gifts themselves and sell them in the shop. Children increasingly play out events and situations in which relationships between different roles become a dominant characteristic. They also play the shopkeeper who writes receipts or gives change. In the house corner the "mother" reads a picture book for her new born baby while "father" reads the cards that have just arrived by post.

Productive Learning Activity

During the development of role-play, a new need arises that marks the transition to a new type of leading activity. The need for pretending in role-play now transforms into a need to act more like adults. In this phase the wish to learn adult cultural tools becomes the most important motive. The child now wants to know things more precisely, wants to be able to act properly, wants to use real instruments and think in an inquiring way. In this stage (mostly at 6 or 7 years old) role-play remains important but now as a learning context for reading, writing and inquiry.

A class of 7–8 year-olds is about to set up a gym. First, the roles are discussed: what kind of people are in a gym? What do they do there? The children make a list including a receptionist, gym teacher, customers and cleaning ladies. The children and the teacher work out a role-board for each role, on which you can see what you can do. The "receptionist" asks the teacher (playing a client) and other customers if they want a subscription. This is the source of various reading and writing activities. The children make their own sports pass with name and full address, stamping the name of the gym or writing it down neatly. They discuss what information it should include about the client: their weight, height, age, heart rate, and so on. The children

Fig. 4.6 (**a**) One of the gym's customers, Cas, makes his own sports pass with the gym's name (the hamster) on it, and writes his own name on the front. (**b**) On the *back* he writes his age, height and heart rate

use a yardstick to measure how tall they are and weigh themselves on a bathroom scale. With a real heart rate monitor (and with the teacher's help) they count their heart rate per minute. All this comes on the sports pass (Fig. 4.6a, b).

Developmental Perspectives in Constructive Play

Constructive play is a specific version of play and has the same kind of build-up: that of object play gradually transforming into designing and creating precise constructions. Constructive play is similar to role-play in that children often make constructions in their role as, for example, architect, brick layer or supervisor.

Object Play

In this stage children explore both large and small objects; they investigate, demolish and restore them in order to find out what they are made of. The materials draw the children's attention; they want to discover what they are, what they can do and what they stand for. Communication is then focused on objects and actions, like piling blocks or making a row of beads.

Discovering a Meaning

In this stage, the focus gradually shifts to materials and tools which require finer motor actions. And, just as in role bound play, the children attach a meaning to the products they – often accidentally – make. They identify their creation: "Hey, this looks like a car". Here the transformation toward self-chosen and deliberate plans for products can be recognised. Communication is focused on naming, discussing and comparing the products and results, followed by conversations about impressions and experiences associated with the activity.

Deliberately Creating

This stage is marked by the children's intention to deliberately make something; a hospital bed for a sick teddy bear out of an empty box, for example, or a garage for parking cars at the hospital constructed out of Lego. In this stage the children learn that planning the activity and predicting possible problems helps to bring the construction to a successful outcome. Using a somewhat systematic approach including planning, reasoning and thinking ahead is the result. Joint activities stimulate the use of new words and concepts necessary to describe the construction process and the reasoning in problem solving (using concepts like "if" and "because").

Products That Enrich Role-Play

Creating products to be used in thematic role-play offers the children a context (the play story) which requires extra efforts. The props must fit with the intentions and expectations of children involved in that role-play. This means even more intensive communication, consultation and detailed planning in different small groups.

After listening to a storybook tale about the hospital for example, a group of children decide to make small ambulances and other props to play with at the story telling table.[3] They make the ambulances from small boxes, paper, corks, etc. They want them to look like the real thing. The first cars are simple, just a plain body with wheels, but they become increasingly better and more complete. Also, some children start building a hospital in the construction corner to play with.

Making Precise Constructions

When the activities in the previous stage develop further, we see how children start making accurate constructions that must meet certain criteria they have in mind. They have a clear mental image of the product they want to make – a hospital for instance – and are able to plan and direct their activity. In this stage they also come to understand the meanings of symbols and signs in more abstract products and plans. The motivation to construct exact products which meet certain standards refers to a next leading activity: the productive learning activity. *The construction of a hospital*

---

[3]The story-telling table is a table where children can replay and retell a story from a (picture) book, in their own way and by using self-made props, miniature figures and objects.

Fig. 4.7 (**a**) The *front* of the building. (**b**) The *back* and the *right-hand side*

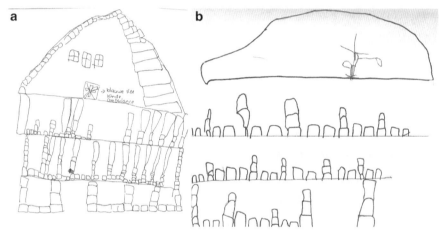

Fig. 4.8 (**a**) A concrete representation of the hospital, showing the different floors and the blue lights of the trauma helicopter. (**b**) A more schematic representation of the different floors and the trauma helicopter on the roof

is a conversation topic that provides good opportunities to talk and think about building things. How many floors does a hospital have and how can we make them? How many cars are allowed in the hospital's parking lot? The teacher photographs the front, the back and the right side of the hospital for a group of children, to acquaint them with making schemes. They are to make maps for the hospital so that they can rebuild it. A real hospital has different floors, but this is difficult to draw. A ruler can help; the children make a straight line on top of the first floor and draw the next floor on top of this line. Most of them start at the front; one boy draws all sides on one sheet and asks the teacher to write "front", "back" and "side" on the sheet (Figs. 4.7a, b and 4.8a, b).

The notion of *stages* must be understood properly. Object play for instance is not replaced by role-play but continues for a long time to be one of the favourite actions. Each new stage originates from a previous one; each is in fact a preparation for the next stage. A second point must be made about the interrelations of the core activities. The airplane theme shows that, in making constructions, role-play and writing texts go hand in hand and influence each other. This example demonstrates that role-play is an important factor in child development, as most of the new qualities necessary for the learning activity already reveal themselves in it. Think of qualities in the domains of communication and negotiation with partners, the use of cultural instruments (writing, numbers, diagrams, etc.), reflection upon actions and meanings, making plans and agreements, obeying rules, etc.

Promoting Play Development

The examples that are used to illustrate the development of role-play and construction play show that object play prevails in the youngest children's activities and conditions in the situation may trigger the transition toward role-play. *Designing a challenging and interesting environment* is one of these conditions. It can be accomplished by adding props, like objects in the sand or household utensils in the house corner. Object play gets a further boost when a story comes into the play, as we have shown in the maternity party.

Providing interesting and meaningful activity settings is a second condition. Such settings provide children with rich opportunities to play act the adults' world, pretending to make cakes from clay or paper or changing the baby's nappy, imitating the actions of the maternity nurse. The motivation to act as the adults do is obviously the forceful developmental drive in all core activities, including reading, writing and mathematics in a play-like manner. We see this when receipts are written in the baby shop and greeting cards are made and read by the receiver. Not only for 3–6 year-olds, but also for older children thematic contexts make productive learning meaningful and interesting.

The *teachers' role* is obviously the most important condition in promoting development through play activities. To encourage play they give the children plenty of initiatives, space and encouragement to explore, invent and enjoy play situations according to their preferences and abilities. If that space is secured, the teacher can join in with children's activities with carefully considered actions that may develop their play, keeping the play perspectives and the educational aims in mind. This task gives teachers a pivot role in child development. To assist them in this task we designed a strategy and tools which will be explained in the following section. Besides that, many practical suggestions and examples are available for teachers to be used in their own classrooms.

Summing up, teachers can learn to support child development in the context of play, by getting them meaningfully involved in rich thematic play activities, and guiding them towards the appropriation of new actions and cultural tools that meet their emerging needs.

A Teacher Strategy for Assisted Performance

In Basic Development the teacher's assistance of children boils down to the question of how teachers can deliberately and systematically promote the development of young children by provoking core activities. In a classroom practice the promotion of children's development should take place in the context of cultural practices in which the child can participate (given its actual level of development), wants to participate (given its orientation to reality), and in which it learns new actions with the help of others, in accordance with the emerging needs of that child in that current cultural practice. Through imitative participation in cultural practices, zones of proximal development can be constructed in the interaction between child and adult, which become valuable contexts for learning, when the child receives appropriate help (see Chap. 2).

Children's participation in core activities does not guarantee that the desired developmental processes will actually occur. Teachers must realise that socio dramatic play, the source and motor of child development, is a result of adult mediation. Therefore, purposeful teacher-guidance is necessary for progress in these activities. In Vygotskian terms, teachers (and other adults) assist children in performing activities, be it indirectly by preparing a rich environment, or more directly in interactions and participation in children's activities. In both ways teachers and children collaboratively construct a zone of proximal development; which offers the most powerful learning opportunities.

The role of the teacher is sketched in guidelines (tools) for the pedagogical-didactic action in practice. Broadly, the teacher's task is to foster a good relationship with the children, create a rich learning environment along with them, guide activities and deploy didactic impulses, plan, observe, register and organise group activities. In the next sections we discuss some tools that are designed for the teacher role in Basic Development.

Didactic Impulses[4]

Besides the opportunities for children to play together, guided activities are important to let the core activities come to full development. To that end, didactic impulses are designed that can be used by the teachers in their work with children. These impulses help to deepen and broaden children's activities and add new abilities and skills. They are not used in a fixed order but employed whenever they are the most

---

[4]"Didactic" is to be taken here in its original old-Greek sense of "showing" (from "deiknumi") with the intention of making others learn something new. This central–European interpretation of "didactics" was elaborated already in the 1970s by German educationalists (see for example Klafki 1976), rejecting the interpretations of the word that later became popular in American educational theory, which referred to imposed learning, training and direct instruction.

necessary and appropriate, according to the teacher's observations and registrations of children's performances. We illustrate the five impulses below, using examples of teachers who work with 3–4 year-old children (Vingerhoets 2010).

Impulse 1: Orientation

Orientation is about the theme itself: what are we playing and talking about? Children must have sufficient opportunities to explore the theme and activities intensively and to feel committed to the activity and to each other. *In the context of the theme of "Doctors", the teacher and children hold a conversation in a small group. The teacher has brought plasters, a plastic syringe and a thermometer and shows them to the children. She tells them about her personal experience, and names the actions and objects. After this, the children easily come up with their own experiences.*

Impulse 2: Adjust and Deepen the Activity

Thematic activities can become richer and deeper with the help of the teacher, so that the children's interest extends and more sub-themes and activities can be added to the original context. Stories from books or personal experiences, for instance, may structure the activity. Interesting materials are important props here. The teacher and children structure their activities together by exploring the actions: where do we want to arrive, which step do we take first? What is the next step? *For example, the teacher brings a new element for role-play into the home corner: she would like to pay a visit to the house. She discusses with the children the roles that can be played. She provides them with a model when she plays out for them what her actions are when she comes to visit.*

Impulse 3: Broaden the Activity

This impulse is to connect the core activities with each other in the activity settings. The teacher helps the children to create new core activities in the thematic settings. *For instance, a teacher plays with the children that they are buying cakes in the bakery. She participates as a father and proposes to make a shopping list in case they forget what groceries they need. She shows how she makes one herself. Through this modelling she stimulates the children's interest in literacy activities.*

Impulse 4: Adding New Learning Opportunities

Adding new learning opportunities means that the teacher gives the children "nudges" towards the desired development by bringing in new opportunities for actions and skills that improve the activity. *A teacher is talking with children in their restaurant/classroom about how to make pancakes. New learning opportunities are offered when drawing a step-by-step recipe on paper. By doing this, she adds making schemes as a new meaningful operation that enhances children's abilities to take part in new activities.*

Impulse 5: Reflection

During all activities the teacher forms for herself an idea about the meanings children attached to this activity and about the degree of their involvement. She helps them to reflect upon their activities and to consider the follow-up. She also reflects upon the effects of her own actions and upon her contribution to the value of the play activity for the children themselves and for their developmental progress.

In the "restaurant" the teacher asks the children what they have been playing there. She finds out what they felt important, what went well and what didn't. She gets good insight into the vocabulary which the children already use to put their experiences into words.

In the end, all didactic strategies and tools rest upon underlying pedagogical motives. Personal interaction and cooperation are strong drives in educational activities, as they rouse new needs and goals in children that call for new cultural tools. A respectful and sensitive attitude is another indispensable aspect of the teacher's relationship with the children, as it strengthens children's confidence in themselves and in the world around them. Fostering high expectations of each child's development is a fundamental pedagogical prerequisite. Only under such circumstances can children rely on adults who keep searching for possibilities to expand children's learning opportunities.

Structuring the Curriculum Process

The core activities are embedded in socio-cultural contents (themes) in a process which we call "thematising". It means that themes are not merely introduced and rigidly carried out as planned by the teacher, but are to be set up and built by children and teacher together. Themes are planned for periods of about 4–6 weeks over which time a theme can expand.

Thematising takes place in phases. Structuring of the process is a collaborative responsibility between teacher and pupils, taking place along the following phases:

Phase zero – Preparation: This is a phase in which teachers choose a meaningful and relevant theme, prepare possible core activities and make a first outline for further elaboration.

Phase 1 – Starting activities: In this phase starting activities are introduced that open the new theme and create involvement. This phase is also important because the

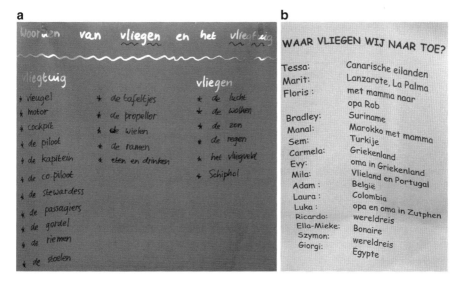

Fig. 4.9 (**a**) When the group is talking about planes and things that can fly, the teacher makes a word-field of the children's ideas. (**b**) Afterwards the group's conversation is about where the children would like to fly to

starting activities give insight into the children's available experiences with the theme. Starting activities help the teacher to discover which ideas and questions arise from the children. On the basis of children's ideas and present knowledge, the teacher can adjust her provisional plans.

In the airplane theme the following starting activities are used. The children and the teacher are taking another look at the plane one of the children made during a previous theme. In the so called "book sharing circle", children read and talk about flying and airports. They talk in small groups and in pairs about objects that have been brought from home; for example, train and flight tickets or suitcase labels. A pilot visits the class to talk about his work and about airplanes. The children have a lot of questions about this, like: The plane goes fast but it seems slow, why? How do you fly a plane? Which buttons do you need to fly? The teacher gains insight into what the children already know. The group talks about things that fly and the children come up with numerous ideas. The teacher writes them down, and organises them into the categories of animals (a butterfly, a ladybug, a wasp, a bat) and machines (airplane, kite, rockets, space shuttle, etc.). She pays attention to the way children come up with personal experiences, listens to what they say and asks questions. She also creates new issues or concerns, like where the children would like to fly to? Children already have experiences to relate to and mention places like the Canary Islands, America or Portugal, a world tour or to visit Grandpa Rob, or other relatives (Fig. 4.9a, b).

Phase 2 – Elaboration: In this phase the teacher makes her plans more concrete. She ensures a rich learning environment and develops play activities with all the previously mentioned core-activities included in them. We call this the elaboration phase of the theme. Children and teacher together elaborate a wide range of activities; for instance play and reading and writing about the airplane, travelling, designing plans for the transport of passengers to the airport. Every day, both children and teacher think of and make plans about the theme and possible activities.

Phase 3 – Completion: The teacher and children gather the outcomes and results of this period and consider involving others, like parents, in the festive closure of the theme period.

Phase 4 – Drawing up the balance: Like phase zero, phase 4 takes place outside the group. The teacher puts all the findings in a row, evaluates the results and sets up new plans for the next theme period.

Thematising ensures that the contribution of the children, their questions and needs, receive serious attention. The group learns together, is aware of shared interests and personal preferences. Learning is active and cooperative in this approach! During the theme the teacher connects children's plans and ideas to her own plans. This characterises the essence of Developmental Education: neither the children nor the teacher decide the programme on their own; it is the teacher's responsibility to create a sound balance between them.

Much attention is paid to how to guide activities and stimulate further development and learning within these activities. Strategies for the stimulation of new learning processes (in the zone of proximal development) are always sought in play activity. However, in our view such learning processes must meet two criteria: they must contribute to the optimisation of the ongoing play activity itself. The children's play must increase in value, a value that they themselves attach to it. And the learning processes to be initiated must be a stepping-stone for future learning, i.e. it should enhance children's possibilities for (peripheral) participation in the activity that is to become "leading" in the next developmental period.

Daily Plans for Supervised Activities

It is important for teachers to make (almost) daily plans for guided activities with a few groups of children she wants to assist. For this purpose, teachers use a logbook in which they make notes in three categories (Janssen-Vos and Pompert 2007, see also Chap. 14 of this volume).

Today's activity settings: The first section concerns the planning of joint activities: which activities, with what intentions and for which group of children? The extent of her personal involvement in the activity is also considered as the teacher plans her interactions, didactic impulses and the use of didactic resources. The teacher also notes points for observation.

Reflection: During activities and afterwards the teacher reflects on the course of the activities, her own intentions and the children's meanings and commitment. She also assesses whether the objectives of this activity came within reach and what the effects of her own contributions are.

Follow-up: Then the teacher thinks about a follow-up. This may be a sequel to the same activity with the same children, or any other activities that fit well in a next moment. It may also be attractive to plan follow-up activities for a larger group. The reflection and ideas for a follow-up lead to planning guided activities for the next day or couple of days, with the same and/or other children.

Usually teachers plan two or three supervised small group activities per period of the day. This is possible when there is a rich environment and all other children are engaged in meaningful activities and can play, work and learn together independently. If this is realised, it is possible for the teacher to intensively engage in an activity with one small group for about 15–20 min.

Observation and Evaluation

Planning depends on observations made during the activities (see also Chap. 14 of this volume). In this way teachers have the opportunity to interact with children, to understand what they want to do and to find out if the play activity is meaningful to them. During the observation they make short notes that they review and elaborate later on. Products or pictures of play activities are included in every child's diary and portfolio. Observation models, related to the core activities and development perspectives, support the teacher's observations. More about observation instruments, registrations and evaluation is to be found in Chap. 14 of this book.

Final Statement

Do we advocate a play-based curriculum for young children aiming at a broad development? Yes indeed, because we take the position that we should acquaint all children with a broad range of learning experiences in different cultural domains, which are established as play and embodied in interesting themes. This is especially important for children who are said to have deficits in language development or suffer from developmental delay and problems. It may seem easy and effective to spend all one's time and energy on training in isolated skills. But the results would be questionable because of the risk that so-called "problem children" would most of all learn that they are not "good enough" to undertake own initiatives and cannot show what they are really able to do and to perform. Their motivation then shifts towards activities that lie outside of the teacher's sight; losing trust and confidence in school can be the result (Allington and Cunningham 2007; Kravtsova 2007).

Opting explicitly for a broad development also reflects our beliefs and hopes for teachers! In our view the pedagogical task of schools is to help children to become responsible citizens (see also Chap. 3 of this volume) and this requires a firm and broad start, as well as responsible teachers that work continuously to further their professionalisation. Hence, valuing a broad development of pupils also characterises our image of teachers: we would like to assist teachers who want to be excellent in their profession, who take children's activities seriously and who wish to develop their pedagogical responsibility for the children's well-being and education. In this spirit we constructed Basic Development as a strategy for the realisation of Developmental Education for young children in the classroom.

References

Allington, R. L., & Cunningham, P. M. (2007). *Schools that work: Where all children read and write*. Boston: Allyn & Bacon.

El'konin, D. B. (1972). Toward the problem of stages in the mental development of the child. *Soviet Psychology, 10*(3), 225–251.

Goorhuis-Brouwer, S. (2008). De mythe van het vroege leren [The myth of early learning]. In *Mythes in het onderwijs*. Amsterdam: Uitgeverij SWP.

Janssen-Vos, F. (2008). *Basisontwikkeling voor peuters en de onderbouw* [Basic Development for preschool and early grades]. Assen: van Gorcum.

Janssen-Vos, F., & Pompert, B. (2007). *Horeb. Handelingsgericht observeren, registreren en evalueren van Basisontwikkeling* [Action-oriented observation, registration and evaluation of Basic Development]. Assen: Van Gorcum.

Karpov, Y. V. (2005). *The neo-Vygotskian approach to child development*. Cambridge: University Press.

Klafki, W. (1976). Zum Verhaltnis von Didaktik und Methodik. *Zeitschrift für Pädagogik, 22*, 77–94.

Kravtsova, E. (2007). Vygotsky's approach to education. In *Rediscovering Vygotsky* (A children in Europe special edition). Edinburgh/Scotland: Children in Scotland.

Pinar, W., & Pinar, W. F. (1995). *Understanding curriculum* (p. 860). New York: Peter Lang.

Pompert, B. (2010). Spelenderwijs wijs [Playing wise]. In A. Beets-Kessens et al. (Eds.), *Hoera! Ik krijg kleuters. Onderwijs aan het jonge kind*. Amersfoort: Thieme Meulenhof.

van Oers, B. (2010). Children's enculturation through play. In L. Brooker & S. Edwards (Eds.), *Engaging play* (pp. 195–209). Maidenhead: McGraw Hill.

Vingerhoets, I. (2010). Spel en taal begeleiden in Startblokken met de vijf didactische impulsen [Guiding play and language in Startblokken with the five didactic impulses]. *Zone, 9*(1), 19–21.

Publications About Basic Development

Bacchini, S., et al. (1998). *De voeten van de kip schminken. Tweede-taalverwerving in Basisontwikkeling* [Making up the chicken's feet. Second language acquisition in Basic Development]. Utrecht: APS.

Fijma, N., & Vink, H. (1998). *Op jou kan ik rekenen* [I can count on you]. Assen: van Gorcum.

Janssen-Vos, F. (2004). *Spel en ontwikkeling. Spelen en leren in de onderbouw* [Play and development]. Assen: van Gorcum.

Janssen-Vos, F. (2008). *Basisontwikkeling voor peuters en de onderbouw* [Basic Development for preschool and early grades]. Assen: van Gorcum.

Janssen-Vos, F., & Pompert, B. (2001). *Startblokken van Basisontwikkeling* [Starting Blocks of Basic Development]. Assen: van Gorcum.

Janssen-Vos, F., & Pompert, B. (2007). *Horeb. Handelingsgericht observeren, registreren en evalueren van Basisontwikkeling* [Action-oriented observation, registration and evaluation in Basic Development]. Assen: Van Gorcum.

Janssen-Vos, F., Pompert, B., & Vink, H. (1991). *Naar lezen, schrijven en rekenen* [Towards reading, writing and arithmetic]. Assen: van Gorcum.

Knijpstra, H., Pompert, B., & Schiferli, T. (1997). *Met jou kan ik lezen en schrijven* [With you I can read and write]. Assen: van Gorcum.

Nellestijn, B., & Janssen-Vos, F. (2005). *Het materialenboek. Een rijke leeromgeving in de onderbouw* [The materials book. A rich learning environment in the early grades]. Assen: van Gorcum.

Pompert, B., Hagenaar, J., & Brouwer, L. (2009). *Zoeken naar woorden. Gespreksactiviteiten in de onderbouw* [Searching for words. Conversation activities in the early grades]. Assen: van Gorcum.

van Oers, B. (Ed.). (2003). *Narratives of childhood*. Amsterdam: VU Press.

van Oers, B., Janssen-Vos, F., Pompert, B., & Schiferli, T. (2003). Teaching as a joint activity. In B. van Oers (Ed.), *Narratives of childhood* (pp. 110–126). Amsterdam: VU Press.

In addition to these book titles many more publications have appeared since 1990 in articles and practice brochures. For more information see: www.de-activiteit.nl

Part II
Good Practices of Developmental Education

Chapter 5
Learning to Communicate in Young Children's Classrooms

Dorian de Haan

Introduction

Communication is the exchange of meaning. Learning to communicate is, therefore, "learning how to mean", which was the title of a now classic study by Halliday (1975). In this study of language acquisition by his son Nigel, Halliday took a "functional-interactional approach". This approach views learning a language as a semiotic process of interaction in which language becomes part of a system of meanings in a functional context. The source of this system is the socio-cultural world in which the child participates. A similar view was also developed by Vygotskij more than 50 years earlier in his writings about the semiotic mediation of higher levels of thought.

Children learn the psychological tools of their culture, which leads to qualitative new levels of mental processes and thus to development. In particular, as neo-Vygotskians have emphasised, children need to learn the *mental procedures of using* these tools in given socio-cultural activities. This cannot be attained by mere exposure: children appropriate these procedures *in joint activity* with knowledgeable others who are sensitive to the child's zone of proximal development (Karpov 2005). The motor of learning in such activity is the emotional involvement of the learner; affective processes make children participate. Fundamentally, Vygotskij considered the dynamic of development to be the result of the development of new motives, personal needs, and interests that emerge in interactions with cultural others.

D. de Haan, Ph.D. (✉)
Department of Developmental Education, Faculty of Learning, Education and Philosophy of Life, Inholland University of Applied Sciences, Haarlem, The Netherlands

Department of Developmental Psychology, Utrecht University, Utrecht, The Netherlands
e-mail: Dorian.dehaan@Inholland.nl; D.M.P.dehaan@uu.nl

B. van Oers (ed.), *Developmental Education for Young Children*, International Perspectives on Early Childhood Education and Development 7, DOI 10.1007/978 94 007-4617-6_5,

Teaching children how to mean is the core of Developmental Education (DE). Communication is at the heart of DE activities. In this chapter I will discuss the following questions: How do children acquire this communicative ability? What role do adults play? How can teachers and peers contribute to this? What practices can be found in Developmental Education?

Learning to Communicate

Assisting children to develop means for communication is an important goal in Developmental Education classrooms. In their work with young children teachers invest a lot of effort in teaching children how to communicate, how to articulate their intentions and what they have in their minds and want to share with others.

Researchers use different perspectives when studying children's acquisition of communicative competence. Some focus on the role of adults in the *guided participation* of the child (Rogoff 1990); others emphasise the child's individual cognitive activity in interaction with the knowing social world in terms of *collaborative constructionism* (Nelson 1996). The common ground among these perspectives is that *shared experience is the foundation of communication*.

Learning to Share Experiences

Cooperative activity involving shared intentionality is considered a uniquely human form of communication, which is referred to as *the Vygotskian intelligence hypothesis* (Moll and Tomasello 2006; Liszkowski et al. 2008). The assumption is that humans are fundamentally motivated to engage in collaborative activity. This engagement is already visible in 12 month-old toddlers when they display their motivation to share attention and interest by pointing, and express themselves as *mental* agents trying to influence the mental state of the other.

The role of adults and children in early communication varies with cultures. A dyadic, face-to-face child-centered style of speaking with babies and toddlers is typical of many Western families. Adults often endeavour to evoke a child's disposition to communicate with them, and by questioning and answering their own questions, they provide their children with the cultural tools that gradually enable them to play their part in this communication. In many cultures, however, adults have other ways of communication (Lieven 1994). In these communities children themselves work hard to make sense of the linguistic communication around them and find ways to participate in shared experiences. They are often involved in polyadic participatory structures. Cole (1985) and Rogoff (1990) account for these ways of learning by specifying the concept of zone of proximal development. Cole broadened the social space by postulating collectively organised activities in which participants have different expertise and responsibilities. Rogoff included tacit and distal arrangements in learning environments. She emphasised children's active contribution as *apprentices* and the learning potential of interaction with peers.

Most research is about adult-child interaction; research on communication between children themselves is rare. However, from a study of families and siblings such as Dunn's (1988), it appears that very young children are also able to collaborate in mutual communicative exchanges with their siblings. She shows that they share playful moods and actions in *rhythmic coaction sequences* (Dunn 1988, p. 111). Some children already recognise and cooperate in a sibling's goal at 14 months old. Dunn observes the positive excitement this cooperation brings, and suggests that it is the emotional resonance that motivates it, referring to Stern's assumption of "affect contagion" as "a basic biological tendency among highly evolved social species" (Stern 1985, cited in Dunn 1988). This brings us back to Vygotskij's intelligence hypothesis, as well as to his view of the importance of emotion, affect, and motivation in the learning process.

In sum, there is clear agreement that children affectionately participate from an early age in, as van Oers (this volume, Chap. 2) labels them, *collaborative processes of structuring current activities*, and that this is a crucial prerequisite in development. Learning how to mean involves collaboration, agency of children, sensitivity and mediation by adults, and passion. This is the core of the Developmental Education approach of communication and learning. But before dealing with communication in DE classrooms, we will first look at how children acquire this communicative ability and what role the adults play.

From Inter- to Intra-mental Functioning

How do children acquire communicative competencies to collaborate? What roles do adults and peers play in children's interactions that have developmental value for the child? What genres are involved?

Language acquisition and cooperative play are important domains in the research on communicative competence of young children. With respect to language acquisition, studies of the dyadic adult-child interaction show how children internalise skills learned in adult-child cooperation and transfer them to cooperation among peers. In *ritual games* with an adult, such as peek-a-boo and hide-and-seek, children display a growing responsibility by initiating turns themselves from 9 months onward. Turn-taking in *conversation* is also an early accomplishment. Initially (Western) adults take the lead in the first months of their children's life. Face-to-face conversations with their baby predominantly serve affective functions from the child's point of view. By 8 months children know how to take turns as a communicative routine. Around the ninth month, children begin to grasp the idea that an adult communicates intentions (Tomasello 2003), and discover the symbolic function of communication. Initially it is the adult who takes care of coherence of topic in the conversation. Only by the age of 3 can children follow turn-taking rules with peers in exchanging information in conversations (Ninio and Snow 1996). Their communication develops from simple adjacency, in which children follow their own track in contributing to the conversation, to contingency of topic (Bloom 1991). According to Nelson (1996), by age 4–5, children engage in conversation on a single topic about non-shared information, without the support of related props. Corsaro and Riszo (1988) have shown how vivid and stylised are the "discussions" between 3 to 6 year-olds in an Italian nursery school. With respect to *problem-solving activities*, children become able to execute coordinated actions involving joint intention and a joint goal non-verbally by 18 months with an adult, and at 24 months in a verbal way; with peers this may not happen before 30 months (Warneken et al. 2006).

Conversations to exchange information and joint problem solving, however, are just two of the communicative genres. Research on the development of cooperative play among peers reveals the importance of other genres, such as imitative and pretend play. As early as 3 months, infants show social interest in one another and display vocalising and reaching to another child (Durkin 1995). An important first form of coordinated action is non-verbal reciprocating *imitation*, which emerges in the first half of the second year (Eckerman and Peterman 2000). In this type of communication, children display abilities of joint action on a common theme, which is the act itself, and show mutual social influence. Their exchanges become semantically related, first in a non-verbal way, and later by integrating language into their coordinated action. They start to direct each other, respond to each other, and a few months later they use words to describe their own acts. In this way toddlers appear to scaffold their efforts at verbal communication with one another. Sharing a theme is also basic to the other genres. Corsaro (1997) found that in nursery school, *play routines* with a simple repetitive structure enable a large number of children to participate and create a peer culture of doing things together. *Pretend play* is another genre in which young children display inter-subjectivity. The recognition and coordination of intention in pretend play among peers initially emerges around the age of 2 (Howes et al. 1992). Göncü (1993) presupposes that this initial pretend play is affective in nature and that development concerns a change in the communicative means to construct inter-subjectivity, from non-verbal ways such as facial gestures and exaggerated movements to verbal communication and meta-communication. There are large individual differences in frequency of social pretence, however. Howe et al. (2005) found that siblings, who frequently engage in pretend play together, were more often able to construct shared meaning than were siblings whose play was less frequent and more focused on agonism and control. Dyads of a kindergartener and a school-age sibling displayed more shared meanings, while dyads with a preschool sibling showed more non-maintenance behaviour. The responsibility for sharing of meanings, development of coordination and a story line in joint play among 25–30 month-old children, is initially taken by mothers and older siblings (Howes et al. 1992).

In sum, although peers of the same age may create their own interactional patterns to share meaning in genres such as imitative and routine play, adults and more expert peers play an important role in the other genres in the child's learning to communicate. Rogoff (1990) conceives of development in the collaborative construction of meaning as a transformation of participation. This is exactly what Developmental Education teachers aim at.

Developmental Education: Communicating to Learn

The first question a teacher in Developmental Education (DE) asks when thinking about any new educational activity is: how will I get children to become meaningfully engaged? One of the first steps is to talk with them. Communication is the backbone of all activities, both oral and written (see also in this volume Chaps. 15 and 16 about learning to read and doing math). It is the point of departure, and at the same time a learning goal. Learning to communicate is one of the main aims of "broad development". This means that children need to learn how to mean in all senses: on the one hand they have to refine their competence in pragmatic functions of language that relate to the instrumental and regulatory use of language, and on the other hand education plays a major role in extending the learning functions of language (Halliday 1975). Halliday distinguishes personal, heuristic, imaginative, and informative learning functions. Children learn language as a means to express their personal feelings, interests, and pleasure, to explore their environment, to create and explore the world of pretence, and to exchange information. So, both learning to communicate and communicating to learn are main objectives. In the early years of educational arrangements, play is considered the means to enable children to appropriate these language functions in order to participate in the activities of their culture (van Oers 2010). Janssen-Vos & Pompert have outlined the main characteristics of DE practices elsewhere in this volume (Chap. 4). The role of the teacher is considered to be crucial. This holds for all the genres and functions mentioned above. The teacher is involved in conversations, problem solving, play routines, and pretend play to challenge children to use the pragmatic and learning functions of language, by designing activities in which children feel secure, emotionally engaged, and curious to participate. In this chapter, I will present our research on the teacher's role in one of the genres mentioned above, namely pretend play, as an illustration to clarify our understanding with regard to communicative development in Developmental Education.

A Case Study of Co-construction in Pretend Play in Developmental Education

In the last few years we have been engaged in research on communication and language in several pre- and nursery schools. This research aims to gain a better view of and contribute to DE practice in collaboration with the teachers, and at the same time contribute to DE theory. Here I will discuss our work in one particular educational good practice at a preschool (the *Voorschool*), working with the programme of *Startblokken* (literally translated as "Starting Blocks", see Janssen-Vos & Pompert, this volume, Chap. 4).[1] Our focus was on pretend role-play,

---

[1] The author would like to thank Jeannette Schut and Jeannette Pals for participating in the data collection and/or the analysis.

since this kind of play is highly valued in Developmental Education for a number of reasons (Janssen-Vos 2004). It is seen as the heart of play development, since it includes all kinds of experiences and skills that children need to develop. It is especially important in the domain of communication, language, and literacy. Several authors have shown the relationship between pretend play and literacy (Pellegrini and Galda 1993; Watson 2001; de Haan 2005). Like a written text, social pretend play consists of a representation of experience. As a type of narrative, it has the cohesive structure of non-random connected sub-events, and often entails meta-communication about roles, props, actions, etc. Pretend play can also offer opportunities for promoting vocabulary growth (van Oers 2010), especially in children for whom the language of the (pre)school is a second language. Teachers may introduce words together with their play actions, which makes their meanings transparent. Bacchini (in prep.) shows that a highly frequent use of words in the input is significantly related to vocabulary acquisition by young second-language learners. Teachers may repeat the most important words of a play topic, and use a great many content words in a short time (lexical density) (Bacchini 2008). So, pretend play offers a number of perspectives to investigate how teachers guide children in "communicating to learn."

The main questions in our case study centre on teachers' collaboration with children: what roles do the teachers take in their play communication with the children, and to what extent do these roles fit the zone of proximal development in which the child and the teacher are involved? How do the teachers encourage children to communicate with one another? What strategies do they use for specific language education goals such as narrative development and vocabulary acquisition?

Method

We interviewed the two teachers and observed them via video in their work with the children on four separate mornings. We used portable wireless audio equipment (Sennheiser, EW 100) and a video camera, and the teachers wore a lapel microphone connected to a pocket transmitter. First we analysed our recordings and selected fragments of pretend play. We transcribed and coded all teacher's and children's utterances in three different play interactions with each teacher (29 and 37 min of interactions with teacher Erika and teacher Barbara, respectively, including 725 utterances by the teachers and 469 utterances by the children), using the software programme Childes (MacWhinney 2000). Finally, we discussed these analyses with the teachers. The children in this preschool were 2 and 3 years old, and all of them had a migrant background, mainly Moroccan and Turkish, with limited command of Dutch (which is a second language for them). In the fragments of pretend play, 11 children were involved in Erika's interactions, and 8 children in Barbara's. Within the general DE framework of the play-based curriculum, the teachers worked with different themes over 6–8 weeks, and played with the children in thematic activity centres (home corner, water table, etc.).

To analyse the teachers' collaboration with the children in the pretend play interactions, we studied their intervention roles. Johnson et al. (1999) and Kontos (1999) distinguish (1) outside intervention – *onlooker, stage manager* and (2) inside intervention – *co-player, play leader*, and *instructor/director*. We then systematised these roles according to five criteria: the *action* the teacher undertakes, the person taking the *initiative* – teacher or child, *which* personal pronouns the teachers use to *address* the children, which *language functions* are used, and the teachers' *attitude* (see Fig. 5.1). We coded the utterances according to who assumed these roles and studied the extent to which the teachers took on the different roles, and in what way these roles were related to the co-construction of the narrative and cooperative play. Except for the instructor/director role, the roles focus on the collaborative development of the narrative.

In the stage manager role, we distinguished between (a) the stage manager who builds up the play setting by discussing props, participants, roles (which is often done with children in DE), and (b) stage manager action, when the participating teacher steps out of her role as a co-player in the narrative to give suggestions about continuing the play, for example, about what the child may say or do.

To study cooperative play, the utterances were coded for *self-directed play, play directed towards an object* (giving an injection to the father-puppet for instance), and *cooperative play directed to another person* (talking about a joint action). Although solitary play (which may be self or object-directed) is viewed as a developmentally lower level than cooperative play, with its complex collaborative interaction, it is valuable on its own and may be rich and intense (Dunn 2008).

Finally, to analyse narrative development, we coded all utterances for the categories of a *(repeated) single narrative act*, which is a play action that stands apart without any connection to a preceding or following action (such as an act of eating), *single scheme sequences* in which the same act is directed to different recipients or different acts that belong to the same script (for instance, when the doctor gives the patient a pill and then a liquid), and *multi-scheme sequences having a logical order* to build a plot (adaptation from Beiser and Howes 1992). Building a plot is the most advanced level.

Two coders independently coded 10% of the utterances to determine reliability of coding; this was sufficient (Cohen's kappa 0.77).

Regarding vocabulary acquisition, we analysed the frequency of important content words. Childes gives an overview of the frequency of all the words in a play file.

Results

Interviews

In the interviews the teachers said that *engagement* and *collaboration* were their main focus. They wanted to connect children to their play and to other children. One

Outside intervention: The teacher is involved, but does not participate in the narrative

	Onlooker	Stage manager
Action	• Observes • Motivates	• Prepares /organizes the play field (attributes, roles) • Gives suggestions, models, proposes content
Initiative	• The children	• The teacher
Address	• "You"	• "You"

Language functions	• Motivate: *That's a nice pie!*
	• Posing questions: *Do you go by bus often?*
	• Describe, label: *You are cooking!*
		• Meta-communication = structuring
		  - Exchange information: *Where are you going?*
		  - Directives: *Doctor, please cure daddy.*
		  - Declarative: *There is the soup spoon*

Attitude	• Look, wait, value, inform	• Involved, advising, organizing

Inside intervention: The teacher is involved, participates/has a role in the narrative

	Co-player	Play leader
Action	• Child's action as the lead, teacher follows and guides in a subtle way	• Teacher takes the lead, enriches the narrative
Initiative	• Balance: child's initiative, teacher follows, assists, adds content in a subtle way	• Teacher
Address	• "We," "I"	• "We," "I"
Language functions	• : *I just listen to my baby in my belly.* • Questioning: *can I have a bit too?*	• Eventcasts; Talk about actions *Oh, just tighten the screw.* • Directing from inside: *We are going to eat.* • Questions: *Do you want a cup of tea?* • Declaratives: *I like pie.*
Attitude	• Teacher as equal partner • Often subordinate role (the child, patient, client)	• Stimulating

Inside intervention: The teacher is involved, participates/has a role in the narrative

	Instructor/director
Action	• Instruction about attributes, organization, word meaning, role • Questioning
Initiative	• Teacher
Address	• " Impersonal," "you"
Language functions	• Questions: *What is that?* • Explanations, declaratives: *That's a cucumber* • Directives: *Give it back, Together*
Attitude	• Teacher

Fig. 5.1 The teacher's roles

main objective was to develop a group feeling and togetherness: "Otherwise they cannot play. Playing means doing the things together." They were convinced that children can learn from each other, and they wanted to teach them to listen to and play with each other. To build possibilities for cooperative play, the teachers created common ground by developing preparatory activities around a theme. The themes have familiar subjects. They bring in objects, label and explore them with the children, act upon them, invite children to talk about their experiences, and give the objects a place in a special corner of the playground, which they build up together. Then the children begin to play and the teachers observe with whom and when they join in. For example, in the theme of the bed room, the teachers started off with a mattress, discussing with the children what was needed to sleep on it; they made up the bed with blankets and a pillow, and then discussed pictures of the blankets at the children's homes, and they played at sleeping with all the lights turned off. Then they made a bedroom in the play corner, discussed the design with night tables and night lamps, etc. The doll house was redesigned and given a prominent place. In the course of the theme period, a picture book was introduced about a family sleeping in a big bed, and a story-telling table[2] was made where props were put in order to rehearse the story and play it out with the children. The teachers played being ill, having a baby, etc., with the children. The teachers justified their choices by referring to the need to create a common ground – *shared meanings* – for play in order to motivate the children to connect to the activities and play together.

Asked about which roles they preferred, the teachers chose roles inside the play, but they also made remarks such as: "meanwhile we also watch the children," and "stage managing we do before and after." With respect to their objectives of guiding the children's communicative and language development, the teachers emphasised the importance of a secure pedagogical climate in which children felt free to express themselves regardless of their limited competence in Dutch as a second language. They selected familiar subjects from the children's socio-cultural world to be sure they understood their meanings, attempted to create real-life activities, and said "*do the words.*" Thus they introduced words in relation to play actions and in discussions around visible objects and the children's experiences. They watched the children and joined in their play scripts.

Observations

To answer our questions about the way DE teachers communicate with children, we studied which roles they took and how these roles supported children in the zone of proximal development. Further, we analysed the way they encourage children to communicate with each other by studying the extent to which the teachers foster cooperative play. Finally, we looked at teachers' strategies to advance narrative development and vocabulary acquisition as specific language education goals.

The Teacher's Role and the Zone of Proximal Development

Our main focus was to analyse whether the use of these intervention roles related to co-construction of the narrative and how the roles relate to the children's zone of

---

[2]For more information about the story-telling telling table see Chap. 4, section "Developmental Perspectives in Constructive Play", note 3.

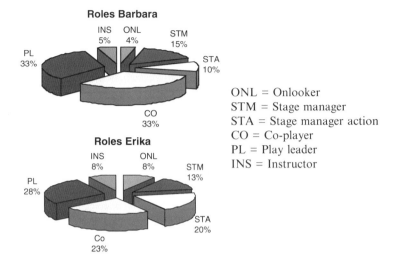

ONL = Onlooker
STM = Stage manager
STA = Stage manager action
CO = Co-player
PL = Play leader
INS = Instructor

Fig. 5.2 Roles of the teacher, percentages of utterances

proximal development. In other words, do the children's level of pretend play and language development influence the teacher's guidance?

We found that the teachers were flexible participants in all roles, as can be seen from Fig. 5.2.

The onlooker and instructor roles were not used frequently. Utterances from the onlooker role were often found at the start of a pretend play, for example, when the teachers asked the child playing in the sand pit: "What are you going to make, Nisa?" But this role has an important non-verbal aspect, which we could not account for since we only analysed verbal utterances. In our interviews the teachers related that they continuously monitored the children's play – "meanwhile we also watch the children" – to be sure they had a common narrative frame.

In just a few cases the teacher gave instructions in an explicit way, for example, when Erika takes the sink bowl from Amin and says "This one has to be in here," and puts it back in the sink, or when she corrects Amin in labelling the roles of the puppets at the story-telling table, "This is mom, look, this is daddy," or when teacher Barbara shows Pedram how to handle the stethoscope. These utterances are often responses to the children's behaviour; they encouraged playing in a more advanced way.

Although both teachers said they preferred to play with the children from the inside roles, we found there were differences between the teachers; teacher Barbara's utterances were largely made as a co-player and a play leader, whereas teacher Erika often played as a stage manager. Upon closer examination, we see that these differences may relate to the play competencies of the children they played with. Most of the time Erika played with the youngest children, especially with Amin who was 2 years, 8 months old; this was true for two of the three play interactions. The following fragments (1) and (2) are about a play situation in which teacher Erika sits in the home corner between Amin, who plays in the kitchen part, and four girls who play with baby dolls, joining the two scenarios in turns. In both cases she takes the role of stage manager. In (1) she adjusts to Amin's limited play and language level by modelling and talking about the step-by-step play actions, guiding him in starting to play, and providing him with the words related to each object and action. Here the stage manager role seems to support Amin's play.

(1) *Doing the dishes.* Teacher Erika and Amin (2 years, 8 months old). Kitchen of home corner. Amin is playing at washing up.[3]

> Teacher: *We take that one off, like this* [She takes the washing-up brush out of the bowl and gives it to Amin]. *You may do the dishes. Look here you have some plates* [Gives him the plates]. *You can wash them up. You turn on the tap* [She pretends this action]. *Then the water runs out. A bit of soap* [She squirts imaginary washing liquid in the bowl]. *Then you may do the dishes* [She takes the brush and shows how to wash-up]. *The front ... The back. ... Do you want to do it, Amin?*
> Amin: [Takes the brush and cleans the plate].
> Teacher: *It is going to get clean, isn't it?*
> Amin: *Yes* [Cleans the plate with the brush].
> Teacher: *You can let it dry here* [Puts a plate in the dish rack]. *You may do that* [Points to the plate].

In (2) teacher Erika addresses Nisa (3 years, 11 months old), with a question about an imaginary past situation requiring a much higher level of play and language. In this case we can see that the stage manager role provides further depth to the child's pretence.

(2) *Baby.* Teacher Erika and Nisa (3 years, 11 months old). Nisa is one of the four girls playing in the home corner:

> Teacher: *Your baby has just had food, Nisa? Your baby has just had food?*
> Nisa: *Yes.*
> Teacher: *Yes. What did you give her? A little drink?*

In these cases the stage manager role might also be prompted by the teacher's position between the two play scenarios: in this way she is better able to monitor both play fields.

The children playing with teacher Barbara in the three play interactions are older, aged between 3 years, 3 months and 4. Barbara takes more of the inside intervention roles to co-construct the pretend play. Fragment (3) is a scenario with Fatima, who already knows how to play and has acquired some Dutch. This fragment shows how teacher Barbara first introduces the role of a doctor for one of the puppets in the doll house as a stage manager and later, as a play leader, she plays the role of the doctor.

---

[3] I have attempted to translate the Dutch of teacher and children as close to the original colloquial speech as possible.

(3) *Daddy is ill.* Teacher Barbara and Fatima (3 years, 6 months old), playing with the doll house. Fatima is playing alone and puts the father puppet in bed and takes a blanket from the doll house.

Fatima: *Daddy is ill, daddy has become completely ill.*
Teacher: *How sad!* (She joins Fatima and is going to sit on the floor). *A doctor has to come.*
Pedram: (Pulls Barbara's arm to come with him to the sleeping room).
Pedram: *Oh, the doctor is coming* (Addressing Pedram, who comes by and looks at the play). *Daddy is ill, says Fatima.* (The teacher tries to involve Pedram). *Where is the doctor? Just searching for where the doctor is.* (Barbara continues her play with Fatima and searches in the doll house for a puppet).
Fatima: *Doctor?*
Teacher: *Doctor. Yes, here is the doctor. Toomtetoomtetoomtetoomtetoom.* (She takes a puppet from the doll house and lets him walk to daddy's bed).
Fatima: *Eh, Daddy is* .... (Teacher interrupts)
Teacher: *Eh, Daddy, what's the matter?* (Low voice of a male doctor).
Fatima: *Eh, euh, tired.*
Teacher: *I am so ill, doctor* (The weakened voice of the sick father).
Fatima: *Eeheheeheh!*
Teacher: *Fatima, what's wrong with daddy?*
Fatima: *Is ill!*
Teacher: *Daddy pain in his belly?*
Fatima: *Yes.*

Both teachers seem to play within the zone of proximal development with the children; both roles fit the children's potential behaviour. The stage manager role of Erika encourages Amin to imitate the play act. He talks hardly any Dutch, and she gives him the words alongside the play actions, without urging him to produce the words himself. The play leader role of Barbara in her initial contribution facilitates Fatima's play: Fatima will imitate the doctor's role in a later fragment of this play moment, when she is playing with the doctor puppet and says "Do you have ill? You have ill?" and then she answers for the daddy puppet who says "yes," and nods his head.

Sometimes it takes time to adjust the children's affective and cognitive levels. For example, at the story-telling table, teacher Erika begins to play the stage manager and instructor roles to involve Amin, asking him questions such as, "Where is daddy, Amin? Are they going to sleep?" Initially she does not succeed in involving Amin, who is just manipulating the puppets, until she switches to the play leader role and *acts* herself: *I am, putting the children in.* ...

(4) *Sleeping story at the story-telling table.* Teacher Erika and Amin (2 years, 9 months old), Meshda (4 years old), Ayoub (3 years, 8 months old).

Teacher: *Is this little child going to sleep too?* (She gives Amin another puppet).
Amin: *Uh?*

Teacher: *Is he going to sleep in the big bed?*
Amin: *Uh?* (Amin puts the puppet in the big bed).
Teacher: *So ..., putting the children in.. This child and this child. ... Look, Amin!*
Amin: *Huh?* (He comes closer with his chair to the story-telling table and looks at the bed).
Teacher: There are four children in it, do you see?
Amin: *Good night* (Amin places the child puppets differently in the bed)
Teacher: *Yes, they are all going to sleep.*

We found that the teachers use all roles in a flexible and functional way, and the roles seem to be appropriate to the children's zone of proximal development for their pretend play. Nevertheless, this finding does not mean that these roles are exclusively related to a particular level of children's play development. The choice of an intervention role is not an all-or-nothing issue and may sometimes be a matter of trying them out: the cognitive level is as important as the affective mood of the child in accepting the teacher's help. Finally, there may also be other pragmatic motives for choosing a particular role, such as teacher Erika's position between two play fields, which hinders her from acting as a co-player.

Cooperative Play

Table 5.1 shows that the percentages of the teachers' utterances with respect to the orientation to self, object, or the other come close to those of the children. For example, 31% of teacher Barbara's utterances are about the child itself, which is exactly the same percentage as the child's self-directed utterances. However, the teachers also seem to encourage the children to play at a higher level, especially with respect to the highest level of cooperative play.

The figures suggest that both teachers often *follow* the children's play choices and join them in their self-directed, object-directed, or cooperative play, and so adjust their guidance to the children's actual development. During the play they may attempt to bring in a higher level by involving an object or another child. In particular, teacher Erika, who often plays with the youngest children, attempts to shift attention away from the self in favour of the higher levels of an object or another person orientation. She arranges a play scene with two or three children, and alternates comments on children's play actions (*Are you going to pour tea?*) with suggestions to cooperate (*Amin, what are we going to eat?*) or taking turns (*He wants to pour a bit. Can he try it once?*). Sometimes she succeeds in involving all children in the same play actions, for example, when all children drink tea or pretend their pizzas are too hot. In other cases children remain focused on their own actions in parallel play.

Both teachers encourage or invite other children to join when they come by and look at what teacher and child(ren) are playing. In fragment (5) teacher Erika invites

Table 5.1 Play orientation of teachers and children; percentages of utterances

	Teacher Barbara		Teacher Erika	
	Teacher (%)	Children (%)	Teacher (%)	Children (%)
Self-directed	31	31	50	64
Object-directed	5	13	14	8
Cooperative play	64	57	36	28

a child to join the play activity. In fragment (6) teacher Barbara, who is playing the doctor's role, immediately gives her doctor's role to Pedram when he suggests playing that role. She tells him to get the doctor's bag to better play this role.

(5) *Drinking tea and eating pizza.* Teacher Erika, Amin, Meshda, and Waiel play that their pizza is very hot, they blow in turns. A child comes along.

Teacher: *Do you want to blow too?* (Addressing a child who is passing).
Child: (Touches the pizza.)
Teacher: *Au, hot!*
Teacher: *Isn't it hot?*
Teacher: *No?* (She blows again and then puts the pan on the table. The child does not join and walks away).

(6) *The doctor comes in.* Teacher Barbara, Pedram (3 years, 8 months old) and Fatima play in the doll house.

Pedram: *I was, I am doctor.*
Teacher: *Oh, are you the doctor! Ooooh! Perhaps you can, you can then get the doctor's case.*
Pedram: (Nods and runs away).
 Meanwhile Fatima takes the mother puppet, the teacher asks her what the mother is telling the doctor, and then Fatima says that *baby is very ill too,* and puts her in bed.
Pedram: *Here is …..* (Arrives with the doctor's case).
Teacher: *Oh look, here is the real doctor!*
Fatima: *Ill and ill and ill!* [Points to all patients].
Teacher: *Doctor, there are two sick people, a daddy and a child are also ill!*
Pedram: *O.K.* (Looks at the beds, opens the doctor's case, and takes the stethoscope).
Teacher: *And another baby is also ill.*
Teacher: *Just sit here doctor.* (She sits backwards, so Pedram has more room).
Teacher: *Then you can heal daddy.*
Pedram: …. (Examines the puppets with the stethoscope).
Fatima: *Uh, here too, little baby.* (Indicates to Pedram where he should listen with his stethoscope).

In general, these 2 and 3 year-old children only occasionally use relevant language in cooperative play among themselves. The teachers seem to have a crucial role in getting them to talk and communicate about their pretend play.

Specific Language Goals

Advancing Narrative Structure

Although, of course, the teachers know how to play out a narrative plot – the highest narrative level – they often join in the children's scenario as is shown in Table 5.2. This means that (the sequence of) their utterances more often express a single act than a logical ordered sequence involving a plot. But the teachers also address children at a higher level. Table 5.2 shows how the teachers' contribution is ahead of the children's narrative structures.

The figures represent mean percentages of the utterances at the group level, and not on the level of the individual teacher-child dyad. Qualitative analysis shows how the teachers often build a narrative from the children's non-verbal play behaviour by bringing in language. For example, in watching Nourdan's and Nisa's play in the sand pit, teacher Barbara discusses what they are going to make, suggests that Nourdan is baking a pie, and she asks whether she can taste it, whether Nisa may taste it, and what's in it. Then she joins the children in baking a pie. When Nisa puts a pan with sand at the border of the sand pit, she sets out the plastic picnic table and suggests they all start to eat. When the teacher joins the pretence of the children, she attempts to elaborate the narrative by suggesting new episodes, for example, treatment with a pill, mixture, and injection by the doctor.

It should be noted that methodological issues may influence the findings. There are differences between teachers' and children's meanings that are scored under single act. Single act utterances by teachers often concern repetitions of utterances when a child does not respond. Explanations by the teacher are also scored under this category. These utterance functions do not contribute further to the narrative plot, but they do not need to be considered as utterances at a simple level in general.

In addition, some scenarios more easily lend themselves to playing a script and single scheme sequences than to a plot. In the home corner the play actions often form a script about eating different things, and in the sand pit pretend play may concern all kinds of cakes (chocolate, strawberry, etc.), whereas the illness-and-getting-better scenario more often evokes utterances involving multi-scheme sequences having a logical order.

We also analysed if it made a difference for the level of the narrative structure whether the teachers intervened from within or outside the play. For these findings we considered only the "pure" co-player and play leader roles as inside intervention (not the director/instructor role). Table 5.3 shows that in general both teachers more often used multi-scheme sequences having a logical order when they intervened from within the play. When we examine the six play interactions separately, however, this does not appear to be the case for all interactions. Especially Erika's

Table 5.2 Type of narrative utterances. Percentages of utterances of teachers and children

	Narrative structure					
	Single act		Single scheme sequence		Multi-scheme sequence logical order	
	Teacher (%)	Children (%)	Teacher (%)	Children (%)	Teacher (%)	Children (%)
Barbara	47	60	25	20	28	20
Erika	40	66	31	20	29	14

Table 5.3 Teachers' roles and narrative structures. Percentages and absolute number of utterances

		Teacher Barbara		Teacher Erika	
		%	n	%	n
Inside intervention	Single act	19	108	25	47
	Single scheme sequence	11	78	18	43
	Multi-scheme logical order	16	102	24	58
	Total		**288**		**148**
Outside Intervention	Single act	33	94	22	69
	Single scheme sequence	13	33	8	48
	Multi-scheme logical order	8	18	4	27
	Total		**145**		**144**
Total			**433**		**292**

interactions differ in this respect: the inside intervention of the *Drinking tea* interaction is most helpful in developing the plot, but in the *Doing the dishes* play, inside and outside interventions advance the plot equally; the *Sleeping story* interaction hardly has any plot.

Vocabulary

Pretend play involving props that may be manipulated enables teachers to use words referring to these props in a meaningful way, which facilitates second language acquisition (L2).

(7) *Drinking tea.* Teacher Erika, Meshda (4 years old), Amin (2 years, 8 months old), and Waiel (2 years, number of months unknown).

Teacher: *I would like to have a cup of tea from you, Meshda.*
Teacher: *Amin, a cup of tea too?*
Amin: *No, no.* (Turns to the kitchen sink.)
Meshda: *Pssss.* (She pours tea and gives the cup to the teacher.)
Teacher: *Thank you!*
Teacher: *Waiel, a cup of tea too?* (Gives him a cup.)
Waiel   (Unintelligible.) (Takes the cup and turns it in his hands.)
Meshda: *Here.* (Gives the teacher another cup of tea.)

Teacher: *Hmmm.* (Drinking tea.) *Do you want to have sugar in it?* (Addresses Waiel, who has his cup in his lap.)

Teacher: *I take a spoon.* (Takes cutlery tray from the cupboard, puts it on the table, and takes a spoon.)

Teacher: *Waiel.* (Gives him a spoon.)

Meshda: *Who wants to have tea?*

Teacher: *Do you want to stir? A little sugar in it?*

Teacher: *No, know how to do sugar!*

Teacher: *Oh, sorry.*

Waiel: (Waves with his spoon for a while, takes sugar from the sugar bowl.)

Teacher: *Are you going to drink a cup of tea?*

Meshda: *Here, you go row.* (In Dutch *stir* and *row* is roe*r*en and roe*i*en respectively; gives the teacher a spoon.)

Teacher: *Are you going to stir?*

Meshda: *You row.*

Teacher: (Stirs her tea intensely, Waiel and Meshda imitate the stirring.) *So, has it been stirred well now?*

Meshda: *Yes.*

Teacher: *Or does it need some more sugar?* (She adds a bit more sugar in her tea.)

Meshda: (She also adds some more sugar in her tea. All children and the teacher stir.)

Teacher: *You are doing a lot of sugar in your tea!* (Addressing Meshda.)

Teacher: *Do you like that, so much sugar?*

In fragment (7) we may see how the words *tea* and *sugar* are often repeated. In the play interaction as a whole, which is about drinking tea and eating pizza, the teacher uses the word *tea* 12 times, *cup* 7 times and *sugar* 8 times. In the pizza scene frequencies are *yummy* 11 times, *eat* 9 times, *hot* 8 times, *pizza*, *blow* and *sandwich* 7 times. It is primarily the oldest child, Meshda, who is using the words *tea, sugar, yummy, pizza,* and *hot* a single time or twice. Waiel's contribution is one time *yummy* and *pizza*. Amin as yet hardly participates verbally. Although the frequency of use of these core words is relatively high, it remains a tough job for L2 children with very limited command of Dutch to acquire these words from a single interaction. According to the theory and empirical research of second language acquisition (Bacchini in prep.), these frequencies are necessary and the words have to be repeated in subsequent interactions to become integrated in a L2 child's passive and active vocabulary. By working with a theme over the course of 6 weeks, in different contexts like the sleeping room, the doll house and the story-telling table, DE makes frequent input of these words possible. In playing with an individual or a small group of children and with props to refer to, teachers may create joint attention and shared meaning. Emphasis on the core words, in short sentences (*Amin, a cup of tea too? Do you want to stir?*) facilitates the L2 child's perception of these words. Table 5.4 about the play-interactions of teacher Erika with the youngest children shows that these core words are embedded in sentences

Table 5.4 Input of words. Absolute number of frequent words of teacher Erika per play interaction

Play interaction	Core words (>5)	Frequency of use	Different words	Total number of words
Drinking tea	Tea	12	173	635
	Sugar	8		
	Cup	7		
	Pizza	7		
	Blow	7		
	Eat	9		
	Hot	8		
	Yummy	11		
Doing dishes	Washing up	5	321	788
	Oven	6		
	Peanut butter	6		
	Pizza	5		
	Tea	8		
Story-telling table	Bed	6	48	151
	Child	5		
	Sleep	9		
	Papa	6		

within a great number of (different) words, so it is important that these core words are salient for the children. In Table 5.4 only core words are presented that have a frequency of more than 5 times; in the *Doing the dishes* interaction this is only true for one word relating to this subject (*washing up*), the interaction then changes to cooking (*oven*) and eating.

In DE, teachers use an observation and registration instrument (see this volume, Chaps. 4 and 14; see also Chap. 6) in order to plan their vocabulary activities with L2 children.

Conclusion

Communication is at the heart of Developmental Education. Teaching both learning to communicate and communicating to learn are major objectives in teachers' educational endeavours. The theoretical basis for this is that communication is learning how to *mean,* which prompts teachers to take collaboration with the children as their lead. To gain a better understanding of the teacher's role in this collaboration, we investigated the way they worked with children in pretend play. Taking the drama metaphor in the intervention roles of Johnson et al. (1999) and Kontos (1999) as our starting point, we found that teachers use all roles in a flexible way to co-construct pretend play. Both outside and inside intervention, roles seem to be appropriate in sharing meanings of the emergent narratives. Our findings suggest that the concept of the teacher's roles is a useful analytical tool for use in teacher training: it reflects on teaching behaviour and helps to make teachers aware of the various ways to collaborate with children in developing narratives in pretend play.[4] The teachers in this study adjust roles, encourage cooperative play, structure narratives, and use vocabulary according to the children's zone of proximal development in the course of play interactions. In "*doing* the words," as they told us, they managed to enhance children's learning to communicate and communicating to learn. The teachers appear to have a crucial role in giving the children language by introducing words and building multiple logical narrative sequences from their non-verbal play behaviour. In this way they also provide them with the tools to bring pretend play to a higher level of communicating their pretence, and so foster their representational and meta-linguistic capacities. This strategy has been found to relate to literacy. In communicating their pretence, the children can expand the use of the personal, heuristic, imaginative, and informative learning functions of language, which Halliday (1975) distinguished. By researching these teaching practices, we hope to contribute to enabling further insights into the Developmental Education approach for advancing children's participation in their socio-cultural world.

References

Bacchini, S. (2008). Schuim op je neus. De stimulering van tweede-taalontwikkeling in het spelcurriculum [Lather on your nose. Fostering second language acquisition in the play curriculum]. In D. de Haan & E. Kuiper (Eds.), *Leerkracht in beeld. Ontwikkelingsgericht Onderwijs. Theorie, onderzoek en praktijk* [Focus on the teacher. Developmental Education: Theory, research and practice] (pp. 116–123). Assen: Van Gorcum.

Bacchini, S. (in prep.). *Eerste hulp bij tweede taal* [First help with a second language]. Dissertation, University of Amsterdam, Amsterdam.

Beiser, L., & Howes, C. (1992). Mothers and toddlers: Partners in early symbolic play: Illustrative study #1. In C. Howes, O. Unger, & C. C. Matheson (Eds.), *The collaborative construction of the pretend* (pp. 25–43). Alban: State University of New York.

Bloom, L. (1991). *Language development from two to three*. New York: Cambridge University Press.

Cole, M. (1985). The zone of proximal development: Where culture and cognition create each other. In J. V. Wertsch (Ed.), *Culture, communication and cognition: Vygotskian perspectives* (pp. 146–161). Cambridge: Cambridge University Press.

Corsaro, W. A. (1997). *The sociology of childhood*. Thousand Oaks: Pine Forge Press.

Corsaro, W., & Riszo, T. A. (1988). Discussion and friendship: Socialisation processes in the peer culture of Italian nursery school children. *American Sociological Review, 53*, 879–894.

de Haan, D. (2005). Social pretend play: Potentials and limitations for literacy development. *European Early Childhood Education Research Journal, 13*(1), 41–56.

Dunn, J. (1988). *The beginnings of social understanding*. Oxford: Blackwell.

---

[4]In our research on teachers' guidance in the inquiry curriculum in the upper grades of DE primary school, we have adjusted the drama metaphor to a sports metaphor: we can use the same criteria to distinguish between outside intervention: a trainer (instructor), coach (stage manager), and inside intervention: captain (play leader) and co-player (van Rijk 2008).

Dunn, J. (2008). Play, drama and literacy in the early years. In J. Marsh & E. Hallet (Eds.), *Desirable literacies. Approaches to language & literacy in the early years* (pp. 162–182). London etc.: Sage.

Durkin, K. (1995). *Developmental social psychology*. Malden/Oxford: Blackwell.

Eckerman, C. O., & Peterman, K. (2000). Peers and infant social/communicative development. In G. Bremner & A. Fogel (Eds.), *Blackwell handbook of infant development. Handbooks of developmental psychology* (pp. 326–350). Malden: Blackwell.

Göncü, A. (1993). Development of intersubjectivity in social pretend play. *Human Development, 36*, 185–198.

Halliday, M. A. K. (1975). *Learning how to mean. Explorations in the development of language*. London: Edward Arnold.

Howe, N., Petrakos, H., LeFebre, R., & Rinaldi, C. (2005). "This is a bad dog, you know...": Constructing shared meanings during pretend play. *Child Development, 76*(4), 783–794.

Howes, C., Unger, O., & Matheson, C. C. (1992). *The collaborative construction of the pretend*. Alban: State University of New York.

Janssen-Vos, F. (2004). *Spel en spelontwikkeling* [Play and play development]. Assen: Van Gorcum.

Johnson, J. E., Christie, J. F., & Yawkey, T. D. (1999). *Play and early childhood development*. New York: Longman.

Karpov, Y. V. (2005). *The neo-Vygotskian approach to child development*. Cambridge: Cambridge University Press.

Kontos, S. (1999). Preschool teachers' talk, roles, and activity settings during free play. *Early Childhood Research Quarterly, 14*(3), 363–382.

Lieven, E. V. M. (1994). Crosslinguistic and crosscultural aspects of language addressed to children. In C. Gallaway & B. J. Richards (Eds.), *Input and interaction in language acquisition* (pp. 56–73). Cambridge: Cambridge University Press.

Liszkowski, U., Carpenter, M., & Tomasello, M. (2008). Twelve-month-olds communicate helpfully and appropriately for knowledgeable and ignorant partners. *Cognition, 108*, 732–739.

MacWhinney, B. (2000). *The CHILDES project: Tools for analyzing talk*. Mahwah: Erlbaum.

Moll, H., & Tomasello, M. (2006). Cooperation and human cognition: The Vygotskian intelligence hypothesis. *Philosophical Transactions of the Royal Society, 362*, 639–648.

Nelson, K. (1996). *Language in cognitive development. Emergence of the mediated mind*. Cambridge: Cambridge University Press.

Ninio, A., & Snow, C. E. (1996). *Pragmatic development*. Boulder: Westview Press.

Pellegrini, A. D., & Galda, L. (1993). Ten years after: A reexamination of symbolic play and literacy research. *Reading Research Quarterly, 28*(2), 161–175.

Rogoff, B. (1990). *Apprenticeship in thinking. Cognitive development in social context*. New York: Oxford University Press.

Tomasello, M. (2003). *Constructing a language. A usage-based theory of language acquisition*. Cambridge/London: Harvard University Press.

van Oers, B. (2010). Children's enculturation through play. In L. Brooker & S. Edwards (Eds.), *Engaging play* (pp. 195–209). Maidenhead: Open University Press.

van Rijk, Y. (2008). Leerlingen doen onderzoek. wat doet de leerkracht? In D. de Haan & E. Kuiper (Eds.), *Leerkracht in beeld. Theorie, onderzoek en praktijk* [Focus on the teacher. Developmental Education: Theory, research and practice] (pp. 168–175). Assen: Van Gorcum.

Warneken, F., Chen, F., & Tomasello, M. (2006). Cooperative activities in young children and chimpanzees. *Child Development, 3*, 640–663.

Watson, R. (2001). Literacy and oral language: Implications for early literacy education. In S. B. Neuman & D. K. Dickinson (Eds.), *Handbook of early literacy research* (pp. 43–53). New York/London: The Guilford Press.

Chapter 6
Assessing Vocabulary Development

Renata Adan-Dirks

Introduction

Globalisation is impacting not only economic and social developments around the world, but also education. As employees of international corporations are transferred to overseas postings and immigrant families seek a better future for themselves in new homelands, ever increasing numbers of children enter schools where the language of education is not the language they speak at home. In the Netherlands Developmental Education schools try to meet the needs of these children through didactic activities based on the pupils' interests and abilities.

Bilingual Children in Dutch Education

As early as 2001 first or second generation immigrants made up more than half of the pupil population in the four largest cities of the Netherlands (Scheffer 2000). Studies show that children raised in immigrant families, or by parents with a limited level of education, often achieve lower results at school (Leseman 2005). Research has shown that immigrant children from non-Western countries have a Dutch language deficit of nearly 2 years compared to native speakers at the beginning of primary school. At the end of primary school achievement of these children is at a level 2 years behind other children in subjects which depend heavily on language skills (Leseman 2005). Bilingual children do not usually catch up with their native speaker peers during the course of primary school.

R. Adan-Dirks, M.Sc. (✉)
e-mail: renata.adan@mac.com

B. van Oers (ed.), *Developmental Education for Young Children*, International
Perspectives on Early Childhood Education and Development 7,
DOI 10.1007/978-94-007-4617-6_6,
© Springer Science+Business Media Dordrecht 2012

Programmes for At-Risk Pupils

Because a deficit in the language of education is seen as a major factor in poor academic achievement, the Dutch government has invested in the development of preschool programmes designed to support those at-risk children. The most common preschool programmes in the Netherlands are Kaleidoscoop and Piramide. Kaleidoscoop is based on the successful high-scope programme in the United States and has a specific focus on language development for bilingual immigrant children (www.kaleidoscoop.org). Piramide is a curriculum-based programme with prescribed lesson plans and learning goals. It is teacher directed and relies heavily on direct instruction (www.CITOgroup.nl/po/piramide/Methode/eind_fr.htm).

Developmental Education is not based on a fixed curriculum with prescribed learning targets. Children are guided towards new zones of proximal development through interaction with teachers and with each other, while engaging in play-based learning activities. In the Netherlands a kindergarten programme based on these Vygotskian principles was developed in the early 1980s. This programme was called Basic Development (*Basisontwikkeling* – see Chap. 4 of this volume). A developmentally focused preschool programme called Starting Blocks (*Startblokken*) was developed in 1996 (Janssen-Vos and Pompert 2000; Janssen-Vos et al. 2006. See also section "Introduction" of Chap. 4, this volume).

In Developmental Education the introduction of various socio-cultural thematic activities provides contexts in which children recognise their need for and are highly motivated in further language development. The shared context also supports language learners in inferring the intention of the speaker and making their own intentions clear. According to Bruner "successful early communication requires a shared and familiar context to aid the partners in making their communicative intentions clear to each other" (Bruner 1983, p. 129).

A four-step approach to new vocabulary education (Verhallen 1995, pp. 63–68) is used in Starting Blocks and Basic Development (Helms-Lorenz and Heerlinga-de Jong 2006; Janssen-Vos 2008, p. 118). The first step is *orientation*: through careful observation as a new theme is introduced teachers determine which words the children already use and which words are unfamiliar. Step two is *semantisation*: helping the children to connect words related to the theme with concepts. This happens best by demonstrating verbs and physically investigating concrete objects. Thirdly, children must practice using the new words properly so they will be able to remember them. This is called *consolidation* and takes place through playing in small groups in the various learning centres of the classroom. The fourth step is *evaluation*, or checking which of the words the children master as the project develops. Teacher observation during participation in children's activities is sufficient to note which words each child understands (receptive vocabulary) and which words the child uses (productive vocabulary) (Janssen-Vos and Pompert 2000).

This four-step approach is also applied during other didactic methods for introducing and practicing new vocabulary, such as interactive reading and the "story-telling table". In interactive reading children do not simply sit quietly and listen to the story but are encouraged to predict events, describe illustrations and interact with the reader. At the "story-telling table" children retell and act out stories related to the current theme using props and actual dialogue from the story. This helps children learn idiomatic expressions and complete phrases with correct syntax as well as increasing their vocabulary and pragmatic ability (Janssen-Vos and Pompert 2000; Nauta 2010). In each of these activities interaction between pupils and teachers provides support for children to reach a new zone of proximal development and progress in their language ability.

Language Development

Although in this chapter we are primarily concerned with accurately assessing vocabulary development of bilingual children, there are several reasons why it is helpful to have some understanding of how one's first language is acquired (see also Chap. 5 of this volume).

First Language Development

There are many similarities between first and second language learning, particularly when the second language is introduced at an early age. Also young pupils are still going through the process of first language development while adding a second language. Teachers are better equipped to distinguish between genuine language development delay and difficulties in second language acquisition when they have an understanding of first language development.

Piaget claimed that language development is a reflection of cognitive development and follows the same behaviourist principle of imitation and selective reinforcement as all other learning. Noam Chomsky cited deviant constructions and neologisms as proof that children do not simply imitate adult speech (van Beemen 1995). He claimed that children have an innate ability to discover structures in the language to which they are exposed and to formulate grammatical rules which they then apply. He termed this ability the Language Acquisition Device (LAD) (Garton and Pratt 1998, p. 21). Errors in over-regularisation far outnumber inaccurate imitations in early speech, which supports Chomsky's theory.

According to Vygotskij, learning to speak is a process of creatively learning to use the language of a community as a communicative tool. Speech enables further cognitive development, rather than being a result of such development (Vygotsky 1987; van Beemen 1995). Vygotskij claimed "thinking in concepts is not possible in the absence of verbal thinking" (Vygotsky 1987). His foundational premise was that like all other psychological or cognitive development, language development takes place through communication within a cultural context. Bruner agreed with Vygotskij's understanding that language is used as a tool and motivated by a need to communicate. He also saw value in Chomsky's LAD theory, but felt it did not sufficiently explain how language learning takes place. Bruner introduced the concept of a Language Acquisition Support System (LASS) which combined the child's inborn tendency toward active social interaction and language learning with scaffolding, or effective help and support from adults (Garton and Pratt 1998). "It is the interaction between LAD and LASS that makes it possible for the infant to enter the linguistic community – and, at the same time, the culture to which the language gives access" (Bruner 1983, p. 19).

Researchers today claim that aspects of all of these theories may be valid at different phases of language development (Hollich et al. 2000). Observation reveals that universally all children go through similar stages in language acquisition. Receptive language always precedes expressive or productive language use (van Beemen 1995). Children can discriminate their own language from another when only a few days old (Bloom 1993). Between 7 and 10 months old all children begin babbling with repetition of short syllabic units. Adequate responses to adult speech indicate that children also understand some words at this age. First words are produced at about 12 months and are nearly all names for specific people, objects and substances which feature prominently in the child's daily activities (Bloom 1993). Between 18 months and 2 years vocabulary acquisition increases dramatically, with estimates of average vocabulary at the age of 2 years ranging between 270 words (McCarthy 1954 in van Beemen 1995) and 500 words (Aitchison 2003). After age 2 vocabulary acquisition proceeds at an ever increasing rate, resulting in the following estimated pattern:

12–16 months	0.3 words per day
16–23 months	0.8 words per day
23–30 months	1.6 words per day
30 months to 6 years	3.6 words per day
6–8 years	6.6 words per day
8–10 years	12.1 words per day

This is based on data from Fenson et al. (1994) for up to 30 months and Anglin (1993) from 30 months to 10 years (as referred to in Bloom 2000).

The amazingly high rate of speech development in young children is attributed to the intensive level of *interaction* between adult and child and the *feedback* more experienced speakers give to reinforce or correct early speech (van Beemen 1995 – her emphasis). Grammatically correct but concise and simplified language input emphasises key words and speech rhythm patterns, and features much repetition which facilitates understanding and later imitation of early words (van Beemen 1995; Garton and Pratt 1998). Parents who are aware of the child's intent will frequently supply the required label for events, actions or objects, supporting lexical development (Nelson 1988). For older children, learning to read creates broad exposure to new words while further cognitive development and metalinguistic awareness enables them to quickly expand their vocabulary levels (Bloom 2000).

Vocabulary Building

Learning new words is a much more complex activity than meets the eye. The four steps of orientation, semantisation, consolidation and evaluation are useful tools for vocabulary acquisition, but they do not explain how words are stored in memory and retrieved when needed. Aitchison (2003) points out that learning a new word involves three separate but related tasks: labelling, packaging and network building.

Labelling, or word-to-world mapping as it is sometimes called (Hollich et al. 2000), takes place when a child recognises that a particular word refers to a particular object in his environment. Initially this may not mean that the child has a complete or accurate concept of the word – a child may believe the word "hot" refers to the stove rather than it's temperature, or may understand "hot" to mean "dangerous, do not touch that". Only when children use a word and have the correct concept of the referent indicated with that word can they be said to be labelling.

Packaging is defining the range or category covered by a word. Two forms of error occur in this stage of vocabulary acquisition: underextension is when the child restricts the use of a word and overextension is when the word is too broadly used. A child may assume that the word "kitty" refers only to the family pet and not to all cats, or she may assume that all four legged creatures, including rabbits and dogs are also called "kitty" (Aitchison 2003; Kienstra 2003). Words are often learned in a particular context and only later applied to a wider situation (Aitchison 2003). Errors in underextension occur even in later language development: some polysemic words cover a much broader range of meaning than is evident in common usage and even native speaker adults can be expanding or refining their understanding of a word's full meaning.

Network building involves understanding which words are related to each other and in what way. This takes place slowly and is an ongoing process. Children often form collocational links, finding relationships between words which frequently occur together. Word association experiments reveal that children link table with eat, dark with night, send with letter and deep with hole, while adults form semantic links, pairing table with chair, dark with light, send with receive and deep with shallow (Aitchison 2003, p. 198).

Many studies verify that words which are semantically related are stored together in a network. In association experiments adults consistently choose objects from the same semantic grouping as the original word, rather than objects with similar appearance. When asked which word came to mind on hearing the word "needle", the adults did not name other long, thin or pointy objects, but rather other objects related to sewing. Secondly coordinates (words which are closely related such as husband/wife or are clearly opposites such as big/small) are closely linked in complex networks and are often named in association exercises (Aitchison 2003, p. 85). Errors or slips of the tongue confirm this theory, as does the process of word-search when a specific word temporarily eludes a speaker.

There is also some indication that different parts of speech may be classified in different ways. In cases where a coordinate is used instead of the required word

90% of the time a different noun replaces a noun and a verb is replaced by a different verb. A required adjective is replaced by a different adjective in 60% of cases, and otherwise by a different noun, but not by a verb (Aitchison 2003).

Finally there is evidence that words which contain similar sounds may be linked as well. Freudian slips are generally phonetically similar rather than semantically related. Most often the required word is replaced by one which contains a similar word outline (beginning letter, vowel and ending letter) but contains some wrong details (Aitchison 2003).

When considering the complexities of labelling, packaging and network building it is truly impressive that young children so quickly build up a large vocabulary in their first language, usually without any intentional instruction. This process of language development is far from completed when children begin preschool, and it is at this point that most immigrant children come into significant contact with their second language.

Second Language Acquisition

When a second language is introduced before the age of 3 this is referred to as "simultaneous bilingualism". The term "successive bilingualism" refers to those situations when a second language is learned after a basis has been established in one's first language (Roselaar et al. 1993). Successful language development and fluency in both languages can be achieved with both simultaneous and successive language learning. The level of success is dependent on how effectively the language learning is stimulated in both languages (De Jong 1986; Roselaar et al. 1993).

In the Netherlands the majority of immigrant children are raised in homes where the parents share a common first language and exclusively use that language in the home. It is estimated that in 70% of immigrant families' homes no Dutch is spoken at all (A. Kant http://www.nieuwsbank.nl/inp/2000/04/0427G020.htm). Children in these families have very limited exposure to Dutch until they begin attending preschool or kindergarten.

Organising Language Systems

It is believed that children growing up with exposure to two languages initially combine both languages into one system. They use vocabulary and pronunciation from both languages but do not have equivalent labels for objects, actions or events in both languages. Somewhere around the age of 2 the child begins to learn that two labels can be applied to the same referent and becomes aware that there are two languages (De Jong 1986; Roselaar et al. 1993; Bialystok 2001).

Unintentionally filling in a gap in one's lexical knowledge of one language by applying a label from the other is known as interference or code mixing. Using verb conjugations from one language with verbs of the other, or plural forms from one language with the other, are also frequent examples of interference. This is seen most frequently when one language is dominant. When a child consciously chooses to use the label from the other language in an attempt to clarify intention it is called code switching. This happens more frequently when there is equilibrium between the two languages (Roselaar et al. 1993).

Aitchison disagrees with the concept of two or more distinct language systems and cites interference or code mixing as evidence of one language system (Aitchison 2003). Interference would be unlikely if the speaker is accessing only one language system when speaking one language. It is also conceivable that when one language is dominant over the other, a required word is subconsciously suppressed and only the word in the language not required comes to mind (Aitchison 2003). This would negatively impact the language ability of children who have insufficient input in their second language.

Various factors affect the ultimate level of fluency reached by second language learners. According to some researchers, cognitive resources largely determine the ease and success of second language acquisition while motivation and contextual factors such as the level of exposure to the target language are of secondary influence (Cummins 1984). Others emphasise that learner characteristics such as extraversion and cognitive abilities affect one's progress in language learning (Fillmore 1994).

Differences Between First and Second Language Learning

When teaching children a second language the processes of labelling, packaging and network building which take place with minimal intentional support during first language acquisition are purposely stimulated and guided. Using the four steps of orientation, semantisation, consolidation, and evaluation teachers help children to rapidly increase their second language vocabulary. In this way pupils are intentionally exposed to and given opportunity to practice the vocabulary they will need for success in school.

In second language education it is at times necessary to explicitly focus on linguistic features which are markedly different than those of the pupil's first language. One of the specific challenges of learning Dutch is grammatical gender. This is a feature of many languages, such as French, Spanish and German, but is not a feature of English or Turkish. Grammatical gender affects the definite article used, pronouns used for objects and the formation of adjectives. Native speakers intuitively use these forms correctly but are often unable to explain the grammatical rules which govern usage. For people who do not have grammatical gender in their first language this can be very confusing and difficult to master. It is important for teachers to emphasise the correct definite article ("de" or "het" in Dutch) and the gender of nouns when introducing new words to bilingual children and to draw their attention to the significance of the distinction.

Another difference between first and second language acquisition is the rate of development. Although there is some variation in how quickly children learn to speak their first language, this generally is limited to a quite small range. In second language development it may take one child 5 years longer to master the new language than it takes another child (Fillmore 1994, p. 61). This must be taken into consideration particularly when evaluating young children who have only had 1 or 2 years of exposure to the second language in a school situation.

On average bilingual children initially have a smaller vocabulary in each of their languages but their combined vocabulary in both languages is greater than that of most monolingual children (Roselaar et al. 1993). Because language testing in primary school only measures the Dutch vocabulary of all children, it is not surprising that the scores of bilingual children fall below the norm of monolingual children of the same age.

Measuring Language Ability

According to Vygotskij, it is important to document what a child can achieve with adequate support, rather than only measuring "the actual level of development". Ideally, a language assessment should evaluate how well a child can communicate, looking at factors such as narrative ability and correct syntax as well as vocabulary levels.

Language Assessment in Developmental Education

In the Netherlands the same summative standardised test is used by nearly all primary schools to measure language ability at the end of kindergarten. This test, the "Taal voor Kleuters 1996" [Language for young children], only measures receptive vocabulary levels and the comprehension of various pre-reading concepts. This type of test is quite contrary to the philosophy of Developmental Education.

The Taal voor Kleuters 1996 test requires that all the children are seated at tables and are required to complete pencil and paper exercises which serve no particular purpose within the context of their play activity. An alternative has all pupils seated at computers and indicating chosen answers with a mouse click. This type of testing is completely foreign to children in Starting Blocks and Basic Development programmes: they are accustomed to being supported by the teacher in order to achieve more than they could on their own, and suddenly the teacher is required to follow a specific script and is not allowed to offer any support. This new type of work form is confusing for many children. Yet, increasingly school inspectors insist that progress be documented by these quantitative test scores, so this test is also used at some Developmental Education schools.

Because in Developmental Education learning is supposed to take place within a meaningful context, with the use of tools and assistance from others, informal dynamic assessment is generally used to monitor the progress of each child (Gipps 2002, see also Chap. 7 in this volume). Ideally, dynamic assessment should take place within the normal classroom context and the pupil would not necessarily be aware that the teacher is specifically assessing his level of independent participation in the activity. Dynamic assessment focuses on the child's zone of proximal development and provides the teacher with much more information than an accumulative test which only reveals what a child can do independently at one particular moment in time. The insight gained into strategies used and where problems occur in completing the task informs the teacher's further input for each individual child.

When dynamic assessment is used instead of standardised tests it appears that Basic Development pupils achieve better results. In a study specifically comparing the effectiveness of this thematic and social approach to second language learning with a direct instruction approach, it was found that the children in the Basic Development kindergarten class learned more target words within the given time frame than the children in the direct instruction class, and used these words in more different contexts (Duijkers 2003). In a related research project a newly developed instrument to measure narrative ability using a thematic illustration was used. This study showed that children in Basic Development classes have further developed language skills than regular testing methods would indicate (Poland 2005; see also Chap. 7 of this volume).

However, in studies where standardised test results are used to compare the success of various approaches to language learning, direct instruction approach programmes consistently score higher. One study compared the test results of Moroccan children in the Starting Blocks programme with test results of Moroccan children in regular schools using the vocabulary section of the CITO test Taal voor Kleuters 1996 [Language for young children] (van Kuyk 1996). This study revealed that the pupils in regular schools scored higher both at the beginning and at the end of Kindergarten, with a slightly greater increase in scores for the children in regular education (Helms-Lorenz and Heerlinga-De Jong 2006, p. 39). One factor which may account for this difference in test results even when looking at pupils from similar backgrounds and comparing the results of the same test is ecological validity. The children in Starting Blocks programmes were not accustomed to pencil and paper evaluations or to assignments being given without a thematic context and they had not been exposed to all the vocabulary items on the test before the test was given. One could contend that the method of testing was ecologically invalid for the Starting Blocks pupils.

Ecological Validity

Ecological validity is concerned with how closely the test situation simulates real life situations and whether behaviours recorded in a test situation accurately reflect the behaviour of subjects in a natural setting (Manstead and Hewstone 1995, p. 191;

Elmes et al. 2003, p. 145). In the field of psychology it has been found that "most treatment research does not permit generalisation to ethnic minority populations" (Bernal et al. 1995). This would indicate that especially when testing children from diverse ethnic backgrounds, care must be taken to avoid cultural bias which could affect results.

In order for a lexical knowledge test to accurately reflect the linguistic abilities of pupils, the test must as closely as possible approximate the normal situation in which children use language, and it must take the previous knowledge of ethnically diverse pupil populations into account. Because the classroom situation and didactic forms prevalent in Developmental Education are quite different from the methods, materials and settings of the CITO Taal voor Kleuters 1996 vocabulary tests, these are considered to be ecologically invalid for pupils in the Starting Blocks and Basic Development programmes. Furthermore the CITO test may be considered ecologically invalid for all children from minority backgrounds, regardless of the type of school they attend, because diverse ethnicity is not taken into consideration in the selection of test items.

There are also other concerns. The CITO Taal voor Kleuters 1996 test only measures receptive vocabulary and is comprised of a list of words without any context or relation to each other. These words are read aloud and the children are required to select and underline the correct illustration from four options for each word. This method of testing places additional demands on children, beyond the recognition of words and connecting these words with concepts. The ability to follow the teacher's instructions, to interpret the drawings, to distinguish between near synonyms and to keep up with the tempo set by the teacher are also being evaluated. The test intentionally includes a range of high to low frequency words so children are being tested on words they may never have encountered before. Furthermore, the test was developed to point out language development delays in native speakers of Dutch rather than to measure second language acquisition.

Designing the Thematic Vocabulary Assessment Test

One of the challenges facing Developmental Education in the Netherlands is the need to find a suitable compromise between dynamic assessment as it is commonly implemented in the Starting Blocks and Basic Development programmes and government dependence on standardised test results to validate the effectiveness of these programmes. In 2007 the Thematic Vocabulary Assessment Test was designed as a first step towards such a compromise (Adan-Dirks 2007).

A Thematic Approach

In designing the Thematic Vocabulary Assessment Test all of the above mentioned concerns with the CITO Taal voor Kleuters 1996 test were taken into consideration and every effort was made to incorporate aspects of dynamic assessment into this new instrument.

The test is based on large illustrations which depict situations familiar to young children and include various items and actions centred on a particular theme. This provides a context and a memory supporting tool to help children access the vocabulary being tested. The assessment is a joint teacher-child activity in which the teacher may provide support, and both receptive and productive vocabulary is measured. The two sections of the Thematic Vocabulary Assessment Test are referred to as the Receptive TVAT and Productive TVAT.

To test receptive vocabulary the tester reads a list of nouns and verbs and the child is asked to point out the item or someone doing the named action in the illustration. A score is given for the number of correct links made between words and pictures. Should the child struggle to find the correct picture the teacher may give one or two small hints to help the child remember the meaning of the requested word. For example, with the verb "spilling" the teacher might add "spilling water" or "spilling water on the floor". When this type of support is needed this is also recorded on the score sheet to give an accurate account of the child's lexical recall abilities. In the productive vocabulary test the child points out various details in the illustration and tells the tester what he sees. The tester may provide assistance by asking questions which elicit further productive language use. This gives the child an opportunity to demonstrate lexical knowledge beyond that covered in the Receptive TVAT. Should the child fail to mention the items already included in the receptive part of the test the teacher can indicate these items in the illustration and ask the child to name them.

With this test it is possible for someone who speaks the child's native language to also ask for the vocabulary items the child is unable to name in Dutch in the child's first language. This would verify whether the child has no concept of the meaning belonging to the word or simply has no access to the Dutch word for that concept. Similarly, in the Productive TVAT it could occur that a child is able to name many items in his first language which he cannot name in Dutch. This could prevent children from being inappropriately labelled as having delayed linguistic development since the first language would be shown to be at the level expected of the child.

Topic and Material Selection

Unlike dynamic assessment, which is ongoing and takes place during each theme, the Thematic Vocabulary Assessment Test is intended to be a summative assessment at the end of kindergarten. It does not need to be based on the theme most recently covered, but to ensure that children have been exposed to the vocabulary which is being tested themes should be chosen which were covered during the Starting Blocks programme. For the pilot testing of the TVAT two topics were chosen which had been covered by both schools participating in the project. The first topic was

The classroom and the second was *The hospital.* A preliminary list of items for the test was compiled from thematic dictionaries. Then suitable illustrations had to be found. The final word list was made up of those words on the preliminary list that were also represented in the illustrations. Not surprisingly the words for the topic *The classroom* were mostly high frequency words, but for the theme *The hospital* there were more low frequency words. The choice of two different topics allows for a broader range of difficulty, facilitating differentiation of scores.

Drawings by Dagmar Stam (a well-known illustrator of Dutch children's books) from a curriculum for learning Dutch designed especially for immigrant children in the Netherlands were chosen as illustrations for the TVAT (Stam 2003, 2004a, b). The posters are simple yet rich in detail, include people of various ethnic backgrounds, and are large enough to easily identify items in the pictures. In the complete series there are 45 illustrations to choose from covering very diverse themes. It would be possible and indeed desirable to expand this assessment instrument with word lists from other themes, so that schools that have not covered the themes chosen for the pilot test could utilise other themes which they have covered.

Once the illustrations had been chosen, the word lists were finalised, including 12 nouns and 3 verbs for each theme. Care was taken to include only monosemous words. Only one word was chosen from word pairs that are closely linked, such as chalk and chalkboard. The highest frequency words were chosen for use as examples at the beginning of each test session. Rather than beginning with easier words and progressing to more difficult words the frequency levels vary throughout the test so that after missing one or two each child still has a chance of succeeding on other items and concluding the activity with a positive feeling. With each pupil *The classroom* was done first because it contained more easy words and would build confidence before introducing the more difficult topic *The hospital.*

During the Receptive TVAT each noun was introduced with the phrase "Where do you see ... in the picture?" Each verb was introduced with "Where do you see someone ...?" A score sheet was developed on which the tester could mark how well the child knew the items on the word list. The score options are:

  G = Good (immediately found item)
  C = Correct (found item after some hesitation)
  H1 = Hint 1 (found item after one hint from the tester or one wrong attempt)
  H2 = Hint 2 (found item after two hints or two wrong attempts)
  X = Unknown (the child could not link an image to the word)
  FL = First Language (the child found the item when the word was said in his first
    language)

This last category can only be used when the tester is someone who speaks the child's first language. Fortunately a growing number of Dutch schools recognise the importance of bilingual assistants in the classroom.

For the Productive TVAT the same illustrations were used. A score sheet was made on which the tester can mark which of the words from the word list are used correctly, which are used while indicating a different item, and any other nouns, verbs or adjectives used. A tally is also kept of correct full sentences used. Because scoring this test is quite intensive a recording device was used to enable the tester to later check the scoring of each child.

Results of the Pilot Project

Two Developmental Education schools in Amsterdam participated in the pilot project of the Thematic Vocabulary Assessment Test in April 2007. The pupils were all bilingual, with most children having either Moroccan Arabic or Turkish as their first language. These pupils had all taken the CITO Taal voor Kleuters 1996 test in January of 2007 and these scores were used as a standard with which their TVAT results were compared.

Upon completing testing, reliability analysis was carried out on both the Receptive and Productive parts of the test. The scores for the two Receptive TVAT topics combined have a Chronbach's alpha of .812 which indicates that it is a reliable test. The Chronbach's alpha score of the Productive TVAT is .855 which also indicates a reliable measuring instrument.

Each child's test results from the receptive vocabulary section of the CITO Taal voor Kleuters 1996 and from the Receptive TVAT were converted to percentages to compare the results of the two tests. At primary school "De Leonardo" 10 of the 12 children tested scored higher on the Receptive TVAT with an average increase of 11.94%. For four of the pupils at this school the Receptive TVAT score was more than 15% higher than their CITO Taal voor Kleuters 1996 score. At primary school "De Pool" results were even more dramatic. All ten pupils scored higher on the Receptive TVAT with an average increase of 48.33%. These results are seen in Figs. 6.1 and 6.2.

These graphs display a clear discrepancy in the lexical knowledge of these pupils when different instruments are used to measure their receptive vocabulary. Unfortunately, based on the lower scores achieved with the CITO Taal voor Kleuters 1996 test many of these pupils are classified as underachieving and the Developmental Education programme they are in is judged to be ineffective. However, the higher scores achieved with the TVAT reveal that these pupils have added many words to their vocabulary through the themes they have covered.

The Productive TVAT results confirm that productive language skills develop more slowly than receptive language skills. However, the results of the Productive TVAT still provide useful insights into the linguistic development of these bilingual pupils. Firstly the number of target words used to label items in each illustration, either voluntarily or when requested by the tester, was measured.

The average score on the Productive TVAT for the theme *The classroom* was 55.55% for children at "De Leonardo". Ten out of twelve pupils tested scored 46.66% or higher. For the theme *The hospital* the average Productive TVAT score was 40%. At "De Pool" the average Productive TVAT score for *The classroom* was 66% with only two of the ten pupils tested scoring below 60%. For the theme *The hospital* an average Productive TVAT score of 47% was achieved.

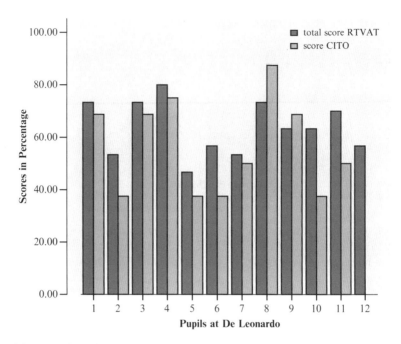

Fig. 6.1 Comparison of RTVAT and CITO scores at De Leonardo

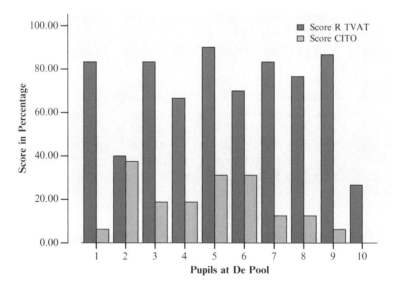

Fig. 6.2 Comparison of RTVAT and CITO scores at De Pool

The score sheet also allowed the tester to note if children used synonyms of target words, which target words the children could retrieve after one or two hints and any additional words or full sentences the children happened to use. Although this did not affect scores, it provides the teacher with insights into each child's language development and informs further teaching. Currently used standardised vocabulary tests focus only on receptive vocabulary, but the above information reveals that much can be gained by assessing the productive vocabulary of pupils as well. It is only when a child knows a word well enough to use it correctly himself that the full process of labelling, packaging and building connections can be seen as completed.

Further Developments

In the years since its initial development the TVAT has been adapted and additional testing has been carried out in the field. Teachers from preschools using the Starting Blocks programme found the original test score sheets too complicated and the testing process too time consuming. In response to these concerns Mariëlle Poland developed a greatly simplified version of the TVAT, the "Woordenschattoets voor peuters en groep 1 tot en met 4" [Vocabulary Test for Toddlers and Group 1 through 4] (Poland 2010). In ongoing field testing, this test is currently being used by five Developmental Education schools in the Netherlands. This vocabulary test is used as a pre-test near the beginning of a thematic unit to help teachers determine how many of the target words they have chosen for the unit are already known. Then at the conclusion of the unit the same test is taken again to measure actual vocabulary growth during the unit. Score sheets for this test simply record whether answers are correct or incorrect.

Teachers generally are pleased with the results their pupils are achieving on these tests. Some schools use this test for each unit throughout the year. Others choose to only do one or two tests a year because they find testing is still quite labour intensive and time consuming. Rather than working with existing illustrations and vocabulary lists, schools are encouraged to accumulate their own visual materials to ensure that target words they want to assess are included in the test. Making new word lists and finding suitable pictures does make it a more time consuming project, but also provides a more rigorous evaluation of actual words covered in the unit. It also makes each test organic and ecologically valid, but removes the possibility of comparing scores from 1 year to another or from one school to another. In the compromise between standardised testing and dynamic assessment the changes to the test move it closer to the side of Developmental Education's principles and away from a standardised instrument which could possibly be considered a valid alternative to the CITO Taal voor Kleuters 1996 test.

Conclusion

Within Developmental Education great strides are being taken towards better assessments of children's vocabulary acquisition. Teachers are being encouraged to document which target words are chosen for each thematic unit. With the "Woordenschattoets voor peuters en groep 1 tot en met 4" an instrument is available to measure the vocabulary growth achieved in each unit. Although the highly organic nature of this test meets the expectations of Developmental Education teachers in being much closer to the dynamic assessment forms they prefer, it is, in my opinion, far removed from the standardised summative tests still expected by school inspectors. The TVAT was designed as a first attempt at a compromise acceptable to both parties and ongoing development and validation of tests will be needed to reach this goal.

References

Adan-Dirks, R. H. (2007). *The thematic vocabulary assessment test.* Master thesis, VU University, Amsterdam.

Aitchison, J. (2003). *Words in the mind: An introduction to the mental lexicon* (3rd ed.). Malden/Oxford/Melbourne/Berlin: Blackwell.

Anglin, J. (1993). Vocabulary development: A morphological analysis. *Monographs of the society for research in child development, 58*(10). Serial no. 238.

Bernal, G., Bonilla, J., & Bellido, C., (1995, February). Ecological validity and cultural sensitivity for outcome research: issues for the cultural adaptation and development of psychosocial treatments with Hispanics – Special issue: Psychosocial treatment research. *Journal of Abnormal Child Psychology, 23*(1), 67–82. Retrieved June 4, 2007, from http://findarticles.com/p/articles/mi_m0902/is_n1_v23/ai_16598567

Bialystok, E. (2001). *Bilingualism in development. Language, literacy and cognition.* Cambridge: Cambridge University Press.

Bloom, P. (Ed.). (1993). *Language acquisition: Core readings.* New York/London/Toronto/Sydney/Tokyo/Singapore: Harvester Wheatsheaf.

Bloom, P. (2000). *How children learn the meanings of words.* Cambridge, MA: The MIT Press.

Bruner, J. (1983). *Child's Talk. Learning to use language.* Oxford/London: Oxford University Press.

Cummins, J. (1984). *Bilingual education and special education: Issues in assessment and pedagogy.* San Diego: College Hill.

De Jong, E. (1986). *The bilingual experience: A book for parents.* Cambridge: Cambridge University Press.

Duijkers, D. (2003). *Betekenisvolle woordenschatontwikkeling, een kwestie van interactie, cultuur en context* [Meaningful vocabulary acquisition, a matter of interaction, culture and context]. Amsterdam: VU University.

Elmes, D. G., Kantowitz, B. H., & Roediger, H. L. (2003). *Research methods in psychology* (p. 145). Belmont: Thomson Wadsworth.

Fenson, L., Dale, Ph.S., Reznick, J.S., Bates, E., Thal, D.J., & Pethick, S.J. (1994). Variability in early communicative development. *Monographs of the society for research in child development, 59*(5). Serial no. 242.

Fillmore, L. W. (1994). Second-language learning in children: A model of language learning in social context. In E. Bialystok (Ed.), *Language processing in bilingual children* (pp. 49–69). Cambridge: Cambridge University Press.

Garton, A., & Pratt, C. (1998). *Learning to be literate: The development of spoken and written language*. Malden/Oxford/Carlton: Blackwell Publishing.

Gipps, C. (2002). Sociocultural perspectives on assessment. In G. Wells & G. Claxton (Eds.), *Learning for life in the 21st century* (pp. 73–84). Oxford: Blackwell Publishing.

Helms-Lorenz, M., & Heerlinga-de Jong, J. L. (2006). *Ontwikkelingsgericht Woordenschatonderwijs, Implementatie en effectiviteit bij Marokkaanse kleuters* [Developmental vocabulary education, implementation and efficacy among young Moroccan children]. Groningen: GION Instituut voor Onderzoek van Onderwijs, Rijksuniversiteit Groningen.

Hollich, G. J., Hirsh-Pasek, K., & Golinkoff, R. M. (2000). *Breaking the language barrier: An emergentist coalition model for the origins of word learning* (Monographs of the society for research in child development, Vol. 65, No. 3). Malden/Oxford/Melbourne/Berlin: Blackwell.

Janssen-Vos, F. (2008). *Basisontwikkeling voor peuters en kleuters* [Basic development for toddlers and young children]. Assen: van Gorcum

Janssen-Vos, F., & Pompert, B. (2000). *Startblokken – De Avonturijn: Een goede start voor peuters en kleuters* [Starting blocks – De Avonturijn: A good start for toddlers and young children]. Utrecht: APS.

Janssen-Vos, F., van Oers, B., & Pompert, B. (2006). Startblokken en Basisontwikkeling de maat genomen [Starting blocks and basic development; taking measure]. *Zone. Tijdschrift voor Ontwikkelingsgericht Onderwijs, 5*(3), 31–32.

Kienstra, M. (2003). *Woordenschatontwikkeling; Werkwijzen voor groep 1–4 van de basisschool* [Vocabulary development; methods for groups 1–4 of Primary School]. Nijmegen: Drukkerij MacDonald/SSN (Expertisecentrum Nederlands).

Leseman, P. (2005). Voorschool: voor- en vroegschoolse educatie voor kinderen in achterstandssituaties [Preschool: Preschool and early years education for children in disadvantaged situations]. In M. H. van Ijzendoorn & H. de Frankrijker (Eds.), *Pedagogiek in beeld. Een inleiding in de pedagogische studie van opvoeding, onderwijs en hulpverlening* (pp. 359–372). Houten: Bohn Stafleu Van Loghum.

Manstead, A. S. R., & Hewstone, M. (1995). *The Blackwell encyclopedia of social psychology* (p. 191). Oxford: Blackwell Publishers.

Nauta, M. (2010). *Spel voor taal. Een onderzoek naar de invloed van de verteltafel op de pragmatische taalontwikkeling van jonge NT2 leerlingen* [Play for language. A study of the influence of the story table on the pragmatic language development of Young DSL pupils]. Master thesis, Faculty of Psychology and Education, VU University, Amsterdam.

Nelson, K. (1988). Constraints on word learning? *Cognitive Development, 3,* 221–246.

Poland, M. (2005). *Het toetsen van narratieve competentie bij jonge kinderen in de onderbouw* [Testing the narrative competence of young children in early years education]. Amsterdam: Vrije Universiteit.

Poland, M. (2010). *Handleiding Woordenschattoets voor peuters en groep 1 tot en met 4 (concept)* [Manual for vocabulary test for toddlers and groups 1 through 4 (draft)]. Amsterdam/Alkmaar: Vrije Universiteit/De Activiteit.

Roselaar, T., Lindijer, H., & Evegroen, R. (1993) *Taalontwikkeling en meertaligheid in kindercentra* [Language Development and Multilingual Child Care Centres]. Alphen aan den Rijn: Samsom-HD Tjeenk Willink.

Scheffer, P. (2000). *Het multiculturele drama* [The multicultural drama]. *NRC Handelsblad, 29* januari.

Stam, D. (2003). *Bas. Waar ga je heen?* [Where are you going?]. Leiden: Groen.

Stam, D. (2004a). *Ik ben Bas* [I am Bas]. Leiden: Groen.

Stam, D. (2004b). *Bas, Ga je mee?* [Bas, are you coming?]. Leiden: Groen.

van Beemen, L. (1995). *Ontwikkelingspsychologie* [Developmental psychology]. Groningen: Wolters-Noordhoff.

van Kuyk, J. J. (1996). *Taal voor kleuters* [Language for young children]. Arnhem: Citogroep.

Verhallen, M. (1995). Woordenschat [Vocabulary]. In R. Appel, F. Kuiken, & A. Vermeer, (Eds.), *Nederlands als tweede taal in het basisonderwijs* [Dutch as a second language in primary education]. Amsterdam: Meulenhoff Educatief.
Vygotsky, L. S. (1987). *Thinking and speech.* New York. Plenum.

Websites

http://www.nieuwsbank.nl/inp/2000/04/0427G020.htm. Retrieved May 21, 2007.
http://www.kaleidoscoop.org. Retrieved May 12, 2007.
http://www.CITOgroep.nl/po/piramide/Methode/eind_fr.htm. Retrieved May 12, 2007.
http://www.sciencedirect.com/science?_of=Mimga&_imagekey=B6W47-4C7WH1P-M-1&_cdi=6535&_user=43300-M. Downloaded June 5, 2007.

Chapter 7
Dynamic Assessment of Narrative Competence

Chiel van der Veen and Mariëlle Poland

Language Use in Socio-cultural Practices

"Anyone who writes something down and assumes that another will be able to understand exactly what the writer means is a fool", according to Plato (Egan and Gajdamaschko 2003, p. 84). One can write something down and feel competent in doing so, but not employ it in a socially appropriate way in order for the reader to understand it. The same holds true for the reader. One can technically be able to read the words, sentences and text, but not comprehend it in a socially appropriate way. According to van Oers (2007, p. 300), "the important point about language use is the ability to employ it in functional and acceptable ways in socio-cultural practices". Within concrete socio-cultural practices, the cultural and personal value (e.g. Leontev 1978) of language as a communicative tool becomes evident. For example, when a pupil has to read out loud and faultlessly a list of words just because his teacher asks him to do so, there remains little to no cultural and personal value (*sense*) within this concrete activity. After all, this activity is not an ecologically valid version of a concrete literacy activity as appears in socio-cultural life (van Oers 2007, p. 301). Of course, in the context of education such activities may be simplified versions of cultural activities, but they still need to exhibit all the defining qualities of the original activity. According to Leontev (1981), neglecting

C. van der Veen, M.Sc. (✉)
Department of Theory and Research in Education, VU University Amsterdam, Amsterdam, The Netherlands

De Activiteit, National, Centre for Developmental Education, Alkmaar, The Netherlands
e-mail: chiel.vander.veen@vu.nl

M. Poland, Ph.D.
Educational and Pedagogical Consultancy, Wieringerwerf, The Netherlands
e-mail: info@praktijkdezilverenmaanvlinder.nl

B. van Oers (ed.), *Developmental Education for Young Children*, International
Perspectives on Early Childhood Education and Development 7,
DOI 10.1007/978-94-007-4617 6_7,
© Springer Science+Business Media Dordrecht 2012

the personal value is the main cause of alienation of pupils from schooling (see also van Oers 2010, p. 1). Therefore, both dimensions of meaning (i.e. cultural and personal) should be taken into account in educational practice. In the case of a pupil writing a letter, the value (cultural and personal) of this concrete literacy activity unfolds in the practice of, for example, a gardening company (Pompert 2004) in which this pupil has to write a letter to the local authority to ask for subsidy for the class' future garden. Due to the context of a concrete socio-cultural practice, this literacy activity is closely related to a real socio-cultural practice and therefore may have much personal value (sense) for the pupil. Without the context of a concrete socio-cultural practice we run the risk of violating both the cultural and personal value of activities in education. In this way, cultural-historical activity theory (CHAT) offers a solution to find the proper balance between both dimensions of meaning.

Becoming Literate

Learning to become literate and to use language in socially appropriate ways, is a complex process that needs careful and sensitive support, as it is essential for the development of thinking and cultural identity. Vygotskij argued that the development of thinking is basically a cultural and historical process, based on the appropriation of language (Vygotsky 1987; Luria 1976). In cognitive development, language functions as "the mediator, the medium, and the tool of change" (Nelson 1996, p. 350). This is in line with Vygotskij, who conceived of language as a sign system that mediates between subject and object (Vygotsky 1978, p. 40). The actions of a subject on an object are mediated through language (as a sign system). It is by language that the subject is able to focus his attention on the relevant aspects of the object(s) in question.

Since the beginning of the twentieth century, there has been a growing interest in language within psychological and philosophical research (see among others Bakhtin 1981; Bruner 1996; Cassirer 1957; Nelson 1996; Tomasello 2010; Vygotsky 1978, 1987). In the past, many studies have been devoted to the relationship between language and the development of memory and thinking. In these studies, language is mainly investigated on an intrapersonal level as a sign system for personal purposes, namely thinking and remembering. However, in most (educational) situations where language functions as a mediator of human activity another agent is also involved, who mediates between the subject and the situation (van Oers 2007; Vygotsky and Luria 1994). "In this case the sign activity is an interpersonal process, where an exchange of meanings between subjects takes places with the help of signs (verbal means)" (van Oers 2007, p. 303). When another subject is involved in a concrete activity, the latter has some degree of influence on the actions of the subject towards an object. For example, when a pupil is preparing a presentation on a specific topic (i.e. is preparing a concrete language activity), another subject (e.g. the teacher) can influence the actions of the pupil by using words or gestures to guide the activity, modelling behaviour, etc. Thus, "language can be said to regulate human object-oriented activity, both on an intrapersonal and an interpersonal level" (van Oers 2007, p. 303). Using language for interpersonal purposes is what we will call communication. According to Vygotsky (1987, 1978), thinking (intrapersonal) and communication (interpersonal) are intrinsically related. In this view, language first appears on an interpersonal level and, after a process of internalisation, can also be used for thinking on an intrapersonal level. Becoming literate in this approach can be conceived of as "building up the generalised ability of using sign systems for personal and interpersonal purposes within specific cultural practices" (van Oers 2007, p. 303). This competence includes not only the mastery of written language (e.g. reading), but also forms of oral language, and theoretical thinking.

In the following we will mainly focus on the use of language as a communicative tool. Communication "is a form of social action constituted by social conventions for achieving social ends, premised on at least some shared understandings and shared purposes among users" (Tomasello 2010, p. 343). Basically, human communication functions as a means to attain and maintain joint attention and, therefore, has to follow some social conventions. After all, the addresser wants the addressee to understand his communicative utterances in order to achieve some social ends. A special feature of human communicative competence is "the ability and disposition to (re)construct and use textual representations for the purpose of clarifying meaning to oneself or others in the context of some socio-cultural practice" (van Oers 2007, p. 304). This ability and disposition is what we will call narrative competence. In Developmental Education narrative competence is considered the core of becoming literate. It encompasses abilities (vocabulary, pragmatics, grammar, and style) and dispositions (attitude, aesthetics) in one complex cultural performance.

Producing Narratives

Narratives are essential in human action, as they function as a tool for giving coherent meaning to reality. They give substance to human experiences within socio-cultural practices and, to some extent, take those experiences beyond the borders of human daily life (Engel 1999). Bruner (1986) made a distinction between logic-paradigmatic thinking and narrative thinking. In logic-paradigmatic thinking, logical relations and theoretical concepts form the basis of thinking processes. This form of thinking is occupied with founding, application, exploration and elaboration of scientific concepts (van Oers 2009). In narrative thinking intuition, associative and aesthetical evaluations, and cohesion determine the progress of thinking. According to Bruner (1990), narrative thinking is the most direct form of thinking. It is related to the situation, to emotions and a person's own language use (van Oers 2009; Egan 2006). Not only is narrative thinking the first form of thinking of human beings, it also relates closely to concrete daily thinking and language use (van Oers 2009). Further, without narratives one is unable to construct an identity and find a place in one's culture, one's society (Bruner 1996, p. 42). With the help of narratives one is able to build one's own consistent story with a certain motive, one's own perspective, and one's own unique role in socio-cultural practices.

The context in which one tells or writes a narrative as a means for thinking (intrapersonal) or communication (interpersonal) is essential in the process of giving meaning. It is the point of view a person takes in his narrative, which gives the listener or reader insight into the narrator's way of thinking, ideas, beliefs, values. Therefore, narrativity can be seen as an important way to understand human action (Pléh 2003; van Oers 2003; Engel 1999). If narratives are important for understanding human action, they should have a central place in educational practice, in order to gain insight into children's development and the nature of their cognitive achievements. It is by the stories children tell and write that one, for example a teacher, has access to information on a child's actual and potential level of development regarding narrative competence. Children's narratives give us a window on their beliefs, thoughts, experiences, language development, etc. (Engel 2003). Therefore, in the context of educational practices children's narratives should be collected as a means to assess their narrative competence. It is through children's narrative competence that one can enter their developmental "world", and learn about their world view, identity, and meanings.

In Developmental Education, a strategy for literacy development has been elaborated over the years which is consistent with the Vygotskian approach (Knijpstra et al. 1997; Pompert and Janssen-Vos 2003; Pompert 2004; van Oers 2007). The core of this strategy consists in adults' and children's interaction for the construction of comprehensible narratives. For elaborations of this literacy strategy in Developmental Education classrooms, we may refer to Chaps. 5 and 15 of this book. In Developmental Education, narratives are a way for children to express themselves, acquire a voice, and make themselves clear. By means of narratives, children are able to understand each other and integrate their own stories with the stories of other children, teachers, books, parents, etc. Therefore, close observation, reading and analysis of young children's narratives is an essential part of Developmental Education. However, the method of assessing children on the basis of their narratives must be consistent with the concept of Developmental Education, and should be consistent with children's learning in and through meaningful socio-cultural activities. It is in the context of these activities that one can observe in an ecologically valid way and assess children's narratives and narrative competence. In the next paragraphs we will present a way in which this can be accomplished.

The Zone of Proximal Development

Before we elaborate a strategy to assess children's narrative competence in a way that is consistent with Developmental Education, we will first explain how we conceive of the zone of proximal development (ZPD) as related to dynamic assessment of narrative competence. As will become clear, the ZPD is the foundation on which the concept of dynamic assessment is built. Referring to Vygotsky's (1978, p. 86) well-known proposition about the ZPD, it is generally taken as the difference between what one can do independently and what one can do with the assistance or mediation of another more knowledgeable agent. Whereas this definition has received divergent interpretations (see van Oers 2011; Poehner 2008), we will further elaborate the concept of the ZPD. According to Vygotskij, imitation is actually the basis of the ZPD. "Imitation not in the sense of meaningless copying of actions but in the sense of meaningful reconstructions of cultural activities" (van Oers 2011, p. 86; see also Chap. 2 of this volume). As stated earlier, the value (cultural and personal) of those imitated activities unfolds in the context of concrete practices, such as a gardening company (Pompert 2004), editorial board of a newspaper (van der Veen 2010), etc. Of course, children are unable to participate completely independently in those imitated activities. It is by the mediation of a more capable social other that the child learns to perform certain new skills independently. The way mediation is understood determines the process leading to progress in a certain activity. For example, consider a pupil preparing a presentation on their research on a rocket that has to fly as high as possible with the aid of baking powder and vinegar. One way for the teacher to mediate this activity could be to prepare the presentation on the pupil's behalf and then simply let them read it out loud. Another option would be to guide the pupil in the process of writing the presentation (for a certain audience), practicing the presentation (mimicry, pronunciation), and finally giving the presentation in front of an audience. In the latter option, the child is involved as an active participant and as such co-regulates the activity. "The ZPD then is about co-mediation between someone who has knowledge or capacity to attain a goal and someone who does not" (Lantolf 2009, p. 359). It is about "social interaction where instruction leads development" (Poehner and Lantolf 2010). It is the task of the teacher to be sensitive to the child's actual level of development in order to mediate the activity towards obtaining some pre-described learning goals and executing a socially accepted imitation of the activity of presenting the results of research. What a child can do with assistance today, he/she can do tomorrow alone (Vygotsky 1978, p. 87). In this approach, the ZPD can be seen as a diagnostic approach to development with a two-step process. First, the actual level of development has to be uncovered. Second, based on the responsiveness of a pupil during mediation by a more knowledgeable agent, the proximal level of development can be unravelled. The former refers to a pupil's abilities that are matured, developed; the latter refers to abilities that are in the process of maturing, are developing. In order to mediate the development of children, we need to understand "the full range of individuals' abilities" (Poehner 2008, p. 42), and – as we would say – their developmental potentials in a certain domain. Developmental potential is related to the child's receptiveness to help, i.e. his capacity to benefit from the assistance he has received from more knowledgeable others.

For the purpose of this chapter, it is necessary to apply the concept of the ZPD and the implied idea of imitation to concrete language activities in which pupils use narratives in order to communicate (or think). As stated earlier, narrative competence is about the reconstruction and use of textual representations in order to clarify meaning on an intrapersonal or interpersonal level in the context of socio-cultural practices. Becoming narratively competent is about the process of building up the ability to use sign systems for communication and thinking. In this process, children are dependent on the mediation of a more capable social other (e.g. the teacher). In the context of children becoming narratively competent, there is another agent involved who mediates between the child and the situation. The ZPD then is about the co-mediation between this more knowledgeable agent and the child to attain the co-construction of some narrative. For example, when a child and a teacher are involved in a joint activity in which they try to understand how to make a schematic representation of the castle built by the child, they co-construct a narrative, which articulates different aspects of the castle (e.g. the mathematical aspects) and helps them understand the world in a structural (mathematical) manner. The mediation of the teacher contributes to the quality of the narrative both to communicate and think about the schematic representation. In the process of co-constructing a narrative in order to understand, for example, how to make a schematic representation of a castle, the idea of imitation plays an important role. As already stated, we conceive of imitation as meaningfully reconstructing cultural activities. It is by the joint activity of narrating that the act of schematically representing a concrete building is meaningfully reconstructed from a structural point of view (see also Chap. 8 of this volume). The activity of retelling how to make a schematic representation – we will again use this example – is not something children learn to do by formal teaching; "rather the adult 'teaches' by leading the child through the activity" (McNamee 1979, p. 65). At some points the teacher may need to ask a lot of questions or take full responsibility for retelling the story. Gradually the child learns to reconstruct the narrative with little guidance from the teacher. In terms of the distribution of responsibilities, it is the child who moves from being a merely peripheral narrator to a more central narrator who finally takes full responsibility in the activity of reconstructing narratives.

Dynamic Assessment

In the preceding, we conceived of the ZPD as a concept that helps us understand how to define mediation between a more knowledgeable agent and a child in some socio-cultural practice. This is in line with Vygotskij's dialectical inter-pretation of instruction and assessment. It is this integration of instruction (as a way of supporting development) and assessment (as a way to understanding development) that we will call Dynamic Assessment (DA) and which is basically a "pedagogical instantiation of the ZPD" (Lantolf 2009, p. 359). The dialectical interpretation of instruction and assessment distinguishes DA from so-called non-Dynamic Assessments (NDA) which are based on a dualistic interpretation of both instruction and assessments (Poehner 2008). As a consequence, non-Dynamic As-sessment characteristically takes assessment outcomes as distinct data, disconnected from the instruction that children have received. Non-Dynamic Assessment at best produces static descriptions of the children's actual level of development.

The term DA was first used by Luria, a colleague of Vygotskij, in the context of identifying children with disabilities for placement in the appropriate school setting (Luria 1961). According to Luria, Vygotskij's elaboration of the ZPD (zone of proximal development) requires that appropriate assistance be given during the actual assessment in order to gain (1) insight into the child's use of assistance and (2) the degree to which the child's performances improved when given assistance (see also Poehner 2008). The assistance of a more knowledgeable agent is aimed at moving "the individual toward independent, agentive performance and to be able to transfer what is appropriated in a given circumstance to future situations" (Poehner and Lantolf 2010, p. 316). This is in line with Vygotskij's notion that higher mental development is originated in interpersonal activity (Vygotsky 1978).

Sternberg and Grigorenko (2002) describe DA as an approach that "takes into account the results of an intervention. In this intervention, the examiner teaches the examinee how to perform better on individual items or on the test as a whole" (p. vii). DA helps the teacher to gain insight into the "developing abilities through intervention" (Lidz 1991, p. 6). When the assessor (i.e. the teacher) gains insight into the developing abilities of the child through a successful intervention, this produces suggestions for future interventions that may promote the development of the child. Over the past decades, two general approaches to DA have been developed (Poehner 2008; Lantolf 2009). "In both approaches instruction as mediation and assessment are fused into a single activity with the goal of diagnosing learning potential and promoting development in accordance with this potential" (Lantolf 2009, p. 360). The two general approaches are mainly distinguished by their conception and realisation of mediation. In the first approach, known as the *interventionist approach*, mediation is based on a standardised and fixed set of clues, hints, and feedback that are offered to the child as they move through a test task. The hints are scaled from implicit to explicit, so the assessor gains insight into the extent of the child's mastery of the task. The use of mostly implicit hints is associated with a higher degree of control over the task (Lantolf 2009). "Thus, the expectation is that as learners move through the test they will require fewer hints and less explicit mediation" (Lantolf 2009, p. 360). This latter tendency is an indication that learners are internalising the skills involved, for example, constructing the correct order in a series of events on the basis of a number of related pictures. This skill may be helpful when they want to compose a message or a short story in a more independent way later on. The great advantages of the use of standardised hints and clues within DA is that (1) it can be executed with high numbers of children simultaneously, and (2) because of the standardised feedback it is possible to express children's abilities in a quantitative manner with the use of psychometric techniques to compare scores. Examples of interventionist DA are elaborated by Guthke and his colleagues (Guthke et al. 1986), Budoff (1987), Carlson and Wiedl (1992), and Brown and her colleagues (Brown and Ferrara 1985; Campione et al. 1984). As Dynamic Assessment is by definition about intervening in developmental processes, we think that *interventionist DA* is a somewhat misleading term. Therefore, in this chapter we will speak of *standardised DA*.

The second approach to DA is known as the *interactionist approach*. This approach focuses on assistance that emerges from the interaction and cooperation between assessor and assessee in order to interpret the development of the latter. Mediation is not standardised and fixed, but rather "negotiated with the individual, which means that it is continually adjusted according to the learner's responsivity" (Lantolf 2009, p. 360). Teacher and pupil cooperate in order to lay down – to use Elkonin's (1998) train metaphor – new tracks leading toward a station that is potentially always relocating. One well-known example of interactionist DA is the Mediated Learning Experience (MLE) which is elaborated by Feuerstein and his colleagues (for example Feuerstein et al. 2003).

Undoubtedly, interactionist DA fits the concept of Developmental Education as it focuses on cooperative dialoguing. However, in the Dutch educational context schools are obliged to use at least some forms of standardised testing that make use of psychometric techniques. The quality of such tests is controlled and registered by the national committee of test matters (COTAN, Commissie testaangelegenheden Nederland) in order to evaluate the quality of public schools (i.e. the more registered tests a school is using, the higher the quality of the school is evaluated by the national inspectorate of education). The problem for Developmental Education is not the use of such non-Dynamic Assessments itself, but rather the need for assessment strategies that can be used by teachers as an instrument to understand the full range of children's abilities and potentials (i.e. matured abilities as well as abilities that are in the process of maturing). Without further discussing the different, mostly paradigmatic elaborations of interventionist and interactionist DA, we will show how the two approaches can be combined. Our goal in doing so is twofold. On the one hand (as already stated) a Dynamic Assessment strategy for narrative competence should fit the concept of Developmental Education. On the other hand, we also need a reliable description of the actual level of development of children's narrative competence. Moreover, given the Dutch educational context, we aim at the construction of a Dynamic Assessment strategy that meets the political requirements and thereby the requirements of the national inspectorate of education. In combining both standardised and interactionist DA, we started out from a sandwich format (or test-train-test design) for dynamic tests in which the assessee first takes a standardised pre-test, followed by an intervention (i.e. instruction), and finally the assessee is tested again on a post-test (Sternberg and Grigorenko 2002). However, we want to go one step further and elaborate the notion of intervention beyond the idea of short-term, more or less standardised assistance or scaffolding. We lengthen the intervention from task intervention, which is often short and bound to a specific task, to an intervention period of several weeks. The main reason for this lengthy intervention is that the development of narrative competence takes more than just a task; it is a competence that develops over time. During this intervention period interactionist DA is used to gain insight into the full range of children's abilities and the development of those abilities over time with the use of cooperative dialoguing. Standardised DA is used to standardise guidance and feedback during the pre-test and post-test before and after the intervention period. (An example of this approach in Developmental Education can be found in Chap. 6 of this

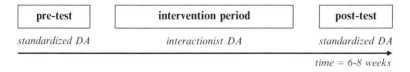

Fig. 7.1 Standardised and interactionist DA integrated in a sandwich format

volume with regard to vocabulary assessment). Both pre-test and post-test produce quantitative information which can be used in addition to the qualitative information gathered with interactionist DA. Together, standardised and interactionist DA give the teacher a valid and reliable image of the actual and potential level of the child's development, as well as the child's sensitivity to certain ways of future instruction. In Fig. 7.1 our integration of standardised and interactionist DA is shown as a sandwich format.

In Developmental Education teachers try to monitor children's literate activities and development by means of an observation system called HOREB (Action-oriented Observation, Registration, and Evaluation of Basic Development; see Chaps. 4 and 14 of this volume). Generally, HOREB aims to observe and register children's development when participating in meaningful activities, in order to monitor their development as well as to gain insight into possible future developmental steps. Therefore, we can consider HOREB as an instrument for DA of children's development. However, an appropriate instrument to measure narrative competence is not available yet. Because we want to give serious attention to the value of narratives, we want to do more than just close-observation. In the next section we will explain the procedure of DA of narrative competence in the context of Developmental Education.

Dynamic Assessment of Narrative Competence in Developmental Education

In Developmental Education, the core lies in the imitation of meaningful sociocultural practices in which children can and want to participate. Concretely, this means that teachers – together with children – build up a theme over a period of 6–8 weeks. All communication and language learning is embedded in thematic activities that make sense for the children. As an example we will refer to the practice of a restaurant. Within this scenario children play roles and use language that is associated with their role. The waitress tells the customers about the menu, makes phone calls, writes down reservations, etc. The chef writes a shopping list, makes a new seasonal menu, gives oral instructions to the other cooks and the waitresses, etc. In the development of a theme, children learn knowledge and skills related to that specific theme and their roles within it, which enable them to become more central participants. This means, for example, that they learn to read and write a menu, make a telephone reservation for dinner, write down the personal experiences they have had when they visited a restaurant, etc.

The notion of a theme over a period of 6–8 weeks is what forms the foundation of our assessment strategy. The following cyclic steps are taken to assess children's narrative competence within those themes: (1) theme planning, (2) pre-test, (3) intervention period, (4) post-test and, (5) interpretation and evaluation. We will further elaborate each of these steps and explain certain steps with examples taken from a theme in which children participate in the practice of a travel agency (see van Oers 2007). We will focus on DA of narrative competence with children aged 4–8. Most children of this age are not (yet) able to write a story that has the qualities of a well-developed written narrative. Therefore, young children are assessed on their narrative competence by telling a story (orally).

The first step is to choose and plan a theme that has cultural as well as personal value for the children. Based on the actual development of the children, possible language activities are planned that could lead to the realisation of certain educational goals. One of these activities could be the making of advertisements for the travel agency with the use of written language. Results on past narrative competence assessments, as well as teacher's classroom observations regarding the narrative competence of children, are taken into account when planning a theme. Second, all children individually take a pre-test in which their actual level of narrative competence within the context of the theme is assessed. In this pre-test the teacher asks the child to tell a story, a narrative about the travel agency. In order to support the child in telling a story, the teacher uses richly illustrated pictures from storybooks which have a central place in the theme. The teacher as co-teller is allowed to ask questions in order to guide the child through the activity of narrating. It is important to observe how much help the child needs and what kind of help or instruction (i.e. modelling, questioning) is needed in order for the child to tell a well-organised narrative. Six different criteria (with sub-criteria) are assessed with help of a score sheet (see Table 7.1), namely: (1) use of a suitable title, (2) addressivity, (3) quality of the story itself, (4) vocabulary and sentences, (5) empathy and imagination, and (6) attitude. Scores on all criteria are added, so the narrative competence of every child can be calculated.

Narrative competence is expressed in an ability score with three levels, namely: high, average, lower than average. The assessment gives the teacher quantitative as well as qualitative information about the development of the child regarding his/her narrative competence. Based on this information, the teacher can reconsider the theme planning to make it fit to the needs of the children and to the aim of contributing optimally to the development of the children's full narrative potential. Third, children (as well as the teacher) participate in different thematic activities which are related to the practice of the travel agency and which are within the children's ZPD. This third step is what we will call the intervention period as it strives to intervene in the children's actual level of narrative development in order to reach their full potential. In this intervention period the teacher plays an essential role in guiding and observing the children's development. Teachers' observations

Table 7.1 Dynamic assessment of narrative competence: some elements from the score sheet

Criteria	Subcriteria	Score
1. Use of a suitable title	Does the child give a name to the story or does the child make clear what the main theme of the story is?	Yes: 1
2. Addressivity	Does the child want to make itself clear?	Yes: 1
3. The story itself	Is it a coherent story, is it fragmented, or is it an enumeration?	Enumeration: 1 Fragmented: 1 Coherent story: 2
	Does the child tell about: who, what, where, and when?	Who: 1 What: 1 Where: 1 When: 1
4. Vocabulary and sentences	Are the sentences logically and grammatically correct?	>80%: 1
	Does the child use jargon related to the theme?	Yes: 1
5. Empathy and imagination	Does the child expresses feelings, thoughts, needs, or wishes?	Yes: 1
	The story is primarily aimed at objects, acts, and events in the present	1
	The story transcends the present	2
6. Attitude	Is the child actively involved in telling the story?	Yes: 1
	The child is eager to tell about the theme or his experiences.	Not: 0 A little bit: 1 Very: 2

are executed and registered with help of the instruments from HOREB (Janssen-Vos et al. 2007). The focus of these observations is on the narrative skills that children exhibit while participating in different activities. These observations are action-oriented, which means that the teacher is at the same time participating in the activity in order to guide the development of the children towards the realisation of their full potential. In this way, instruction and assessment are integrated in an interactionist manner. Fourth, the children take a post-test at the end of the intervention period (theme) in which their level of narrative competence is again assessed. The format of this post-test is the same as the pre-test, as we want to gain insight into how the development of the children has been affected by the intervention. Fifth, the scores on the pre-test and post-test as well as teachers' observations are evaluated and interpreted. Difference scores on the post-test and pre-test evaluate to what extent the child has become more competent in telling a narrative over the intervention period. Together with the observations, these difference scores give the teacher both qualitative and quantitative information regarding the narrative development of the child. Based on this information the teacher identifies a child's developmental potential and needs in order to promote development in accordance with this potential (Lantolf 2009). In the next theme (first step), the teacher can co-construct new activities with children, in which they are offered the help they need for building up their full narrative potential. Based on available time, teachers can choose whether they repeat the whole cycle every theme or only take post- and pre-tests once or twice a year. Of course, observing the development of children's narrative competence in an action-oriented way is something teachers should do throughout the whole year.

Some Preliminary Experiences

"Our experience up to now shows that it is possible to make a valid and reliable instrument, although many trials still have to be done before we can definitely qualify the instrument" and get the instrument registered by the national committee of test matters (COTAN) (van Oers 2007, p. 311; see also Poland 2005). Based on a few pilot studies the following preliminary results can be presented:

- The present instrument to assess children's narrative competence turned out to be reliable (Poland 2005);
- Validity is high, because the instrument directly measures what it is supposed to measure, namely children's ability to tell or write narratives. Because of the active role of the assessor (guidance, feedback, questions, modelling) – which is closely related to Vygotkij's notion that a child's level of performance with help is indicative of his/her future independent performance – children are able to demonstrate their full narrative competence. Complicating factors for the child's narration, such as memory, attention, and subject-related knowledge, are excluded or taken over by the teacher who gives guidance and/or temporarily deals with difficult episodes in the storytelling. The focus is meant to be exclusively on children's narrative competence *per se*;
- Dynamic Assessment of narrative competence is consistent with the concept of Developmental Education as it is a whole-language approach. Many other language tests fragment language into several sub-skills such as spelling, vocabulary, attitude, etc.;
- Inter-rater reliability turned out to be acceptable for the instrument as a whole, as well as for most of the six different sub-scales (the criteria). Reformulating the criteria in scale five (empathy and imagination) is necessary as the inter-rater reliability for this scale is low;
- Teachers are positive about the instrument because it also gives them information to evaluate their own instruction. In addition, the instrument is of great help when planning future educational activities that promote children's narrative development;
- Since our instrument tends to be subjective, i.e., it has no definite or standard answers for the way teachers have to score the different criteria in an objective manner, the standardisation of the scoring procedure is a point of issue. The instruction manual as well as the different criteria have to be rewritten with the addition of concrete examples, so that teachers understand how to score the criteria as objectively as possible and avoid multiple interpretations;

- Teacher's skills are of great importance for the proper use of the instrument as assessment and instruction are integrated. This dialectical view of instruction and assessment, although fitting the concept of Developmental Education, is new for most teachers. Therefore, teachers should be guided in assessing children's narrative competence by trained professionals (see for example Chaps. 12 and 13 of this volume) in order to change their view of and attitude towards assessment;
- Finally, we have to point out that using this instrument can be time consuming. Many teachers in our pilots were unfamiliar with Dynamic Assessment (see also the previous point) and were not aware of the importance of narrative competence and therefore they did not always see the advantages. Because most of the teachers were obliged to use some standardised and COTAN registered tests, they could not fully focus on assessing children's narrative competence.

In the near future the instrument will be further developed in order to make it suitable for a wider group of teachers. Objectivity, reliability, and validity will be reconsidered in several pilots. In those pilots teachers will be specifically trained to use the instrument in a proper manner in order to develop children's full narrative potential.

Final Remarks

In Developmental Education, Dynamic Assessment of narrative competence is an important activity in which both teachers and children are active participants. This instrument offers schools an alternative to standardised tests which only provide information about children's matured abilities. Dynamic Assessment of narrative competence helps teachers to understand children's full range of abilities and potentials. Undoubtedly, our current instrument has great advantages for both children and teachers; children can show their full narrative potential and teachers gain insight into children's abilities, as well as their own instruction that may lead to the development of children's potential. However, future research is necessary for the improvement of the instrument and to make it more practical for use in classroom situations.

References

Bakhtin, M. (1981). *The dialogic imagination* (M. Holquist, Ed.; C. Emerson & M. Holquist, Trans.). Austin: University of Texas.

Brown, A., & Ferrara, F. A. (1985). Diagnosing zones of proximal development. In J. V. Wertsch (Ed.), *Culture, communication, and cognition. Vygotskian perspectives* (pp. 273–305). Cambridge: Cambridge University Press.

Bruner, J. S. (1986). *Actual minds, possible worlds*. Cambridge, MA: Harvard University Press.

Bruner, J. S. (1990). *Acts of meaning*. Cambridge, MA: Harvard University Press.

Bruner, J. S. (1996). *The culture of education*. Cambridge, MA: Harvard University Press.

Budoff, M. (1987). The validity of learning potential assessment. In C. S. Lidz (Ed.), *Dynamic assessment: An interactive approach to evaluating learning potential* (pp. 52–81). New York: Guilford.

Campione, J. C., Brown, A. L., Ferrara, R. A., & Bryant, N. R. (1984). The zone of proximal development: Implications for individual differences and learning. In B. Rogoff & J. V. Wertsch (Eds.), *Children's learning in the "zone of proximal development"* (pp. 77–91). San Francisco: Jossey-Bass.

Carlson, J. S., & Wiedl, K. H. (1992). Principles of dynamic assessment: The application of a specific model. *Learning and Individual Differences, 4*, 153–166.

Cassirer, E. (1957). *The philosophy of symbolic forms (Vol. 3): The phenomenology of knowledge*. New Haven/London: Yale University Press.

Egan, K. (2006). *Teaching literacy. Engaging the imagination of new readers and writers*. Thousand Oaks: Corwin Press.

Egan, K., & Gajdamaschko, N. (2003). Some cognitive tools of literacy. In A. Kozulin et al. (Eds.), *Vygotsky's educational theory in cultural context* (pp. 83–98). Cambridge: Cambridge University Press.

Elkonin, D. B. (1998). Epilogue. In R. W. Rieber (Ed.), *The collected works of L.S. Vygotsky. Vol. 5: Child psychology*. New York: Plenum.

Engel, S. (1999). *The stories children tell. Making sense of the narratives of childhood*. New York: W.H. Freeman and Company.

Engel, S. (2003). My harmless inside heart turned green: children's narratives and their inner lives. In B. van Oers (Ed.), *Narratives of childhood. Theoretical and practical explorations for the innovation of early childhood education* (pp. 39–50). Amsterdam: VU University Press.

Feuerstein, R., Feuerstein, R. S., Falik, L., & Rand, Y. (2003). *Dynamic assessment of cognitive modifiability*. Jerusalem: ICELP.

Guthke, J., Heinrich, A., & Caruso, M. (1986). The diagnostic program of "syntactical rule and vocabulary acquisition" – A contribution to the psychodiagnosis of foreign language learning ability. In F. Klix & H. Hagendorf (Eds.), *Human memory and cognitive capabilities. Mechanisms and performances* (pp. 903–911). Amsterdam: Elsevier.

Janssen-Vos, F., Pompert, B., & van Oers, E. (2007). *HOREB-PO. Handelingsgericht Observeren, Registreren en Evalueren van Basisontwikkeling* [Action-oriented observation, registration, and evaluation of basic development]. Assen: Van Gorcum.

Knijpstra, H., et al. (1997). *Met jou kan ik lezen en schrijven. Een ontwikkelingsgerichte didactiek voor het leren lezen en schrijven in groep 3 en 4* [With you I can read and write. Developmental didactics for learning to read and write in grades 1 and 2]. Assen: Van Gorcum.

Lantolf, J. P. (2009). Dynamic assessment: The dialectic integration of instruction and assessment. *Language Teaching, 42*(3), 355–368.

Leontev, A. N. (1978). *Activity, consciousness, personality*. Englewood Cliffs: Prentice hall.

Leonfev, A. N. (1981). *Problems of the development of the mind*. Moscow: Progress Publishers.

Lidz, C. S. (1991). *Practitioner's guide to dynamic assessment*. New York: Guilford.

Luria, A. R. (1961). Study of the abnormal child. *American Journal of Orthopsychiatry: A Journal of Human Behaviour, 31*(1), 1–16.

Luria, A. R. (1976). *Cognitive development. Its cultural and social foundations*. Cambridge, MA: Harvard University Press.

McNamee, G. D. (1979). The social interaction origins of narrative skills. *The Quarterly Newsletter of the Laboratory of Comparative Human Cognition, 1*(4), 63–68.

Nelson, K. (1996). *Language in cognitive development. The emergence of the mediated mind*. Cambridge: Cambridge University Press.

Poehner, M. E. (2008). *Dynamic assessment. A Vygotskian approach to understanding and promoting L2 development*. New York: Springer.

Poehner, M. E., & Lantolf, J. P. (2010). Vygotsky's teaching-assessment dialectic and L2 education. The case for dynamic assessment. *Mind, Culture, and Activity, 17*(4), 312–330.

Poland, M. (2005). *Het toetsen van narratieve competentie bij jonge kinderen in de onderbouw* [Assessing young children's narrative competence in early childhood education]. Unpublished master's thesis, VU University, Amsterdam.

Pléh, C. (2003). Narrativity in text construction and self construction. *Neohelicon, 30*(1), 187–205.

Pompert, B. (2004). *Thema's en taal* [Themes and language education]. Assen: Van Gorcum.

Pompert, B., & Janssen-Vos, F. (2003). From narrator to writer. Promoting cultural learning in early childhood. In B. van Oers (Ed.), *Narratives of childhood. Theoretical and practical explorations for the innovation of early childhood education* (pp. 127–145). Amsterdam: VU University Press.

Sternberg, R. J., & Grigorenko, E. L. (2002). *Dynamic testing. The nature and measurement of learning potential*. New York: Cambridge University Press.

Tomasello, M. (2010). *Origins of human communication*. Cambridge, MA: The MIT Press.

van der Veen, C. (2010). *Towards abstract thinking in a fifth dimension site: Children taking the role of junior editor at a news-paper.* Unpublished master's thesis, VU University, Amsterdam.

van Oers, B. (Ed.). (2003). *Narratives of childhood. Theoretical and practical explorations for the innovation of early childhood education*. Amsterdam: VU University Press.

van Oers, B. (2007). Helping young children to become literate: The relevance of narrative competence for developmental education. *European Early Childhood Education Research Journal, 15*(3), 299–312.

van Oers, B. (2009). Narrativiteit in leerprocessen. *Pedagogische Studiën, 86*(2), 147–156.

van Oers, B. (2010). *Imitative participation and the development of abstract thinking in primary school.* Internal Publication Department Theory and Research in Education. Amsterdam: VU University.

van Oers, B. (2011). Where is the child? Controversy in the Neo-Vygotskian approach to child development. *Mind, Culture, and Activity, 18*(1), 84–88.

Vygotsky, L. S. (1978). *Mind in society. The development of higher psychological processes*. Cambridge, MA: Harvard University Press.

Vygotsky, L. S. (1987). Thinking and speech. In *L.S. Vygotsky, collected works. Vol. 1* (pp. 39–285) (R. Rieber & A. Carton, Eds.; N. Minick, Trans.). New York: Plenum.

Vygotsky, L. S., & Luria, A. R. (1994). Tool and symbol in child development. In R. van der Veer & J. Valsiner (Eds.), *The Vygotsky reader* (pp. 99–174). Oxford: Blackwell.

Chapter 8
Promoting Abstract Thinking in Young Children's Play

Bert van Oers and Mariëlle Poland

The Unending Query of Abstraction

One of the missions of Developmental Education is to prepare children to deal with a variety of complex tasks that occur in their cultural environment. Complexity is generally considered to be confusing and difficult to handle, and the ability to deal successfully with complex situations is seen as a slowly growing process that comes with age. Particularly young children are considered unable to cope effectively with complex situations.

One strategy for dealing with complexity, which has been given much attention in the literature on thinking and problem solving, is the systematic reduction of the number of features of the situation or object. Usually this process is referred to as *abstraction*. Although the phenomenon of abstraction has raised much debate since the ancient Greek philosophers, the Aristotelian view is still broadly accepted, i.e. the assumption that abstraction results from the focus of human attention on the essence of objects, acts and events. Children are supposed to become acquainted with the essential properties of the world by mastering abstract academic (scientific) concepts, which are supposed to summarise what scientific history has identified as true knowledge, representing the essence of things.

The mastery of abstract scientific concepts was for Vygotskij an important aim of education and cultural development (see for example Wertsch 1996). The goals of

B. van Oers, Ph.D. (✉)
Department Theory and Research in Education, Faculty of Psychology and Education,
VU University Amsterdam, Amsterdam, The Netherlands
e-mail: bert.van.oers@vu.nl

M. Poland, Ph.D.
Educational and Pedagogical Consultancy, Wieringerwerf, The Netherlands
e-mail: info@praktijkdezilverenmaanvlinder.nl

B. van Oers (ed.), *Developmental Education for Young Children*, International
Perspectives on Early Childhood Education and Development 7,
DOI 10.1007/978-94-007-4617-6_8,
© Springer Science+Business Media Dordrecht 2012

education nowadays consist to a great extent of references to the mastery of abstract knowledge. However, many children have difficulties with successfully dealing with such abstractions in ways that make sense to them.

Davydov (1972) has already convincingly explained that the problem of abstraction in school children is a result of the way children get to know abstractions. Teaching abstractions by letting children discover the essential qualities of things without pedagogical guidance, often results in irrelevant notions and will not contribute to flexible understandings that are compatible with the outcomes of cultural history. Teaching abstractions by imposing cultural categories (direct instruction) upon children will in most cases not contribute to meaningful understanding either. Davydov demonstrated that assisting children with the employment of theoretical models for the interpretation of cultural reality will lead to the mastery of meaningful and functional abstractions. However, Davydov was persistent in his assumption that the theoretical models should be handed out to the pupils as cultural tools for their interpretations of reality. His approach did not clearly explain the process of formation of the theoretical model in a meaningful way. As van Oers (1987) put it, Davydov concentrates on the appropriation of theoretical structures instead of the development of the ability of theoretical *structuring*. The collaborative structuring of experience through discourse (see Carpay and van Oers 1993) was later only hesitantly accepted by Davydov (1996, p. 226), although the dynamics of discursive construction of abstractions and theoretical models still remained unexplained in his works. Nevertheless, Davydov's work was an important step forward, as he demonstrated that the adopted view of abstraction itself determines how abstractions are promoted in children. So the question about the nature of abstraction and abstract thinking is primordial to education and to the development of abstract thought by education.

The nature of abstract thinking, however, has been the cause of numerous disputes over the past 20 centuries. It is impossible to give an overview of the debates here (see for example Bolton 1972; Il'enkov 1991). Common to all views on abstraction is that it represents a particular way of perceiving and conceiving of reality. The core of the problem of abstraction then is how the outcomes of abstraction processes relate to the realities they are assumed to refer to. Basically, we can distinguish two types of relationships. On the one hand, abstractions, as the name already suggests, are conceived as *drawn from* certain more complex realms of experience (concrete-material or mental) either by successively eliminating irrelevant features, or by directly seeing the essence of situations, things, processes or events (intuition). On the other hand, abstractions can be seen as cultural conceptions (models) that are *added to* reality in order to understand its concrete nature in a consistent, theoretical way. In dialectical logic (see for example Il'enkov, Davydov) this latter interpretation of abstraction refers to a process of theorising reality, or "ascending from the abstract to the concrete" (Ilyenkov 1977; van Oers 1987, 2001). Both approaches to the phenomenon of abstraction, however, still make a distinction between the abstract and the concrete. Yet in our view, the abstract and the concrete are inseparable and intrinsically intermingled dimensions (see also Roth 2004; Roth and Hwang 2006a, b).

In this chapter we develop an argument that demonstrates that even young children can actively participate in activities that include abstract notions, if meaningfully embedded in their own playful activities. We describe the potential in young children to think abstractly and we will outline an approach to assist children in appropriating this type of thinking. We start with some brief notes on the development of abstract thinking and a clarification of our notion of abstraction. Subsequently, we will focus on the concept of schematising activities as a possible way for children to deal with abstraction processes. By means of schematising children learn to represent thoughts and ideas as self-invented and cultural symbols and schemes. Through participating and problem solving in collaborative activities children also encounter cultural symbols and abstractions, and can learn to acknowledge the need and function of symbolism. We will present part of our research on schematising and abstract thinking, conducted in Developmental Education classrooms (ages 5–6/7), and demonstrate that schematising, when meaningfully embedded in play activities, can improve children's mathematical thinking.

The Potential of Abstract Thinking in Young Children

The faculty of abstract thinking is usually, and has for many years been seen as an ability that emerges relatively late in children's thinking development (see for example Piaget 2001). Piaget acknowledged that young children can pay attention to specific aspects of reality due to the different effects these aspects have on their actions, and he called this "empirical abstraction". Real abstract thinking in his view, however, is closely dependent on formal operational thinking which occurs in his view from the age of 12 years old.

Despite the numerous critical evaluations of Piaget's theory (see for example Davydov 1990; Egan 1986, 2002) the idea of abstraction as a difficult achievement for young children is deeply rooted in our culture and is still a strong and persistent assumption, hard to expel from educational thinking and practices. Nevertheless, schools continuously confront (young) pupils with quite formal activities that are generally acknowledged to be abstract, such as mathematical operations or grammatical parsing. Unfortunately, many children already have difficulties with abstractions at the start of their school career (Hughes 1986; van Oers and Poland 2007; Poland 2007).

In order to prepare children for independent participation in our culture (including the use of abstractions), schools have to help children with understanding abstract theoretical concepts. The so-called "gap" between concrete practical thinking and abstract logical thinking needs to be bridged (Dijk et al. 2004). At this moment, however, the development of abstract thinking is an implicit task of education, and very little explicit attention is given to how tools and strategies for abstracting can be formulated in pupils. In order to develop a pedagogy that is able to help children develop abilities for participation in complex cultural practices in which abstract thinking is needed, we have to investigate how abstract thinking develops and how children from an early age can be taught to develop this ability. Davydov (1972, 1990) demonstrated that children in the age group of 8–10 are able to think abstractly. In his view, children can think abstractly if they have models for the analysis of the concrete world. If children get models "to think with", they can ascend from the abstract to the concrete. According to Egan (1986), such model-based abstract thinking can only become a meaningful activity if children are emotionally involved in the act of understanding a concrete situation (see also van Oers and Poland 2007). If children are engaged in activities, they are able to see reality from specific perspectives and go beyond the boundaries of the multi-faceted concrete. According to Egan, children are able to deal with abstractions from an early age, as long as these abstractions are meaningful to them. The research of Carruthers and Worthington (2003), Gravemeijer (1994), Hughes (1986), and van Oers (1994) also demonstrates that children have the capability to make their own representations of aspects of reality *if* these representations are functional tools in children's activities.

A Cultural-Historical View of Abstraction

In our conception of abstraction we start out from the work of the neo-Kantian philosopher Ernst Cassirer, as interpreted by van Oers (1987, 2001). Cassirer points out that abstract thinking is basically an act of taking a partial point of view (Cassirer 1923, 1957). Cassirer argues that "the general is not the end result of an abstraction process; rather, some general principle is always the beginning. An abstract concept then is not so much a reproduction of reality, but actually establishes a point of view that guides our thinking" (van Oers 2001, p. 284). So, abstracting can then be defined as a process of constructing relationships between objects *from a particular point of view* (van Oers and Poland 2007). Abstractions are products of human creativity that are added as new dimensions to concrete reality. Cassirer also argues that abstraction always includes taking a point of view from which the concrete can be seen as meaningfully and coherently related (van Oers 2001; van Oers and Poland 2007). However, finding an appropriate point of view depends on the contextualisation of someone's actions, and is strongly dependent on cultural conventions and structures. We conceive of abstraction here as a dialectical process between concrete objects and the abstract representation of them. For example, if someone has to find red things, he takes "redness" as his particular point of view. The objects he has to select from are compared and related from his point of view: redness. Redness in this case is the abstraction and the diverse objects to choose from are the concrete. This dialectical process (abstracting red things from the collection of objects given) includes two processes: going from the concrete to the abstract and from this abstract to concrete again. Abstraction always has a relation with the concrete reality.

In a publication of 2001 (p. 288) van Oers already explained that: we must conceive of abstract thinking as a new type of activity emerging from a concrete situation. Abstract thinking is a state of being highly involved in a theoretically construed world, based on explicitly used relations, logical rules, and strict norms of negotiation. This new activity is not a detached way of acting but a new cultural activity driven by both cultural contents and human desires.

Abstraction can then be seen as taking "a partial point of view from which the concrete can be understood in its systematicity, as well as a point of view that is not particularised in all its details, and that is uncomplicated by deforming influences" (van Oers 2001, p. 287). Abstraction qualifies the diversified concreteness.

Schematising Activities

From previous observational studies, it could be concluded that young children are able to look at their play and play situations from a specific point of view. It emerged that perceiving reality from a structural angle, and articulating from that point of view the relationships between concrete objects with symbolic means, is an accessible activity for children (see van Oers 1996). They can, for example, draw a map of their classroom from the point of view of "routing", and construct a reduced representation of their classroom with the help of symbolic means for finding a hidden treasure. The act of drawing such "reducing" representations from a structural point of view is what we called schematising. Making and reading schemes is a form of abstracting that is accessible for young children (in our research already at the age of 5 years old).

The concept of schematising in young children's mathematics education is receiving more attention than ever before (see Carruthers and Worthington 2003). The construction of schematic representations is an important form of abstraction. A schematisation can be described as a symbolic representation of reality, by which one can make specific statements about that reality (Poland 2007). By means of symbolic representations, people can organise their knowledge and thoughts. We consider a schematising activity to be every cognitive activity aimed at the construction and the improvement of reduced and symbolised representations of an element of the physical and socio-cultural reality. In a schematic representation, people represent part of their situation from a particular point of view. They represent the main relationships from their point of view between the concrete objects they see in an abstract way. The representations are always partial, because they are given from a particular point of view and that is what makes the representations abstract.

An example of a schematising activity is as follows. A teacher (in grade 2; 5 year-olds) selected three children in the classroom to build St. Nicholas'[1] ship. The children were shown a construction plan of St. Nicholas' ship and were required

---

[1] St Nicholas is a popular myth in the Netherlands. On the celebration day of St Nicholas (December 5th), people in the Dutch speaking part of Europe exchange gifts, and write poems for each other or (particularly children) for St Nicholas. Months before this date, most shops are filled with all

Fig. 8.1 The building design
of St. Nicholas' ship

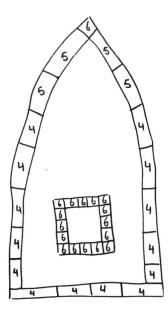

to "read" this schematisation and build the ship according to this construction plan
(Fig. 8.1). Afterwards, the children were asked to schematise their own construction
plan or to schematise the actual construction they created during the activity.

The teacher inquired whether the children knew what the numerals in the drawing
meant. At first they had no idea. The teacher then explained it to them by saying,
"The numerals in the drawing, in each of the blocks, mean that you have to stack
that many blocks upon each other. So, if there is a number 4 in such a little box
in the drawing, you have to put 4 blocks on top of each other." Evidently, all the
children understood this and no one posed any further questions.

In the next step, the children had to discuss in advance which blocks they wanted
to use before they started building, partly according to the construction plan and
partly according to their own representation. The children demonstrated that they
were fairly good at interpreting the building design with regard to the numerals.
They knew exactly how many blocks had to be put on top of each other because
they knew what the numerals meant. The teacher then reminded them of the number
of blocks that had to be next to each other. After this prompt, they started counting
the number of blocks in a row. When the children had been building for a while, they
suddenly realised that they would not be able to get in and out of the ship, because
there was no door indicated on the design. Moreover, it turned out that there were
not enough blocks to build the ship exactly like the one in the picture. The fact that
there were not enough blocks was part of the teacher's plan. She wanted the children

kinds of gifts and candy, especially for children (for more information see: http://en.wikipedia.org/
wiki/Sinterklaas).

Fig. 8.2 St. Nicholas' ship
drawn by Maudy

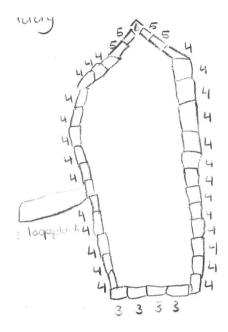

to discover this and to think of a plan B. Hence, they would be stimulated to change their original plan, intervene, build a new ship and represent a new building design. The children decided to make an opening in the ship that could serve as a door and they kept on building their own ship.

Since there were not enough blocks at the end of the activity, the ship was not built exactly like the one in the design. Therefore, the teacher asked the children to draw a new construction plan of the ship to reflect the one they had actually built (Fig. 8.2).

In previous case studies van Oers (1994, 1996) demonstrated that schematising as an activity is accessible for young children (from the age of 5) when schematising is a meaningful and integral part of their play activities. If children are asked to draw their classroom in order to make treasure maps which they need to play "finding a treasure", children are motivated to do this and it is meaningful for them. While drawing, they will soon discover that it is not very useful to include everything in their drawing. So, they will make a decision about what to draw and what to leave out, dependent on their purposes and point of view. By the use of such schematisations during play activities, children are able to represent what they think or what they mean; they can represent their view of the concrete reality in their drawings and the symbols within it. They can draw what they see and invent their own symbolism to point out what they think is important. These abstractions, made by children themselves (in interaction with more knowledgeable others) serve as useful tools for them in handling the complexity of the concrete reality (a new ship for St. Nicholas has to be designed, because the old one has a leak) in the context of the play activity (building the ship).

Schematising as a Way to Improve Mathematical Thinking

Many children have difficulties with formal mathematics upon reaching grade 3 (approximately age 6) (see Hughes 1986). The most important goals of education in grade 3 include teaching children to read, to write, and to develop elementary mathematical skills. In that school year, children are taught many new skills. These skills often have to be learned using different methods than those children became accustomed to in their previous years of schooling. In early childhood, many skills are taught in the context of play activities. However, in grade 3, knowledge and skills are taught using more structured methods. As a result, a gap develops between the way children learned and reasoned in early childhood education and the way they have to do this in grade 3. In our view, school requires children to look at reality from a mathematical point of view, without supporting children in the process of abstraction itself.

Mathematical understanding requires mathematising. Mathematising is, according to Freudenthal (1973), the ability to organise one's own field of experiences by constructing a new object that is open for mathematical refinement. In mathematics education, children are often asked to organise quantitative or spatial data in order to solve problems. Moreover, children are often required to interpret symbols for organising or understanding a situation or process. This means that children have to reorganise, translate or transform functionally related data into new forms or configurations. Children are required to transform data or thoughts into symbolic representations and then translate symbols back into data or statements. This process is very difficult for young children because, in early childhood, children lack familiarity with consistently organising and structuring data using mathematical thinking and symbols. According to Cobb et al. (1997), "the struggle for mathematical meaning can be seen in large part as a struggle for means of symbolising" (p. 161), i.e. as an activity of organising data that come about when we look at reality from the perspective of quantity or spatial relations with the help of symbolic means.

When children are given a mathematical task, they have to first establish the context from which the question arose. Then they have to translate this into a mathematical question, correctly reason from this question and calculate. Last, but certainly not least, children need to translate the result of the calculation back into the concrete context (what does it mean?). The latter step is especially hard to accomplish if a task does not emerge from a real–life context (Poland 2007). If an activity makes sense to them, children are motivated and interested and are therefore willing to demonstrate their capabilities (Hughes 1986). When children are curious, they are optimally motivated to learn. Activities that do not make sense to them are probably the most fundamental problem of mathematics education. Hughes (1986) illustrates this problem in his research. When Hughes asked the children in his study to make a representation of the number of blocks that were in a pile and of changes in the quantity of the blocks in the piles, the children were expected to use sums containing the symbols "+" and "−" to represent these numerical concepts. However, not a single child used the symbols "+" or "−" to represent addition and subtraction or the change in the number of blocks. This is remarkable, because these children had been using these notions every day in their mathematics lessons. Hughes contended that the problem was rooted in the fact that, "these children clearly did not regard these symbols as relevant to the problems facing them" (1986, p. 74). Additionally, before children enter school, they become accustomed to making their own problem solving strategies at the level of complexity required for solving problems that arise (Siegler 2003). They construe their own ways to represent their reality. The gap between the way children have learned and reasoned before they started school and the way they are supposed to learn and reason once they commence school is overwhelming. Children have to learn to translate between "the language of mathematics and their ordinary knowledge about familiar things and situations" (Hughes 1986, p. 44). Using words to describe how to build a ship is a far more concrete activity than reading a construction plan that uses symbols, numerals and other devices to describe the same task. Tools (like schematisations) can be used in teaching children how to translate between abstract and concrete representations (Poland 2007).

In our research project we worked in six Developmental Education schools. During our research, we created an experimental group of pupils who were guided in the production of schematic representations during play activities. During one school year, a teacher trainer assisted the teachers in three experimental schools with teaching their pupils (N = 75, grade 2, age 5–6) to participate in schematising activities as an enrichment of their play activities. In the control groups, schematising rarely took place, and if it did so spontaneously, it was not guided by the teachers. In these schools, the teacher trainer only gave general support for the implementation of the Developmental Education approach and did not pay attention to schematising activities. In this research project, we conducted a longitudinal study and were able to empirically demonstrate the value of early schematising for later mathematical thinking. We demonstrated that the children in the experimental condition who were repeatedly involved in meaningful schematising activities outperformed their counterparts in the control group in grade 3 on a standardised mathematics test. In this standardised test, the pupils were tested for their abilities on counting, ordering, adding, and subtracting (see also van Oers and Poland 2007).

The request for schematising encouraged the pupils to take a particular perspective in play activities, and to represent particular relationships that were relevant to their purposes. If children are taught the function of symbolical representations by means of schematising, they will gradually see the necessity of learning to schematise and they will also develop abilities in structural thinking that help them to deal with mathematical structures. Schematising can help to improve children's learning outcomes and processes in mathematics. Below we will describe and illustrate how young children can become involved in schematising activities in the classroom activities of a play-based curriculum.

Schematising in the Context of Meaningful Activities

We will start this section with an interaction that occurred during a schematising activity in one of our research schools. One of the children's classmates, Danil, had been involved in an accident and the whole class visited the location of the accident after the pupil's recovery. All the children were deeply affected by what had happened. The teacher decided to create an activity around this incident, following up on the strong impressions the accident had made on the pupils. The class visited the location of the accident and the children attempted to make a map of it during the visit. The teacher noticed that although mapmaking was already a meaningful activity for the children, it was still very difficult. Therefore, the teacher decided to enrich the activity by taking several photographs of the accident location, after which she discussed them with the children and helped them to make new maps. We describe the interaction that occurred during this activity below. It begins as the teacher presents one of the photographs she took of the accident's location. Each child in the class appeared in one of the photographs. The teacher invited the children to look for the photograph in which they appeared.

Teacher: This is about the place of Danil's accident.
Children: Yeah.
Teacher: Well, I have been making photos and I want you to look for a photograph in which you are busy making a map of the place of the accident.

The children looked at the pictures and after a moment, the teacher continued. She wanted the children to interpret the photographs. The children were expected to determine where the teacher was standing on the map of the location when she took that particular photograph.

Teacher: Now, we are going to do something else, did everybody find a picture of himself?
Teacher: I first want you to take a look at your photo. ... Look, what kind of photo do I have here? What do you see in this photograph? Damian? What is Danil doing?
Damian: *Points at the place where Danil is in the photograph.*
Teacher: He is pointing at the place of the accident. Well, shall we now take the map?

After this, the teacher got a map that one of the children drew when the class was at the accident's location (see Fig. 8.3). The schematisation shows how the accident has happened. This was discussed with the teacher:

Teacher: This schematisation was not very good, was it? But we are going to make a new one in a minute. The place where the accident actually happened was represented clearly. If you look at his picture, can you see where Danil is standing with his wheelchair? Can you point it out in the map, Jake?

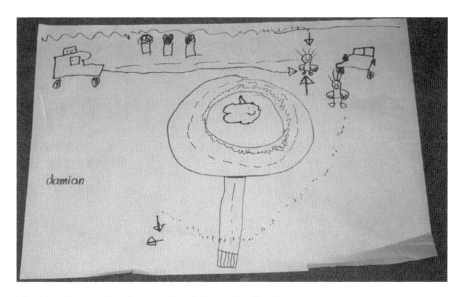

Fig. 8.3 The map: the schematisation of the accident location

Jake: *Does not point at the right place. The teacher tells him so and explains which place Jake was pointing at. Nigel points at the road. The teacher asks him to have a closer look at it. They decide that Danil was standing on the pavement.*

Teacher: Danice?

Danice: *Points at the right place.*

Teacher: Yes, he is standing here, isn't he? Yes, over here and he points at the place of the accident, you see?

Ok, I will look further. This one, look, what is going on in this picture?

Jake: A car, you cannot see the car!

Teacher: Yes, and where is the car, can you show that on the map?

Jake: Somewhere over here. (*He does not know exactly*).

Teacher: We were standing here, because we were going to cross the street at the place of the accident and where was the red car standing, Damian? Point it out on the map.

Damian: *Points at the right place.*

Teacher: Yes, and he was standing here, so if the red car was over here, he was standing here and he wanted to cross the street and then?

Jake: He did not see it!

Teacher: No, you see that very clearly in this picture. What does it mean if you can't see anything if you want to cross a street, Merijn?

Merijn: That you have to look very carefully!

Teacher: It is a very dangerous place!

Fig. 8.4 Another schematisation of the accident location

Teacher: And when I made this picture, where was I standing at that moment? First you have to look. Just think about it. You look at the picture and then you think about Thursday, where were we? And then you look at the map and you think about where I made this picture. Merijn?

Merijn: *Points at a wrong place.*

Teacher: What do you see in this picture? Where is this building you see here? *Merijn points out wrong again. Merijn tells what she sees and points at the map; all the children take the wrong perspective.*

After discussing that particular picture and others, the teacher handed out the other maps drawn by the children when they were at the accident location. She then asked them to redraw the maps because their spatial understanding of the location was much better now. Merijn and Yasmin cooperated on this activity. Their map is shown in Fig. 8.4. While making this map the children had the following conversation:

Merijn: Wait a minute, now the water.

Yasmin: You can do that. It should be little, shouldn't it?

Merijn: Yes, the last time, it was too big. You can make the circle. (*The circle is representing a parking place which is called the "Fish market"; the children represent this by drawing a little fish*).

Merijn: Now, the pavement.

Yasmin: Yes. I won't draw the circle very big.

Merijn: Yes, it is all right like this, that's the right way!

Merijn: Now the car, that ran over Danil. (*She gets a pencil*).

Yasmin: No, a red one!

Merijn: No, look, Damian also has this, there was a little white in it!

Merijn: Here the car should be, no, that is the place of the ambulance and there the car should be. Do you draw Danil? But not too big!

Yasmin: Look, Femke (*the teacher*) is always doing it like this. (*She is drawing the car*). And there should also be a dent in it, doesn't it?

Merijn: And also a window, otherwise he can't watch.

Yasmin: You should draw Danil over there.

Yasmin: Now, the ambulance is coming from here. And there should be a cross on it.

Teacher: How do I know which direction the ambulance is going? How can I see that?

Merijn: *Draws a long arrow and says*: Arrow!

Teacher: That is smart!

Merijn: *Also draws an arrow in front of the car.*

Teacher: Well, this is going great! Are we also able to see from which direction Danil is coming?

Merijn: Yes, from this direction. (*Draws an arrow behind Danil*).

Teacher: Yes, and where did he want to go to?

Merijn: Here.

Teacher: Yes, and did that he succeed?

Merijn: No.

Teacher: Why not?

Merijn: Because, he is run over.

Teacher: Can you draw a cross where he was run over?

Merijn: Yes, that's easy.

Teacher: You should discuss that with each other. Where do you think that has happened? Then you have to think about where we were, because he showed it, didn't he?

Yasmin: Yes, because he was rolling further with the car.

Teacher: He did roll further with the car.

Yasmin: So, it should have been somewhere here. (*Draws a cross*).

Teacher: So, that is the place where the cross is drawn where everything went wrong actually.

Yasmin: That is where he was run over.

Teacher: Well, I think you did a wonderful job, girls! Well done!

This activity clearly shows the children's engagement. The activity was meaningful for them, because they were all deeply affected by the accident that involved their classmate. It was interesting for the children to map the accident's location as it allowed the children to learn several notation systems for making their own representations of the location. Yasmin and Merijn were prompted to use arrows in their map by the teacher who asked, "How do I know which direction the ambulance went?" As a result of this activity, the children learned how to represent action, movement and direction (see Poland 2007 for a full description of this activity). In any case, their representations were always the result of a specific point of view of the situation.

Conclusion

In this research project teachers were taught to develop and guide schematising activities in the context of play. This is characteristic for schools in Developmental Education. In Developmental Education, schools work with about 5 or 6 theme periods per school year. During a theme teachers and children try to establish a socio-cultural practice, such as "The restaurant", or, "The hospital", or "The zoo". In order to make such a socio-cultural practice work, children need to learn a lot of skills like counting, reading, writing, interacting with customers and staff, the integration of several skills from several domains, etc. In some cases children need to think about what to represent and what not, depending on the purposes they have in their play. What symbols can be used and what quality is needed in order to make the map clear to other people? In such play activities there are many opportunities for children to schematise and practice with ascending from abstract to concrete by using their schematic representations for the organisation and interpretation of concrete reality. There are many opportunities to invent their own symbols and construct their own representation from their perspective on the concrete reality.

The role of the teacher, the adult or the more knowledgeable other is very important in these activities. Only when the teacher gives meaningful feedback on the actions of children in these activities, children can give a certain meaning to what they are doing. If the teacher, for example, does not "bring in" interesting problems in the play activities, the activity will not develop automatically. If children play in the zoo and the teacher mentions that it might be interesting to design a map of the place for visitors, this is an enrichment of the play activity and schematising can occur. But whether this happens or not depends on the interaction between teacher and children. When children start to schematise, the teacher can react to these schematisations in a variety of ways, including a mathematical way, asking children about the numerical aspects. Then, children's actions begin to gain mathematical meaning related to their schematical representations of reality. In fact, the numerals introduce new dimensions to reality through these representations. Through participation in such interactions within these activities, the children may meaningfully acknowledge mathematical contents for the orientation in reality, and finally for the regulation of their own actions as well (van Oers 2012).

References

Bolton, N. (1972). *The psychology of thinking*. London: Methuen.

Carpay, J., & van Oers, B. (1993). Didaktičeskie modeli i problemy obučajuščej diskussii [Didactical models and the problems of developmental discourses]. *Voprosy Psichologii, 4*, 20–26.

Carruthers, E., & Worthington, M. (2003). *Children's mathematics. Making marks, making meaning*. London: Paul Chapman Publishing.

Cassirer, E. (1923). *Substance and function and Einstein's theory of relativity*. New York: Dover.

Cassirer, E. (1957). *The philosophy of symbolic forms* (The Phenomenology of Knowledge, Vol. 3). New Haven: Yale University Press.

Cobb, P., Gravemeijer, K., Yackel, E., McClain, K., & Whitenack, J. (1997). Mathematising and symbolising: The emergence of chains of signification in one first-grade classroom. In D. Kirshner & J. A. Whitson (Eds.), *Situated cognition. Social, semiotic, and psychological perspectives* (pp. 151–233). Hillsdale: Lawrence Erlbaum.

Davydov, V. V. (1972). *Vidy obobščenija v obučenii. Logiko-psichologičeskie problemy postroenija učebnych predmetov* [Types of generalisation in education. Logical-psychological problems of the construction of subject matter]. Moscow: Pedagogika.

Davydov, V. V. (1990). *Types of generalisation in instruction: Logical and psychological problems in the structuring of school curricula* (Soviet studies in mathematics education, Vol. 2; J. Kilpatrick, Ed. & J. Teller, Trans.). Reston: National Council of teachers of mathematics. (Original work published 1972)

Davydov, V. V. (1996). *Teorija razvivajuščego obučenija* [The theory of developmental education]. Moscow: INTOR.

Dijk, E. F., van Oers, B., & Terwel, J. (2004). Schematising in early childhood mathematics education: Why, when and how? *European Early Childhood Education Research Journal, 12*, 71–83.

Egan, K. (1986). *Teaching as story telling. An alternative approach to teaching and curriculum in the elementary school*. Chicago: University of Chicago Press.

Egan, K. (2002). *Getting it wrong from the beginning*. New Haven: Yale University Press.

Freudenthal, H. (1973). *Mathematics as an educational task*. Dordrecht: Kluwer Academic Publishers.

Gravemeijer, K. P. E. (1994). *Developing realistic mathematics education*. Utrecht: Freudenthal Institute Utrecht University.

Hughes, M. (1986). *Children and number: Difficulties in learning mathematics*. New York: Blackwell.

Il'enkov, E. V. (1991). *Filosofija i kultura* [Philosophy and culture]. Moscow: Isd-vo Političeskoj Litertury. (Also spelled as Ilyenkov).

Ilyenkov, E. V. (1977). *Dialectical logic. Essays on its history and theory*. Moscow: Isd-vo Političeskoj Litertury. Also spelled as Il'enkov.

Piaget, J. (2001). *Studies in reflective abstraction*. Hove: Psychology Press.

Poland, M. (2007). *The treasures of schematising activities*. Enschede: Ipskamp.

Roth, W.-M. (2004). What is the meaning of "meaning"? A case study from graphing. *Journal of Mathematical Behaviour, 23*, 75–92.

Roth, W.-M., & Hwang, S. W. (2006a). On the relation of abstract and concrete in scientists' graph interpretations: A case study. *Journal of Mathematical Behaviour, 25*, 318–333.

Roth, W.-M., & Hwang, S. W. (2006b). Does mathematical learning occur in going from concrete to abstract or in going from abstract to concrete? *Journal of Mathematical Behaviour, 25*, 334–344.

Siegler, R. S. (2003). Implications of cognitive science research for mathematics education. In J. Kilpatrick, W. B. Martin, & D. E. Schifter (Eds.), *A research companion to principles and standards for school mathematics* (pp. 219–233). Reston: NCTM.

van Oers, B. (1987). *Activiteit en begrip* [Activity and concept]. Amsterdam: VU University.

van Oers, B. (1994). Semiotic activity of young children in play: The construction and use of schematic representations. *European Early Childhood Education Research Journal, 2*(1), 19–34.

van Oers, B. (1996). Are you sure? The promotion of mathematical thinking in the play activities of young children. *European Early Childhood Education Research Journal, 4*(1), 71–89.

van Oers, B. (2001). Contextualisation for abstraction. *Cognitive Science Quarterly, 1*, 279–305.

van Oers, B. (2012). How to promote young children's mathematical thinking? *Mediterranean Journal for Research in Mathematics Education, 11*(1–2).

van Oers, B., & Poland, M. (2007). Schematising activities as a means for encouraging young children to think abstractly. *Mathematics Education Research Journal, 19*(2), 10–22.

Wertsch, J. V. (1996). The role of abstract rationality in Vygotsky's image of the mind. In A. Tryphon & J. Vonèche (Eds.), *The social genesis of thought* (pp. 25–44). Hove: Psychology Press.

Chapter 9
Teaching Arts: Promoting Aesthetic Thinking

Lieke Roof

Current Situation in Arts Education Compared to Arts Education in Developmental Education

Developmental Education aims to promote broad development in pupils (see Chap. 4 of this volume), covering all aspects of identity development that may be relevant for pupils' participation in diverse cultural practices. Vygotskij (see for example Vygotsky 1997) emphasised the importance of aesthetic development, both at a personal and a cultural level. In his view, art is a cultural technique for emotional expression that comes about – like all manifestations of human life – through creative activity. In school he was strongly against the idea of arts education as a form of relaxation or for the ornamentation of life. Arts education not only facilitates emotional expression, but also strengthens creativity. In his view, creativity is the essence of human life and is involved in the innovation of all dimensions of culture.

A similar stance on the intrinsic relationship between art and the development of the socio-cultural mind is nowadays also taken by some modern authors (see Eisner 2002), who believe that arts education can help people to develop a disposition to tolerate ambiguity, to deal with uncertainty, and to exercise free judgment.

In this chapter I start out from similar assumptions. In Developmental Education arts education is considered an important dimension in pupils' broad cultural development (van Oers 2004). I will demonstrate here how arts education can be realised in Developmental Education, taking mostly the visual arts as illustrative examples. However, the starting points underpinning the approach described in this chapter are assumed to be relevant for other artistic expressions (music, literature, poetry, dance, sculpture, etc.) as well.

L. Roof, M.Sc. (✉)
Primary school "De Groote Wielen", Rosmalen, The Netherlands
e-mail: Liekeroof@hotmail.com

B. van Oers (ed.), *Developmental Education for Young Children*, International Perspectives on Early Childhood Education and Development 7, DOI 10.1007/978-94-007-4617-6_9, © Springer Science+Business Media Dordrecht 2012

Most schools nowadays teach from a cognitivistic approach in which the main objective is the acquisition of knowledge and skills by pupils. There is no difference when it comes to arts education: the basic idea in today's arts education is usually that the main aim consists in getting to know the materials and to apply skills and competences for the production of a work of art. Teachers take the materials, skills and techniques as the basis for their teaching activities, rather than focusing on how this makes sense for the child's creative activity. Teachers often use a curricular programme which determines what kind of skills or techniques should be presented in 1 year. This approach separates assignments from each other and forces children to apply specific skills and techniques to serve isolated products. Working like this does not give proper attention to the creative process underlying the activity. This is at odds to the approach of Developmental Education, where the development of pupils in the context of meaningful activities is the basic principle. The activities that children become engaged in should result from something that they wish to create themselves. In other words, children are sometimes inspired by things in their environment, become affectively engaged with them, and undertake initiatives to create something new using the skills and techniques they have learned from the teacher. An obvious difference exists here between the traditional and Developmental Education approaches. The following sections will offer an idea of teacher behaviour in arts education in Developmental Education, and clarify how to implement arts education in the classroom, using examples from the teacher's practice.

The Teacher's Perspective

The intervention of a teacher is essential in the artistic development of children, just as it is in other developmental areas. The teacher's focus should be on helping children find their own definition of beauty and art, through developing personal ways of looking, judging and creating art. The child should be in the artist's frame of mind, making his own fantasy perceptions of reality and the teacher should be there to lead the child into this lifelong process, starting in the primary school. In his psychology of art, Vygotsky (1971) points to the important cultural role of the art critic, who brings products of art into a process of public reflection enhancing the social meaning of a piece of art as emotional expression. Teachers in Developmental Education both encourage pupils to produce art, to strive for perfection, to find their personal definition of beauty and art, and also initiate public reflection of artful expressions. The teacher's role as a reviewer is crucial in this process.

Focusing on children's creative activities from a developmental perspective, the teacher needs to be focused on three things in arts education: development of aesthetic thinking in children, development of skills and competences, and development of a personal progressive oeuvre (van Oers 2005). In the following sections I will clarify the meaning and relevance of these three issues with classroom

Fig. 9.1   Talk about painting

examples. The purpose is to give an idea of classroom practices that hamper aesthetic development, and of how the Developmental Education approach can affect classroom practices positively and foster pupils' art development.

Development of Aesthetic Thinking

Central to the development of aesthetic thinking is the review or judgment of a work of art in progress or completed, and the process that underlies this review or judgment (van Oers 2005). Van Ipkens (2004) investigated young children's aesthetic judgment. In her research she reviewed famous paintings with children, encouraging them to make these paintings "more beautiful". By doing so, the question "Is this beautiful art?" was reflected on by the children. The research showed that children were able to assign personal meanings to works of art. A similar activity was carried out at another Dutch primary school. It showed children, in the 11–12 age group, paintings of famous painters. By putting themselves in the role of these famous painters the children actually felt in control of the artistic process and they developed aesthetic judgments to refine these works of art. By discussing their artistic products with other children and parents at an art exposition, called "museum night", they showed their development in aesthetic thinking by talking about what made the work of art complete (see Fig. 9.1). Their improved versions of famous paintings or changed judgments of these paintings can be considered a momentary personal definition of what art was for them at that particular moment.

Classroom Examples

A teacher of a group of 26 children aged between 6 and 8 years old organises a discussion group on some pictures. Together, they reflect on the works of art made by other children.

Teacher: Daisy, can you point to the work of art that attracts your eyes?
Daisy: (*Looks around and points.*) This one.
Teacher: Tell me what you see?
Daisy: Lots of colours and nice fluffs.
Teacher: Well, Daisy, look at it again. What comes to your mind?
Daisy: I like it very much. It makes me happy inside here (points to her chest).
Teacher: How is that possible? Why does this masterpiece give you this sensation?

By asking questions about a work of art, the teacher elicits an aesthetic judgment from the child about it. She asks open questions and waits for the child to value a way of looking at this piece of art. This judgment prompts an emotional judgment, something that should be the beginning of discovering art (van Oers 2001). In this conversation the teacher is not yet aiming to connect it to the context and search for deeper levels. This should be the aim in the interaction between the teacher and an individual child.

In our classroom observations, we also found, however, how easily this process of public reflection can go astray in our rationalising culture. In the class of teacher Peter a conversation begins between himself and two children, Mike and Eva, regarding a painting assignment. The children painted their feelings about a word that they chose themselves, for example the word angry, happy, scared or sad. Talking about it, they discuss several paintings.

Teacher: Mike, which painting do you like most?
Mike: This one.
Teacher: And why do you like it the most?
Mike: If you look very well you see little illustrations in it.
Eva: Yes, that looks like a rabbit and that's a sea monster . . . if you look at it from this way.
Teacher: Eva, you see models in it. And what about the colours? Do they match the word?
Eva: Yes, I think so.
Teacher: Why do you think so?
Eva: Black and brown look sad to me.
Teacher: You think those are sad colours? For what kind of things would you use these colours?
Eva: For darkness.

Fig. 9.2 Painting flowers like
van Gogh's

In this conversation the teacher immediately asks his pupil a "why" question. Asking "why" in an aesthetic judgment is a trap for many teachers. Aesthetic questions like "do you like it?" or "what's your feeling about it?" are questions that don't appeal to reasoning. A "why" question gives a rational dimension to the question, and that is not the primary aim in arts education. This gives another twist to the conversation and usually this leads to a dead end. It is important that teachers avoid this in their discussions with children about works of art. A child should be able to verbalise an aesthetic judgment without that rational dimension, but only if the teacher asks for the background of the child's judgment. We should bear in mind that the verbal comment is basically a secondary aesthetic statement. The art production itself is the child's first statement on beauty and art (his so-called *ostentative* definition of art). An ostentative definition of art is a child's way of *wordlessly showing* to the world in a work of art what she or he takes as a statement of perfection, beauty or art. The teacher's aim to develop the child's aesthetic thinking is only successful if the teacher has insight into this basic aspect of the child's aesthetic development (Fig. 9.2).

Another example of a missed chance to stimulate the development of aesthetic thinking is manifested in the following observation. In a classroom a teacher is working with a group of 6 year-old children. They are painting by using a straw which they blow through. The teacher gives instructions.

> Kate puts down her straw and looks at her painting. She's clearly considering how it looks. The teacher reacts enthusiastically by saying that the result looks very nice and puts down a new blank piece of paper for the girl. The girl hesitates and then starts working on a new painting. After 2 min she starts to look around the classroom and loses interest in the activity.

The teacher undoubtedly has good intentions, but it's a pity that she is stepping in at a moment when the child is still considering her work of art. She interferes in the child's aesthetic thinking by deciding for the child that the work of art is completed. By doing so, the teacher deprives the child of the opportunity to make an aesthetic judgment about her work and maybe to make it "more beautiful", i.e. to make it fit better with her personal feeling of perfection at that moment. In this case, the teacher decides whether the work is finished or not, when such a decision should be in the hands of the child.

Conclusions About Development of Aesthetic Thinking

Developing an aesthetic judgment with children seems automatically associated with art perception. It is more than just a judgment from a child regarding a work of art. When exploring a child's aesthetic judgment, a teacher should try to discover the needs and motives of the child's expressions and the need to bring these to further perfection. In exactly this way, development can be evaluated. By exploring the child's artistic activity, the teacher can ascertain what the child's needs are in terms of new techniques or knowledge and by doing so identifies a zone of proximal development of the child in the area of arts education. In this way the teacher is able to determine whether development in fact is taking place. This is possible without attaching a rational dimension to the aesthetic judgment. The "why-question" should be avoided by the teacher above all. Besides, it is important that the teacher leaves the moment of judgment to the child during the process of creating. Thus the child (rather than the teacher) determines when a work of art is "right". Giving the child control of the process should not be confined to the beginning of the artistic activity, but should still be the case at the moment an aesthetic judgment is made about the process and the final product.

Development of Skills and Competences

Besides developing aesthetic thinking, it is important to develop a child's skills and techniques for producing new works of art as a way of better exhibiting aesthetic judgments. If children get the opportunity to discover that and how they can improve a work of art, the motivation to actually do this will strengthen.

Classroom Examples

Teacher Alice, responsible for a group of 11–12 year olds, was inspired by the article from Van Ipkens (2004). With her pupils she reviews the painting "Sunflowers" by Vincent van Gogh. She instructs the children to draw it after a model. In doing so, they are asked to conserve the aspects they like about the painting and change the aspects they like less. In a conversation with a child, the teacher reacts to it:

Teacher Alice:	Amy, what do you like about the painting by Van Gogh?
Amy:	I like the flowers and you can see depth.
Teacher Alice:	Is there also something you don't like and want to change?
Amy:	I don't like the colours and the flowers all seem dead. Also, they really look the same way. That's boring.

Reviewing her own result, Amy is initially not very satisfied. She asks the teacher how to draw depth. Teacher Alice explains the technique of overlapping to her.

This example shows that the child needs to extend her skills and techniques in order to bring her work of art to further perfection. This child's need arises from the assignment and the frame that the teacher has offered. By following the child's need and development, the teacher is able to impart the knowledge or technique meaningfully at the right moment.

This demonstrates the essence of Developmental Education: due to this strategy the child's development will be stimulated in close connection to the needs of the child. In this example, Amy wishes to enrich her work and bring it closer to her personal intuition of perception, but she lacks the skills to do so. The teacher takes notice and offers help by showing the technique of overlapping to suggest depth in a painting. The development of the child is shaped by the intervention of the teacher: Amy adjusts her work with the newly learned technique.

Another example shows that the teacher's interference is not always beneficial. A group of 26 children aged between 6 and 8 are working on a plastic art assignment. One group of five children works on a painting assignment and they're using paintbrushes. A boy, named Sven, is going to work on his idea by experimenting with creating an animal.

Teacher:	Sven, what are you making?
Sven:	I don't know yet. An animal, but is doesn't look real to me.
Teacher:	Yes, it does. It does to me.
(*Silence.*)	
Sven:	No, the skin doesn't look real to me.

Sven is trying to make the animal look as realistic as he can, but he doesn't feel that he has yet succeeded. The teacher saying that he did succeed doesn't really help him. Sven is obviously not at the point where he can determine his work as "finished"; he is not yet satisfied. In this case, the teacher misses an opportunity to discuss the technique of using "structure" in Sven's painting. It would also be a good suggestion to let Sven paint with other equipment than just a brush. This encourages more experimentation with materials, equipment and techniques and thus gives rise to new possibilities. Helping Sven to expand his repertoire of techniques helps him to approximate his idea of what the final product should look like.

Conclusions About Development of Skills and Competences

Developing skills and techniques, according to the theory of van Oers (2005), should derive from the child's own need and request to improve his abilities so that he can express his private ostentative definition of beauty of perfection. The teacher's role is very important here, because he has to present a new skill or technique at the right moment. To be able to do this, the teacher is expected to accompany the child in the learning process. In this way the teacher can determine when the right moment arrives.

Development of a Progressive Oeuvre

As the third point of interest, van Oers (2005) mentions the development of a progressive oeuvre. By this he means that children should remain actively working with art in a reflective way, while their emotion and evolving aesthetic judgment remains central in the reflection. By building a progressive oeuvre artists may permanently improve their expressions of their ostentative definitions of art and beauty. Children need to constantly explore more options to record their emotions; they have to build on earlier experiences and creations. When this building on earlier experiences consists of improving themselves, making something even prettier, then children will exhibit the need to learn new skills and techniques for optimising their creations. The progress in a child's oeuvre closely follows the ongoing need for perfection and is driven by the child's (artist's) judgment about the elements that deserve a follow-up to achieve new perfection and find new ostentative definitions of art.

Classroom Examples

A group of children aged between 6 and 8 is working with a mailbox system in the classroom. Every child has his own mailbox, and he receives mail in the box at the beginning of the week. The teacher uses this system to let the children build on a work of art that they receive from another child. They can build on it by creating something plastic or literary. The purpose of the assignment is to create a chain of stories or creations with other children. Referring to "the new mail" the teacher starts a conversation with the whole group in a circle around the creations found in the mailboxes.

Teacher:	Nina, would you read aloud for us what you found in your mailbox?
Nina:	Geel-meel-veel. (*Meaning "yellow", "flour", "much" – in Dutch these are rhyming words.*)
Teacher:	What do you think it's about?
Nina:	About yellow, the colour.
Teacher:	How do you feel about the colour yellow?
Nina:	It's nice.
Teacher:	Imagine picking a word for this colour, which word matches for you?
Nina:	Nice colour.
Teacher:	Let's do this together! Everybody close your eyes. What comes to your mind, when you think of yellow?
Reactions:	The letter 'ee', a giraffe, a yellow paper, egg yolk, French fries, a little chicken, a tiger, the sun.
Teacher:	Nina's yellow paper makes us think about very different things. Isn't that weird?

After the conversation, Nina starts writing her poem. Because the children explored new options to record their emotions or feelings about this piece of mail, Nina has a lot of ideas to start her own poem. She wasn't the creator of the mail she received, but by interacting with the teacher and other children Nina is recreating the original creation. By starting to work on her own creation as a follow-up from the mail, she builds on an earlier creation. She wants to enrich the creation, after finding it in her mailbox by writing a poem about it.

In teacher Peter's classroom a conversation is going on between the teacher and Tessa, referring to paintings made by 9 year-old children. The children painted their feelings about a word that they chose themselves. Talking about it, they discuss several paintings (Fig. 9.3).

Teacher Peter:	Let's review another one. Yes, that one 'fire'. I really liked that one. Who also thinks this is the best? Just Tessa? Do you also like this one the most? Can you tell me why?
Tessa:	Yes, the colour really fits the word 'fire'. And yes.....I just like it.
Teacher Peter:	What's different about this painting as compared to Tom's painting?
Tessa:	He uses fewer colours.
Teacher Peter:	And if we compare this to the painting 'evil'?
Tessa:	The colour is different.
Teacher Peter:	Right, the colour is indeed different.

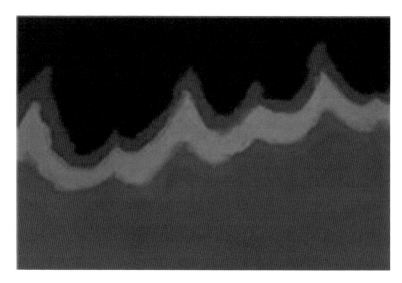

Fig. 9.3 Fire

For building up a progressive oeuvre, a child should have the ability to build on earlier creations (including works of great painters), and possibly improve these expressions of beauty in the course of their evolving oeuvre. Moreover, he should be able to compare creations with one another from his own framework of thoughts. In the classroom example the teacher attempts to let the child think about this. Unfortunately the child does not go beyond comparing colours. A lot of chances are missed by the child and, most of all, by the teacher to expand the child's oeuvre. The child mentioned "colour", but a lot of other aspects remain unreflected, such as: composition, lighting, shape and texture.

Conclusions About Development of a Progressive Oeuvre

Developing a progressive oeuvre means that children are in search of new possibilities to capture their emotion with increasingly sophisticated means. Herewith they build upon earlier creations, with the purpose of improving themselves in producing new creations. All this should be supported by interaction between the teacher and child and this interaction needs to be based upon the child's learning processes and development. Exploring new possibilities together can help children to take the next step in the creation process. In this process the great works of art can also be meaningfully integrated.

Interaction Is the Key

Taking note of the classroom examples and connecting this to the role the teacher plays, it can be postulated that a lot of teachers tend to take the lead in the conversation with children on their pieces of art. Consequently they are not optimally stimulating the children to ask the questions themselves. This leads to a one-way communication, instead of a genuine interaction between teacher and children in the process of collaborative aesthetic reflection. This creates a passive attitude in the child, while an active attitude towards the subject matter is important in Developmental Education. At the same time, teachers don't always see the opportunities within the interaction with a child. Apparently it is hard to ask the right questions, so that the child can arrange and develop his thoughts. For this purpose teachers need ideas and examples, but they also need guidance in communication skills to be able to hear what the child is actually saying and to determine what the child needs next.

Arts education in a way that fits with Developmental Education is not highly developed in many elementary schools (Roof 2009). It is not only creating art that is important. Reflectively discussing and judging art is particularly essential for the aesthetic development of a child. In these discussions there are no wrong answers or strange questions. Hopefully this chapter is an incentive to educational managers and teachers to approach arts education from the perspective of Developmental Education.

References

Eisner, E. W. (2002). *The arts and the creation of mind*. New Haven/London: Yale University Press.

Roof, E. N. L. (2009). Waar gaan jouw ogen naar toe? Kunstzinnige vorming in Ontwikkelings-gericht Onderwijs [Where are your eyes going? Arts education in Developmental Education]. *Zone. Tijdschrift voor Ontwikkelingsgericht Onderwijs, 8*(3), 4–7.

van Ipkens, J. (2004). Wat vind jij nou van kunst? [What do you think about art?]. *Zone. Tijdschrift voor Ontwikkelingsgericht Onderwijs, 3*(3), 4–7.

van Oers, B. (2001). Tekenen van ontroering. Kunstzinnige vorming in Ontwikkelingsgericht Onderwijs. [Signs of emotion. Arts education in Developmental Education]. *De wereld van het jonge kind, 28*(10), 301–304.

van Oers, B. (2004). Op naar Helicon! Kunstzinnige vorming in ontwikkelingsgericht onderwijs. [To the Helicon! Arts education in Developmental Education]. *Zone. Tijdschrift voor Ontwikke-lingsgericht Onderwijs, 3*(3), 8–11.

van Oers, B. (2005). Minerva's Queeste [Minerva's quest]. In B. van Oers (Ed.), *Dwarsdenken, essays over Ontwikkelingsgericht Onderwijs*. Assen: Van Gorcum.

Vygotsky, L. S. (1971). *The psychology of art*. Cambridge, MA: MIT.

Vygotsky, L. S. (1997). *Educational psychology*. Boca Raton: St. Lucie Press.

Chapter 10
Every Child Is Special: Teaching Young Children with Special Needs

Barbara Nellestijn and Isabel Peters

Different Children, Similar Aims

Every child is different. This makes teaching challenging, but sometimes difficult as well. Particularly in schools for special education, it looks as if every pupil needs a different approach. In Developmental Education a teacher fine-tunes her interactions with children habitually to the needs and abilities of each individual child. In Developmental Education it is no exception that teachers have to cater for a wide range of differences among children in their classrooms. The question then is, how does she keep the pupils together as a group? Children at risk require different teacher assistance than other children. What does this assistance look like in Developmental Education? In this chapter we will show how teachers can fine-tune their interactions to the interests and abilities of young children with special needs, in order to get them successfully engaged in meaningful learning processes. The chapter discusses how teachers, starting out from Vygotskij's "compensation hypothesis", can deliberately promote the learning of these children with the help of a specific interaction model, while still maintaining the pedagogical aim of promoting broad and meaningful development in *all* children.

Learning together in a heterogeneous classroom is an important tenet in Developmental Education. In principle, every child's development can be stimulated and every child can be educated (Nellestijn and Peters 2008; Nellestijn et al. 2009). However, children do not all develop in the same manner. In Developmental Education, teachers deliberately make use the differences between children. Differences

B. Nellestijn, M.Sc. (✉)
De Activiteit, Alkmaar, The Netherlands
e-mail: b.nellestijn@de-activiteit.nl

I. Peters, M.Sc.
De Activiteit, Alkmaar, The Netherlands
e-mail: ija.peters@kpnmail.nl

B. van Oers (ed.), *Developmental Education for Young Children*, International
Perspectives on Early Childhood Education and Development 7,
DOI 10.1007/978-94-007-4617-6_10,
© Springer Science+Business Media Dordrecht 2012

are allowed and can be made productive for children's development (see also Tharp et al. 2000)! But interpersonal differences are not easy to deal with in a developmentally productive way. Children who have difficulties with picking up the content of teaching, children who show disruptive behaviour or hardly participate in activities, children who face difficulties in reading or mathematics, all these children require specific teacher assistance. In this chapter we will describe how teachers in Developmental Education, by using an interaction model, are able to fine-tune their meaningful interactions to the needs and abilities of the children and foster their development. All children are different, but the pedagogical aims of teachers in Developmental Education schools are similar: promoting broad development in *all* children.

Development by Interaction (The Case of "Special" Children)

Several studies show that there are a number of conditions in a child's life that may presage problems in learning and development in primary school (see for example Sylva et al. 2004). The attendance of preschool classes, the financial-economic situation of the family, and the educational level of the mother turn out to be among the main predictors for problems in learning and development. For the teacher in the classroom, however, these conditions cannot be easily influenced or changed. Teachers must find ways to compensate for these conditions if they want to promote the development of at-risk children.

Vygotsky (1978, 1994) emphasised the important role that the environment plays in a child's developmental process. According to him, development is always socially mediated. The environment not only shows children the ideal form of action in a certain situation (how things should be done, said, written etc.), but also informs children about how an action can be carried out by helping them to use the cultural tools properly. Each child is born with specific physical and neurological characteristics, but most of the time these are not in themselves a cause for "developmental problems" (Janssen-Vos et al. 2000). Problems mostly arise through the ways the social environment deals with these characteristics and values them. A handicapped child is often not directly aware of his handicap, but experiences the problems that his handicap brings along in his or her interactions with the social environment. This child is approached and treated differently than the other children around him and he feels a social pressure to adjust to the desired (ideal) forms of action of this social environment. For example, a child diagnosed with ADHD is put in a special position because of his handicap and his divergent way of acting. Within his family, his position will be different from that of his siblings. Also at school he will be put in a special position; he may even go to a school for special education. It is precisely through this special position that a child comes to notice his handicap. As a consequence, he also runs the risk of developing an "inferiority complex": he is "special", "different" from other children. In this manner, problems can be socially created, according to Vygotskij.

Coles (1987) also states that the cause of the difficulties children face most of the time does not lie within the child, but in his environment. Traditionally, special pedagogies often look for the cause within the child. Coles calls this *blaming the victim* (p.25). This point of view often results in individually rectifying pedagogical procedures, rather than in fundamental social changes. *Victim-blaming* encourages individuals to accept their handicap or disability and make the best of their lot.

Research by Peters and van Oers (2007) shows that teachers indeed adopt a different approach towards children they consider to be at-risk. Teachers use several strategies in their goal-oriented interaction with these children, so that the pupils end up in less meaningful activities in which they get no room to use their own initiative or negotiate meaning. The teachers do not challenge the children and often even place them outside the community of learners. In this way, the educators actually contribute to the emergence of a learning problem, and render the child "problematic" or "at-risk".

According to McDermott (1993), schools create (learning) problems by the way their education is organised. When teachers look at the progress a child actually makes, and not just at the results in comparison to other children, hardly any pupils with learning problems exist. Every child learns, in his own manner and at his own pace.

Compensation

Of course, some handicaps, like a visual handicap, have a biological cause and not a social one. However, according to Vygotskij, Coles, and others education should not so much be focused on the biological factors, but rather on the social consequences the handicap brings along. This is not to deny or ignore possible influences of bio-neurological factors! The main goal, however, is to correct the flaws in the social interaction with the environment by following a different path, and not to force the child to adapt to the conditions that are developed for and by people without a handicap and the corresponding bio-neurological conditions.

Vygotsky (1993) claims that the underlying principles of development are basically equal for every child. However, children with a handicap or learning problem usually need different means to reach similar outcomes. In order to explain his point of view, Vygotskij introduced the notion of *compensation*. When development is complicated by a defect, on the one hand this means a limitation, a delay in development. On the other hand, it also stimulates development, because the defect creates difficulties that call for new developmental formations. Every handicap creates stimuli for compensatory processes, according to Vygotskij (see Vygotsky 1993, p. 32). The decreased value of a certain faculty may be fully or partially compensated for by the stronger development of another faculty. As an example Vygotskij refers to the development of blind children. A blind child may lack sight, but he/she compensates for this deficit with an increased ability to perceive meanings through touch. By the use of Braille, the blind child is able to read. If a blind child reaches a similar developmental level as a child with sight, the blind child reached this stage by means of a different way and different tools.

> Compensation, the individual's reaction to a defect, initiates new, roundabout developmental processes – it replaces, rebuilds a new structure, and stabilises psychological functions (Vygotsky 1993, p. 34).

Vygotskij was first of all interested in children's capabilities and not in their shortcomings. Educators should find alternative ways for helping children; they should not start by "treating" the handicap. On the basis of Vygotskij's compensation theory, educators can maintain high expectations for the children's developmental potentials.

Reaching Higher Together

We have to look for alternative paths and instruments to make children with special educational needs participants in our cultural practices. Here lies an important role for educators. By participating as a partner in socio-cultural activities with pupils, a teacher can create a zone of proximal development through prompting new actions that are significant for their shared activity. Step-by-step she lays out a learning route ("curriculum") that is tailored to the needs and abilities of the children (Peters 2003). Through such assisted "imitations" of cultural practices, the child is stimulated to make transitions from his actual level of performance to new actions he has not yet mastered. "Imitation" here definitely does not mean mechanically copying isolated actions or operations; rather, it means participating in already existing socio-cultural activities. The child learns specific new skills in a meaningful manner within a relevant context. The teacher takes into account the actions the child is not yet able to perform on his/her own, and takes care that the activity continues to be a coherent whole. All the actions the child undertakes should be meaningful to him/her and should make sense in the ongoing activity. In the following example, a teacher in a special needs group creates a zone of proximal development in which she helps the child to improve his participation in an important activity and provides him with the means to take part more independently (Peters 2003, pp. 177–178):

The children are sitting in a circle. After the teacher has told them what they are going to do today, Carlos (5 years old) points at a book he wants to read to his classmates. The teacher places a chair next to her, which she calls the "reading-chair". Carlos is a bit shy, but the teacher says that she will help him. Carlos sits down and pretends that he is reading to his classmates. He shows the book to the children and turns the pages. The teacher reads the text because Carlos is not able to read yet, but he finishes the teacher's sentences.

Carlos is very proud that he has read the story to his classmates. To keep the reading activity as authentic as possible, the teacher takes care of the actions Carlos is not (yet) able to perform by himself.

By participating in shared activities, the teacher can ascertain the actual level of the child's performance and find out what personal meaning the activity has for the child. At the same time, the teacher is in search of "development signalising data", for new actions a child may be able to accomplish with a little help (van Oers and Pompert 1991). In the shared activity, the teacher introduces new tools and ways of acting, and assists the child while he explores and learns to use them. The teacher remains alert to the personal meaning of the activity for the child. Does he still want to participate? Does he enjoy the activity? The teacher's interventions make sense to the child and fit into the activity. She should not deal with individual actions separately and expect that in due course the child will be able to put the actions together into one coherent activity. The teacher accounts for the actions the child is not yet able to perform in the course of the ongoing activity, so that this activity continues to be a coherent whole.

For children with special educational needs it is even more important not to simplify or reduce the meaningfulness of the socio-cultural activities they participate in only for the reason of meeting their "special features". Activities that are especially made up for these children make them special (Janssen-Vos et al. 2000).

Assisting Activities

An important aspect within the zone of proximal development is the interaction between the child and a more capable partner. Wood, Bruner and Ross call the assistance the adult offers *scaffolding* (see Bodrova and Leong 1996; Stone 1993). Scaffolds are temporary appliances to assist the child's learning process. With scaffolding the task itself is not reduced, but it should be made easier for the child through the help he gets. The assistance a teacher offers can vary, from focusing a child's attention on an important aspect of the activity, to explicitly demonstrating the execution of a certain action (*modelling*). For example, the use of pictograms to clarify the sequence of a task could help children to perform the task better. As Daniels (2001, p. 107) also points out, a scaffold should not simplify the task or the activity itself, but support its accomplishment by suitable help. The level of assistance gradually decreases as the child takes more responsibility in performing the task. In the course of time, the scaffold will not be needed anymore, for the child has internalised the actions and its external supports, and is now able to perform these actions independently. In this sense, scaffolding can be seen as a pedagogical strategy for the realisation of Vygotskij's compensation hypothesis in individual cases.

However, scaffolding should always be used with care and never be applied as a procedure for direct instruction. The scaffold should make sense to the pupil (Stone 1993). If the scaffold is built up without the pupil, it may be meaningless to him or even alienating. Such learning probably results in learning that changes pupils' behaviour, but does not promote development in a way that makes personal sense for them. Pupils must have possibilities to try alternative ways of structuring (van Oers and Wardekker 1997). Children are not in control of the activity if they do not know where they are aiming for, that is, what the activity's objective is. Communication between the child and the more capable partner about the scaffold must be such that the child can give personal meaning to the scaffold. Scaffolding should not only inform pupils about how to act, but also about why it makes sense to do so in the prospect of a wider goal. In this way, scaffolding becomes a social activity in which several children can participate, and in which questions and needs of the separate members can be pooled. Moll and Whitmore (1998) refer in this case to the concept of a collective zone of proximal development.

Interaction Is the Foundation

It is highly important that the educator pays due attention to every child and that she is able to make real contact with the child. Children are not identical. Every child develops in his own way and learns in his own manner. By having conversations in shared activities, the teacher can ascertain the personal meaning the activity has for the child, as well as find out how the child acts and tackles problems. Interaction is the foundation for further development. Only by real interaction with children and by having good relationships with them, the teacher can create a zone of proximal development with them. In Developmental Education we employ the following interaction framework to analyse interaction:

Framework of interaction:

- High expectations – real attention – taking time
- Establishing personal meanings
- Receiving and following
- Joint interaction
- Building up understanding
- Adding new points of view
- Evaluating and follow-up

In order to create a solid foundation for children's participation in shared activities, a teacher should tune in to the knowledge and abilities of that child, and to his motivations and his skills. To promote the child's development the teacher can also introduce this child to new areas of knowledge and skills that he/she needs to perform his or her task in that shared activity. In the following we present the teacher skills that are needed to create that solid foundation, in particular focusing on special needs children, following the interaction framework given above:

High Expectations – Real Attention – Taking Time

Children with special educational needs have often experienced failure in classroom activities. They know they are different and they act accordingly. Sometimes they seem passive or not interested in school activities. Or worse: they refuse to participate in school activities and resist in every possible way. Children with special educational needs depend more on their teacher than other children do. They depend on the time and the goal-directed support that the teacher gives to them (Stevens 1997). They often feel incapable, because they compare themselves with other pupils in their class. The relationship with the teacher can become stressful because the teacher may have the feeling that she has to devote all of her time to the children that are left behind. As a result, these children become more passive. van der Aalsvoort (1998) refers to this as a "paradoxical situation". Because of the extra help the teacher gives, the children become more dependent on that help and lose sight of their own learning capacities.

To get children more involved in the activities, teachers have to ascertain the personal meaning children can give to these activities, and find out how children can get personally involved in them. The pupils have to be intrinsically motivated to participate. This is an important step for teachers when they want to promote the development of children's abilities. It is not always easy to see children's personal meanings. The teacher has to take time and effort to understand the stories children tell or want to tell. Children want to feel that they are worth listening to, that the teacher is really trying to understand them (Peters 2003). The teacher must maintain high expectations for all children, by all means for the children she considers to be at risk (see Weinstein 2002). Only then will children feel confident enough to tell what is on their mind, even when they do not yet have the words to do so.

On the other hand, a teacher needs to be sensitive to the signals children give. This is impossible if the teacher is always running around the classroom, making sure everybody is at work with the right material. A sensitive teacher takes the time to have a conversation with a small group of children or an individual child. She makes real contact and gives the children the feeling that they are welcome and that she appreciates what they are saying.

Another way to get children more involved is to create "togetherness". Togetherness generates a bond of solidarity in a group and the feeling that each person wants to stay a member of that group. It prevents activities from breaking down when problems arise and need to be faced (Hännikäinen 2008; van Oers and Hännikäinen 2001). In a community of learners, where children learn with and from each other, togetherness is the basis for activities. Children need to work together; they should be willing to share their understandings and keep on doing so despite possible disagreements (Peters 2003).

The teacher can create togetherness when she helps children in their thinking process, in putting ideas into words, and discussing these ideas with other pupils. Togetherness exists more easily if the pupils work together within the same context or thematic activity. They understand each other more readily and they are together responsible for the outcome of their activities. For example, in a school for special primary education, a group of children, aged between 6 and 8, have decided to set up a bakery:

Eight children are sitting in a circle to make dough for the bread. Their teacher, Jacqueline, wants to let them know that they all matter, that they can all help. The group has read the recipe to make dough. Paul asks: "Can I help?" Jacqueline: "I would appreciate that, because we have a lot to do." The pupils help to sift the flour. Jacqueline asks them questions and by so doing she keeps the attention of all children. Together they take decisions. A pupil fills a cup with salt. Jacqueline asks: "Do we have to sift the salt too?" "Yes," says Paul. But Marie disagrees. She says: "No." Jacqueline: "Paul thinks we have to and Marie says "no", what shall we do?" Marie says: "There are no lumps in the salt, so we don't have to sift." Jacqueline: "What do you think, Bart?" Bart: "I think Marie is right. If there are no lumps, we don't have to sift." "Well, Paul, what shall we do?" Paul: "I don't know. Maybe there are lumps." Jacqueline asks the others what they shall do. "Let's sift to be sure," Nicole says. Everybody is happy with this decision and they can continue to follow the recipe.

Activities in small groups amplify the feeling of togetherness. The children feel that they are responsible for their bakery: if they do not manage to bake bread, the bakery cannot open. Jacqueline has high expectations for the children and she states that she has confidence in them ("You can do that"; "Would you mind filling this cup with water?"). The children experience that they can really contribute to the activities that are needed for the bakery, with and without the help from Jacqueline.

Establishing Personal Meanings

Activities have to be meaningful to children. They have to be connected to the child's own world of experiences. Sometimes the teacher has seen a glimpse of this world since she has visited the child at home, but she does not know what particularly attracts the child in the activities in his home environment. The best way to get that clear is to invite children to speak their minds. For young children, it is important to start from their daily actions and routines. This also applies for children with special educational needs, because more care is required to make them feel safe and recognised. The attitude of the teacher in those interactions has to be sensitive. She wants to understand what the child is doing and can actually "read" what a child means by his actions, the things he says, the activities in which he wants to participate, and what he has in mind. van den Heijkant and van der Wegen (2000) describe sensitivity as a teacher's capacity:

- to see the signals a child gives out;
- to interpret signals in the right way;
- to estimate the emotional aspect of the signals.

The teacher has to imagine herself in the child's situation. She seeks activities which make sense to the child. She explores the personal meaning the child attaches to the activity, and the experiences the child already has with it (Peters 2003). For example, teacher Daphne has many interesting objects to show to her group of special needs children (age 4–5):

The children and Daphne are sitting in a circle. Daphne says: "It's almost my birthday and I want to look pretty. I have brought all kinds of stuff with me. Could you help me?" She takes several objects out of a plastic bag: a brush, a comb, yellow hair gel with glitter, hair clips, rubber bands, perfume, an aerosol blue hair paint; but also a skirt, a sweater and a suit. "You have to put on the skirt," Tim says. "The suit is nice," Anass says. Tina adds: "Shall I comb your hair?" Daphne decides to continue this conversation with Tim, Anass and Tina. The other children play in the classroom under supervision of a teaching assistant.

Anass, Tim, Tina and Daphne look at the things Daphne brought from her home. "What is this?" Tim asks, taking the hair gel with glitter. "I don't know," Daphne says, "Shall we open it?" Daphne puts a blob of hair gel in each child's hand. Then she puts one in her own hand too. "Grouse, it sticks," Tina says. Daphne: "You're right, it sticks. Does it also stick to your hands, Tim and Anass?" Tim nods. Anass says: "I know what it is . . . hair gel! My brother has this at home too." Tim looks at his hand, brings his hand to his hair, and puts the hair gel in it. Anass imitates it. "Nice," Tina says, "do you want some too?" and she looks at Daphne. Daphne nods "yes" and a few seconds later, her hair is greasy, but the children love it.

Because Daphne has brought all those objects to school, the children can more easily tell what they know about them. They can touch them, smell them and feel the hair gel. It brings back memories from home, which they tell their teacher. It opens a window to their personal worlds.

Receiving and Following

When a child lets the teacher know what he is thinking, it is important that he has the feeling that the teacher has heard him and is trying to understand him. The attitude of the teacher needs to be responsive (van den Heijkant et al. 2000), meaning that the teacher:

- reacts often and directly upon the signals of the child;
- lets her reaction correspond with the signals of the child;
- lets her reaction correspond with the initiatives of the child.

In addition to a teacher's sensitivity, a responsive attitude is also important for all children, particularly for children with special educational needs. These children are often less open, take fewer initiatives and communicate less with adults. The teacher can be responsive when she makes real contact with the child, but also when she plays with him or participates in the child's activities. She can help the child when he cannot manage the activity or when he ends up in a conflict situation. She can also involve him in conversations with other pupils.

In Jacqueline's group, the children are starting a bakery. One morning, all children are sitting in a circle and Jacqueline shows them a shopping bag. She takes out a little bag of white powder and asks: "What do you think is in this bag?" "Sugar," David says. Jacqueline confirms this: "Sugar? That's possible, isn't it?"

"Seeds," Iris says. Jacqueline responds: "Shall I open it?" She opens the little bag and pours some of the contents into a cup. The children respond: "Sugar!" "No, it's powder." "Maybe it is powdered sugar." Jacqueline shows the white powder to the children and says: "Powdered sugar? Well, let's taste it. Then we'll know." Davis puts his finger in, then licks it and pulls a face. Jacqueline: "Why do you pull a face? Isn't it good?" She gives Iris a lick and she also pulls a face. All children get curious now. Jacqueline asks David: "Don't you like sugar?" Iris reacts: "This isn't sugar!" All the other children want to taste it. Peter says: "It's from the sea." Jacqueline answers: "Yes, it tastes like it comes out of the sea. It looks like sugar, but it tastes different." "It's from the sea," Jessie says, "It's salt!"

This example shows that Jacqueline really listens to the children. She notices how they react, she expresses what she sees in their faces and she responds accordingly. The children examine the powder together; they want to know what it is and they are not afraid of saying wrong things. Everything they say matters, there are no wrong or right answers. The children feel that and want to take part in this conversation. Joining in conversations and getting sensitive responses is a starting point for meaningful learning.

Revoicing

When several children interact with each other, it is the teacher's role to let every child understand what the other is meaning. A way of doing this is to use "revoicing" (O'Connor and Michaels 1996). By revoicing the teacher refrains from evaluating the child's utterances as right or wrong, but reformulates them in a way all children understand. The teacher can use revoicing to relate the pupil's contribution to the ongoing activity or to the utterances of other pupils. O'Connor and Michaels call the latter "aligning". Aligning describes the act of positioning pupils relative to one another, by placing their contributions to the discussion alongside or opposite to the other contributions. Such revoicing also creates a slot for the pupils to agree or disagree with the teacher's characterisation of the pupils' contributions, thus ultimately crediting the contents of the reformulation to the pupils themselves. Reformulating and recasting of a child's contribution can be conceived as an attempt to "give a bigger voice" to a child's contribution. The contribution is necessarily transformed: it can be uttered more succinctly, loudly, completely or in a different register. Thus, revoicing is not just repeating a pupil's contribution; by revoicing the teacher puts a surplus in her reformulation and still credits the utterance to the pupils themselves.

For children with special educational needs it is very important that the teacher stimulates their speaking through revoicing. If used in the proper way, it gives the children the feeling that it does matter when they say something. And although they may not have said it properly, the teacher was able to understand what they wanted to say and they can confirm the revoicing. It is also an opportunity for them to hear the proper way of speaking (Peters 2003). In the previously given example about salt, Jacqueline uses revoicing when she says: "Yes, it tastes like it comes from the sea. It looks like sugar, but it tastes differently." She shows that she understands what Peter says. She repeats Peter's contribution and puts it in a better-structured and more complete utterance. She also adds a new perspective: she compares it with sugar. In this way, she gives a "bigger voice" to his contribution so all the pupils can hear and understand more clearly what he has said. After Jacqueline's contribution Peter nods. By doing this he approves of the reformulation. Peter gives out a signal of agreement, crediting the content of Jacqueline's reformulation.

A teacher can also use revoicing to draw other pupils into the conversation. This is called "animation". She can reformulate the contribution of a child and ask another child what he thinks of it. In this way the conversation can take place among pupils instead of only back and forth between the teacher and individual pupils. Pupils learn to understand each other and react in an appropriate way.

Building Understanding

When children participate in a shared cultural activity, there are parts they can do by themselves, but other parts they only can do with the help of an adult or more knowledgeable peer. The teacher must take an active role in the activity and in the conversation about what they are going to do. For the time being, the teacher can take responsibility for the actions that a pupil is not yet able to perform independently and consequently acts as a model the pupil can imitate ("modelling", see Tharp and Gallimore 1988). Modelling is a powerful tool, especially if the teacher accompanies her acts with words. She demonstrates how to tackle a problem and explains out loud how she does it. Through participating in the conversation pupils imitate the teacher's activity and also use the words she has used. They imitate the teacher's manner of speech and actions and interiorise them in due course with appropriate help. By repeating the teacher's utterances while acting, they ultimately develop their "inner speech".

The teacher can also help children to master the situation by structuring their ideas and thoughts, and getting them engaged in the right actions in that activity. For the teacher, structuring an activity means that her actions are focused on clarifying actions to the children, making the activity well-organised, and giving it coherence. Structuring concerns the handling of the teaching situation, not the handling of the child (van den Heijkant et al. 2000). This means that the teacher has to clarify and publicly organise the activity, so that the situation becomes understandable for the pupil and the teacher (Peters 2003). It is important to point out here, that the teacher must take care that the process of structuring in itself should be a meaningful process for the children, so every step in the structuring must be clear for the children and functional for their shared activity and its purpose (see Stone 1993).

In Daphne's special needs group, they have celebrated a lot of birthdays in the little house in the classroom. Each time when pupils play in the house, Daphne participates in that play. Activities arise, like laying the table, decorating the house, and writing invitations. After each play activity Daphne discusses with the children what they have played. They discuss the order of activities. Together they put small pictures that are characteristic for the activities on a sheet of paper. These pictures form a play script for the next time they will play. The pictures hang nearby the house, but Daphne also has little ones which she can use when they are sitting at a table. This way, the next time they are going to play in the house, they can discuss in advance how they will play. The pictures regulate the play in a general way, without determining children's actions. They also help the children to talk more easily about their play. They have literally something in their hands to talk about.

This example shows different ways of structuring an activity. Daphne participates in the children's play. She is a role model and speaks out loud the actions she undertakes. By asking questions and giving them suggestions, she can assist the actions of the pupils. But she also brings in a tool that can help the pupils the next time they play, when Daphne is not around: the play script. This script has taken shape in collaboration with the pupils and therefore has personal meaning to them. It structures their own play activities, not the activities the teacher wants to see.

Adding New Points of View

A teacher does not merely adjust her pedagogical interactions strictly to the natural developmental rhythm of the child (see Chap. 2). She wants to promote children's development and create a zone of proximal development to let children grow. In joint activities she can introduce new points of view and new ways of acting in a meaningful and comprehensible way. She can confront the pupils with open problems: problems with multiple solutions. In this manner, the pupils have to deliberate and reason before they can act.

Earlier we saw Jacqueline. She shows the children that there are lumps in the flour. She asks the children if that is a problem when they are going to bake bread. Together they come to the conclusion that it is better when there are no lumps in the flour, because the bread might taste funny then. Jacqueline asks: "How do we get the lumps out of the flour?" Tim says: "With a spoon." Lisa thinks that you can squeeze them with your fingers. Then David says: "My mother has a thing, umh, where she puts the flour in and then she shakes it." David shows what he means with his hands. "Do you mean this?" Jacqueline asks, and she pulls out a sieve. "Yeah, that's what I mean!" David takes the sieve and starts shaking it. "What shall we do now? We have three ideas: using a spoon, with our fingers or using the sieve." All children are unanimous: they want to sieve the flour.

By introducing the problem with the lumps and keeping a sieve behind, Jacqueline enriches the activity for the children: she opens new actions that make sense for the pupils within the activity of baking, and also enriches the children's vocabulary with new words ("sieve"). This increases the children's motivation and self-confidence to participate (Janssen-Vos 2008; see also Chap. 4 of this volume, especially on the concept of didactic impulses).

Evaluating and Follow-Up

Evaluating an activity can take place during and after an activity. During the activity, in interaction with the children, the teacher can observe the children's level of involvement, and find out what their personal meaning and motives are. Evaluation when the activity is finished gives information about the effects of the teacher's intervention and may also establish whether the interventions had the desired outcome for the children. What have they learned and how would they deal with the activity the next time? Through such conversations the teacher can deal explicitly with the problems the pupils faced and with the progress of their development in the broad sense. Evaluation often leads to ideas about new activities for the children, but also gives data about their developmental processes. Children learn to look back at their activity and give words to their actions (see the example of Daphne with the play script). We think that this may enhance the children's autonomy and meta-cognitive development. Carefully valuating activities is important for all children, but especially for children with special educational needs. The teacher participates in the evaluation activity and helps the children to give words to their actions, tells them what they have done right and what they could improve next time. She can also tell the child what she considers the greatest learning achievement in that activity and what skills the child has learned (Janssen-Vos 2008).

All Children Are Special

The different interventions of the teacher with the help of this interaction framework ensure that the pupils feel better understood, that they understand themselves and the world around them better. Children also build up the confidence that they will receive help when they need it. That is exactly what we want to accomplish in Developmental Education: broad personal development for all children (see Chap. 4 of this volume), as well as promoting children's domain-specific learning, their control of emotions and explorations, their participation and feeling of togetherness in group activities, and their making sense of curriculum materials.

Teachers in Developmental Education reject stigmatisation of children on the basis of actual qualities or handicaps. They start out from an optimistic view of development and always look for ways to get round children's developmental barriers (if any). By sensitively observing and listening in their interactions with children, teachers are able to construct a good relationship with the group as a whole, as well as with the individual children, and collaboratively create a specific zone of proximal development with each of them. The use of Dynamic Assessments (see Chaps. 6 and 7 of this volume) is a powerful tool for teachers to accomplish this.

With all their unique characteristics (special needs) children need assistance in finding out how to participate to the best of their abilities in cultural practices. Every child is special; every child is different. Developmental Education is sensitive to differences among children, and aims to use this diversity for the benefit of all children. Every child can take and improve his/her own particular role in a shared cultural activity, in accordance with his/her available knowledge, skills, interests, handicaps and talents.

A teacher's responsibility is to offer pupils the gift of confidence (Mahn and John-Steiner 2002) and support them with properly tailored help on the basis of sensitive observations, by participating in meaningful activities, and by interacting with the pupils, taking into account all their special qualities. Interaction is the foundation for meaningful learning in diverse communities, for all children!

References

Bodrova, E., & Leong, D. J. (1996). *Tools of the mind. The Vygotskian approach of early childhood education.* Englewood Cliffs: Prentice-Hall, Inc.

Coles, G. (1987). *The learning mystique. A critical look at "learning disabilities".* New York: Fawcett Columbine.

Daniels, H. (2001). *Vygotsky and pedagogy.* London: Routledge Falmer.

Hännikäinen, M. (2008). Saamhorigheidsgevoel in de klas [Togetherness in the classroom]. *De wereld van het jonge kind, 36*(4), 18–21.

Janssen-Vos, F. (2008). *Basisontwikkeling voor peuters en de onderbouw* [Basic development for three to eight year-olds]. Assen: Van Gorcum.

Janssen-Vos, F., van Oers, B., & Schiferli, T. (2000). Eén voor één maar niet alleen. Een ontwikkelingsgerichte pedagogiek voor jonge (risico) kinderen [One by one, but not alone. A developmental pedagogy for children (at risk)]. *Tijdschrift voor orthopedagogiek: Themanummer: Opvang van jonge risicokinderen: onderwijs als aanknopingspunt? 39*(7/8), 300–312.

Mahn, H., & John-Steiner, V. (2002). The gift of confidence: A Vygotskian view of emotions. In G. Wells & G. Claxton (Eds.), *Learning for life in the 21st century. Sociocultural perspectives on the future of education* (pp. 46–58). Oxford: Blackwell.

McDermott, R. P. (1993). The acquisition of a child by a learning disability. In S. Chaiklin & J. Lave (Eds.), *Understanding practice. Perspectives on activity and context* (pp. 269–305). Cambridge: Cambridge University Press.

Moll, L. C., & Whitmore, K. F. (1998). Vygotsky in classroom practice: Moving from individual transmission to social transaction. In D. Faulkner, K. Littleton, & M. Woodhead (Eds.), *Learning relationships in the classroom* (pp. 131–155). London: Routledge.

Nellestijn, B., & Peters, I. (2008). Omgaan met verschillen. Verslag van een ronde-tafelgesprek [Dealing with diversities. Report of a round table]. *Zone, 7*(2), 28–31.

Nellestijn, B., Peters, I., & Koster, G. (2009). *Uitgaan van verschillen. Ontwikkelingsgericht Onderwijs in het speciaal basisonderwijs [Dealing with diversity. Developmental Education in schools for special education].* Alkmaar: De Activiteit.

O'Connor, M. C., & Michaels, S. (1996). Shifting participant frameworks: Orchestrating thinking practices in group discussions. In D. Hicks (Ed.), *Discourse, learning, and schooling* (pp. 63–103). Cambridge: Cambridge University Press.

Peters, I. (2003). The roles of a teacher in a play-based curriculum in special education. In B. van Oers (Ed.), *Narratives of childhood. Theoretical and practical explorations for the innovation of early childhood education* (pp. 176–186). Amsterdam: VU University Press.

Peters, I., & van Oers, B. (2007). Teachers' action strategies in goal-oriented interactions with young children at risk. *European Early Childhood Education Research Journal, 15*(1), 21–136.

Stevens, L. (1997). *Overdenken en doen. Een pedagogische bijdrage aan adaptief onderwijs [To consider and act. A pedagogical contribution to adaptive education].* Den Haag: Procesmanagement Primair Onderwijs.

Stone, C. A. (1993). What is missing in the metaphor of scaffolding? In E. A. Forman, N. Minick, & C. A. Stone (Eds.), *Contexts for learning: Sociocultural determinants in children's development* (pp. 169–184). Oxford: Oxford University Press.

Sylva, K., Melhuish, E. C., Sammons, P., Siraj-Blatchford, I., & Taggart, B. (2004). *The Effective Provision of Pre-School Education (EPPE) project: Technical paper 12-the final report: Effective pre-school education.* London: DfES/Institute of Education, University of London.

Tharp, R. G., & Gallimore, R. (1988). *Rousing minds to life. Teaching, learning, and schooling in social context.* Cambridge: Cambridge University Press.

Tharp, R., Estrada, P., Dalton, S., & Yamauchi, L. (2000). *Teaching transformed. Achieving excellence, fairness, inclusion and harmony.* Boulder: West View Press.

van der Aalsvoort, G. M. (1998). *Kwetsbare jonge kinderen: diagnosticeren en handelen [Young children at-risk: diagnosis and action].* Leiden University, department Orthopedagogiek. Lecture Conference OGO-Academy.

van den Heijkant, C., & van der Wegen, R. (2000). *De klas in beeld. Video Interactie Begeleiding in School [The classroom in focus. Video Interaction Guidance in School].* Heeswijk-Dinther: Uitgeverij Esstede.

van Oers, B., & Hännikäinen, M. (2001). Some thoughts about togetherness: An introduction. *The International Journal of Early Years Education, 9*(2), 101–108.

van Oers, B., & Pompert, B. (1991). Kijken naar kinderspel: een beschouwing over ontwikkelingsgericht observeren [Looking at children's play: A reflection on development-oriented observation]. *Vernieuwing, 50*(7), 3–8.

van Oers, B., & Wardekker, W. L. (1997). De cultuurhistorische school in de pedagogiek [The cultural-historical school in pedagogy]. In S. Miedema (Ed.), *Pedagogiek in meervoud* (pp. 171–213). Houten/Diegem: Bohn Stafleu Van Loghum.

Vygotsky, L. S. (1978). *Mind in society. The development of higher psychological processes.* Cambridge, MA: Harvard University Press.

Vygotsky, L. S. (1993). *The collected works of L.S. Vygotsky* (The Fundamentals of Defectology (Abnormal Psychology and Learning Disabilities), Vol. 2). New York: Plenum Press.

Vygotsky, L. S. (1994). The problem of the environment. In R. van der Veer & J. Valsiner (Eds.), *The Vygotsky reader* (pp. 338–354). Oxford: Blackwell.

Weinstein, R. (2002). *Reaching higher. The power of expectations in schooling.* Cambridge, MA: Harvard University Press.

Chapter 11
Fostering the Teacher-Parent Partnership

Frea Janssen-Vos and André Weijers

A Plea for Educational Partnership

A few years ago a Dutch study showed that parents' interests in their children's school were decreasing (Overmaat and Boogaard 2004). That parents nowadays are far too busy to get involved in school matters was, and still is, the complaint. On the other hand, the government and schools increasingly urge parents to take courses in order to gain more parenting skills. Especially when schools experience difficulties in the language development of children from non-Dutch backgrounds, or when they struggle with children's behaviour and learning problems, they appeal to the parents' responsibilities. We are not convinced of parents' indifference to their children's education and think it is time to find new inspirations to improve parent-school contacts, and build developmentally productive educational partnerships.

Parent involvement can take different forms. In the Netherlands, three possibilities for parents' participation in school matters exist (Onderwijsraad 2010). First, parents have legal rights to be involved in school matters. For instance, each school has a school board (in Dutch: "Medezeggenschapsraad") in which representatives of the parents are members. A second possibility concerns the cooperative partnership in the children's upbringing. Thirdly, parents assist the school in daily school practices as members of a parent community. In this chapter, we discuss the second and third parent positions.

Many schools work at improving their relations with parents for the benefit of children's broad cultural development. They more or less need to do so, because

F. Janssen-Vos (✉)
e-mail: janssen-vos@planet.nl

A. Weijers
De Activiteit, Alkmaar, The Netherlands
e-mail: a.weijers@de-activiteit.nl

B. van Oers (ed.), *Developmental Education for Young Children*, International
Perspectives on Early Childhood Education and Development 7,
DOI 10.1007/978-94-007-4617-6_11,
© Springer Science+Business Media Dordrecht 2012

nowadays children, their parents and modern society require new relationships with schools and teachers. In turn, schools want closer contacts with parents because of their joint educational aims and responsibilities. More than ever, teachers want to build up caring relationships with children and support children's independence, participation, cooperative learning, and democratic behaviour (Hargreaves 2003). Increasing emphasis is being placed today on broad development and social competences, as well as academic achievements in school. Moreover, it is widely acknowledged that the way in which children are raised at home can greatly impact their success at school.

These educational intentions overlap parents' responsibilities and educational values. As a consequence, bringing up children is no longer just the responsibility of parents alone; schools are equally concerned with these matters. Such new joint perspectives can, however, be difficult for teachers and for parents. Teachers, for instance, may find that parents are failing in their pedagogical efforts, and parents may feel that teachers do not pay due attention to their wishes or questions. Hence, it is obvious that we cannot neglect the need for new forms of parent-school relationships and must admit that taking each other's viewpoints into consideration is becoming essential (Moore and Lasky 1999).

A strong motivation for parental involvement lies in the benefits this may have for children. The Dutch *Onderwijsraad*[1] (2010) cautiously refers to the results of research that show the positive effect of parental involvement on children's achievements, social competence and motivation in school. However, it must be admitted that research results are sometimes hard to interpret, as it is not always clear what kinds of parental involvement have what kinds of effects on children (Smit et al. 2006). Scientists and educational experts do agree that children profit from a good relationship between their parents and school, because a certain mutual adjustment promotes the children's learning and school career (Booijink 2007a, b). A sceptical reaction is to say that research models are based on high social economic class' expectations and wishes. As a result social inequality is reproduced as children are made more dependent on their parents' ability to give content to their relation with the school. The best answer to this problem is to go to greater efforts to give parents with a lower social economic status a role in their children's school career. Decisive in this discussion is probably that a good parent-school relationship has often turned out to have more positive effects on children's careers than learning achievements alone. Studies prove that parental support affects their pedagogical practice. Moreover, parental involvement improves the school's climate and creates more openness of schools towards the children's home environments (Epstein 1995; Smit et al. 2006).

We conclude that in today's education fostering teacher-parent contacts is absolutely necessary. Moreover, the definition and the potential prospects of this partnership should be unambiguously defined. We find interesting opportunities and potential in what is called "educational partnership". This concept denotes a

---

[1] A national council that advises the Minister of Education in matters of education and schooling.

relationship between parents and teachers, founded on a joint concern to create optimal conditions for children's development and learning in the context of school and family. Educational partnership aims at the collaborative realisation of goals that emerge from this shared concern; it is a relationship in which equal participation is the predominant ideal (de Wit 2005; 2008). Ultimately, parents are responsible for their children's upbringing and education. They claim this responsibility for instance when choosing a school, or leaving it when they differ in opinion about what is right for their child. The school's responsibility lies in the arrangement of educational content and curricula at school, in maintaining the quality of the education and taking parents seriously.

Educational Partnership in Developmental Education

The ideal of educational partnership fits with (multicultural) Developmental Education schools that feel a bond with parents in their joint responsibility for young people in our society (de Wit et al. 2007). Obviously this requires strong motivation on the part of both school and parents, and each of the partners must be aware of this shared responsibility for the children. Moreover, the Vygotskian perspective asks for specific accents in parent-school relations. A partnership assumes that school and parents take each other seriously, respect the other's autonomy, and make efforts to listen to and understand each other's traditions and conventions. This is no easy ambition. Therefore we prefer to speak in terms of a *developing partnership*.

How can we promote the development of an educational partnership in the context of Developmental Education? What are we striving for? We propose the following aims:

- The school shows openness towards parents, genuine interest in their children, and gives them and their children a warm welcome.
- The school communicates well with parents, invites them to say what is on their minds, and undertakes special efforts when the parents' language is not yet sufficient for mutual understanding.
- The school provides parents with information and insight into class practices, and clarifies the (theoretical) backgrounds of its educational concept.
- The school invites parents to attend classroom activities regularly and to participate in them; be it through assisting in organisational matters or acting as "expert", or "guest teacher".
- The school invites parents to discuss pedagogical and other issues of mutual concern.
- The school gives parents an account of the children's developmental and learning progress and searches with them for solutions should questions or problems arise.
- The school makes every effort to reflect the children's life situations and backgrounds in school, and invites the support of parents to bring this intention into practice.

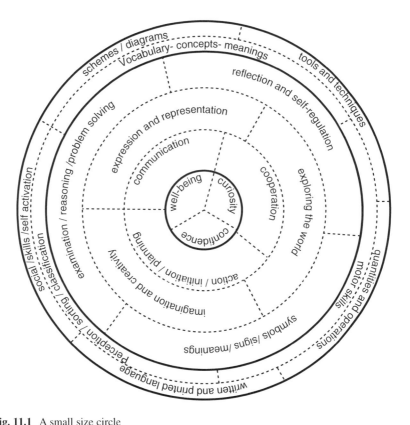

Fig. 11.1 A small size circle

- The school offers parents a room in the school for meetings amongst themselves and with teachers, in order to discuss possibilities for more involvement.
- The school informs parents about planned thematic class activities, invites them to take part and to make contributions or proposals for elaborations.
- The school tries to find ways (in the school itself or by reference to other institutes) to help parents who want pedagogical support and to find answers to their questions and personal learning needs.

It is important here to draw attention to the aims of Developmental Education as expressed in the circle diagram of Basic Development (see Chap. 4), as they are relevant for the educational partnership as well. Feeling welcome, self-esteem and eagerness to learn are the psychological conditions for learning (the core of the circle; see Fig. 11.1), both for children and parents. Improving communication and interaction, and understanding children's development from parents' and teachers' perspectives are examples of a broad developing partnership (the middle circle). Furthermore, specific skills in teachers and parents need to be developed to form the desired partnership. Think of social skills and skills for coaching parent groups (the outer circle; see Fig. 11.1).

Zones of Proximal Development

Not all parents or schools will immediately be in favour of or able to achieve all these aims. But we think it reasonable to consider them as necessary elements of a developing partnership which all schools should be able to realise in due course. This is also true for multicultural schools where creating a relationship with parents from non- Dutch origins is often considered hard to realise. It is true that parents in multicultural groups often need more of the teacher's support and attention. Communication can be difficult and more complex, while prejudices and differences in expectations can hinder contacts. Research shows, however, that the majority of the parents from ten different ethnic groups are very much interested in their children's education at school (Smit et al. 2005; van Kreveld 2004). They are involved and are eager to participate, but encounter problems in the sphere of communication. They may seem to be less interested because of their poor command of the Dutch language, but they really do support their children.

Thinking of the many differences between schools and parents, we may see the aims listed above as stepping stones towards improving the partnership between schools and parents. From a Vygotskian perspective, we suggest that meaningful practices should be arranged for interaction between parents and teachers which create new learning opportunities (zone of proximal development). Such practices indeed offer valuable contexts for learning when appropriate help is available. An important precondition for this is, however, that the school has (or acquires) sufficient professional understanding and skills to initiate and guide teachers' and parents' activities, in particular for making parents feel welcome and letting them feel that they are appreciated as partners in education.

Meaningful Activities and Content

In the next section we describe some proposals for meaningful activities which can promote further development of an educational partnership. We must be modest and admit that in this we are all beginners. All participants need time to get used to such shared responsibilities, to a different way of interaction and cooperation, and must find the time and expertise to grow in the desired direction.

Activities are to be elaborated in a developmental way, articulating that communication and interaction are the heart of any developing partnership. Activities which help to explore children's growing up and education from both sides can be seen as primary in this partnership. The previously described aims offer guidelines for parents and the school to attain the necessary motivation, insight and skills towards productive partnership.

layer 3. ego states	parent-role	child- role	adult-role
layer 2. body language	first position: me	second position: you	third position: the whole
layer1. welcome	giving a heartily welcome	limitation means growth	autonomy

Fig. 11.2 The three layers of the communication wall

Creating a Strong Foundation. Building Up Reciprocal Communication

A good relationship with parents is important and depends upon a positive communicative attitude on both sides. To achieve such communication with parents, it is necessary to make a start within the school team and improve the teachers' abilities to communicate with each other and with parents.

In his work at Developmental Education schools one of the authors (André Weijers, subsequently referred to as the coach) has been particularly concerned with the team's relationship with parents. He coaches teams of teachers in the improvement of their reciprocal communicative abilities with parents. In his approach he introduces a strategy to improve the communicative quality of teams (Weijers 2009a).[2] He tells the team they are going to build a "communication wall" which consists of three layers each with three different kinds of brick (see Fig. 11.2). The members of the team are asked to reflect on their own attitudes and wishes. They are encouraged to talk about their professional attitude, about dealing with emotions and critics, and to determine for themselves which aspects of the foundation have already been acquired and which need improvement.

In his introduction of a project with a school team, the coach presents several short stories or personal experiences to help the team understand the meaning of the bricks and to stimulate interactions. The following gives a description of the communication wall as it is introduced to the teachers.

The First Layer of Bricks

Brick 1. *Giving a warm welcome. The phase of acceptance*
    Making others feel welcome is essential for a healthy contact, because this shows that the other persons matter and are valued. We, adults, have acquired many non-verbal rituals for this welcome: shaking hands, looking the other person in the eye, or offering a seat. Teachers are aware of the importance of these courtesies and yet at the same time realise that such a welcome is often lacking. This may be due to past conflicts or misunderstandings, or simple oversight.

---

[2] At the time of this work, André Weijers was internal coach of a primary school in Amsterdam.

Brick 2. *Limitation means growth. The phase of exploring the subject*

"Welcome" goes together with "limitation". As it is for children, it is also important in the teachers' contacts with parents that boundaries are set and restrictions made in order to have an overview and create safety. It is of essential importance for teachers to be absolutely clear about the purpose of the contact and, at the same time, to make the parents feel welcome.

Brick 3. *Autonomy*

This brick refers to autonomy (taking and giving of self-government) of parents, teachers and children. The power of strong relationships with parents exists in the fact that parents and teachers are considered equal and maintain their autonomy. Nevertheless, teachers sometimes encounter difficult situations, for instance, when parents treat their children in a way that they consider inconsistent with the school's pedagogical purposes. Mostly they are reluctant in such situations, because they do not want to interfere in parents' responsibilities. On the other hand, they also realise that they, as teachers, are jointly responsible and must protect the child. As a matter of fact, it is a teacher's responsibility to create optimal conditions for each child's achievement and development (see also Chap. 3 of this volume). In cases of such pedagogical tensions it is necessary to speak with the parents in order to understand why they are acting as they are. Then they can explain why certain actions are not beneficial for their child and suggest alternatives. It is quite understandable that teachers hesitate to interfere, but they also must realise that this child, and all the others, need to feel that they are understood and that not all adult reactions are helpful for the child's broad development. And of course, the reverse is also possible: parents may also disagree with some of the teachers' acts. In these cases it is important that a climate of openness is created in which the parents feel at home (brick 1), and free to discuss the issue with the teacher.

The Second Layer

This layer of bricks concerns different foci on the participants, including the awareness of body language and the non-verbal aspects of communication.

- The first focus is "me": awareness of space and attention for "me". In this position the coach is prominent as a leader: he undertakes action, makes decisions, and draws the lines. The benefits of this position are clarity and an ability to take matters into one's own hands. The risk is appearing abrupt or moving forward too quickly. This "me"-position is important in the contact between parents and teachers. People tend to appreciate the security conferred by clear guidelines. If the teacher cannot provide these conditions, parents will take over the lead, determine the agenda, and consider when and how their issue can be discussed. Hence, the teacher must be clear from the beginning about the aims of the conversation. Nevertheless, parents should also have the opportunity to bring in their agendas and consider when and how their issues can be discussed.

- The second focus is "you": space and attention for the other. Here, the other (the parent) takes the primary position. The teacher listens actively, tries to put herself in the parent's position and to show empathy ("This must be very hard for you ... "). The benefit is much attention and support for the parent; the risks are getting too personally involved and not enough space for the teacher.
- The third focus is "the whole": space and attention for overview. This position is the one of the camera. This creates distance and space to overview the whole situation. The benefit is that overview and insight into the issue being discussed is gained without immediate judgment. Overview helps to create distance in order to reflect on experiences and consider a follow-up. The risks are too much distance and complacency.

Teachers are often the least aware of this position and must realise that in conversations with parents it is necessary to take time for this reflective overview.

The Third Layer: Ego-States

The roles that can be taken in communication form the bricks in the third layer.

- The parent-role. One can act as the "nurturing" or the "critical" parent. The nurturing parent gives attention to positive care and encouragement: a compliment, a reward, a hug. He touches, appreciates and protects. The critical parent notices what goes wrong, criticises, takes note of failures and makes remarks like "you shall never succeed". He is never satisfied.
- The child's-role. The role of the child has three positions. The free child is spontaneous, flexible, playful, emotionally free and active. The socially adaptive child is constantly aware of others' reactions to his behaviour, adjusts itself to these reactions and wants to be one of the group without a demand for autonomy. The rebellious child will do anything to be noticed and cannot function without the others.
- The adult-role. The adult role is directly in line with the nurturing parent and the free child. He is independent, equal, able to negotiate and intermediates in solving problems.

Which of these positions do teachers take in contact with parents? As soon as a parent enters the room a position is inevitably taken. How do you see this person? Do you regard her or him in a critical way or with a nurturing attitude? Or do you present yourself as a mediating adult? Some teachers start a conversation from one of the child-positions and adjust to the situation or become rebellious. Imagine that the teacher contributes to a conversation from the role of the critical parent. Then the other feels forced to act in one of the child-roles. His reaction will be either very socially adjusted or completely rebellious. Neither reaction is satisfactory. However, suppose that one person acts from the adult-role, autonomous, active and on the basis of equality; and the other person acts from the same position. Then, communication on the basis of mutual respect, action, and problem solving can be predicted.

The three bricks of the ego-states complete the illustration of the aspects of communication. In our experiences with this wall of communication model, we noticed that many teachers said that the building bricks are well-known. But they also admit that they are not always aware of the effects of the different ways in which the communication processes take place.

Being aware of the essentials of communication with parents, teachers can improve their skills. They enhance their communicative efficiency by consequently planning the purpose and subjects of the meetings, as a guideline during the conversations. Afterwards, they reflect on their learning experiences and draft a report. Next, they discuss their experiences and questions during intervision sessions in the team. Sometimes teams decide to speak with parents in pairs, taking turns in the conversation. Afterwards they reflect together and learn from each other's actions and remarks.

Collaboratively Exploring Children's Development and Education

Every school organises meetings with parents in order to explain and discuss educational philosophies and activities. What information is relevant for parents who are considering enrolling their children in a Developmental Education school? And how can these initial meetings be followed up once the children are pupils of this school? Several educational issues can be addressed in these meetings with parents. The following section illustrates three of the main topics that have turned out to be important issues for parents with young children in Developmental Education schools (play, learning to read and write, and learning opportunities at home).

An Introduction to Play and Development in Young Children's Classrooms

One of the schools organises informative meetings twice a year (Hagenaar 2009). The parents are invited to visit a photographic exhibition which depicts several educational moments in various early years groups. They give their first impressions and ask questions. Before answering these questions, the teachers take the parents to different classrooms. Here they find for instance a corner where the current thematic activity is displayed, the role-play corner set up as a home or a shop and the story table with picture books and stories the children have written or drawn. Examples of the teacher's work, such as observation systems and children's portfolios can also be examined. After this tour everyone returns to the meeting room where questions are answered and written information is handed out.

What Kind of Information Is Important?

On the basis of their experience, teachers have a notion of the kind of information parents probably want. They always want to be assured that the teachers are kind and will make their child feel safe and welcome. They also want to understand why children play so much in Developmental Education schools and what the teacher does to be sure that children learn enough. These concerns form the basis of a presentation about educational beliefs. Teachers illustrate the information with a power point presentation with photos or video clips with examples of good practice.

Important topics are:

- The basis: safety and trust.
  Home and school should be places where children can find shelter and feel safe. The school meets this fundamental need by making children feel welcome and ensuring that teachers listen, understand and care.
- How can development occur?
  Children learn from participating in meaningful activities that represent the social-cultural world of adults. Because they want to be "big" and do what adults do, they try to find out how they can participate in the adult world. Teachers create situations in which the child can "play the world". Parents easily recognise this in their home situations when the teacher explains that all their children's activities can have a play character. This makes it easier for them to understand why children play at school and why teachers join in in order to find good opportunities for teaching their children new things that make sense to them and that will make them more able participants.
- The teacher's role
  Play development is not an autonomous process. That is why the teacher is important (see for example Karpov 2005). She creates play situations, fosters a positive atmosphere and provides interesting materials and themes. She joins in with the children's play to communicate, to make activities more meaningful, and to identify opportunities for new learning moments.
- What are the objectives?
  Developmental Education schools first of all strive for a broad development (see Chap. 4 of this volume). Children not only need to acquire oral language skills or motor skills; they also learn to take initiatives, make plans, explore the world, feel a shared responsibility and learn to communicate in various ways. All of these aims are based on personal qualities such as self-esteem, curiosity and a sense of well-being.
- What are the effects?
  Teachers observe children's activities, by which they can follow and evaluate their progress. They record their conclusions and plans in a class logbook and in diaries kept for each child (see also Chap. 14 of the present volume). Progress is documented in portfolios. This results in narratives for parents about their children' developmental progress, and indicates any possible problems.

Follow-Up Information. How About Learning to Read and Write?

Some time after the children's entrance into the school, parents can attend meetings to learn more about the classroom practice. Informal conversations with parents and teachers' experiences help in the choice of meaningful topics. For instance, teachers notice that parents of the youngest children are very interested to hear when their child will learn to read and write. This urgent interest explains why they sometimes have doubts about the time spent on play activities. For this reason teachers decide to take this concern as one of the topics in parent-teacher meetings (Weijers 2009b).

The introductory presentation of the coach explains the relation between play and learning to read and write. He stresses the following aspects in the information he provides by referring to many classroom illustrations.

In play activities young children show who they are and what they can do. By joining in children's play, teachers have the opportunity to challenge them, expanding their interests and motivation to be engaged in new experiences. As play activities are the source of meaningful learning, the teacher can explain how reading and writing arise from play. Illustrations of children's activities can be shown, where they tell stories or express their experiences through drawings as they play in the house corner or in the baker's shop, etc. This makes it easier for parents to understand that play and making drawings are important factors in language, communicative and intellectual development.

During the presentation parents are encouraged to ask questions and talk about their experiences at home. They are also encouraged to interact with each other, as they are members of the same group. The teacher takes notes on a large wall chart, showing that every input is taken seriously. Parents are reminded of the intention of the discussion, namely helping them recognise the importance of role-play and make-believe writings, of the importance of books, paper, letters and writing materials in the classroom.

Using real anecdotes of classroom experiences, teachers can speak with parents about the way they assist the children in their awakening interest in reading and writing. For instance, they ask children to tell the "story" they have drawn; through genuine interest and interaction the children will feel encouraged to go on talking and telling. Next, it can be explained to the parents how and why adults can eventually suggest writing down some elements of the child's story. In cases where the child replies that they cannot write, the adult can offer to write what the child wants to write for them. In fact, they make the child a "partner-in-writing".

At this moment parents probably want to ask questions, give examples of their own children's actions, or ask for more explanation. Then a next step can be mentioned, namely reading the written story aloud with the children so that they may recognise the correspondence of the story they told with what is written on the paper. Most children are amazed when they hear the adult read their story for real (see Chap. 15 of this volume)!

In the explanation for parents the importance of being an active listener must be stressed: what is it this child is telling me? What experience lies behind the words? Parents should be sensitive in interactions and suggestions; it is important to invite children to undertake activities rather than pressing them. Teachers can explain this, by giving the children's products a place in the classroom. As a result children can see the value and importance of their work. Teachers can also point out how important it is that adults and children do serious work together, referring to the picture books they made with the children of the children's own stories. Showing these picture books to parents often reassures them that play indeed leads to creative and intellectual experiences, and to progress in reading and writing.

In the context of picture books a next step in the learning process becomes visible. Now, the teacher refers to the children's curiosity about the symbols used for writing. This is a special moment for drawing attention to the correspondence between spoken and written words and stories. Teachers may ask parents if their children like to write at home and what their ideas are about children's scribbles. They can join in with the parents' discussion and confirm that most children at a very young age want to write, often starting with writing their own names. Adults' writings make children eager to "write" words themselves. At this point parents may react and maybe want to understand what it is wise to do. Eventually it can be explained that various materials (like letter stamps or Lego-letters) help children to make words and texts without having to write formally themselves. Examples of these materials and of children's texts illustrate what young children like to do and can do. It must be emphasised that all depends on the children's choice of the way they want to "write", "scratch" or draw messages, letters or shopping lists. The numerous examples of different kinds of writings in their environment often encourage children to try new and different kinds of writing themselves. At school, teachers can offer help whenever they observe that children are in need of some material or skill. By helping children with the accomplishment of new actions or with the use of new tools within their collaborative activity, teachers create a zone of proximal development with the children.

If parents appear very interested to hear and see more, the moment is there to create a new zone of proximal development together. Parents discuss their wishes and ideas for activities and topics, and teachers connect them with their ideas. "Question walls" easily enable a teacher to do a quick survey of questions and proposals, giving him an opportunity to finish the presentation and to offer help by preparing a follow-up meeting and/or circulating information on paper.

Teachers Examine Children's Learning Opportunities at Home

When parents are well informed about the way their children learn at school, the teachers in their turn are in a position to learn about the children's developmental opportunities in their own home environments. They can attain information in the following ways:

- They may ask parents to take pictures of learning situations at home. Parents who are not in the possession of a camera can be given one, as a present or just to borrow. The teacher also asks the parents to write down why they took precisely this picture.
- Another possibility is to invite the parents to a meeting in school where they can talk about these particular pictures. By doing so, teachers meet the needs of parents for whom writing is for some reason difficult. Moreover, they also learn about children's home situations and mutual relations. Maybe informal contacts before or after school time can be used for this purpose.
- Then the teachers make picture books with the parent's photo's and narratives, written by them or with the teacher's help.

The objective of this team activity is that teachers express and share their expectations and opinions about learning moments in the children's home situations. It is important here, that they keep the social-economic situations of the families in mind. Next they compare their expectations (and possible judgments) with the pictures and narratives in the photo books. Then they have the opportunity to correct their images and find better adjustments between educational activities at home and at school.

Comparing and discussing photo books also creates a rich source for communication among parents. It is a challenge to exchange ideas about what parents see as important for their children and about their opinions and questions. Most parents like to learn more about each other's experiences and activities at home. Exchanging these ideas helps them to become acquainted with each other as partners in education. Teachers can extend parents' ideas by helping them to learn more about their children's educational activities at school. This can be achieved, for instance, when parents participate in classroom activities (as a guest or guest teacher), when they attend a conclusion of a thematic period or a presentation of children's activities, or with descriptions of classroom examples in school magazines. In such occasions, teachers are models for parents. Another possibility is to use the picture books in group activities in the classroom, as a new source for children's discussions, play, reading and writing.

Propositions like these are based upon Marilyn Fleer's study (2005). She refers to Vygotskij's statements about the relation between scientific and common sense (everyday) concepts, and about the significance for a cultural pedagogy in the early grades. She concludes that learning experiences offered at school must be related to children's learning outside school, at home and in the real world. Fleer mentions that research outcomes clearly show that the majority of the families undertake all kinds of joint activities with their children; activities which are mostly connected with housekeeping and daily routines like shopping, cooking, on their way to school etc. Parents certainly consider these events as important for children's learning to read, write and calculate.

Sharing Educational Issues. A Safe Pedagogical Climate

How can dialogue and an exchange of ideas be initiated between school and parents? What can serve as a starting point? Debate propositions? Press cuttings? Perhaps a personal experience? The following is an illustration of how this could be organised, taking the building-up of a safe pedagogical climate as an example.

The coach proposes that his team bring the pupils into a situation where structure and laws do not exist (Weijers 2009c). The teachers are to discuss such situations with them: what are the positive aspects, what is not agreeable and needs to be improved? In the end, a special school committee will construct an inventory of rules. All children, even the young ones, are going to vote for eight basic rules of their school, with the youngest children being assisted by older pupils. The whole process will be recorded on film, to be shown and discussed in a meeting with parents.

Building up such a safe pedagogical climate is a whole-school commitment. The upper grades (grades 7–8; in the Netherlands this refers to pupils aged 11–12) teachers take their pupils on an outdoor trip. There they bring the children into a problem situation: no adults take care of organising their lunch, the pupils are to find out by themselves how to share the food and drinks. There are no rules, and chaos and hostility are the result. Afterwards, in the classroom, teacher and pupils watch the film one of the teachers made of this situation; they discuss what happened and what rules they see as important.

The teachers of middle groups (5–6) invent a story about a boat in which children end up on a deserted island. They want to escape and with the help of parents they build a ship at least 10 m long. The children write logbooks and rules about how to get along with each other on a boat. This process is also recorded on video.

The teachers of the 4 and 5 year-old children take the story of Pippi Longstocking (by Astrid Lindgren) as a starting point. Pippi has no parents and makes all the necessary rules herself in her own self-centred way. The classroom functions as Pippi's house "Villa Villekulla" for a while; the children invent rules and agreements as if they were in charge of the villa.

As planned, the committee takes all the rules from all classes and compiles a list of 16 basic rules. One day all the children vote by choosing (ticking) eight out of these. The youngest ones do so by means of pictograms on their voting ballots and by putting stickers on each rule which they think is important.

As a completion of this project many parents attend a meeting with teachers and the children. They enjoy the children's activities as shown in the film and admire their products. They are also very interested in the rules they have chosen and ask the children to tell them more about their ideas.

Later on, parents and teachers have a follow-up meeting. Now it is the teachers' challenge to start a dialogue with the parents. The above described situation is about how to create a safe pedagogical climate in school. This team started the project with a meeting where the teachers themselves expressed what they see and don't see as a safe climate. To start the discussion they watched a film about the behaviour of a group of school children. After that, they showed parents the same film and gave their opinions of what is safe for their children at school and what is not. Their ideas are the trigger for parents' reactions and questions. The discussion leads to an explanation of the school's strategy to consider and discuss emotional and social safety at school with the children. This is done step by step and as concretely as possible. The parents then watch film clips showing how children and teachers are involved in activities and discussions. After that parents and one of the teachers continue the discourse in small groups. Differences in opinions about rules and how they are to be implemented in everyday practices are respected and discussed.

In this meeting everybody seems to be convinced that a school climate which rests upon self-chosen basic rules is very important. A safe pedagogical climate is indeed a subject that will return in many more future meetings and discussion.

Involving Parents in Educational Activities

There are several ways to involve parents in their children's educational activities. These vary from giving a helping hand on special occasions to serving as "guest-teachers" with special talents, hobbies or knowledge. Teachers experience that once parents are more familiar with the children's activities and interactions in school, their interests in what is happening there increases, and they become eager to know more about the why's and how's. From that moment on, information and explanations about young children's development and education become more meaningful for them. We will mention some possible parental activities which may promote the developing partnership:

- Parental involvement in the class' theme
- Coffee meetings
- Learning more about language development
- Pedagogical support
- Teaching parents

Parent Involvement in the Class' Theme

In planning parent involvement in classroom activities the phases in the thematic approach offer structure to the teachers' interaction with parents (van Brandwijk 2009).[3] In accordance with the process of thematising, parent involvement can be structured as follows:

---

[3] See Chap. 4 for the phases in thematisation.

Information About the Theme

Teachers often create a kind of "information centre" about the theme they have in mind with pictures, objects, books and a list with new words, for example. With this information, parents become aware of the children's interest and this makes it easier to communicate about what is going on at school. They can for instance help to find objects or supplies which may fit in with the theme and can be taken to school.

Participating in Themes

Parents can be asked to *assist with special events* like educational walks or visits to places of interest in the context of the theme. In one of the schools parents accompanied children on a visit to a sweets shop where they saw what kind of sweets were on offer and which they could make and sell in their own shop at school. Afterwards, with the assistance of the accompanying parents, the children played in their class sweets shop, making use of what they learned.

Parents can also *join in* the children's group activities. As the children's partners they may read picture books or stories with them in the book corner, play the role of customer in the hairdressers' shop or assist the brick layers who are creating "a super large football stadium". Their possible contributions are carefully planned beforehand with the teacher, and sometimes also rehearsed.

Parents who are known to have special interests or expertise can be asked to act as *guest teachers*, again in close contact with the teacher. Think of a sculptor, a hairdresser or shopkeeper. In the theme "Babies" for instance, the children visit an infant welfare centre. Afterwards the centre's infant nurse visits the school and participates in the children's role-play. She demonstrates how to bathe the baby, how to hold and dry it, how to control the temperature of the bath water and so on. In this way the children learn many new roles, words and concepts. The children have lots of opportunities to use what they have newly learned. Another example is a parent teaching children how to use a sewing machine in order to make fancy dresses for a fairy play. She helps children to take measurements, draw designs, choose the right materials etc. She lends a hand when some techniques are too difficult. In one of the other schools a father acts as expert when making tepee's with the children, for their play in the theme "Indians". In a multicultural school during the theme "My family", one of the fathers plays with the children some of the games he knows from his own childhood and which he also plays at home with his children. In "Professions" one of the mothers owns a hairdresser's shop and is a favourite guest who shows how to create different Surinam hairstyles. One can imagine how fascinating all this is for young children, how many new words are added to their vocabulary and how "big" they feel when they play hairdressers themselves.

All of these examples not only stimulate contacts between school and parents, but also improve mutual interest and contacts between them (Fig. 11.3).

Fig. 11.3 One of the mothers helps in the class' kitchen

Concluding a Theme

At the end of a theme period, parents often assist in concluding the theme with an exhibition, a show or performance for all children and their parents. At that moment not only teachers and children reflect on what they have undertaken and learned; the participating parents do the same. Attending the presentations and watching their children and other parents' reactions often results in closer contacts with the school.

Coffee Meetings About Educational Practices

When parents are a little more acquainted with classroom activities, they often have questions, comments, or suggestions. Therefore many schools organise so-called coffee meetings (originally set up as informal contact venues for parents) to discuss important developmental issues like children's language, literacy development, or religious education (Peters 2009). This is the place where parents and teachers bring in their concerns or ideas. Usually one of the teachers participates and takes care of constructing a meaningful programme and presentation, and sometimes external guests are invited, depending on the point of interest.

Of course coffee or tea comes first, after which different kinds of activities take place like observation in classrooms, trying out children's materials, sorting out picture books, a visit to the library and so on. The parents ask questions and discuss with the teacher what they have heard and seen. The teacher answers questions and explains, stimulates the parents' narratives and connects comments and opinions. The intention is to promote the parents' input, to reflect that opinions can differ amongst people, and to emphasise the value of differences in a learning community.

An example is the theme "Clothes". In the classroom a clothes shop and a shoe shop are set up where children can play. A small group of parents joins in with role-playing. Children and parents show each other the clothes they like to wear and exchange ideas about their favourite dresses and shoes. After school time all parents are invited to attend play activities in a clothes market in the school building. Yet another example we want to refer to is from the theme "All children in the picture". Teachers present group activities they have filmed, e.g. activities which are more or less focused on spoken language; for instance play at the story table with picture books, or (pretend) reading and writing in the kitchen corner. Observations of the ways teachers interact with the children to promote language development provide parents with a role model for their interactions at home. Observations and discussions help parents to recognise their children's language development and to reflect on the important role of adults in this.

Teachers notice that parents who attend the coffee meetings now talk to each other more often. They recognise each other's experiences and like to talk about their children, about educational matters and their own backgrounds. It becomes easier for them to approach teachers with questions or shared experiences, for instance about vocabulary and language matters.

Through these events and narratives parents become increasingly involved in education at school and understand more easily what their children experience.

Parents Learning More About Language Development

Inviting parents to join in with meetings as described above, is in fact a very delicate matter. Teachers should avoid the impression that they intend to instruct parents on how to rear their children. On the other hand, parents often do want to learn more about ways to support their children's development and learning. In our experience, schools can safely appeal to parents' interest and responsibilities in educational matters, if they make real efforts to explain their own motivations for working with children in the way they do. Because of these honest explanations, parents will easily be prompted to refer to their own experiences with their children's vocabulary or special interests. In such cases it is only natural to exchange ideas about interactions and activities between parents and children at home.

The following is an example from a school that takes initiatives to involve parents in matters of children's language development (Hagenaar et al. 2008). The school wants to bring language development and literacy to the parents' notice. During six meetings they explore issues like television programmes for children, going to the library, buying children's books, using play scripts, and literacy in everyday events.

After welcoming the parents, the teachers take care of several explorative activities in the groups. Parents can examine children's play and work, and may join in with thematic activities, particularly looking at language issues. They may visit a library with a group of children, look at an exhibition of children's work or at the theme books that are on display, and read information about the importance of reading together and about the library's services.

When concluding the theme, there is always something for children and parents to take home.

Pedagogical Support for Parents

The coordinator of a multicultural Developmental Education school, Stiena, notices that parents talk spontaneously with her about child rearing issues at home (Duijzer 2008). In everyday contacts they readily speak about the problems they face at home, and ask the teacher how to manage difficult situations. Therefore, Stiena considers offering parents pedagogical support and thinks about ways to do this. She does not approve of currently available training strategies and decides to construct a new course for parents. Her course consists of ten meetings and starts with a group of ten parents, seven Dutch and two or three from different cultural origins. She prefers mixed culture groups because this supports cultural integration through cooperation and learning together. The course takes place in the school building.

During the first meetings the parents themselves are at the centre: the conversations focus on who they are, on their own upbringing, and how they were as children. Then they discuss at length how they communicate with their own children and talk about building up a sound relationship, actively listening to the children, and being responsive to them. The topics for the following meetings are: what is it you strive for in bringing up your children? Which options do you choose? The parents are asked: suppose you wish your children to become self-supporting and independent. Then the teacher helps them to understand that this choice means that parents must encourage their children to do things by themselves. In this way the parents are prompted to reflect on what upbringing actually means and on the different ways in which they can raise their children. They begin to realise that the confidence they instil in their children may stimulate them to build up positive self-esteem and to become independent and responsible for themselves.

In every meeting the parents make plans for what they want to try out and practice at home. Their questions are the starting point for the next meeting and the teacher joins in with the parents' positive experiences to keep the reflection process going. For instance, they can discuss the effects of positive attention and giving compliments. Sometimes, Stiena stimulates the discussion by bringing in examples from pedagogical situations with her own children. She also provides books and magazines that give information about child rearing issues, ranging from professional literature to popular magazines. She considers this important, because information can open discussions about differences and similarities in pedagogical matters, and about the question of how the parents would like to act themselves. Finally, suggestions for home work activities are matched with the discussion outcomes. The parents formulate assignments for themselves about what they want to practice. For instance: "Next week I shall try to listen more actively to my children".

This approach is clearly based on Developmental Education principles. Remember the developmental prerequisites like self-esteem (see for example Chap. 4) for young children. Parents too must have a sense of well-being and involvement in order to be able to improve the relationship with their children. Joint discussions about child rearing issues are a meaningful activity in which the teacher mediates. When this is stimulated, the parents' motivation to participate can grow. Their questions are followed up by discussions and information on new insights and experiences. They are encouraged to try out what kind of actions or decisions are most appropriate in their home situations. The parents also keep logbooks or diaries about their actions and learning experiences.

In her evaluation of the course, Stiena comments that she can follow the parents' development. They become more self-confident and talk about child rearing with more pleasure than before. "I have learned a lot and am more aware of my role as a parent", one of the parents writes in an evaluation. Even at school these parents act differently and seem to have fewer problems with the children. Finally, they are really "in charge" as parents.

Educating Parents

Coach Adèle and her colleague Vera work at an almost completely "black" school and made a plan for the improvement of parent contacts. Every month these non-Dutch parents are invited for a coffee meeting and to suggest topics for conversations. Additionally, Adèle and Vera arrange theme mornings. They lead these mornings themselves, and sometimes guests from outside the school are invited to do so. Their ultimate goal is to strengthen parental commitment. The topics at these morning meetings are always about actual themes in the children's classrooms. During the theme "The market", for instance, a real market stall with different kinds of fruit gives parents the opportunity to do their shopping and use Dutch in the interactions. In pairs they tell each other about the fruit they chose. Then they make drawings of the fruit and consider a recipe for a fruit dish, with the help of both coaches and cookery books. After that the whole group talks about making fruit desserts. Later on they visit the classrooms to watch the children and teachers work together about the market in the neighbourhood.

Another example is the theme "Going to the zoo". Parents are encouraged to make word fields, just like the children do. They take a look at the theme's exposition table in the classroom and choose the animal that most appeals to them. In pairs they tell each other why they chose this particular animal. Next they discuss what else they would like to know about it and then use information books to find answers to their questions. If necessary, both coaches help, being their more knowledgeable partners, for instance by reading the texts and writing the answers with them. In the end all parents come together to look at each other's work and to discuss the outcomes of investigations. And later, back at home, they continue the discussion with their own children.

Regularly, guests from outside the school join in the morning meetings to offer information. A library employee, for instance, talks about her favourite book and serves as a model for the parents at the same time. Pairs of parents then choose two books; they discuss the content and what they like about them, or what they find rather difficult. Afterwards the interactions continue, now about the response to this meeting: what was appreciated and what was new for the parents?

Guests often come to the school but it also happens that parents pay a visit to a specialised person or a particular institute, for instance a local health centre. The coaches themselves are often a source of information for the parents who, for instance, would like to know more about the care for children with learning problems and about schools for special education. These points of interest are often welcome, as parents sometimes tend to be concerned about their child needing extra help. Now there is an opportunity to correct certain prejudices about children with a handicap or a behaviour disorder. Parents actually learn that in Developmental Education each child is considered special (see also Chap. 10 of this volume).

Conclusions

Educational partnership between parents and school is for the benefit of children's development. The examples drawn from Dutch Developmental Education schools strengthen our conviction that this claim can be realised. When the school takes parents seriously and makes them feel welcome, the basis for joint responsibility is laid. When parents become meaningfully involved in their children's activities and development at school, the need for reflecting the children's developmental opportunities at home is born. When parents join in classroom practices, a new zone of proximal development opens in both parent and teacher development in becoming educational partners.

We hope and expect that these perspectives of a Developmental Education approach also increase the parent's self-esteem and even support the "empowerment of parents". Ultimately, the children will benefit from this.

References

Booijink, M. (2007a). *Handreiking: Terug naar de basis. Mogelijkheden voor het verbeteren van de communicatie tussen leerkrachten en allochtone ouders in het primair onderwijs* [Helping hand: Back to the basics. Possibilities for improving communication between teachers and parents from other origins in primary education]. Leiden: Leiden University.

Booijink, M. (2007b). *Onderzoeksrapport. Terug naar de basis* [Research report. Back to the basics]. Leiden: Leiden University.

de Wit, C. (2005). *Ouders als educatieve partner. Een handreiking voor scholen* [Parents as educational partner. A hand out for schools]. Den Haag: Q*Primair.

de Wit, C. (2008). *Partnerschap tussen ouders en school* [Partnership between parents and school]. 's-Hertogenbosch: KPC Groep.

de Wit, C., Beek, S., & van Rooijen, A. (2007). *Samen kun je meer dan alleen. Educatief partnerschap met ouders in primair en voortgezet onderwijs* [Together one can do more than alone. Educational partnership with parents in primary and secondary education].'s-Hertogenbosch: KPC Groep en Q*Primair (Den Haag).

Duijzer, S. (2008). Opvoeden, een kwestie van respect [Bringing up children. A matter of respect]. *Zone, 4*, 16–18.

Epstein, J. L. (1995). School/family/community Partnerships. Caring for the children we share. *Phi Delta Kappan, 76*(9), 701–712.

Fleer, M. (2005). *A socio-historical analysis of the formation of everyday knowledge and schooled knowledge in economically disadvantaged communities. Cognitive blocks and pedagogical gaps*. Melbourne: Monash University.

Hagenaar, J. (2009). Spelen en leren in de onderbouw [Play and learning in the early grades]. In *Samen, oudercontacten in ontwikkelingsgerichte scholen*. Alkmaar: De Activiteit.

Hagenaar, J., Pompert, B., Weijers, A., & Peters, I. (Eds.). (2008). *Levensecht Leren. Verslag van het GOA/BSN Project Samen investeren in ontwikkelingskansen van de Capelse jeugd* [Lifelike learning. Report of a project about investing in development]. Alkmaar: De Activiteit.

Hargreaves, A. (2003). *Teaching in the knowledge society. Education in the age of insecurity.* New York: Teachers College Process.

Karpov, Y. Y. (2005). *The neo-Vygotskian approach to child development.* Cambridge: Cambridge University Press.

Moore, S., & Lasky, S. (1999). Parents involvement in education: Models, strategies and contexts. In F. Smit, H. Moerel, K. van der Wolf, & P. Sleegers (Eds.), *Building bridges between home and school* (pp. 13–18). Nijmegen/Amsterdam: ITS/SCO-Kohnstamm Instituut.

Onderwijsraad. (2010). *Ouders als partners. Versterking van de relaties met en tussen ouders op school* [Parents as partners. Enforcing the relations with and between parents at school]. Den Haag: Onderwijsraad.

Overmaat, M., & Boogaard, M. (2004). *Neemt ouderparticipatie af? Stand van zaken en tips voor ouderraden* [Is parent participation receding?] Amsterdam: SCO-Kohnstamm Instituut.

Peters, I. (2009). Koffie-ochtenden in de groep [Coffee mornings in the group]. In *Samen, Oudercontacten in ontwikkelingsgerichte scholen*. Alkmaar: De Activiteit.

Smit, F., Driessen, G., & Doesborgh, J. (2005). *Opvattingen van allochtone ouders over onderwijs: tussen wens en realiteit* [Opinions of parents from different backgrounds : Between wish and reality]. Nijmegen: Instituut voor Sociale en Toegepaste Wetenschappen.

Smit, F., Sluiter, R., & Driessen, G. (2006). *Literatuurstudie ouderbetrokkenheid in internationaal perspectief* [Literature study on parent involvement in international perspective]. Nijmegen: Institute voor Sociale en Toegepaste Wetenschappen.

van Brandwijk, D. (2009). Ouders doen mee in thematische activiteiten [Parents participate in thematic activities]. In *Samen, oudercontacten in ontwikkelingsgerichte scholen*. Alkmaar: De Activiteit.

van Kreveld, M. (2004). *Migrantenmoeders doen mee op school. Kansen en werkwijzen voor ouderparticipatie op multi-ethnische basisscholen* [Migrant mothers participate in school. Chances and methods for parent participation in multi-ethnic primary schools]. Utrecht: APS.

Weijers, A. (2009a). Aan de basis. Bouwen aan communicatie [At the basis. Buiding at communication]. In *Samen, oudercontacten in ontwikkelingsgerichte scholen*. Alkmaar: De Activiteit.

Weijers, A. (2009b). Van spelen komt lezen en schrijven [Play leads to reading and writing]. In *Samen, oudercontacten in ontwikkelingsgerichte scholen*. Alkmaar: De Activiteit.

Weijers, A. (2009c). Werken aan een veilig pedagogisch klimaat [Working at a safe pedagogical climate]. In *Samen, oudercontacten in ontwikkelingsgerichte scholen*. Alkmaar: De Activiteit.

Part III
Implementing the Play-Based Curriculum of Developmental Education

Chapter 12
Coaching the Transition Towards Developmental Education: Exploring the Situation with Teachers

Lorien de Koning

Changing Society

In our society we can observe various expressions of the deeper changes that are occurring. Children choose the clothes they wear, they use the computer if they feel like playing a game, they own a mobile phone for contacting their friends, and they use the internet if there is anything they want to know. Thomas Ziehe has summarised phenomena like these into two cultural changes influencing the relationship between young people and school (Ziehe 2000):

- Popular culture has become leading: Expressions of a consumption-based society, like pop music and video games, are now accepted worldwide and have become part of the dominant culture. This popular culture is not a negative phenomenon as such, but the effect of its increasing dominance implies the devaluation of the traditionally esteemed types of higher culture, such as art and science. The mental distance between young people and the established culture has become greater. The attitudes that are associated with the established ("higher") culture, such as elaboration and delight, are in danger of disappearing from the lives of young people.
- The personal life-world of the individual has replaced higher culture as the norm: young people nowadays have their own life-world, influenced by peer groups, the internet, media and pop music. This popular life-world has become the new ground on which decisions are based, such as whether something is interesting, relevant or fascinating enough to get involved in. Young people have become cultural self-suppliers. Everywhere they go, they take their life-world with them: to the sports club, the discotheque, and even the school. This life-world has

L. de Koning, M.Sc. (✉)
De Activiteit, National Centre for Developmental Education, Alkmaar, The Netherlands
e-mail: L.dekoning@de-activiteit.nl

B. van Oers (ed.), *Developmental Education for Young Children*, International
Perspectives on Early Childhood Education and Development 7,
DOI 10.1007/978-94-007-4617-6_12,
© Springer Science+Business Media Dordrecht 2012

become the centre of these young people's world view, resulting in a higher degree of freedom. However, the drawback associated with these changes is that the distance from other sources of knowledge, like the school and the teacher, has increased.

Young people's centeredness on their life-world is coupled with their orientation toward social relations. Young people connect to others who share key aspects of their life-world, leading to a decrease in opportunities for meaning-making. This is captured in the concept of tunnels of relevance. Young people's life-worlds are admitted into the popular culture, but not the immediate world, such as the culture of the family, the neighbourhood, or the school. In this way, the school runs the risk of becoming more and more of an isolated institution.

These cultural changes result in increasing alienation between the pupil and the teacher. In the classroom we can observe three kinds of problems, according to Ziehe (2000):

- Pupils do not accept "the unfamiliar". They only want knowledge that fits with their life- worlds – if it does not fit it is boring. This makes life difficult for teachers who were used to teaching without thinking about their pupils' intentions. They used to teach in a frontal way, offering the same knowledge to all pupils. Moreover, the distance between pupils and school books has increased, as many pupils no longer understand the formal language of these books very well.
- Social forms are changing, becoming altogether more "relaxed" in a way that fits with popular culture. Strict etiquettes, disciplinary rules and rigid behavioural norms are rapidly becoming the exception rather than the rule. Average everyday school situations are more open-ended, and also more diffuse. Pupils have less self-control, particularly in group settings, and may behave in ways that are under-structured. Of course the teacher has to find ways of dealing with all of this. Pupils are increasingly skilful with the use of new media like the internet, but less and less able to structure the avalanche of information they produce or encounter.
- The relation to the self is also changing. Young people have become better at observing their own and others' feelings, emotions and preferences, but it is harder for them to choose and to make decisions. Motivating oneself is not easy for these young people, making them more likely to want to escape or be mentally absent. They start doubting their decisions as soon as they have taken them, wondering whether they made the right decision, or feeling inadequate. Young people feel much more observed by themselves, their friends, and their parents. It is hard to accept not being perfect. Underneath their self-doubt there is a deep longing to be proud of oneself.

Modern schools in industrialised societies have to cope with the changes described by Ziehe. These changes in society demand a different approach in schools, as the problems in the classroom may result in pupils being less prepared for living their lives in our traditional society. The demands of the information society require excellence in performance and put their own claims on individuals, which are often at odds with the evolutions of popular culture. Pupils cannot handle all of this on their own, without support from a learning environment. The mission of Developmental Education is to support pupils in resolving tensions between these two contradictory developments. This concerns all school teams, teachers and parents. They need a new approach and a new conception of their responsibilities (see Chap. 3 of this volume), which should take into account that:

- Schools must work on helping their pupils accept in critical ways "the unfamiliar" that is offered to them by the surrounding established culture. Pupils need skills to be able to do this: to become good readers and writers, to change their attitude, to be capable of abstract thinking, to learn to accept that they can't succeed instantly at everything.
- Schools must create structured learning situations. Teacher and pupils are responsible for structuring the activities, which arises in interaction between teacher and pupil. The teacher furthermore is responsible for representing the cultural values, and simultaneously sticking to his or her personal pedagogical goals and values. Pupils, in turn, bring their own goals, interests, and possibilities (van Oers 2002). The focus is on the joint structure. Teachers in Developmental Education aim to do justice to pupils and their popular youth culture, and at the same time they want to prepare their pupils for critical participation in the information society. To do this, pupils have to build up knowledge and skills at a high level.
- Teachers must help their pupils broaden their range of vision in (self-) critical ways. They have to fulfil a bridging function between their pupils' life-worlds and the strange domains.

These are some tenets of the Developmental Education approach, which propagates the idea that education is more than the transmission of knowledge and skills to pupils; it includes giving attention to the personal development of the pupil. Pupils need to understand the cultural meaning of being human in a pre-given cultural environment. Development occurs by means of appropriating cultural tools and rules: the achievements of others must become part of oneself (Wardekker 2009). Learning, however, is not confined to knowledge of how the world is objectively put together. It is just as important to learn how to build self-confidence, awareness of situations, and ways of critically acting on them. The knowledge we possess is a product of previous generations. It consists of the designed and tested theories and solutions of previous generations for problems in everyday life. Our knowledge of the world is always connected to human practices and problems, so knowledge can be understood as a tool (e.g. historical or geographic) that enables us to understand our world better. We know that Amsterdam is not next to New York, because we possess information about the distance between these two cities (around 3,700 miles). These facts are mostly part of a scheme or model, like the knowledge about Amsterdam and New York as part of our global model of the world. In addition to children learning these facts, it is at least as important that they learn how to find them, and to decide in which situations to use them. Otherwise they cannot apply the knowledge they possess. To achieve this, children should learn skills and knowledge collaboratively in authentic situations, which they get offered from their society.

Education needs to be embedded in socio-cultural activities in which children get in touch with the cultural context, and get involved with meaningful and current issues in the world (see also Chap. 2 of this book).

Starting with Developmental Education

Schools that consider changing, or radically innovating, their educational approach have different reasons for doing this. In the initial stages of the innovation process it is important to take the school's reasons for innovation into account.

Why Do Schools Adopt Developmental Education?

Some newly established schools immediately chose Developmental Education and work with this approach from the very start. Management and teachers are familiar with the concept and are enthusiastic about it. They organise their school in line with the ideas propagated by Developmental Education. Over time, they continuously improve the ways in which they practice Developmental Education.

However, most of the schools adopt Developmental Education at some later point in time, after years of working from a different perspective. Today, about 5–10 % of all primary schools in the Netherlands have adopted Developmental Education. The most common reason for schools to implement Developmental Education is that they have motivational problems with pupils (see the three kinds of problems in the classroom in the previous section). Another common reason is that schools want to work with a shared and explicit educational concept. They explore different educational concepts and adopt Developmental Education when they conclude that it accords most with their own current views on good education.

In some cases the school management advocates Developmental Education because it acknowledges the potential of this concept for innovation and improvement of the teaching-learning process in the school. The approach requires collaboration between teachers, and engaged involvement with each other and with each other's work. The teacher takes a more pro-active role and is more involved with the organisation as a whole. It also tends to diminish "the cultural islands" to which teachers retreat as soon as they enter their own classrooms (Pompert 2004).

Implementing Developmental Education

Developmental Education is not implemented overnight, so schools have to make a decision about where they want to start. Most schools start with the implementation of Basic Development in the lower grades (see Chap. 4 of this book for more information). After a few years, they take a next step by introducing the concept in the higher grades of the school. After making a conscious decision about where in the school the implementation should start, the school decides which component of Developmental Education they want to implement first. As the Developmental Education approach advocates a play-based curriculum, the implementation in the lower grades centres on "the play activities", while for the higher grades, the implementation's core component concerns "the inquiry activities". These core activities connect to other core activities, such as reading and writing, mathematics, or dialogue. The implementation, however, is not imposed on the team or the teachers, but collaboratively constructed by the teachers and the guiding coach. The actual quality of the implementation depends on the personal skills and intentions of the teachers. Teachers change their educational approach in close collaboration with both their colleagues and their pupils. Furthermore, it is strongly recommended that Developmental Education is implemented with professional support. The teacher must work together with someone who is not part of the school staff in order to find ways to change and improve the teaching approach on the basis of new concepts and values. This does not mean, however, that it is a top-down approach: "[The implementation] should be a joint activity, in which the innovator accepts responsibility for the quality of teaching, significantly supports the teacher, and reflects on the teaching as well as on his or her own activity. By participating in such innovative activities, the teacher becomes more of an innovator" (van Oers et al. (2003, pp. 112). In each case, a zone of proximal developmental is constructed in a collaborative manner (see also Chap. 2 of this book). The biggest challenge of these joint activities is to reflect on the teacher's practice as well as on the fundamental concepts of the teacher (see also Chap. 13 of this book). After many years of interdisciplinary working with schools, and exploring this challenge with a number of people from different professional backgrounds (teachers, innovators, teacher trainers, school counsellors, and academic researchers), van Oers et al. (2003, pp. 114) set up a support strategy consisting of three phases:

1. First the teachers have to recognise basic elements of Developmental Education in their own teaching actions and their own practices, and learn to appreciate their potential value for the solution of their classroom problems.
2. In the second phase, teachers shift from mere reflection on classroom activities towards the actual implementation of some elements of Developmental Education in their own classroom.
3. Finally, in the third phase, teachers analyse and reflect on their own role as educators. They learn how to reflect on their education activities and interactions with pupils, and understand how to improve their activities and how to draw conclusions for further action.

Starting with Developmental Education in School

There are several ways to start working with Developmental Education. On the basis of many years of experience in guiding schools in the implementation process towards applying the Developmental Education approach, we have been able to identify a number of important conditions for successful implementation:

- Implementation of a new educational concept is a collaborative process that teachers engage in together with their colleagues and all the other members of the school team. Working with Developmental Education means changing the culture of the school in a fundamental way. Instead of emphasising only the subject matter of teaching, it means customising the subject matter to the specific interests of the pupil. If teachers want to teach something to a pupil, they need to know what is on the pupil's mind and what is interesting for him or her. This means they need to change their approach from transmission to guided co-construction. And this is not just a matter of a change in the classroom, but also of transforming the school system as a whole to create a favourable institutional context that promotes ongoing learning in both teachers and pupils (see also Chap. 17 of this volume). Such a whole-systems change is possible only if everybody is involved. Furthermore, the necessary cultural change in the school can succeed only if everybody supports it. Is it also important for teachers to have "buddies" in the learning process? This enables them to establish a zone of proximal development in their shared activity, and to become a community of inquiry. A community of inquiry connects those who are exploring the same subject through their joint activities and questions, such as: "How can I implement Developmental Education in my classroom?" In a community of inquiry, all the participants collect knowledge about this issue, starting out from their personal questions.
- Everybody, from teacher to principal, has an active role to play in the transformation, because they are all involved in maintaining the school's culture, and therefore in any change of that culture. If the implementation is to succeed, everybody will need to develop new skills and knowledge, and assume responsibility for their own development. Of course, there is also a shared responsibility, as the school's goals can only be achieved if everybody is willing and able to work towards them.
- Teachers and coaches need to start with a collaborative exploration of Developmental Education with the school team as a whole, before implementing it. Why? Because in every school team each member of the team has a different view of what this concept means and what its implications are. Therefore, it is critical for the team to build up a shared understanding of Developmental Education. The best way to do that is by participating in good practices of Developmental Education (see also Chap. 1 of this book). By so doing the teacher will gain personal experience of the difference in educational approaches. Of course, as was mentioned previously, the teacher needs to be guided in this process by a more experienced and informed learning partner. Moreover, it is important to come to an agreement on the duration of the implementation. That means a rigorous agreement stating which part of the day the teacher can work on these practices, and which education goals must be achieved in this period. In addition, the agreement should also include the specific questions a teacher has about working with Developmental Education, and information on how the teacher is going to explore these questions. The experience the teacher builds up needs to be framed in a theoretical conception, so the teachers can develop a realistic view of Developmental Education, together with the other school team members.

- Teachers and coaches have to acknowledge that each individual is at a different level of development, but that together they are working towards the same goals. The school team has a shared goal, but all the members of the team take individual steps to achieve that shared goal. It is important to clarify these steps and the expectations about them, so everybody understands where their colleagues are in their own development.

  Teachers need to take ownership of their own development. A good way to do this is by working with inquiry questions (Pompert 2004). First, they formulate all their questions about Developmental Education. They then continue to formulate a way of finding the answer for each of their questions. Next is the drafting of an inquiry plan, and taking action to accomplish it. This produces a lot of data which teachers will need to interpret. For the interpretation of the data, teachers need a critical friend or an experienced learning partner.

The principles for promoting developmental learning among pupils then, are valid for the teachers' developmental learning as well (also see Chap. 2 of this book).

An Example of Implementation in a Dutch School

A number of years ago a school in Gouda, a city in the mid-western part of the Netherlands, decided to innovate its educational approach. After several years of working with a traditional curriculum they began to experience its drawbacks. The most important of these concerns were their pupils' lack of involvement with their own learning process, which was overly centred on the teacher's transfer of knowledge. As pupils learn in a variety of ways, and at very different speeds, this approach no longer fit their pupils' needs. Based on these experiences, the school team started exploring different educational approaches. After a few years of exploration, supported by a number of educational consultancies, the school team decided that Developmental Education best fit their educational needs, values and expectations. The school wanted to implement Developmental Education in both the lower and the higher grades, so the whole school was involved in the implementation from the start, and all teachers joined the process. The school decided that professional support was necessary for this innovation to be successful. They turned to "De Activiteit" (National Centre for Developmental Education) for professional guidance. The author of this chapter was one of the employees of "De Activiteit", who was in charge of this implementation.

The Intake

We started the implementation process with an intake conversation, in which all members of the school team (from principal to teacher) got the opportunity to ask questions and to share hopes and expectations. This can be done in a group conversation, but it is often more effective to have private conversations, since people generally speak more freely about their thoughts and personal concerns. In addition to these conversations, we visited all the classes to observe teachers' current ways of working. Together, these conversations and observations formed our baseline assessment of the teachers' skills and knowledge. We considered:

- *The learning environment*: Were thematic books used in the classroom? Did pupils share their questions and interests in the classroom? Was there a place for play activities? Were there interesting props for play activities? Were the materials accessible for the pupils? Were pupils involved in the work activities?
- *The teacher role*: To what extent were the following capabilities present and visible: deliberately grouping pupils, working with the group as a whole, working in small groups or pairs, giving different types of instructions, designing meaningful activities, making connections between the different activities, observing and registering pupils' development, being aware of pupil interaction?

Everything we observed in the classroom, we shared with the teacher. This also led to interesting new questions and perspectives. At the school we observed a lot of the core components of Developmental Education in the learning environment. Teachers were already trying to stage play activities in their classrooms and had built some knowledge and skills in doing so. Based on their experience, they had questions such as: How do I involve all pupils in the play activities? How do I keep their attention for the activities for a period of 6 weeks? How do I prepare a theme period together with the other teachers? These questions were great starting points for a shared exploration among the teachers. The teachers had to recognise the questions their colleagues were wrestling with, and figure out the position of their team as a whole. So after the individual conversations and the consultations, we arranged a meeting with the whole team where we shared our initial questions about Developmental Education. We stuck the team's questions up on the wall and let teachers present their queries to each other (Pompert 2004; Janssen-Vos 2008; Kramer 2009):

Why do you as a teacher want to work with the Developmental Education approach?
What are your personal questions about Developmental Education?
What are the most important topics we discussed after the consultation?
What questions remain?

The questions that remained after these deliberations became the departure points for the next meeting for the exploration of Developmental Education. For the teachers of the school in Gouda, the shared questions turned out to be very important. They wanted to make them visible in the school, so they set up their own "wall of questions" in the coffee room.

In addition to the exchange of these questions, for the intake to be concluded it was important to agree on the specifics of the implementation process. Together with the whole school team, we found agreement on the following questions:

- What are we going to do precisely?
- How much time are we going to take for this work?
- How much room is there for our personal development?
- What are our goals?
- Which of these goals needs individual work, and which of them relates to our personal development?
- What would be the design of the implementation process?

This agreement constituted a shared foundation for the start of the implementation. With the school in Gouda we agreed on the following workplan:

- In the first year of implementation we would start with an exploration of Developmental Education that would involve the whole team. This exploration would be anchored in one theme that we would accomplish together with the whole school team.
- We would be working on this school theme for 8 weeks.

   - The goals for the lower grades were:

     (a) Working with the themes in play activities, particularly focusing on literacy activities that followed from them.
     (b) The following teacher skills:

       - working with themes and building up a theme in several stages.
       - using instruments of Developmental Education for clarifying the educational goals for a theme and activities, such as the circle of Basic Development (Janssen-Vos 2008) and the HOREB models of observation (Janssen-Vos and Pompert 2007; also see Chap. 4 of the present volume).
       - designing play activities so that all pupils could join in and be involved.
       - designing functional reading and writing activities in line with the theme and the play activities.
       - guiding the play activities and knowing when to follow the pupil's initiative, when to join in, and knowing how to design a cognitive challenge in the shared activity.
       - guiding collaborative learning.
       - learning how to use a journal and specify the planning of guided activities.

Besides the goals for the lower grades, we also made specific goals for the teachers of the higher grades (de Koning and Poland 2009). From this agreement, all members of the school team started with formulating learning goals and creating a plan on how to achieve them, with one condition: their goals for personal development should align with the school process. After 8 weeks of exploring, we evaluated the process and agreed on the next implementation steps.

Table 12.1 Stages in thematic activities

Stage 0	Stage 1	Stage 2	Stage 3	Stage 4
The preparation stage:	The exploration stage:	The implemen-tation stage:	The concluding stage:	The evaluation stage:
Did we chose the right theme? Were there enough good materials?	The teacher introduced the theme in the classroom.	The play activities went into full swing.	The teacher concluded the theme with the children.	The teacher registered the output and experiences.

The First Year of Exploration

We started the exploration with a team meeting, in which we presented some basic principles of Developmental Education. Just as pupils needed to learn skills and knowledge in authentic situations, the teachers also needed to learn about Developmental Education in ways that were embedded in their own teaching activities. Therefore we designed activities for this meeting that combined classroom work with an understanding of the theoretical framework. In this way, the teachers got involved with the concept of Developmental Education through meaningful activities. In this meeting, they personally experienced the activities that they would be undertaking with their pupils. The teachers found this very valuable. To begin with, we gave the teachers a theoretical framework about how to work with themes in their classrooms during a period of 6–8 weeks. However, during these weeks teachers were not performing the same activities all the time, because the theme was built up in five stages: the preparation stage, the exploration stage, the implementation stage, the concluding stage and the evaluation stage (see Table 12.1).

In our experience, these stages gave teachers a handle on working with themes. Once they knew how to build up a theme, they needed to learn what types of activities fit in with each of the five stages. The best way to learn about these activities is to experience them. So for the school in Gouda we set up a theme for this first meeting. We chose to use the theme "Chocolate", because we worked with the school team in December, a month which includes several holidays that are traditionally celebrated by eating chocolate, among other things (e.g. Sinterklaas, Christmas, and New Years' Eve).

The teachers could not learn all the activities belonging to all five stages in one meeting. In this first meeting, we started working on the activities belonging to stage 0 and stage 1, since these covered the activities that the teachers would need first. In a later meeting, we worked on activities from stages 2, 3 and 4. Our educational counselling for the school team in Gouda had the following design (Table 12.2).

The activities in stage 1 of the theme we called the introductory activities. They were intended to provoke shared explorations by the teacher and the pupils on the new theme. They should trigger certain thinking processes and help create a shared foundation.In order to trigger these processes, the introductory activities had to meet a number of specific requirements (Janssen-Vos 2008):

Table 12.2 Working schedule in the first year of implementation

Date:	Activity:	Result:
November	Intake with the whole school team	Baseline measurement of the knowledge and skills of the teachers
		Any questions by the team about Developmental Education had been clarified
		Everybody was aware of the next steps in the process and there was clarity around the goal
December	First meeting with the whole school team	Theoretical framework
		Teachers learned activities for stage 0 and 1
First week of January	The teachers introduced their theme in the classroom	Start of the theme
Second week of January	Every teacher got a personal consultation in the classroom	The teacher got improvement suggestions
		The teacher asked practical questions
Third week of January	Second meeting[a]:	Theoretical framework
	1: with the teachers of the lower grades	Teachers learned activities for stage 2
	2: with the teachers of the higher grades	
First week of February	Every teacher got a personal consultation in the classroom	The teacher got improvement suggestions
		The teacher asked practical questions
Third week of February	Third meeting[a]:	Theoretical framework
	1: with the teachers of the lower grades	
	2: with the teachers of the higher grades	Teachers learned activities for stage 3
End of February	The teachers concluded the theme with the children in the classroom	End of the theme
March	Final session with the whole school team	Teachers learned activities for stage 4, the evaluation stage
		Theoretical framework of Developmental Education after having had the experience
		We discussed the next step of implementation

[a]For this meeting we split the school team in two groups: the teachers of the lower grade and the teachers of the higher grade. We worked in this meeting with both groups separate

- They were challenging;
- They raised new questions;
- They gave insight into what knowledge and skills the pupils already had;

- Together, they had a certain cohesion and dynamic;
- They illuminated new perspectives on the chosen theme;
- They were interdisciplinary;
- Pupils would be actively exploring the new subjects;
- Pupils would be working together in varying groups.

To ensure that the teachers included all these characteristics in their design of their introductory activities, they had to experience the activities themselves. Therefore, in the first meeting we started with the model theme of "Chocolate". I brought in different types of chocolates that Dutch people eat when they celebrate the December holidays. I chose one chocolate and shared my personal experience associated with this piece of chocolate with the teachers. Many teachers recognised my experience and started to share some of their experiences around it. Ten minutes later, all teachers had chosen a piece of chocolate and shared their personal experience with their colleagues. After this exchange, I paired up the teachers and instructed them to choose one of their two chocolates, to observe it closely and to answer the following two questions:

- What do you already know about the object?
- What would you like to know about it?

I then put two pairs together, so they formed a group of four persons. In this group they summarised their answers in two word fields. One word field contained everything they knew about chocolate, while the other word field contained everything they would like to know about chocolate. The teachers then returned to their pairs and chose their favourite question from the word field. After choosing their question, the teachers returned to the whole group and presented it to their colleagues.With the group we clustered the different questions. As a facilitator, I then stepped into a teacher role and asked them: "Imagine we want to know all this about chocolate: how is it made, how long does it take to make chocolates, what is in the chocolate, and what is the difference between milk chocolate and dark chocolate? Finally, what kind of socio-cultural practices do we need in the classroom that may help pupils to develop these understandings?"

"A chocolate factory" said one of the teachers. "Yes, indeed!" I answered. "And in addition to learning about chocolate in this play activity, pupils can also work on their literacy, conversations and numeric-mathematical activities!"

Now the teachers understood the essence of the introductory activities and had learned how to introduce the theme to their pupils. Now it was time to return to the teachers' daily practice. They chose their own theme subject, and by doing so, completed the preparation stage of the theme (stage 0). In our experience, many teachers find it difficult to choose a good theme. Sometimes they feel hesitant to make a choice, thinking that their pupils should choose the theme, as they are the ones who should find it interesting. Obviously, it is only natural to take the pupils' interests seriously into account, but it is still the teacher who has to decide on the theme, because he or she will be setting and monitoring the educational goals. For choosing a workable theme, the following should be taken into account:

- *The meanings for children*: What do they talk about amongst themselves? What catches their interest?
- *Current events*: What's happening in the world around us? What's in the news?
- *The intentions of the teacher*: What subject matter do you want to introduce? What are the educational goals?
- *The socio-cultural practices:* Can you connect the theme to familiar socio-cultural practices, like: the chocolate factory, the book-store, the fashion show, the tourist information office, the restaurant, the art gallery etc.?
- *A broad theme:* How easy is it to connect different subjects to the theme?
- *Look beyond the interests of the pupils*: Will the theme open up a new world for the pupils? Will the theme enable you to connect new knowledge to the things your pupils already know?

Using this summary, the teachers in Gouda were able to choose a workable theme. In the lower grades, some teachers chose to use the theme "The animal doctor", while other teachers chose "the museum". In the higher grades, some teachers chose to use the theme "The newspaper", while other teachers used "Elections". After choosing a workable theme, the teachers proceeded to work on stage 0, the preparation stage. The first ideas about subject matter, goals and interesting issues were put down on paper. From these first ideas, the teachers started to design the introductory activities. This was followed by the exploration of the theme with the pupils, ending with a summary of what they already knew about the theme and what they would like to know. The introductory activities gave teachers a sense of what would be interesting for their pupils, allowing them to go back to their original plan and adjust it as needed.

The teachers of the school in Gouda enthusiastically introduced the new themes into their classrooms. During the first week, they carried out six introductory activities to explore the theme with the children, supported by personal consultations with their coach in the classroom. We observed the introductory activities and discussed the outcomes, giving the teacher the opportunity to make immediate adjustments. When the teachers were ready to proceed to stage 1 of the theme, we set up the next team meeting to help them through it. We evaluated the introductory activities and connected their experiences to our shared understanding of Developmental Education. We also had a look at our "wall of questions" to see if there were any questions we could now answer. Then we were ready for the next step, in which the teachers practised the typical activities belonging to stage 2, the implementation stage. The teachers had to design play activities in such a way that all pupils would be able to join in, and link functional reading and writing activities to these play activities. We worked with the following cycle:

1. Explore the new piece of knowledge or skill, using the theoretical framework for the play activities (Janssen-Vos 2008; see also Chap. 4 of this volume).
2. Recognise the play activity in a video clip of a good practice we developed at "De Activiteit", and articulate what has been recognised.
3. Promote hands-on experiences during the meeting.
4. Implement the new skill in your own practice.
5. Evaluation and reflection.

During the implementation of the activities in their own practices, the teachers got a new personal consultation in the classroom. We observed the play activities and discussed their outcomes. The teachers worked on their personal learning points, and when we came to the end of the theme a few weeks later, we had the third meeting. This was a similar kind of meeting, but now the emphasis lay on the activities the teacher needed to perform in stage 3 of the theme, the concluding stage. After this meeting, the teacher was able to conclude the theme with the pupils. When all teachers concluded their themes, we organised the final session with the whole school team. We looked back at the themes and evaluated educational goals and subjects. We summarised teachers' experiences: Did they get to observe new behaviours or aspects of their pupils? Did they feel their themes worked successfully? The teachers of the school in Gouda were very enthusiastic, and had even arranged an open evening for all the parents to share the theme's outcomes. One of the teachers told us that her pupils had become much more involved in the classroom activities, and that they took much more initiative. Just before the open evening, we were hit by the news of the Haiti earthquake. Pupils were shocked and wanted to find a way to contribute to the aid effort. One of them came up with an idea: to ask the visitors to the open evening to make a contribution to the fund for Haiti. The teachers agreed with this proposal and the pupils further developed the plan. All of the school's pupils were involved in thinking about and designing activities (besides presenting their theme) that would bring in money for Haiti. Some pupils had made jewellery to sell, others sold snacks and drinks, there was art for sale; some pupils took care of pets, others sold the newspaper or gave a performance of some kind. In total, these activities brought in a total of € 5.000 for Haiti! Parents, teachers and pupils were very proud of the contribution they had been able to make, and the theme was concluded successfully.

The school team was particularly content with:

- The results in the classroom
- Links and connections between the subjects
- The meaningful and useful activities
- Proud and involved children
- The ability of the teachers to manage by themselves the process and the themes
- Teachers finding ways to deepen a subject without time pressure

The year after, the school team continued the process of implementing Developmental Education. They took the next step by increasing the number of themes from one to three per year. Working with these three themes, they wanted to develop their teachers' skills in designing theme activities. Moreover, they wanted to deepen the theme activities so that they would be useful and could be broadened to other functional activities. In order to achieve this, the teachers had to learn how to observe the development of their pupils closely, to register it and to design functional follow-up activities (compare Chap. 14 of this volume to see in more detail what this implies).

In the Classroom: The Teacher and Developmental Education

Adopting Developmental Education in the school leads to some challenges for teachers (see Chap. 13 of this volume for elaborations). The approach requires an attitude of inquiry in pupils, but also in the teachers. The biggest learning opportunities lie hidden in uncertainty, and tackling them requires courage. One director of a school for educational innovation once described three big challenges that lie ahead of teachers who step onto this path (van Dijck 2007):

- The teacher must learn to adopt the role of a conductor and change his ways of thinking and behaving. He can no longer take a rigid, timetable approach to his teaching. In this new role he must match the teaching to the characteristics and contributions of his pupils. The teacher will need to make his own choices about his teaching offerings.
- The teacher has to change his methods and organisation, in order to create space for experimenting with new methods.
- Engaging in a shared learning process together with all school team members. Aligning each person's ambitions and learning pace to form a cohesive team can be challenging.

These challenges came up in the work of teacher Leonie from the school in Gouda. In the early stages of her theme, Leonie was very reluctant to take initiatives, because she believed that all initiatives had to come from her pupils. She understood her role as a teacher to be one of a passive observer. After we observed the situation in Leonie's class for the personal consultation, we discussed the outcome of the activity with her. Leonie could accurately describe what she had seen in class and with individual pupils. But when she was asked about her next step and follow-up activity, Leonie looked puzzled: "Should I be thinking of that beforehand? The pupils should make the next step by themselves, right?" I explained to her that pupils will only take the next step if the teacher plays an active role in the activity. The teacher must prompt a zone of proximal development in the activity and encourage pupils to explore new action potential (see also Chap. 2 of this book). After having explained this, I supported Leonie in planning the follow-up activity for the play activity with "the animal doctor". On that day, Jorg, Anne and Samuel were engaged in the play activity. Samuel was the vet, and we observed that he had a hard time. He had several patients, but he could not remember which pet had which problem. So what were we going to do as a follow-up activity? Leonie suggested she could be part of the play activity to support Samuel in dealing with the trouble he was having. And that is what Leonie did. She played the role of doctor's assistant, so she could discuss with Samuel how he could remember all the different pets in his medical practice. This turned out to be a big step forward for Leonie. She made changes in her role as a teacher and experienced that this required a different way of thinking and behaving.

In addition to the changing nature of the teacher role, Developmental Education also requires a different learning environment. Play activities must become the centre of the learning environment. This means that, when you come into the classroom, you should be able to see instantly what the play is about. Besides being aware of where every activity takes place in the classroom, the teacher should also be looking at the materials that are being used in the activity. When the teacher adds paper, pencil, and an agenda to the play activity setting, the play will change and the pupils usually start drawing and writing things down in their play (Peters 2002).

It is also important that the pupils recognise the materials that are used in the play activities, so we recommend using real-world materials as much as possible, instead of toy materials (Nellestijn and Janssen-Vos 2005).

Another big challenge for the teacher in Developmental Education concerns the conversation activities. Because the curriculum is built up in the classroom, and teachers will want to involve pupils in the education activities, they need good conversation skills. They have to stimulate free communication, because it is important for all pupils' voices to be heard. Pupils should be able to create their own stories, in which they can learn how the language of our culture works. This will also enable them to learn thinking out loud so they can share their ideas for the theme and deepen them (Pompert et al. 2009). This means that the teacher needs to design a framework for the conversation, so that every pupil knows what is expected of him and what behaviour is allowed. The teacher manages the pupils taking turns and listens carefully to the ways in which pupils are thinking about the subject. Together, teacher and pupils try to come to a shared opinion on the subject, delivering new input for the play activity. The level of the teacher's involvement in the conversation depends on the teacher's goals. If he wants the pupils to develop their own constructions, then the teacher would not have much input in the conversation. He would only support the pupil in thinking out loud, and make sure that other pupils understand the constructions. The teacher can also add something to the conversation that the pupils do not know. In that case, the teacher has a different goal and therefore a different role in the conversation, e.g. a language-related goal such as vocabulary extension. Janssen-Vos (2003, p. 102) has developed these teacher's roles further into five "didactic impulses" (see also Chap. 4). All in all, the adoption of Developmental Education can be quite challenging for the teacher. However, teachers are not alone in meeting the challenges, as they can work together with colleagues, pupils, and coaches on developing an attitude of inquiry. And that can be a lot of fun!

References

de Koning, L., & Poland, M. (2009). *HOREB 2. Het Activiteitenboek* [The Activity Book]. Alkmaar: De Activiteit.

Janssen-Vos, F. (2003). Basic development: Developmental education for young children. In B. van Oers (Ed.), *Narratives of childhood* (pp. 93–109). Amsterdam: VU Press.

Janssen-Vos, F. (2008). *Basisontwikkeling voor peuters en kleuters* [Basic Development for preschool and lower grades]. Assen: van Gorcum.

Janssen-Vos, F., & Pompert, B. (2007). *HOREB-PO. Handelingsgericht Observeren, Registreren en Evalueren van Basisontwikkeling* [Action-Oriented Observation, Registration, and Evaluation of Basic Development]. Assen: van Gorcum.

Kramer, M. (2009). Van betekenisvolle vragen naar nieuwe kennis [From meaningful questions to new knowledge]. *Zone, 8*(1), 23–25.

Nellestijn, B., & Janssen-Vos, F. (2005). *Het materialenboek* [The Materials Book]. Assen: van Gorcum.

Peters, L. (2002). Bewust bemoeien: een leerkracht in ontwikkeling [Deliberately interfere: A teacher in development]. *Zone, 1*(4), 16–18.

Pompert, B. (2004). *Thema's en taal* [Themes and language]. Assen: van Gorcum.

Pompert, B., Hagenaar, J., & Brouwer, L. (2009). *Zoeken naar woorden* [Searching for words]. Assen: van Gorcum.

van Dijck, M. (2007). In een ontwikkelingsgerichte school trekken schoolleiding en team samen op [In a Developmental Education school, management and team collaborate closely]. *Zone, 6*(1), 25–26.

van Oers, B. (2002). Structuur in onderwijs. Orde en volgorde in ontwikkelingsgericht perspectief [Structure in education. Order and sequence in development-oriented perspective]. *Zone, 1*(1), 4–8.

van Oers, B., Janssen-Vos, F., Pompert, B., & Schiferli, T. (2003). Teaching as a joint activity. In B. van Oers (Ed.), *Narratives of childhood* (pp. 110–126). Amsterdam: VU Press.

Wardekker, W. (2009). De rol van kennis in OGO. [The role of knowledge in OGO (Developmental Education)]. *Zone, 8*(4), 4–6.

Ziehe, T. (2000). School and youth – A differential relation. Reflections on some blank areas in the current reform discussions. *Young, 8*(1), 54–63.

Chapter 13
Creating Knowledge and Practice in the Classroom

Bea Pompert

Characteristics of the Implementation of Basic Development

Building up a meaningful implementation trajectory for Developmental Education in the early years (Basic Development) takes at least 2–3 years. Our work in this area is consistent with innovative approaches that have been proposed by several cultural-historical researchers, like for example Tharp and his colleagues (Tharp and Gallimore 1988; Tharp et al. 2000), Wells and Claxton (2002) and Engeström (2005). We too take an explicit stance in the cultural-historical approach.

Fundamental principles are:

- Improving teaching and schooling is a joint activity in which all participants share their goals and also take a part of the responsibility.
- All participants work together as partners, helping each other in a continuous process of acting and reflection.
- All actors and actions in the system – the school – are committed to improving the learning processes of the children, including their broad development.
- The teachers take an active part in their own development and at the same time develop as participants in a community of practice. They develop inter-subjectivity at the levels of organisation, goals, practice and values. The teacher trainer is also a partner and participant in the classroom practice, clearly in a specific role and with her own responsibility to monitor the use of conceptual means.
- Discrepancies and differences of opinions are a rich source of opportunities to make real changes in the classroom.
- Teachers attach their own meanings to the given support and seriously take it into account for their own performance.

B. Pompert, M.Sc. (✉)
De Activiteit, National Centre for Developmental Education, Alkmaar, The Netherlands
e-mail: b.pompert@de-activiteit.nl

B. van Oers (ed.), *Developmental Education for Young Children*, International Perspectives on Early Childhood Education and Development 7, DOI 10.1007/978-94-007-4617-6_13,

The implementation trajectory itself is an outcome of continuous discourse among teachers, management team and teacher trainer (see also Chap. 12 of this volume for more details).

Redefining Effective and Responsible Teaching

During the past 20 years we have gained a rather good insight into the ingredients of successful developmental trajectories. In those schools teachers acquire important knowledge and competences on six main aspects of Basic Development:

(a) Play as a format for all children's activities;
(b) Embedded instructions in the context of play;
(c) Instructional conversations and revoicing;
(d) Developing a community in the classroom;
(e) Activity-oriented observation to build up learning trajectories for all children;
(f) Organise classroom activities in a flexible way: balance between whole class, small groups, pairs and individual activities.

While working with teachers on these issues over the past decades, it became clear that these six aspects can indeed be effectively employed by teachers in order to enact a form of developmentally appropriate teaching that they considered relevant for their own pedagogical responsibilities and for the children's future cultural participation as autonomous cultural identities. At the same time, however, it became clear that teachers often had to innovate many of their deeply rooted conceptions for a successful enactment of this form of responsible teaching in the context of Developmental Education (see also Chap. 3 of this volume).

I will discuss each of the above mentioned issues further below.

Play as a Specific Activity Format

Play is at the heart of Basic Development. In our work with teachers we bring in the conception of play as formulated by van Oers (see Chap. 2 of this volume; also van Oers 2010). We take play as a basic format of all core activities in the early years. This idea is evidently difficult for a lot of teachers. They have to change their ways of thinking on several aspects of teaching. In the first place they need to understand the parameters of play as a format, namely the type of rules that constitute the activity, the degrees of freedom that may be permitted to children, and the level of personal involvement that is necessary for meaningful learning. In the second place the teachers need to develop new insights into the relationship between play, development and learning processes.

Many teachers need time and support to acknowledge the richness of play and recognise the teaching opportunities and learning processes embedded in play.

For young children, fundamental learning is intrinsically related to meaningful play activities. Pretend play activities such as the shoe shop, the vet, living in a castle, and building a garage give the children a chance to operate in their role as the shoemaker, the patient, the knight or the motor mechanic. New knowledge and skills can deepen these roles, and the children are able to learn these in a meaningful way, especially when the teachers join in and relate their interventions to the questions the children generate.

An example:

In one of the schools we support, two teachers are working with a group of 6 and 7 year-olds. They work on the theme "Living in a castle". The teachers and the teacher trainer discuss all kinds of possible play activities and other core activities. The children build castles with blocks and construction materials, little clay stones and real building stones. Reflecting on these activities makes it possible to communicate about the number aspects of the constructions, and integrate mathematics into the activity, for instance, using schemes, reading floor plans, using special concepts and numbers to indicate the measurements of the building.

The teacher trainer acts as a partner in designing and models ways of relating this play to mathematics learning.

During the theme period the teacher trainer visits the teachers in their classroom.

One morning, one of the children brings in a problem. She wants to build a round tower, but does not know how to do so. The teacher shows interest and subsequently asks her pupils what they think about this problem. An interesting conversation unfolds and at the end of it, the group gives the following directions:

- You have to draw circles to build on;
- You can use a plate to make circles on cardboard;
- You need as many cardboard circles as the number of floors you want to build.

After this, three girls build the round tower, and one of them writes an account of their building activity. At the end of the morning the girls are invited to report their findings to the whole group (Fijma and Pompert 2002).

Afterwards the teacher and the teacher trainer discuss and reflect on this activity. They analyse the play characteristics, the mediating role of the teacher and the learning experiences of the different children. Together they try to define elements that may enhance the quality of future play activities.

Embedded Instruction

A lot of teachers believe in the direct-instruction model or recitation script for teaching children, especially if the children are believed to have low cognitive potentials or poor social capabilities. However, commitment to the Developmental Education point of view requires adjustments in teachers' assumptions about development and a change in the nature of their purposeful interactions. Teachers then must adopt a responsive and interactive way of instructing. Teaching should be accomplished as an act of "assisting performance" (Tharp and Gallimore 1988).

In order to achieve this, the teacher trainer brings in an important teaching tool: namely five didactic impulses that the teacher aims to employ in the interaction with pupils (Janssen-Vos 1997; see also Chap. 4 in this volume). The use of these multi-dimensional teaching strategies helps the teacher to assist children in their paths through their zone of proximal development. It gives information on how to build a balance between the actual potentials and meaning-making qualities of the children, and the developmental perspectives of the children and their achievement goals. The impulses are:

- *Orientation:* encourage pupils to reflect in advance on their ideas and plans; this entails deliberate attempts to build on pupils' previous knowledge and experience.
- *Deepening and structuring:* help to see the point and structure of the activity, the appropriate actions and language register.
- *Extension to other core activities:* help to connect to skills and knowledge from other activities for the enrichment of pupils' initial activity, for instance: connecting pupils' garage building with writing activities, such as making tickets and information posters.
- *Adding new actions:* introduce by modelling, instructional conversation or direct instruction new actions within the child's ongoing activity. These new actions should correspond with the motives of the child to accomplish the activity in the best way.
- *Reflection:* take every opportunity to look back on the activity. What went well, what steps were made, what problems needed an answer? Also try to look forwards: what lessons can we draw from specific reflections?

Teachers receive support in accomplishing these five impulses and relate them to embedded instructions on language, literacy, social studies and science.

Embedded instructions are defined as teaching activities that are:

- functional and meaningful for the pupils;
- related to various activities in the classroom;
- adaptive to different children and their learning styles;
- up-to-date: modern didactic strategies are combined with teaching opportunities.

Instructional Conversations and Revoicing

Basic Development comes to life in the classroom if the teacher succeeds in creating a safe and challenging culture of dialogue and polylogue. Pupils need to argue and discuss a lot both with each other and with the teacher. Instructional conversations are used to integrate actions and language and to ensure that children's everyday concepts become interrelated with new concepts and thoughts. One of the most important competences for the teacher is to revoice (O'Connor and Michaels 1996; see also Chap. 10 of this volume). "Revoicing" is a powerful instrument in the interaction with pupils. It starts with receiving the message of the child who is actively trying to speak out. Then the teacher reformulates the child's utterance in a specific way, without judging it as correct or incorrect. The reformulation is more than literal. By rephrasing the child's utterance the teacher returns the utterance for the child's evaluation and makes this utterance accessible for open discussion. The teacher deliberately revoices the child in such a way that his utterance becomes understandable to the other children and suitable for further meaningful conversation. The revoice is also important for the classroom conversation, because it aligns different points of view and gives children a chance to give a reaction and, if necessary, to reformulate the original utterance.

Children often highlight aspects of the utterances or deepen the utterances, and collaboratively give an appropriate response. Most teachers find revoicing a complex skill to apply and need supervision and support. The teacher trainer and the teacher together review a videotape of an instructional conversation and analyse elements of revoicing in order to become aware of possible improvements and formulate new steps.

Developing a Community in the Classroom

In Basic Development pupils may cooperate with their classmates in activities that are more complex than what they can understand when playing and working on their own. Therefore teachers need to build up a real community in their classrooms. There are a number of organisational measures that can be taken to build up an engaged community of learners through inquiry that goes beyond being merely a collection of pupils:

- *Meetings with the whole group.* These daily meetings create a safe and lively platform for all children to tell their personal stories and talk about the concerns and questions they have. Children experience the value of storytelling and listening to stories. Storytelling is an accessible form of language use for making sense of our lives. We use stories to give our lives form and structure. By structuring events and relationships in a story we understand things better. We understand each other better, because stories can connect minds and souls. Especially personal narratives about shared experiences establish inter-subjective affinity and empathy with others. The central meetings are also meant for making plans for future activities, and to evaluate and present results from play and work.
- *Instructional conversations in small groups.* Here instruction and conversations are woven together. Pupils learn to exchange their perspectives and understand-ings, accept joint meaning negotiation, and learn from each other. The teacher helps the pupils in weaving new concepts and ideas into existing knowledge.
- *Expert work.* Expert work is a form of cooperative learning. It is used to organise the exchange of understandings in the classroom. Pairs or small groups study a different subject or text. In a way, they become experts and prepare a presentation

for their classmates to discuss their findings. At the end all children participate and make use of all the knowledge they now collectively have. Expert work involves:

– question-generating;
– predicting and hypothesising;
– use of comprehension strategies;
– summarising;
– presenting;
– reflection and evaluation.

To build up a community of learners the teacher needs to understand that she herself is a member of this community, a member with a special role. She takes a mediating position and serves as a more knowledgeable partner, seeking every opportunity to improve the quality of the interaction. The teacher is an active participant and has a central role in arranging all kinds of social contexts for learning.

Activity-Oriented Observation to Build Up Learning Trajectories

In collaboration with their pupils, teachers need to construct specific and developmentally appropriate learning trajectories. Central to the design of such learning trajectories is the core ability to observe the pupils in their activities. This implies that teachers develop an ability to work and think simultaneously on two levels: they have to act as participants in the children's activities and at the same time reflect on the teacher-child interactions, think about productive questions and reactions, and keep in mind specific intended learning outcomes (van Oers and Pompert 1991). In such joint productive activities with the children, teachers can attach more and new cultural meanings to children's activities and promote the emergence of inter-subjectivity (see also Tharp et al. 2000). At the same time the teacher observes the child's performance and evaluates the ways in which the child adopts new actions from the teacher. By doing so, the teacher can also formulate new steps for future learning. These steps are actually hypotheses about the appropriate way children's development can be promoted. These new steps in the learning process have to be put into practice to see whether they are adequate and the guidance suitable. Reflection in action is crucial (see also Chap. 14 of this volume for further clarification).

This differs from most teachers' common practice: that is, assessing and controlling the results of the children's independent activity, individually and momentarily. Traditionally, teachers are trained to evaluate each child's performance in a static way. As a result, teachers don't use their knowledge about children's meanings nor take their own mediating role into account for the evaluation of the child's learning, or for the planning of further learning processes.

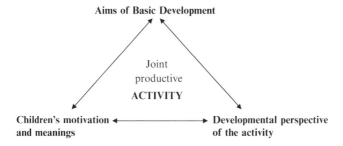

Fig. 13.1   Evaluation triangle for Basic Development

To help the teachers in creating new understandings of the evaluation and planning of learning processes in the classroom, the teacher trainer supplies this triangle diagram (Fig. 13.1).

In the centre we see which activity is taken as relevant for both the teacher and the pupils (for instance: playing in the shoe shop, constructing a race-track, writing a story). Working with this triangle gives the teacher insight into the following aspects and the relations between them:

- How does the child respond to this activity: participation, use of language, actions, meaning-making (is it correct and does it make sense?).
- The developmental perspective of the activity: empirically informed images of how the child should (and probably will) carry out this activity in the near future, when helped appropriately.
- How does it contribute to the aims of Basic Development (see Chap. 4 of the present volume).

The triangle-diagram has proven to be an effective tool for evaluating observational data from the classroom to make better decisions for appropriate learning trajectories for different groups of children.

Flexible Organisation

For effective participation in children's development, it is of course necessary that the teacher manages classroom activities and creates many opportunities for constructing pupils' zone of proximal development. Therefore the teacher has to organise classroom activities in a flexible way:

- Balancing between class work, work in small groups, and individual work.
- Balancing between homogenous and heterogeneous grouping.
- Balancing between independent and joint activity.

Fig. 13.2 Diagram for
organisational options

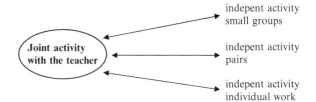

We know from our experiences that there are two important problems to overcome: "being everywhere and nowhere" and "speaking above all heads". Instead of wandering around the classroom or giving time consuming explanations, teachers need to join in the children's activities and seriously participate as a group member for a longer period. This is a necessary condition for the implementation of developmentally appropriate ways of guiding and directing, especially instructional conversations and dialogues (Tharp and Gallimore 1988).

Children need to learn to give substance to their own work for increasingly longer periods of time. Hence, they also have to learn how to solve problems independently, and make plans and exchange ideas with other children.

We use the following diagram for reflection on the available organisational options (Fig. 13.2).

The challenge is to use this diagram in an ongoing process of negotiation of meaning with other teachers. This negotiation process is in fact a joint reflection on theory concerning effective learning environments and improvements in the classrooms.

The teachers share their learning stories with each other. They highlight communalities and differences. Next they seek consensus about the differences and make new plans for further exploration in their own classrooms. Finally they evaluate their experiences personally, with the teacher trainer and in the group. This process continues until the teacher and the teacher trainer reach the point where they see better results for the children (see also Chap. 12 of this volume for further details on the implementation process).

Guiding Teachers on the Job

Implementing Basic Development (see Chap. 4 for further information about this programme) is a process characterised by *shared responsibility* based on the idea that teaching is not an individualistic project but basically a collective cultural-historically developed (and developing) practice (van Oers et al. 2003). We have to professionalise teachers by supporting them in those parts of the teaching activity they cannot yet do on their own (Tharp et al. 2000). So teaching is learned through participation in a teaching practice, in which responsibilities are shared and know-how is exchanged. Through empowerment of the teacher by multi-perspective assistance we create "extended teachership" (van Oers 2005), referring to teachers who have learned to integrate understandings from different resources into a possibly hybrid but coherent teaching practice, that is consistent with the basic assumptions of cultural-historical theory and with the local constraints of the situation. Communication and acceptance of shared responsibility are the core elements of the innovation process.

The teachers use the manuals we have written to organise the learning processes of the pupils. These manuals offer instruments and give insights into the objectives and aspects of designing and guiding meaningful activities. They also offer concepts and instruments for activity-oriented assessment. These instruments are meant as tools for thinking, not as teaching devices. That's why the style of the communication in these interactions is very important. The challenge is to bring these manuals into a process of negotiation of meaning with the teachers. To ensure the success of these negotiations, it is necessary to establish collaboration and exploratory discussion among teachers and teacher trainers. Teacher and teacher trainer are both responsible for bringing in their own ideas, interests and questions. The inter-professional communication between teachers and teacher trainers in the process of team discussions and individual coaching is characterised by rules that regulate the communication and innovations (van Oers 2005, 2009).

Rules of Communication and Support

In these communicative rules the teacher trainer really mediates between concepts and the ongoing practices in the classroom. The challenge for the teacher trainer is not to impose new ways of teaching, but to co-construct them until the point is reached when all participants feel the chosen solutions fit in satisfactorily with their conceptual framework and answer their individual and collective needs.

Teachers acquire new views, new ways of thinking and acting, and new means for promoting development in pupils. They have to make a radical change: allowing pupils to participate in relevant socio-cultural activities with a play character instead of using a fixed day-to-day programme for teaching prescribed knowledge and skills.

The teacher trainer gives assistance through a wide range of activities for individual teachers and the team.

Work with the Teachers in Their Own Classrooms

Teachers operate in their own specific ways. Their performance consists of all kinds of material and mental actions that relate somehow to Basic Development. For some of them Basic Development is close by, for others there is still a long way to go.

The teacher trainer serves as a partner for the teacher. Together they construct an assistance plan for a year and describe the new competences. They also address the real problems and specific questions of the individual teachers and define their expectations for the pupils' development. The teacher trainer visits the teachers in their classrooms on a regular basis to observe their performance of the teaching skills of the current focus. After the visit, feedback is given in an instructional conversation. The teacher is invited to formulate results and new questions. Together they decide on the next goals for the teacher's own learning and make a plan for the children for the next period (see also Chap. 12 of this volume).

Videotapes and photo reports support this process because seeing the images and listening to the interactions makes the analyses more precise. Floor training is also arranged when needed. If the teacher indicates that a demonstration of a new skill or specific activity could help, then the teacher trainer or one of their colleagues gives a demonstration.

Videotapes, photo reports and demonstrations support the process of reflection, encourage the formulation of alternatives for performance, and indicate where the teacher trainer needs to intervene. These interventions essentially make sense for the teachers as they arise from their actual needs and goals.

Reflect with the Teachers Using the Theory-Based Instruments

In Basic Development concept-based teacher manuals are available, including:

- curriculum ingredients for a play-based approach;
- an outline of relevant areas of learning and learning goals;
- tools for designing learning trajectories;
- tools for observation, registration and evaluation;
- instruments for self-evaluation to focus on their own learning processes.

The teacher trainer is responsible for introducing these instruments and for using them in the proper way. In using them the teachers integrate concepts into their changing practice and learn to justify what they are doing.

Develop New Strategies for Classroom Activities

Innovation of teaching and schooling is a difficult and hybrid process that takes place in complex and varying situations. The teacher trainer is aware of this and therefore supports the teachers in focusing on their own role and the results of the pupils. A teacher must become aware that interaction between teacher and pupils is the basic unit of analysis in Developmental Education, and that interventions for the improvement of these interactions are crucial.

This way of defining quality needs to be captured by a lot of teachers who are used to working with fixed programmes and predetermined general definitions of quality. Consequently, they are used to reflecting on pupils' outcomes only in terms of success or failure.

An example:

Teacher Nadia is accustomed to teaching her children (6 year olds) reading and writing using a programme. She is not satisfied with it, because she observes a lack of involvement in the reading lessons. She discusses her queries and ideas with the teacher trainer. Together they analyse the problems and design a learning trajectory for 3 weeks without using the fixed programme.

As a replacement of the standard programme they develop role-play activities and narratives about "Problems in the palace": Santa Claus has lost all his lists of gifts wanted by the children, and frantically wonders what to do to solve this serious problem.

The children create all kinds of narratives, and write letters, poems and lists. During these activities the teacher trainer visits the teacher in her classroom and supports her in organising the activities and assisting the pupils. Especially the five previously mentioned didactic impulses are an issue of common concern. They pay a lot of attention to the impulse for adding new actions in an embedded and functional way. At the end of the intervention period they reflect on the whole process and the teacher talks about her new sense of ownership:

> This way of teaching makes me much more watchful. I consider the utterances of my pupils seriously and discover that their potentials go far beyond the objectives of our reading programme. They learned much more about reading and writing than usually. They wrote more and varying texts and started to read earlier in books about Santa Claus. A lot of interesting language goals became meaningful, also aspects that in the programme are reserved for the second part of the school year. Mathematics became functional too in our play activities, through such activities as wrapping gifts at the packing table. Especially pupils who experience difficulties with the basic skills of reading, writing and mathematics profit most!

Assist the Teachers and Provide Models

Implementation trajectories need to be as concrete as possible. It is only then that the teacher trainer is able to assist appropriately and provide well-tailored models.

An example:

In one of the Developmental Education schools teachers formulate their needs for better authorship of young pupils and enriched language in their texts. Together with their teacher trainer they discuss their common practice and come up with a critical view of it. Teachers come to realise that they have to change their conventional concepts about writing a text and see it rather as a very complex problem-solving task. Consequently they will have to innovate their instructions and instructional styles as well. Then they formulate a hypothesis that they could probably get better

Table 13.1 The five didactical impulses

5 impulses	Teachers role	Instruction style
Orientation	Build up meaningful writing activities	Instructional conversations
	Finding a good idea and a good reason	Story-telling
	Rousing the stories of the pupils	
	Assisting to tell the stories	
Deepening and structuring	Assisting to make the transfer from telling to writing	Instructional conversations
	Assisting to clarify the aim of the writing and writing strategies	Modeling writing strategies
	Assisting by focusing on the context of the writing	Direct instruction
Extension to other core activities	Assisting in reading back	Coaching
Adding new actions	Assisting in revising and correcting	Coaching
		Instructional conversation
		Direct instruction
		Modeling
Reflection	Assessing writing process and product together with the pupils	Instructional conversation

results if they succeed in combining the five didactic impulses with instructions on vocabulary, writing strategies, grammar and spelling. They design a matrix for action and reflection (see Table 13.1), which becomes a comprehensible instrument that all teachers and the teacher trainer can use and discuss.

Using this matrix also gives participants a hold for strict monitoring and precise evaluation. The teacher trainer can provide models by means of videotapes, good practices on paper and demonstrations on the floor, in accordance with the individual learning needs of each teacher.

Share the Outcomes: A Narrative Approach

Teachers share their individual progress with each other by telling their learning stories. By telling their stories using a video clip, a photo report or examples of pupils' work or pupils' outcomes, the teachers can identify with each other and give mutual support. In the best scenario they explore new possibilities and good practices. These conferences are meant to clear up uncertainties, to ask and answer questions, and to give meaning to results and further plans. Together they create the platform that is needed for mutual confidence and for the innovation of their initial assumptions about teaching. Within such a community of inquiry the teachers learn how to create new concepts for teaching in a Developmental Education classroom. By doing this, the "I-story" of the individual teacher becomes a "we-story" of the team. A jointly constructed story about new concepts and strategies in the classroom gives the best guarantee for a sustainable innovation.

Encourage the Team to Become Self-supporting

Teachers need time and professional support to become committed to their new practices. (See Chap. 17 for further description of the conditions for successful implementation of Developmental Education in schools.) The teacher trainer understands the importance of working with the whole system of teachers and their pupils, internal supervisors, and school principals.

Final Remarks

Teachers and their trainers work together in constructing learning trajectories with high developmental value for all children. This is a complicated process and certainly not without difficulties and critical moments. The most important problems have to do with lack of knowledge and the fear of losing control.

To build up learning trajectories for heterogeneous groups of pupils and for individual pupils in the group, a lot of knowledge about the developmental pathways and educational content is necessary. The teachers need to integrate children's motives with specific learning objectives. They also have to recognise that a shared meaningful activity setting can contain a variety of learning processes and outcomes for different children.

For instance: A group of 5 year olds is playing "silent pussy-cats". It is obvious that the different motives of the children lead to different results. One of the boys is constantly talking about the play theme and he is reflective on the roles. Two girls are laughing together without making any noise. They are practicing their silence as pussy-cats.

Two other boys are running away and turning back. They practice their motor skills intensively and go on and on, until they are tired and plop down on the playground.

The teacher needs to reflect on this play activity in terms of teaching opportunities, drawing from her available knowledge about learning areas for young children.

Another important quality for the teacher to develop has to do with opening up the existing and spontaneous concepts of the children and using them in building bridges to academic learning. Making a double move in teaching (Hedegaard 2002) requires a lot of time and energy from the teacher and the teacher trainer in most implementation trajectories.

Finally, knowledge and competencies of the teacher during the implementation process must also be evaluated.

To do this we use evaluation forms with an overview of the teachers' competencies. Teachers discuss this overview with the teacher trainer or colleague, and score their outcome with:

L: for learner, or apprentice:	this means that the teacher is learning a new ability and still needs the help of others;
G: for gezel (craftsmen):	this means that the teacher is already practicing this ability in her classroom but needs feedback to appropriate and refine it further;
M: for master:	this means that the teacher has fully appropriated the ability, can flexibly apply it ("can play with it"), and is able to help others with it.

Over the last years we have used this instrument in many schools, with hundreds of teachers. It seems an effective way to help teachers to reflect on their own learning processes. It also helps to create an ongoing reflective climate in the team or early years department. Further research is needed to validate this way of evaluating results.

Most teachers find it hard to build up a dialogic culture in their classroom. A fundamental activity setting for that purpose is the instructional conversation. This setting relates thinking, acquiring concepts, language development and literacy in a broad sense (also mathematics). We agree with Tharp and Gallimore (1988) that most teachers are not capable of giving effective assistance because they lack the time to interact in a way that can direct a negotiation of meaning in small groups.

This requires a high level of instructional and organisational competence. Therefore it is necessary to give a lot of attention to the implementation of instructional conversations (IC) on both dimensions. Teachers need to know several aspects of these dimensions:

- grouping: knowing when to group homogeneous and when heterogeneous and selecting the children;
- planning: every child meets in an instructional conversation for at least 20 min a day;
- defining purpose and goal-oriented observations;
- building up an IC using discourse skills, like modelling, revoicing, feedback and questioning.

In one of our projects, seven schools worked together on the improvement of their reading results in the early years. In this project we tried to implement instructional conversation on reading narratives and information texts. We interviewed the teachers about the process they were involved in and asked them to point out its most demanding aspects. They mentioned three main points:

1. keep a good view of your group as a whole and of individual pupils;
2. create time to reflect and make new plans for different groups of pupils in IC;
3. handle loss of control in favour of better and more initiatives of the children.

Teachers need to cope with a certain amount of uncertainty. Too much of it paralyses and creates fear of failure. Knowing this, the teacher trainer listens very carefully and takes the teachers' questions and problems seriously. Together they try to find a way through the ZPD of the teacher and find a new starting point.

Assisting teachers in a supportive way for the creation of new knowledge and practices basically consists in finding and constructing joint activities, in which the voice of the teachers really meets the actual value of theoretical concepts, and finally integrates the cultural demands of society with the personal interests of the pupils.

References

Engeström, Y. (2005). *Developmental work research: Expanding activity theory in practice* (Vol. 12), Republished by Georg Rückriem, 2005. Berlin: Lehmanns Media – LOB.de.

Fijma, N., & Pompert, B. (2002). *Unity in pedagogical concept; diversity in teaching methods in dealing with heterogeneity.* Paper 5the ISCAR conference Amsterdam.

Hedegaard, M. (2002). *Learning and child development.* Aarhus: Aarhus University Press.

Janssen-Vos, F. (1997). *Basisontwikkeling in de onderbouw* [Basic Development in the early years]. Assen: Van Gorcum.

O'Connor, M. C., & Michaels, S. (1996). Shifting participant frameworks: Orchestrating thinking practices in group discussions. In D. Hicks (Ed.), *Discourse, learning, and schooling* (pp. 63–103). Cambridge: Cambridge University Press.

Tharp, R., & Gallimore, R. (1988). *Rousing minds to life.* Cambridge: Cambridge University Press.

Tharp, R., Estrada, P., Dalton, S., & Yamauchi, L. (2000). *Teaching transformed: Achieving excellence, fairness, inclusion and harmony.* Boulder: West View Press.

van Oers, B. (2005). *Carnaval in de kennisfabriek* [Carnival in the knowledge factory]. Inaugural Lecture. Amsterdam: VU Press.

van Oers, B. (2009). Developmental education. Improving participation in cultural practices. In M. Fleer, M. Hedegaard, & J. Tudge (Eds.), *Childhood studies and the impact of globalisation* (pp. 293–317). New York: Routledge.

van Oers, B. (2010). Children's enculturation through play. In L. Brooker & S. Edwards (Eds.), *Engaging play* (pp. 195–209). Maidenhead: McGraw Hill.

van Oers, B., & Pompert, B. (1991). Kijken naar kinderspel [Observing children's play]. *Vernieuwing, 50*(7), 3–8.

van Oers, B., Janssen-Vos, F., Pompert, B., & Schiferli, T. (2003). Teaching as a joint activity. In B. van Oers (Ed.), *Narratives of childhood. Theoretical and practical explorations for the innovation of early childhood education* (pp. 127–145). Amsterdam: VU Press.

Wells, G., & Claxton, G. (Eds.). (2002). *Learning for life in the 21st century.* London: Blackwell.

Chapter 14
Evaluation of Learning and Development

Ester van Oers

Introduction

In the first grade of a Developmental Education school, the children (4 year-olds) are involved in an activity that invites them to examine in dyads different seeds. The teacher tells an exciting story about a frog and a toad, who plant seeds in their garden. After the story, each pair of children receives a number of seeds. First, the children feel and look at the seeds. Some children smell them too. After the first exploration, each pair of children receives a sheet of paper with a number of observation questions. The teacher discusses these questions and shows the children an example of how to use the sheet. The teacher asks: "What is the shape of the seed? What colour is it? How does the seed feel?" After this, the children work with their own seeds and answer the questions.

This is a type of activity that is quite common in Developmental Education (Basic Development). The described activity took place in the first week of a new thematic activity that introduced the children to a new cultural practice: "The garden centre". The teacher had deliberately chosen this activity with specific educational purposes in mind, which she planned to realise in the coming weeks. In advance, she has reflected on the possible meanings this topic might have for the children in her class. What will be interesting for the group, how can the children's interest be aroused, and how can we encourage them to be involved in the garden centre?

E. van Oers, M.Sc. (✉)
De Archipel, Amsterdam, The Netherlands
e-mail: e.van.oers@askoscholen.nl

B. van Oers (ed.), *Developmental Education for Young Children*, International
Perspectives on Early Childhood Education and Development 7,
DOI 10.1007/978-94-007-4617-6_14,
© Springer Science+Business Media Dordrecht 2012

A Tool for Planning and Evaluation in Basic Development

For planning and formatively evaluating activities like the one described above, Basic Development has introduced an instrument that can be used by teachers as a tool in their teaching activity. That instrument, called "HOREB" (an instrument for Action-oriented observation, registration and evaluation in Basic Development) helps teachers to organise activities for children in the age group of 3–8. With this tool the teacher can plan, observe, register and evaluate intended activities (Janssen-Vos and Pompert 2007a, b; van Oers 1999). Teachers continuously follow the guidelines of this instrument, and take the steps in planning, performing and evaluating accordingly. HOREB is inextricably connected to Developmental Education (and in particular to Basic Development, see Chap. 4 of this volume). Basic Development cannot be validly implemented without HOREB.

HOREB is an open, strategic instrument consisting of a number of specific tools: an *activity book* is used for the planning and evaluation of activities over a period of 6–8 weeks; additionally, *a logbook* is used by the teacher to plan and evaluate the daily activities. Furthermore, *diaries* are used for registering in detail the actual developments of pupils.

Another important feature of HOREB is the contextual link to activities as opposed to fixed developmental areas, as practised by many other observation instruments. In Developmental Education, for example, the teacher observes reading skills in the context of writing a shopping list for the supermarket, instead of testing this skill in isolation without a meaningful context. Teachers will participate in such activities, and through interacting with the children they will learn a lot more about children's development than they would by just using a standard check list. By so doing, the teachers primarily apply a type of dynamic assessment in evaluation (as described by Vygotskij and Lurija; see also Chaps. 6 and 7 of the present volume), which qualifies children's developmental *potential* in a given domain, rather than simply fixing their attainments.

HOREB consists of several components, which will be clarified over the course of this chapter:

- the activity book;
- the logbook;
- the observation models;
- the children's diary and the evaluation instruments.

In this chapter I will explain these components in the context of the previously mentioned "garden centre".

The Activity Book

In Basic Development the teacher starts a thematic period by choosing a theme and content together with the children, and transforming these into activities (and related roles) that presumably interest them. The activity book presents the resources and tools which can help teachers in selecting a suitable theme, planning the activities, choosing the goals for this period, and evaluating afterwards. The book provides the teachers with a number of forms (see below) that can support their decisions. These forms help teachers to prepare and make plans that constitute the guidelines during that period. These plans also establish the content of specific precursory activities that are meant to capture the interest and experiences of the children. It sets the general outline for plans which can be adjusted at a later stage.

The activity book contains the following forms:

- Preparation of themes and activities;
- Matrix with living areas and resources;
- Web model or designing scheme;
- Word list;
- List of reading strategies;
- List of different text forms;
- Evaluation form.

In the following sections the use of some of these forms will be illustrated.

Planning a Theme

This designing phase is called the zero-phase (see Chaps. 4 and 12 of this volume for further information). This is the stage where a concrete plan is made for a new period and its thematic activity. In this preparation period teachers think carefully about the possibilities of a theme for their group.

Teachers at a Developmental Education school always plan a meeting to prepare the new theme together. First they brainstorm about the subject. For example, they ask: "What comes into your mind when you think of the garden centre?" and "What experiences do you have?" The teachers' coach (or supervisor), joins in during this meeting and has a coordinating role. For the garden project the supervisor reads a famous Dutch poem to her colleagues about a frog who wants a kitchen garden. Afterwards they talk in pairs about their own gardening skills. It is important for teachers to recall their own experiences, because this influences the way in which they present the theme in their classrooms. When teachers are enthusiastic about a subject, they will be more likely to pass this on to their group of pupils.

After the brainstorming session they fill out the form for the preparation of themes and activities (see Fig. 14.1).

In completing the form, teachers first think about the content of the theme. The choice of a subject connected with nature suggests new contents to the teachers.

Preparation of themes and activities

titel   de pizzeria
Omschrijving restaurant
Startdatum   08-09-2010
Einddatum   08-09-2010

What are you thinking in selecting and preparing a theme?
Content of a theme

Meanings and experiences of the children

Intentions of the teacher with this theme

Fig. 14.1 Fragment of the preparation form for themes and activities

Table 14.1 The completed matrix for the theme "The garden centre"

Resources	Living areas Primary needs	Trade, economics engineering	Stories, religion, culture, science
Real life situations	What do you eat from your garden	The garden centre in your neighbourhood Redesigning your own garden	Care for nature
Actuality	Miscellaneous plant and flower species	The garden at school	Spring has begun
The broader world	From a seed/bulb to plan	–	Art and flowers
			Healing flowers

Previous topics used by the teachers have not addressed this subject. The topic also fits well with the time of year: it is spring, many people work in their gardens in the spring, and the garden centre can be a crowded place. A useful scheme for checking if there is enough variation in the themes is the matrix which can be found in the activity book (see Table 14.1). The topics in the matrix are arranged into life areas (basic needs, technical/trade/economics and culture/art/religion) and sources (real life situations, current events, wider world). Thus, a range of subjects ensures that broad subject areas are covered throughout the school year.

By filling out the matrix, the teachers already begin to think about important sub-themes. They are keen to focus on the spring, the growth of bulbs, and on relevant knowledge of different flower species.

The next step of the preparation form is to think about the meanings and experiences of the children with regard to the activities in this thematic period. Teachers often try to make use of the home experiences that children and their parents can contribute (see also Chap. 11 of this volume). In this first grade, there is a girl whose parents own a garden centre. The girl will probably be able to say a lot about it and it may be a good idea for the class to visit this garden centre.

One of the teachers has noticed that the children are very interested in growth. There is a tape measure in the classroom, and every week a group of children measure themselves. The teachers decide that the children may also find it interesting to observe the growth of a plant. The theme, and particularly the issue of growth, thus creates good opportunities to join the world of the children.

Of course teachers have their own intentions for this theme: they have clearly in mind what they want to achieve. To make their intentions more concrete the teachers use "The Circle of Basic Development" which provides an inventory of basic conditions, broad developmental aims and specific objectives that guide the concrete organisation of early years classroom activities (for this circle see for example Chap. 4). From this circle, the teachers choose some of the broad developmental aims that they consider relevant for the present project, such as combining play and work, exploration of the world around you, and expressing yourself in words and shapes. Further, they also want to help the children with learning how to care for nature.

The teachers also identify the more specific goals they want their pupils to achieve during that period. For example, they want the children to learn more about the different growth stages of bulbs and seeds. There will be a story-telling table in the classroom. On this table children can reconstruct situations from a book they have read, and act out the story of that book with the help of different materials, figures and props. Teachers often use this table specifically for the children who need additional language support.

In the context of the garden centre, the teachers also want to integrate the goals for mathematics for the coming period. The teachers notice for example that calculating with money is still difficult for many children. This theme-based activity provides an opportunity to give some extra attention to these children within the meaningful context of tending the cash register in the garden centre. The teachers also choose a number of spelling categories which are to be explained, using frequently used words in the garden centre.

The next step is to think about what kind of activities would arise in the classroom. The teachers use the so-called web model to help them think about those activities (see Fig. 14.2). The web model is a designing scheme from HOREB, which is segmented into the following core-activities (see also Chap. 4 of this volume):

- Object play and role-play;
- Reading and writing;

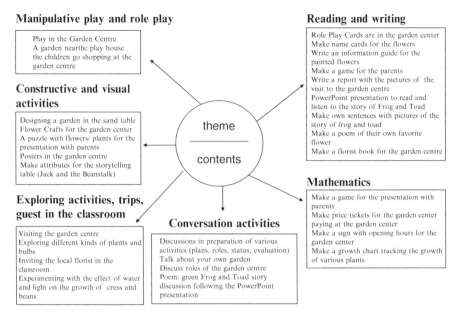

Manipulative play and role play

Play in the Garden Centre
A garden near the play house
the children go shopping at the
garden centre

Constructive and visual activities

Designing a garden in the sand table
Flower Crafts for the garden center
A puzzle with flowers/ plants for the
presentation with parents
Posters in the garden centre
Make attributes for the storytelling
table (Jack and the Beanstalk)

Exploring activities, trips, guest in the classroom

Visiting the garden centre
Exploring different kinds of plants and
bulbs
Inviting the local florist in the
classroom
Experimenting with the effect of water
and light on the growth of cress and
beans

theme
———
contents

Conversation activities

Discussions in preparation of various
activities (plans, roles, status, evaluation)
Talk about your own garden
Discuss roles of the garden centre
Poem: green Frog and Toad story
discussion following the PowerPoint
presentation

Reading and writing

Role Play Cards are in the garden center
Make name cards for the flowers
Write an information guide for the
painted flowers
Make a game for the parents
Write a report with the pictures of the
visit to the garden centre
PowerPoint presentation to read and
listen to the story of Frog and Toad
Make own sentences with pictures of the
story of frog and toad
Make a poem of their own favorite
flower
Make a florist book for the garden centre

Mathematics

Make a game for the presentation with
parents
Make price tickets for the garden center
paying at the garden center
Make a sign with opening hours for the
garden center
Make a growth chart tracking the growth
of various plants

Fig. 14.2 The completed web model of the "The garden centre"

- Mathematical activities;
- Conversation activities;
- Constructive and visual activities;
- Exploratory activities, trips, guest in the classroom.

In the Developmental Education curriculum, play is considered the leading activity for young pupils and a productive context for meaningful learning. The teachers use their theme as a first step to reflect on what kind of cultural practice will be organised in the classroom. The teachers using the setting of a garden centre include in their planning a reflection on the roles children may play, such as: a customer, salesman and maybe someone who takes care of the plants. Next, they think of the actions characterising each of these roles: What do you do when you work in a garden centre? What kind of tools do you need?

The connection is then made with other activities which could take place in a garden centre. The garden centre will need posters with "deals" and also a price list. They will need pots to put the plants in. Together with the children, the teachers make plans for all the different role-activities. As a result, there will be many conversations to plan. The teacher plans all these activities in the logbook, which will be explained in more detail in the next section.

None of the activities are entirely fixed. In the first one and a half weeks the teacher plans different activities to arouse the children's interest and to learn more about their experiences. Sometimes it happens that new subjects arise, which the teacher had not anticipated. This orientating period is called Phase One of the theme. With the outcome of these orientation activities the teacher can make a precise plan of the theme in cooperation with the children. The teacher can use the scheme for the further planning of goals and activities (see Fig. 14.2).

In the planning process, the teachers also make a word list. On this list they mark the target words which the children are supposed to learn during this theme. The teacher makes a distinction between children who have a large vocabulary, and children for whom Dutch is a second language.

HOREB also has a list of reading strategies and a list of different text forms. On this list the teacher can note down his/her plans during this new thematic period. At the end of the theme the teacher has an overview of the strategies and text forms offered.

In the finalisation of every theme, teachers fill out the evaluation form. On this form they write down which contents have been offered and which activities the children found most interesting. The teachers also make an overview of the goals that have been achieved and the goals that remain on the child's agenda. They also plan what methods or materials they want to use again in the next theme; the story table, for example, was a big success, therefore the teachers decide to include another one in the next theme.

The Logbook

Observations are necessary for designing appropriate activities in the classroom. The main goal of a logbook is to register observational data and connect these to the next planned activities. Teachers use the logbook to plan and reflect on the supervised activities. They also participate in children's activities and by doing so learn more about the development of the children. The active role of the teacher within the activities is very important in order to take the children into their zone of proximal development, encourage them to try new actions, and establish if the children are ready to become engaged in those actions and are receptive to the help they get. That is a fundamental rule for Basic Development: with the teacher's instruction and guidance, the children can do more than they can on their own.

In this process of stimulating and guiding pupils in their activities, teachers make use of a logbook to register the children's actions, interests, successes and failures. The logbook has three sections (see Table 14.2 below). In the left section a teacher writes the plan for some supervised activities, the right section is to reflect on the actually performed activities, and the third section is to indicate the focus of subsequent plans.

Throughout the theme, the teacher makes plans for groups of children. These plans are more concrete than in the activity book and are tailored to selected groups of children.

Every day the teacher plans two or three supervised activities with small groups of children, particularly focusing on each child's "zone of proximal development".

Other children can continue their thematic activities in their own small groups. For guiding the teacher's work with the children, a conceptual scheme (the square)

Table 14.2 Example of an activity planned in the logbook, including the reflection and the follow-up plans

Planning	Reflection
1. What activity?	1. Was the activity meaningful?
Make a garden game to play with their parents during the final presentation	The four children were all very excited to design a game for their parents. They were very involved during the making of a plan.
2. Which children?	2. Development of activity
E, C, K, D	K. immediately had many ideas for a game and he could clearly explain this to others.
3. What is my role?	D. was particularly interested in the existing games and wanted to play these games.
Showing examples of existing games	C. was really focused on the goal of the activity. She thought about how many parents had to play and if the game could really be made by the children.
Make a link to mathematics during the making of the game	E. listened to the others, but after a while he brought in some good ideas.
Fostering cooperation and mutual consultation among the children	3. Were my intentions realised?
Ask questions to support the children to regulate their thoughts and intentions	K and C took many initiatives and immediately wanted a real game for the parents. C wanted to make it very precise.
4. Observation points	E. did not show much initiative, but he thought of using a tally to keep track of how many pictures on the cards we had to make
Do the children taking part in conversation stay focused on the topic and input from the others?	For D. the activity was still too abstract. He wanted to play the game and could not imagine the game that we ourselves were making.
Do the children take initiatives to develop a game idea?	4. Was my role helpful?
How are the children focused on making the game precise and do they check themselves to make sure it is correct?	The existing games were a big support for the children to bring up their own ideas for a game.
How do they describe the computational problems that we encounter during the creation of the game and how can they explain this?	During the activity I have managed to reformulate the thoughts of the children and kept them involved with each others' ideas. This was truly a collaborative process.
	For D. I was able to be more specific with more visual support referring to the game that we have made during the theme of animals.
	Follow-up plans:
	With D. I am going to take the first game we made to explore this and make it more concrete.
	With K en C I plan a moment next week to develop a real game from this idea and present it to the other children.

is developed with four questions to support teachers while planning an activity (see Fig. 14.4).

This scheme constantly reminds the teacher to ask four specific questions while going through the planning of this activity. The questions are:

> *Which activity* am I planning and what is the goal of this activity?
> *For which children* am I planning this activity?
> *How will I support* the children during this activity?
> What are my *observation points*?

The Observation Models

The time has now come to track down data that indicate the development of the children. Here the teachers can use the observation models included in the HOREB-instrument. With the observation models the teacher can explore which activities and interactions are in the zone of proximal development of the children. It is important that the teacher knows the developmental perspectives of each of the core-activities. In these perspectives, the development of each core-activity is described for the ages of 3–8 years old. Early mathematics is implicitly embodied in the actions and thoughts of young children, for example, while endlessly pouring coffee into a cup. When children get older, mathematics becomes more explicit, functional and meaningful in the context of role-play; for example, the guests in the restaurant have to pay correctly for their meal. Step by step, the activity becomes more realistic. The children gradually develop a mathematical attitude that helps them to see the mathematics in new situations and deal with it properly.

If the need for more "real" actions and mathematical acts gets stronger, some children learn and practice the mathematics more independently from the context of play. Mathematics then becomes a conscious learning activity. In such cases, for example, children are introduced to the multiplication tables while making out a prescription in the pharmacy; one spoonful three times a day. Afterwards the teacher gives an instruction on the table of three.

In practice, not every teacher has these perspectives readily available. This problem can be solved by using the new digital version of HOREB which gives a teacher access to an extensive range of devices for planning, evaluation, and registration of children's actions, problems and progress. On every screen page there is an information button (see Fig. 14.3). When users click on this button, they find a list with all the resources they need to fill out on this page, for example, the forms for identifying developmental perspectives or the observation models.

The observation model helps the teacher to identify the intended development in children. Every observation model is divided into five parts:

A. The meanings and motives of children: Do they enjoy the activity? Are they interested and involved? Do they take their own initiatives? These are

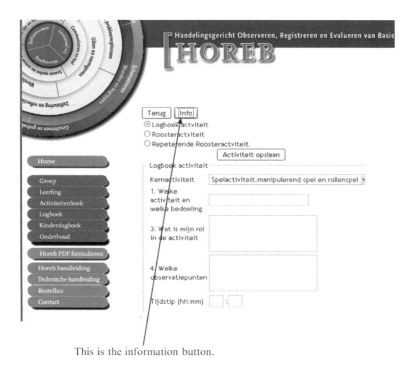

This is the information button.

Fig. 14.3 A screenshot from the HOREB-programme (see www.HOREB-po.nl)

fundamental conditions for children's meaningful participation in activities and
their development within the activities.

B. The development of the activity: The teacher focuses on the activity itself. Does
   it evolve in the direction of the developmental perspectives they have in mind
   with this activity?
C. The development of language and thought: How is language used in the activity
   and what thought processes can be witnessed during this activity?
D. The broad development: Which general developmental qualities are addressed
   and encouraged by the teacher within the core activity? For example, the focus
   on working together or reflecting one's own actions.
E. Specific knowledge and skills: Which skills specifically should be used or practised within the activity? For example, certain spelling categories or vocabulary
   expansion.

Each developmental perspective is to be accomplished within a concrete activity
with the children. For example, within the theme "The garden centre", the teacher
plans to make a garden game with the children, which they can play with their
parents during the final presentation at the end of the theme-period. The teacher
plans this activity in the logbook, using the following format (see Table 14.2). In the
first column (left) the teacher writes down specific decisions about the activity she

Planning an activity

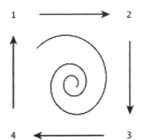

1. Which activity am I planning and what is the goal of this activity?

2. For which children am I planning this activity

3. How will I support the children during this activity?

4. What are my observation points?

Fig. 14.4 The square model of the logbook

wants to realise with the children. In the second column (right) the teacher writes down the observations she has made in the course of the activity, and that she may need in further planning of activities with (some of) these children.

After this guided activity, the teacher plans a follow-up activity. In this example, the teacher explores an existing game that was produced in a previous thematic activity, in order to help one of the children by providing him with a concrete example. The teacher also makes a plan for getting other children involved in the construction of a real game from this game idea. For this activity the teacher selects other goals. This whole process is circular. The teacher plans the activity, the activity is executed, and then the teacher reflects. This process can be shown within the square model of the logbook, by drawing a spiral (see Fig. 14.4).

The Children's Diary

For each child a diary is used to note observations during an activity. In this diary the teacher writes down remarkable findings about the development of the child. Every child has a personal diary which contains sections for the different core activities. In the new digital HOREB, observations from the logbook can be automatically transferred to the child's diary. Formerly, this used to take a lot of the teachers' time, because everything had to be written by hand.

To write in the children's diary requires a time investment from the teacher. For newly qualified teachers it is difficult not only to formulate concisely, but also to use the language of the observation models. With practice, it becomes much easier.

Some of the new observation models in the digital HOREB have now underlined key words, to support teachers in their own formulations. In the digital version of HOREB, teachers can easily have the models close to hand by using an information button on each page of the programme.

In the children's diary, the teacher can also keep additional material, such as photos, video clips and written texts related to a specific child. In this way the teachers can build a portfolio for each child. It is important that the work gives a realistic insight into the development of the child and that the child does not make things just for the sake of their portfolio.

In addition to the described reflections per core activity, the children's diary consists of several other (evaluation) forms:

1. The entry form

    When a child starts school, the teacher may want to collect data on the early development of the child. When a child is registered in a school, the teacher plans an entrance interview with parents or carers.

    The focus for this conversation is the form "This is me", which includes personal data on the child, for example name, date of birth, gender, etc.

    The second focus is on the life of the child so far: health, stay in kindergarten or child care, brothers and sisters, development information related to emotional stability, independence and social skills, play and language development (first and second language).

    It is important that parents or guardians really feel able to talk about their child. When parents have confidence that the teacher and school are seriously interested in the child, there is a good chance that key information about the child will be discussed.

    The key points during the interview are filled in on the form. The information from the parents is then used to determine in which group the child is best placed and if necessary, what specific arrangements need to be made.

2. Status after the first 3 months (or 6 months with toddlers)

    An entry period of 3 months gives the teacher and the child time to get used to each other and to get to know each other better. When a child has just started in the group, the teacher doesn't know much about his development. It is only when a child feels safe that he will begin to realise his potential. In those 3 months, both children and teachers have the opportunity to build a good basis for the coming period. In this first period, the observations are focused on how the child functions in the group and how he or she participates in the activities offered in the group. For that purpose a special observation model is designed for the entry period.

    The first 3-months period ends with a first evaluation (see Fig. 14.5). The teacher now has enough information to write this evaluation of the child's development on a special form. Based on this form, the teacher makes plans for a follow-up learning-teaching trajectory. On this form the teacher makes statements about the child's school life, with comments on:

Entry Period. Progress review after 3 months substructure

Name	L.
Date	xxxxx
Name teacher	xxxxx

The child and life in the group
L plays in the various corners. She very much likes to observe the play of the other (s) and occasionally joins this play. She easily starts a conversation during the play and also talks about the play itself. Other children react well and let her join their play. L. follows the play of the others. At other times she likes to play by herself. L. chooses what she wants to do and does this independently. She makes good choices. She can manage herself.
Meanings and motives
L. undertakes some activities in which she experiments with the material. But, she often knows what she wants to make and she can well describe what she is doing. If the teachers gives a defined instruction for an activity L. is very focused for a long period on this activity. Within these activities L works independently.
Development of play
L. likes to dress up and likes to play roles. She likes to participate in activities in which the teacher has a guiding role. She picks up new skills or instruction quickly and easily. When L played in the pizzeria, she chose the role of a waitress. She showed great initiative and she remained in her role. She used thematic role play and role dialogues. In order to write down the order she said she did not know how to write it. I said just pretend and she draw three circles for the 3 pizzas.

Fig. 14.5 A fragment of an evaluation form after the first 3-months-period

- The basic characteristics: does the child feel at home (socially-emotionally) in the group?
- Participation in group life and the school community.
- Frequency of attendance and an impression of the involvement of parents or carers.

The teacher also writes about the child's development:

- Play activities: role-play and construction play. Did the child have interest in new activities and materials and did he want to participate in the games of others? How is the use of language in the play activities?
- Language use and vocabulary: How is the use of language and vocabulary in the first language and in Dutch as a second language (NT2)? How is participation in discussion activities? How is the early literacy?
- Specific knowledge and skills. How are the gross and fine motor skills? How are the social skills?

Semi-annual Progress Reports and Evaluations

Twice a year the teachers make an overview of the total development of each child. The children's diary and portfolio contain notes about the remarkable

Situation of literacy
Transfer Form

| Print | Info | Sla het formulier op |

Naam van het kind: Lieve Konings
Geboortedatum: 24-09-2006
datum invullen: 21-12-2010
Ingevuld door:

Letterkennis	+/-	eventuele opmerkingen
Active letter knowledge	- ○ + ⦿	She reads short words. She has a little trouble mixing up the ou and au.
		B *I* U ABC ↻ ⤶ | ☰ ☰ | 📋 HTML 🖼
Passive letter knowledge	- ○ + ⦿	L knows all letters in a passive way. She can point them out and easily copy them.
		B *I* U ABC ↻ ⤶ | ☰ ☰ | 📋 HTML 🖼
Distinguish sounds	- ○ + ◉	L. analyses words in separate auditory sounds and she can join separate sounds into a word. She can rhyme.
		B *I* U ABC ↻ ⤶ | ☰ ☰ | 📋 HTML 🖼

Fig. 14.6 A fragment of the transfer form for literacy

developmental moments. The teachers make a summary for each core-activity. Sometimes it is necessary for the teachers to plan extra activities and do additional observations to fill the gaps in the data. There are a few instruments developed to fit into the developmental approach. These instruments are sometimes used to give the teachers extra data, for example, on the vocabulary development of the child (see also Chap. 6 of this volume), or narrative competence (Chap. 7 of this volume).

The digital version of HOREB also contains a number of different forms. The teacher can easily use these forms by ticking boxes for special skills per core activity. For example, in the form for mathematics, skills are listed such as counting to ten, synchronous counting, comparing quantities, or adding by counting forwards etc. These forms are intended to be supplementary to the written observations of the teachers (see also Chap. 16 of this volume for further descriptions of the assessment of mathematical development).

3. Transfer forms

In promoting children to another grade, transfer models may be useful for making decisions, as these forms summarise children's learning outcomes in a certain area. This is the case when toddlers are going to make the transition from a day care centre to school. For this goal a transfer model was designed. Below is a transfer form focused on literacy for children who are going to first grade and will learn to read and write (see Fig. 14.6).

The Introduction of HOREB in School

The use of HOREB in Developmental Education (Basic Development) is not an easy matter, but it can be learned with appropriate support (see B. van Oers 2000a, b). Our experience tells us that problems inevitably arise when HOREB is offered separately from the daily work with Basic Development. Teachers should be allowed to get ample experience working with HOREB instruments in their daily work. In Basic Development it is essential that teachers deliberately promote development and take the children carefully to the next step in their development. This can be done by using the logbook and the observation models. HOREB therefore, is at the heart of Basic Development.

The role of the supervisor in a planned introduction of HOREB in a school is crucial (see E. van Oers 2008a, b). He or she can create time and optimal conditions for teachers to work with HOREB seriously.

It takes time and investment to learn and work with HOREB. It is advisable not to do everything at once, but to make choices and set priorities. These choices are generally associated with other developments in the school. For example, when the collective focus of the team is on improving the didactics in mathematics, teachers can choose to make a start with planning the mathematics activities in the logbook. A teacher in kindergarten can start to plan play activities in the logbook and describe the development of embedded mathematical actions in the children's diary (see Chap. 16 of this volume; also Fijma 2003).

If this goes well, the teacher can choose another core activity. Because play development is a key issue in Basic Development, it is advisable to start with play.

It often helps, for example, when an entire team or a group of colleagues get started together, so they can talk with each other about the things they encounter and collaboratively reflect on their own actions (see also Chap. 12 of this volume). Some schools plan HOREB time with the team in their weekly schedule. During these meetings there is time and space for teachers to talk about their personal experiences. It is also beneficial to practice together with a planned logbook activity on paper, produced by one of the teachers, and then watch the video of the related activity as a group. Teachers can then complete the logbook, plan together and ask each other questions, such as: what do you actually write in your child's diary and how do you use the HOREB vocabulary?

It is highly recommended that HOREB is introduced with the help of a supervisor or external teacher trainer. It is a good idea to get support from someone who is familiar with HOREB and who can give an overview of the goals and potentials of HOREB. A coach within the school ("internal facilitator") may also introduce the whole process to see, for example: what are the teachers' different writing styles? What is feasible for each teacher? What are the problems and needs of each teacher?

On the basis of our own classroom and team experiences, we can say that one thing is certain: HOREB is an essential part of Basic Development and everybody can learn it!

References

Fijma, N. (2003). Mathematics learning in a play-based curriculum. How to deal with heterogeneity? In B. van Oers (Ed.), *Narratives of childhood*. Amsterdam: VU University Press.

Janssen-Vos, F., & Pompert, B. (2007a). De nieuwe HOREB. Nog beter werken aan Basisontwikkeling [The new HOREB. Working better with Basic Development]. *Zone, 6*(1), 4–8.

Janssen-Vos, F., & Pompert, B. (2007b). *Handelingsgericht Observeren, Registreren en Evalueren van Basisontwikkeling. Handleiding* [Action-oriented observation, registration and evaluation of Basic Development. Manual]. Assen: Van Gorcum.

van Oers, B. (1999). Quality of diagnostic teaching abilities in early education. *European Early Childhood Education Research Journal, 7*(2), 39–51.

van Oers, B. (2000a). Het oog van de meester (m/v). Toetsen en observeren in het onderwijs [The eye of the teacher (m/f). Testing and observing in education.]. *De wereld van het jonge kind, 27*(5), 146–150.

van Oers, B. (2000b). Observeren kun je leren! Pleidooi voor een brede professionalisering van leerkrachten. In F. Janssen-Vos (red.), *Tien jaar Basisontwikkeling: Het maakt verschil!* [10 years of Basic Development: It makes a difference]. Utrecht: APS.

van Oers, E. (2008a). Werken met de digitale HOREB [Working with the digital HOREB]. *Zone, 7*(1), 20–22.

van Oers, E. (2008b). Handelingsgericht Observeren en Evalueren. In de Haan, D. & Kuiper, E. (eds.), *Leerkracht in Beeld. Ontwikkelingsgericht Onderwijs: theorie, onderzoek en praktijk* [Teacher in the picture. Developmental education: Theory, research and practice]. Assen: Van Gorcum.

Website: www.HOREB-po.nl.

Chapter 15
Teaching Reading by Writing

Bea Pompert

Language and Literacy Development

In Developmental Education learning processes are always embedded in activities that make sense to the children. Imagine the following scenes from a classroom that follows the Developmental Education approach of Basic Development (see Chap. 4 for further information about Basic Development):

"We are vets!"

In a kindergarten group, the teacher Dorien and her pupils are working on the theme "Pets". In the classroom there are two interesting play corners: the pet shop and the veterinarian. Dorien plays in the vet corner with four children. The teacher is the vet and Corine (4 years old) is her assistant. The other children visit the vet with their sick pets. Tobias' dog has a broken paw, Rubia's cat is ill and Salma, who has just started school, accompanies Rubia. She looks around and pats all the animals. An interesting play arises wherein the children talk about the animals and their ailments. And, of course, the animals are examined. In her role as the assistant, Corine hands over all the items that are needed, like the bandages and plasters for Tobias' dog "Spot". While doing this, she names the functions of these props. She also fills in the client treatment card. On this card she puts a cross for the treated pet and she writes down the given treatment and the prescribed medicines in her own

B. Pompert, M.Sc. (✉)
De Activiteit, National Centre for Developmental Education, Alkmaar, The Netherlands
e-mail: b.pompert@de-activiteit.nl

B. van Oers (ed.), *Developmental Education for Young Children*, International
Perspectives on Early Childhood Education and Development 7,
DOI 10.1007/978-94-007-4617-6_15,
© Springer Science+Business Media Dordrecht 2012

idiosyncratic scribbles. After the consultation hour she talks with the vet about the number of animals that came to be treated today. She draws some signs, intending: 1, 2, 3, and 4.

"Opening Hours"

Sander, (5 years old) wants to make a board that shows the opening hours. Sander and Dorien discuss this with the rest of the group. They talk about what to write on the board. Looking at the weekly calendar, they check out for each day at what time they can play in the vet corner. The teacher writes these days and hours on a flip-over. In this way she creates a reminder for Sander. Then, before Sander begins, he and the teacher have a little talk about the board. The teacher stimulates him to consider his approach by asking him the following questions: "Sander, do you know what you are going to do now? Can you start now, without my help?" And "If you don't know how to write something, do you know where to find it?" After this conversation he starts with his board.

The previous examples illustrate the starting points for language acquisition and language education in Basic Development:

- Language education remains connected to the play character of activities in interesting themes in the group.
- We learn to use language in real life situations, together with others in a community of language users; a community that treats you as if you are proficient, although you are just a beginner. You can always participate, and you are never too young to do so.
- We learn language by communicating (speaking, writing and reading) with others, while we all concentrate our attention on the same object or topic.

In Basic Development, language education essentially aims to improve the communicative skills of young children so that they can participate in a variety of cultural practices, in a world of stories and language play (de Haan 2008).

In the vet play, we see how children understand each other in the play script and align language and action to each other. But that's not all; they also build up their world knowledge and the associated language genres. For instance, they learn to distinguish between a description ("this is how a sick cat looks like") and a theory ("when you suspect that a dog has a broken paw, an x-ray is useful; but when he's nauseous it isn't.") In the playful activities in and around the vet corner, it is possible to create a zone of proximal development, wherein language and thought processes are brought to a higher level. The play activities provide children with opportunities to give meaning to activities like reading and writing, but also to receive help when needed.

In the play in the vet corner, many children learn to fill out the treatment card, but they also write (and read) other texts, like a report about a visit to the real vet, and booklets for the play in the vet corner that give tips about various animals.

In building a language community, the adult plays a specific role. The teacher ensures that the interaction is developmentally orientated and directed to language acquisition. That is to say, the teacher is focused on creating zones of proximal development in conversations with groups of pupils, wherein the voices of the children are called up and expanded with the help of the teacher or the children's peers. The teacher challenges children to use language and responds to them. The pupils' language production is the basis for building up an instructional conversation together, whereby the topic (what exactly are we talking about?) is investigated by talking and questioning. The teacher stimulates the children's language learning mechanism through fine tuning and feedback (Damhuis and Litjens 2001).

A Broad View of Literacy

Acquiring good reading and writing skills is essential for every young child. A child who doesn't learn to read and write properly in his early years, will encounter problems later in life. The risk of a less successful school career increases for children that are labelled as poor readers in their first years of education (Au 1993). Appropriate help in the use of language as a personal means for communication, observing the conventional rules, is crucial for all children to become proficient readers and writers (Pompert 2008).

For becoming proficient at literacy education in Developmental Education, teachers often have to revise their basic educational conceptions (see also Chap. 13 of this volume). In the area of literacy education, teachers must dismiss the idea that reading is merely a technical accomplishment. It is a form of communication too, closely related to writing. In this section I will clarify the view of literacy education in Basic Development.

Reading and writing in Basic Development includes four combined areas of competence that ensure that young children become good readers and writers:

- Narrative competence
- Literary competence
- Visual competence
- Informative competence

Narrative Competence

Narrativity is an aspect of human nature (see also Chaps. 5 and 7 of this volume). Everything we see, hear, feel and experience produces stories. By telling stories we give meaning to things and create coherence and continuity in our experiences. Our stories give much information about how we think about things and what kind of meaning we assign to them. Children are participants in narrative activities from the beginning of their lives and soon also become narrators themselves (see van Oers 2003). They talk about what happens, about their concerns, their feelings and their experiences. For example, in Dorien's class the children talk about their own pets, they make texts for the pictures of the visit to the vet, and for pictures of their sick teddy bear. Young children benefit from telling their own stories and listening to other peoples' stories. Through listening to stories and telling stories children become able to understand literate language. By telling their stories they learn to express events in language. They learn to hold on to the perspective of the story, to name place and date, to follow a chronological order and to indicate relations. Personal narratives can be used as a basis for text comprehension. The spoken stories of the children are worth capturing in texts or drawings. These written and drawn versions of the story provide an excellent stepping stone for children to learn to read themselves. Indeed, by capturing narratives and reading them back, pupils are able to communicate messages more precisely: to themselves and to others. This is why the texts of the children in Dorien's group always come back as presentation text or as read alouds in the whole group.

Literary Competence

Literary competence for children at this age is about reading picture books. The children learn to contemplate a picture book and take account of literary aspects like the narrative perspective, character indications and narrative strategies (like the way the excitement span is built up). They read the picture book and talk about these literary codes. In Dorien's class, for instance, they read the book *De jongen en de vis* (*The boy and the fish*) by the Dutch author Max Velthuys. The boy catches a big fish and in doing so, fulfils his dream. The boy doesn't want to sell the fish to the fishmonger but rather takes it home with him. Back home he puts the fish in a bath tub of water, but it is very small for the fish. The fish is unhappy so the boy tries to cheer him up. The next day, the fish is ill and the doctor gives him a medicine. The fish dreams he can fly, but unfortunately he's still in the tub and still sick. He tells the boy he is homesick. The boy understands and takes the poor fish back to the lake. In the conversation about the story, the children talk about the boy, why he loves the fish so much, why the mother is okay with the fish staying in the bath tub, why the fish is homesick, and why the boy tries to cheer him up and comfort him. This manner of reading and talking about books enables children to think about (read aloud) stories and draw conclusions about the main characters, the place and time of the action and the plots of a story. Moreover, research shows that young children are able to distinguish properly between the world of stories and the real world due to this way of dealing with pictures (van der Pol 2010).

Visual Competence

Learning to use visual language is becoming more important as many messages are communicated in pictures. Think about prints, photos, videos and all kinds of visual symbols. Young children must learn to use illustrations as an aid to remembering stories. They don't always automatically do this in a right way (Nelson 2007). Besides, illustrations often only add details that do not help in remembering the storyline. Visual competence is about being able to perceive carefully and naming and describing the subject of the picture. For this, we use questions such as what do you see, what shapes, structures, colours, what parts can you see clearly and brightly, and what is less clear? After this, it is about finding out what the image means and how it affects you.

Dorien's group is talking about an illustration in the picture book about the boy and the fish. In the illustration they see how the boy holds the fish under his arm while he walks through the city. They look carefully at who the boy meets on his way, and further on they discuss why nobody speaks to him.

Informative Competence

Informative competence is about reading and writing in order to gain and process knowledge about the world. Young children explore their direct environment and encounter other people, animals and objects within it. They experience all kind of things they want to know more about. Stories and books give them this opportunity. Reading informational texts requires specific skills. In the first place it's about learning to use what you already know about the subject of a text, so you can make connections with your own knowledge and the questions you have. While reading, it is important that you build up – and watch over – your comprehension of the text. After reading, it's important to look back and review what you have come to know and what not. Moreover, reflecting on the reading process and evaluating whether this approach has been effective also ensures an attentive reading attitude. In Developmental Education reading informational texts includes writing: before, during and after reading the children submit their ideas and thoughts. For example, they note their questions before reading or they make a semantic map. While reading, they write down key words. Afterwards they make their own text, a report, or they write down the answers they found to their questions. Understanding is achieved through talking about what you read. The pupils are being challenged to exchange views and build up understanding, with the teacher, in small groups or in pairs. Obviously, vocabulary and word knowledge play a major role in the understanding of especially informational texts. Oral vocabulary and stimulating oral communication improve informational competence, because they positively influence reading comprehension. To really understand texts, it is essential to read together and to reason, judge and sort things out in dialogue.

The children in Dorien's group read a variety of informational texts about animals, the work of a vet and animal rescue. In Basic Development the above mentioned competences are dealt with in joint activities wherein young children are directed to real literacy activities. You are never too young to be a real reader or writer, and communicate ideas in written form.

Writing Comes First

The way people in a child's environment talk, read and write with young children is of major influence for children's literacy development. Becoming literate is a cultural and not a natural process. The contribution of adults is crucial. Through interaction with adult readers and writers young children enter a new world of literate meanings. Telling stories, writing texts and reading aloud together constitute challenging zones of proximal development for starting readers.

Because developmental processes have an open character and can go in many unpredictable directions, it is necessary to maintain an overview of the developmental perspective by building up long-term learning routes for literacy for 3–7 or 8 year-olds. The learning route for reading starts with oral interaction and stories, then moves on to messages and texts on paper, to reading back together, and reading aloud until, eventually, the stage of reading by yourself is reached.

At the age of approximately 2 years old, children start to gain more specific skills and knowledge about language, which give them access to more complex communicative activities, such as the ability to tell small narratives. The stories of toddlers obtain increasingly more content and show a clearer construction: that is, they have a beginning, a middle and an end. It is almost always worthwhile to draw or write these personal stories. Also in role-play activities, the children find plenty of reasons to write. With the theme in the Dorien's kindergarten group children write all kinds of things:

- treatment cards;
- informative booklets (see below: tips for the guinea pig);
- reports about the visit to the vet;
- animal passports;
- labels for the medicines (see below Fig. 15.1).

This writing builds on the capabilities that the children already have in the field of oral and pictorial communication, and in putting their thoughts, moods and intentions into words. In our view, writing is a continuous extension of communicating with pictorial means. This is consistent with Vygotskij's claim that the formation of writing ability should be meaningful for children, based on a need to communicate with new means. In his view, children's written communication should be developed on the basis of guided attempts to "cultivate" previous means

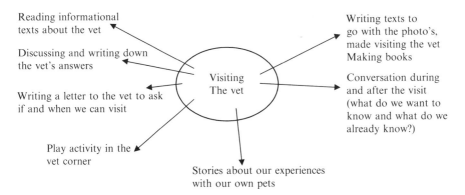

Reading informational
texts about the vet

Discussing and writing down
the vet's answers

Writing a letter to the vet to ask
if and when we can visit

Play activity in the
vet corner

Visiting
The vet

Writing texts to
go with the photo's,
made visiting the vet
Making books

Conversation during
and after the visit
(what do we want to
know and what do we
already know?)

Stories about our experiences
with our own pets

Fig. 15.1 Scheme of literacy activities

for communication, rather than replacing children's old means of communication by imposing new cultural tools (Vygotsky 1978, p. 118).

This explains why in our view writing comes before technical reading (van Oers 2008).

By reading back their own texts and the texts of others, pupils become participants in meaningful literacy activities. This is the moment when the need emerges to become more precise and more conventional, both in writing and in reading back, as well as in reading together. Now there is a fertile soil for children's first reading efforts. The skills and knowledge required for this, such as letter knowledge and phonemic awareness, are timely and functionally addressed in this way (Ehri 2001). Reading several books together with other children and with the teacher remains important. At this stage, the children read books for beginning readers on their own, and they read picture books, stories and informational books with the help of their teacher. This keeps the development of reading and writing connected, which ensures that reading and writing mutually reinforce each other in powerful ways (Suhre 2002).

Meaningful Reading and Writing Activities

The reading and writing activities in Basic Development are always linked to activities with a play character and to interesting themes that play a role in the group. The children read and write about topics they care about. The topics and themes are related to events in their direct environment, to current situations and issues, to texts and to books that are brought into the group, to excursions outside the school and to the stories of others.

In Dorien's group, the children have told stories about sick pets and injured animals. They know that these animals need to go to the vet for treatment. They get very curious about the work of veterinarians and wonder if they could maybe even visit one. The teacher thinks that this should be possible. Together with the group, she designs a range of literacy activities around the vet that can be schematically represented like in Fig. 15.1.

With these activities the teacher gives shape to a literacy curriculum with the following characteristics:

1. Reading and writing activities are meaningful and interrelated. They are real for the children and functionally embedded in their ongoing activities. At the same time they focus on realising important literacy aims in learning to read and write. For example: the animal information booklets have a function in the play in the pet shop. They are used and sold to customers. If a customer buys a guinea pig he gets a free information booklet. Information booklets are widely read and some specific words from the books are used to expand children's alphabetic knowledge and to teach them decoding skills. Explicit attention to the achievement of language goals remains attached to communicative and meaningful contexts.

2. Reading and writing activities are communicative activities, i.e. they are inter-active and dialogic. They develop through numerous instructional conversations before, during and after reading and writing. The teacher ensures that she varies interaction styles and that she has the knowledge about when direct instruction is useful and needed, and when coaching and conversation is more appropriate.

3. Pupils actually have a voice in the decisions about the suggested activities, whilst the teacher keeps sight of necessary goals and developmental moments for all children. Language skills that should be addressed are learned as much as possible in meaningful contexts and communicative activities. There is a balance between authenticity and conventionality.

4. Different types of texts are offered from the outset. Starting readers are chal-lenged to read all kind of texts besides special books for beginning readers that focus on reading fluently and quickly. Pre-eminently, informative books on the themes in the group and children's own questions help to develop an optimal reading attitude.

The books are also rich sources for the children for writing their own texts related to the topic involved. For example, in Dorien's group the texts are made with speech bubbles, inspired by a comic book that turned out to be a real hit in this class.

The Teacher's Role

The teacher creates meaningful and coherent reading and writing activities and uses the four-field scheme (see Figs. 15.2 and 15.3 below) for integrating and contextualising necessary instructions, mini-lessons and instructional conversations (Fijma and Pompert 2007). This scheme concentrates on the four main aspects of teaching literacy in context:

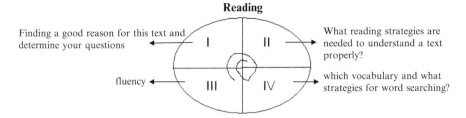

Fig. 15.2 Main objectives for reading activities

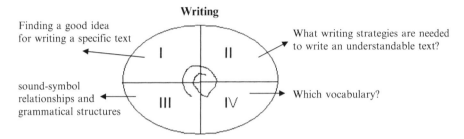

Fig. 15.3 Main objectives for writing activities

I. motivation;
II. comprehension;
III. vocabulary;
IV. language conventions.

The four-field schemes given above are used for the reading (Fig. 15.2) and writing activities (Fig. 15.3). They give an overview of the important language aims for all activities in the theme period.

The realisation of these goals requires a lot from teachers. In the first place they have to keep in mind that writing and reading stay connected to each other within the thematic activity of the group. By giving writing a central place, the reading activities become more useful and effective.

Before reading, pupils write down their own stories and the knowledge they have already acquired about the topic. The teacher encourages oral negotiations of the meanings represented in the texts or drawings. For example, in Annemarie's group of first graders (4–5 year olds) the theme is: "What jobs do our parents have?" First the children talk about what they want to be. They come out with wonderful stories. They compose numerous texts about professions and make rich semantic maps about what they already know about a secretary, policeman, doctor and lifeguard. The information books that they read after examining these professions become more understandable through these advance organisers, and thus are read with more enthusiasm. The children are already familiar with the new words in the books, so understanding the texts becomes easier. During reading, they pause to write down important things (with the help of the teacher). They do this by making small texts, taking notes, remember-lists or underlines. After this, it is important for pupils to discuss the written text, not only verbally, but also by making written reflections. Think of comics, answers to questions, a report or summary, a poster or a personal text on the subject or read story.

In Gerlanda's class (second grade) they are working with the theme "Professions" and the children set up an employment agency in their classroom. The idea is to make an information paper about the job vacancies. Of course this requires further investigation. The group will visit shops in the city where parents work and they will visit a labour and employment agency. Parents are interviewed about their work. One of the activities is to write a profession card. First the children interview a parent and they make notes on the profession card. Then they read an informational text about this job to be able to complete the profession card. The interview and the information from the text are also incorporated into the text for the job information paper (Fijma and Pompert 2007).

The teacher uses her daily logbook to plan the reading and writing activities and reflects on her instructional role for all the children (for the rationale and use of logbooks see also Chap. 14). She prepares to engage her pupils in an instructional conversation that both builds knowledge of the subject matter, and strengthens their vocabulary, comprehension strategies, motivation and use of language conventions.

Instructions are tied to collaborative literacy. Reading and writing are practised as social and joint activities with a lot of exchange between the children and the teacher. The teacher uses flexible grouping as a dynamic approach to learning, which involves the formation of many group arrangements to tune in with the children's needs and the teacher's goals. Flexible grouping involves grouping by interest, homogeneous by instructional needs or heterogeneous by language level. It is through interaction with others – peers and adults – that the children are able to expand their thinking and language use. The teacher varies her instructional style to achieve the balance between the active negotiation of meaning by the children, and her explicit educational goals and expected results.

She uses three instruction types:

1. *Instructional conversation*

The teacher converses with a small group of pupils on a specific academic topic or a literacy problem. The teacher elicits pupils' talk by listening, questioning, rephrasing or modelling.

Together they are "weaving new information into existing mental structures" (Tharp and Gallimore 1988), to ensure that the interface between emergent schooled concepts and everyday concepts is provided. Instructional conversations are necessary before, during and after reading and writing activities. In the pre-writing phase they are used to activate or build up background knowledge about the writing topic, to get ideas for the stories during writing and afterwards used for feedback on work in progress, suggestions for revision and reflective talk about the final drafts.

Also for reading activities the teacher uses instructional conversations for:

- exploration of the theme of the text;
- activation and use of background knowledge and questions;
- discussions and elicitation of arguments and ideas about the text.

2. *Participating and scaffolding*

By active participation the teacher is able to scaffold the writing and reading activities of the children. She uses dialogues and small group talks to fine-tune on the language and actions of the pupils.

An example:

A group of eight pupils is writing a text about how life was when they were a baby and how life is now. They all have a piece of paper with two photographs of themselves, one as a baby and one at the age of about 6 years old.

They are working in dyads, talking about their photographs.

The teacher is participating and she assists the children in telling their stories by asking questions such as:

"Joep, where is this? What did you do here?"

"You smile in your photograph? Why is that? Have you already told this to Charlotte?"

After the duo-talks the pupils are going to write their stories and again the teacher participates.

Ellis is writing a story about her baby photo. She needs help from the teacher (T).

T: "Ellis, can you read what you already have written?"

E: "I only have ... my rubber pacifier"

"I always spit it out, my rubber pacifier"

T: "You know why you did that?"

E: "Yes because I liked to suck on my thumb"

T: "So ..."

E: "For I did not liked my rubber pacifier"

T: "Then you can write that now. Two lovely sentences"

3. *Explicit instruction*

Explicit instruction, like modelling, is necessary for implementing new reading and writing strategies.

The teacher uses responsive and interactive instruction. She knows which strategies are useful for small groups of children from observing the joint reading and writing activities and the interactions among the pupils and between herself and the children. She uses these data for selecting goals and specific instructions for different pupils.

Teacher Dorien is using her logbook in the following a way:

"Play with Corine. I am the vet. Corine is my assistant.

I'm going to assist her in:

- extending her role;
- filling in the card (writing the words);
- sorting out the medicines.

Tobias, Salma and Rubia will visit us. I'm going to assist them in rousing their stories."

For gathering the right data the teacher uses observation models for language and literacy. These models are part of the observation manual (HOREB) used in Basic Development (see Chaps. 4 and 14 for further information). With this instrument the teacher makes registrations of the pupils in a diary and tries to infer the needs for new steps from these observations.

The registrations in the children's diaries are completed with performance samples, such as semantic maps, graphic organisers, narratives and journal writings.

Alternative criterion-oriented tests for vocabulary and narrative competence provide for supplementary data (see Chaps. 6 and 7).

In this way the teacher builds up a dynamic assessment strategy in which hypothetical learning trajectories have to be put into practice to find out how pupils respond.

Our Research and Results

In the 1990s we started research on the implementation and further development of literacy activities within Basic Development. The still ongoing research activities include three main issues:

1. The implementation of this form of developmental teaching in different schools. Are the teachers able to appropriate this Vygotskian paradigm on literacy in their classrooms and schools?
2. Evaluation of the outcomes in terms of progress of the pupils in reading and writing.
3. The support and assistance teachers need to improve their work in this way.

Re 1. In the first years we focused on questions about the changing role of the teachers. We conducted several case studies to find out whether the teachers were able to design literacy activities with a play character, and whether they were able to participate in these activities so that new cognitive instruments could be made interesting for the pupils, through which the transition to the more conscious learning activities can be made in due course.

This concerns symbol use, printed text, writing messages and playing and telling narratives (see for example Pompert and Janssen-Vos 2003). Later on evaluations were conducted both by researchers committed to Developmental Education, and non-committed researchers from a more distanced point of view (a.o. Harskamp and Suhre 2000; Suhre 2002). Their research indicated that the teachers were able to improve literacy activities in this way. They internalised most aspects of the concepts and were able to execute them in practice with diverse groups of pupils.

Re 2. From the year 2000 we also evaluated in terms of learning outcomes. In several schools we looked at the results on literacy. We used standardised tests on fluency, vocabulary, text production, and comprehension (van Oers 2002; Duijkers 2003; Fijma and Pompert 2002). This research indicated that the pupils benefit from our curriculum, especially in the field of vocabulary and comprehension. Research by Harskamp and Suhre (2000) shows that 50 % of the pupils from our classes (in this case n = 67) score above the national average norm.

Poland (2007) reported on longitudinal research at four schools. These schools had been implementing developmental literacy education over a period of 4 years. This study showed that the results on vocabulary, fluency, text production and narrative competence were better and that the schools succeeded in preventing children from dropping out of the reading and writing activities at an early stage.

Re 3. Implementing this approach is a complex task and a process that requires a strong and reflective teacher. It goes without saying how important research is on the support that a teacher needs to acquire new views and ways of thinking in order to master the concept and to act on it in their daily work. We as teacher trainers develop instruments for planning and designing, observation and evaluation. Research focused on the use of these instruments such as the 4-field-scheme shows that co-construction in joint activity in the classroom with a participating teacher trainer, creates the best results. It is in the context of such joint, reflective activity that teachers can attribute personal meaning to these instruments (Fijma and Pompert 2007; Pompert 2004). This way of professionalising teachers requires mutual interest for lasting improvement of both theory and practice.

Improving reading results remains a central topic in the ongoing political and social debates in our country about the quality of primary education. Much emphasis nowadays is on evidence-based reading research with a strong focus on explicit instruction in the skills and concepts that are considered the best predictors of later reading achievement. A lot of research has identified the core content that young children need to learn, to become successful fluent readers.

In Basic Development we see it as a challenging task to integrate effective strategies and rich, meaningful reading and writing activities.

References

Au, K. (1993). *Literacy instruction in multicultural settings*. Fort Worth: HBJC Publishers.

Damhuis, R., & Litjens, P. (2001). *Creating practices with real opportunities for oral language learning*. Presentation 11ᵉ EECERA-conference 2001, Alkmaar, the Netherlands.

de Haan, D. (2008). Leerzaam en betekenisvol taalonderwijs [Informative and meaningful language education]. In J. van der Zwaard, S. van Oenen, & M. Huisman (Eds.), *Zonder wrijving geen vooruitgang* (pp. 75–81). Apeldoorn: Garant.

Duijkers, D. (2003). *Betekenisvolle woordenschatontwikkeling, een kwestie van interactie, cultuur en context* [Meaningful vocabulary acquisition, a matter of interaction, culture and context]. Amsterdam: VU University.

Ehri, L. C. (2001). Phonemic awareness instruction helps children learn to read. *Reading Research Quarterly, 36*, 250–287.

Fijma, N., & Pompert, B. (2002). *Unity in pedagogigal concept; diversity in teaching methods in dealing with heterogeneity.* Paper 5ᵉ ISCRAT-congress 2002 Amsterdam.

Fijma, N., & Pompert, B. (2007). *Assisting young writers in meaningful play-board activities.* Paper 17e EECERA-conference 2007, Praag.

Harskamp, E., & Suhre, C. (2000). *Praktijkbrochure Ontwikkelingsgericht lezen. Lesportretten en leerresultaten* [Promoting reading development in school – a practical brochure]. Groningen: GION.

Nelson, K. (2007). Entering the symbol world. In K. Nelson (Ed.), *Young minds in social worlds* (Chap. 6, pp. 149–178). Cambridge, MA: Harvard University Press.

Poland, M. (2007). Bergopwaarts in taalontwikkeling. Ontwikkelingsgericht Onderwijs [Reaching higher in language development in Developmental Education]. *De wereld van het jonge kind, 35*(3), 79–82.

Pompert, B. (2004). *Professional growth of teachers: How to create a zone of proximal development.* Paper 14ᵉ EECERA-conference Malta.

Pompert, B. (2008). Een goede schrijver ben je niet, dat word je [One isn't a good writer, but becomes one]. In D. de Haan & E. Kuiper (Eds.), *Leerkracht in beeld* (pp. 124–133). Assen: Van Gorcum.

Pompert, B., & Janssen-Vos, F. (2003). From narrator to writer. Promoting cultural learning in early childhood. In B. van Oers (Ed.), *Narratives of childhood* (pp. 127–145). Amsterdam: VU University Press.

Suhre, C. (2002). *Functioneel lezen en schrijven in de groepen 3 en 4* [Functionally reading and writing in grades 3 and 4]. Groningen: RION.

Tharp, R. G., & Gallimore, R. (1988). *Rousing minds to life: Teaching, learning, and schooling in social context.* Cambridge: Cambridge University Press.

van der Pol, C. (2010). *Prentenboeken lezen als literatuur* [Picture book reading as literature]. Delft: Eburon.

van Oers, B. (2002). Portfolio's. Naar een andere manier van kijken naar kinderen [Portolio's: towards a new way of evaluating children's work]. *Jeugd in school en Wereld, 87*(4), 37–40.

van Oers, B. (2003). Multiple narratives of childhood: Tools for the improvement of early childhood education. In B. van Oers (Ed.), *Narratives of childhood* (pp. 9–26). Amsterdam: VU University Press.

van Oers, B. (2008). Continuïteit in ontwikkelingsgericht onderwijs [Continuity in Developmental Education]. In D. de Haan & E. Kuiper (Eds.), *Leerkracht in beeld. Ontwikkelingsgericht Onderwijs: theorie, onderzoekpraktijk* (pp. 13–20). Assen: Van Gorcum.

Vygotsky, L. S. (1978). The prehistory of written language. In L. S. Vygotsky (Ed.), *Mind in society: The development of higher psychological processes* (Chap. 7, pp. 105–119). Cambridge, MA: Harvard University Press.

Chapter 16
Learning to Communicate About Number

Niko Fijma

Introduction

In the process of learning to participate in cultural practices, pupils have to learn how to communicate about the numerical and spatial aspects of cultural reality. Teachers in Developmental Education try to teach mathematics within meaningful activities on the basis of classroom conversations on solutions of diverse problems with the help of mathematical means. These activities provide a context for appropriating significant mathematical knowledge and skills. For the young pupils in primary education (4–7/8 year olds in the grades 1–4) play is a so-called leading activity (see Elkonin 1972). Participation of the pupils in such playful activities is assumed to open possibilities for creating zones of proximal development in which the pupils can appropriate (with the help of the teacher and peers) the cultural tools for mathematising in a meaningful way.

This Vygotskian activity-oriented view of development and learning also calls for an activity-based view of mathematics. In this perspective, mathematics is conceived of as an activity of mathematising, i.e. systematically constructing methods for problem solving with symbolic tools (van Oers 1996a, b, 2002; Fijma and Vink 1998). It can be further characterised by its pursuit of certainty. It comes down to a way of solving quantitative and spatial problems with both the help of reasoning with variables and their relations, and of schematic tools (see also Chap. 8 of this volume). Collective reflection and communication on those relations and tools is important for further improvement and schematisation. In Developmental Education we assume that teachers in the lower school grades (4–8 year-olds) stimulate both the general dimensions of mathematical activity like schematising (making schematic representations), attention to relations, the interest

N. Fijma, M.Sc. (✉)
De Activiteit, National Centre for Developmental Education, Alkmaar, The Netherlands
e-mail: n.fijma@de-activiteit.nl

B. van Oers (ed.), *Developmental Education for Young Children*, International
Perspectives on Early Childhood Education and Development 7,
DOI 10.1007/978-94-007-4617-6_16,
© Springer Science+Business Media Dordrecht 2012

in questions of certainty, and the more specific content-oriented skills like counting, adding, subtracting, multiplying, etc. In Developmental Education teachers teach mathematics by (communicatively) mathematising relevant contents and raising interest in the activities on these contents.

In this chapter I will give examples of teaching mathematics in early years classrooms in a developmental way. Important teacher skills are:

• to design and plan a range of meaningful mathematical activities;
• to guide the activities in such a way that they get added value for the children and are in line with the teacher's intentions;
• to observe actively intensive interactions of and with children.

Each of these will be discussed in this chapter. First of all, however, I will further clarify the assumptions of teaching mathematics in a developmental way.

Mathematics in Developmental Education

In Developmental Education the teacher tries to connect mathematics with interesting themes from children's lives and other core activities in the classroom. The teacher avoids isolating mathematics from young children's everyday life.

Learning Mathematics Is Connected to Diverse Relevant Activities and Interesting Themes

In a group 3 (6–7 year olds) the teacher (Jannie) and the children work with the theme "Toys" for about 7 weeks in the months of November and December, the period with the feasts of St Nicholas[1] and Christmas. Teacher Jannie has explored the goals, meanings and possible activities of the theme by means of a scheme derived from HOREB (Janssen-Vos and Pompert 2007; see also Chaps. 4 and 14 of the present volume). She is going to set up a toy shop with the children. At the start of the theme the children and the teacher compare their wish lists of gifts. The lists are discussed and they make an inventory of the kinds of toys they want. Earlier the children have been involved in learning to use different kinds of representational tools (like maps, construction plans, graphs) and they use this knowledge to make a graph of the inventory. Then the children look at a large copy of an illustration from the book "Sinterklaas" (Dematons 2007). This is a cross-section of the part of St Nicholas' castle in which the toys are stored. The children look closely at the toys in St Nicholas' castle and compare it with their own inventory. The children also want to draw a floor plan of the whole of St Nicholas' castle. After that, three

---

[1] For an explanation of this phenomenon see note 1 (Chap. 8).

children build the castle with the help of this floor plan and the illustrations in the book. The next day the children and the teacher make a plan for setting up a toy shop in the classroom. They discuss with each other the lay-out of the shop and the kinds of toys they are going to sell. The children are enthusiastically involved. They are also eager to invent and to make games to sell in their shop. Moreover, they also plan a visit to a toy factory, about 10 km from their school.

After setting up the toy shop in the classroom the children can play in it. To be able to play well in the toy shop, the teacher encourages the pupils to get engaged in several activities in the group, such as writing wish lists, designing and making wrapping paper, designing and making new games, determining the prices of the toys, making the price list, drawing up sales slips. Also, the children write letters to St Nicholas and they write poems. They also make a list of questions in preparation for the visit to the toy factory.

During these weeks the teacher uses these activities as opportunities for teaching mathematics too. For example, she connects learning to count with counting in steps of two in order to make their inventory of kinds of toys. The children are eager to learn to count in steps of two as it helps them to count the toys quickly. Furthermore, the teacher connects spatial orientation to making the floor plan of St Nicholas' castle.

Mathematical activities and their included goals are closely linked to other core activities and interesting themes. Themes usually cover a longer period of 6–8 weeks. Working with themes gives teachers opportunities to become curriculum-makers themselves, taking the actual interests of children seriously into account. Children have the time "to get acquainted" with a theme in order to become aware of their growing possibilities to participate better in the activities. Learning mathematics embedded in meaningful activities is an important principle in Developmental Education, because it appeals to the children as agents and therefore gives a better guarantee for broad meaningful (mathematical) development. In that way the children integrate the narrative of mathematics more and more into their own narratives. They are more able to comprehend the (mathematical) aspects of cultural practices. In Developmental Education the teacher takes care that learning mathematics leads to socio-culturally acceptable mathematical stories, told in a socially negotiable context (Burton 2003).

Learning Mathematics in a Play-Based Curriculum

In Developmental Education the learning of mathematics by young children is always embedded in children's imitative participation in meaningful cultural practices. According to Elkonin (1972), the leading activity of young children (2–8 year-olds) is to be characterised as play activity. Young children's mathematics learning should be inherently related to their play activities.

That's why teacher Jannie wants to set up a toy shop with the children as described in the previous section. In their role-play activities children imitate cultural practices (in this case a toy shop), which constitute contexts for (mathematical) learning. The children determine the prices for the things to sell in the shop. The clients have to pay for these items. The shopkeeper writes a sales slip, etc.

Learning mathematics in a playful way, however, means more than just practicing mathematics embedded in the role-play activities. As van Oers described in Chap. 2, playfulness is a characteristic of children's activities. That means that the teacher and the children take the *rules* that constitute the activity seriously. Making a floor plan of the castle, for example, means that the children try to make it "as real as possible". But it also means that the children have some *degrees of freedom*. The children may act freely to a certain extent. The floor plan is their own schematic representation. They are personally involved in the construction of the schema and the high level of *involvement* helps them to carry out and learn these mathematical actions as actions of their own.

This is a fruitful basis for further development. The teacher is focused on improving the children's abilities to participate in this mathematical activity. Teacher Jannie helps the children to draw the floor plan "in the flat plane". In her communication with the children she uses concepts such as "floor plan", "length" and "width", for example: "Okay, you said we must draw this side longer. You are right. This long side of the castle is the length of the castle". She stimulates the children to use these concepts in their communication, for example: "Tom, please ask John to help you with drawing the floor plan". The children "accept" her help because it takes place in the context of an activity that makes sense to them, and helps them to improve their ability to participate. Teacher Jannie's approach gives opportunities to integrate mathematical meaning and personal sense.

Learning Mathematics in Communication and Cooperation with Others

Learning mathematics is basically a matter of learning to communicate with mathematical means about problem solving, and constructing (new) means for communicating with oneself and with others about mathematical notions like numbers and spatial orientation. In teacher Jannie's group the children learn to communicate in a culturally acceptable mathematical way about the graph with the inventory of kinds of toys, about the floor plan of St Nicholas' castle, about the price list, the sales slips in the toy shop, etc. They appropriate mathematical means like numbers, prices and values of money to be able to communicate in particular practices, like the toy shop.

In Developmental Education the teacher conceives of heterogeneity as a source for individual development. Children learn from and with each other. Cooperation is important: one needs others to develop. The children in teacher Jannie's group 3 are going to make Christmas games. The visit to the toy factory was a big success! The children discovered that the factory doesn't produce Christmas games. So the group decides to produce four games: happy families, a memory game, a puzzle and a game of goose. Teacher Jannie forms heterogeneous groups regarding social skills and level of mathematics. After making plans the groups start to produce the games. Lisa and Femke are members of the group that aims to make the game of goose. Lisa is a vulnerable pupil who has difficulty with counting and with writing numbers. Lisa and Femke make the floor plan of the game. Femke helps Lisa with counting and writing the numbers on the floor plan of the game of goose. Lisa is proud of her work after she has finished making the floor plan.

Learning Mathematics with the Help of a More Knowledgeable Other, e.g. The Teacher

The role of the teacher is essential in Developmental Education. From a Vygotskian point of view the emergence of mathematical thinking in young children is a culturally guided process, wherein mathematical meaning is assigned to (spontaneous) actions of children in the context of their play (see van Oers 2012). These actions can be further developed through collaborative problem solving with more knowledgeable others in the contexts of activities that make sense to the children. The teacher is always looking for meaningful teaching opportunities that contribute to the improvement of children's ability to participate in mathematical activities in their play or classroom conversations.

Teacher Jannie reads aloud a letter from St Nicholas. St Nicholas has lost a lot of his maps! He is still able to find the village, but he probably won't be able to find the school without a map of the school's neighbourhood. In the letter he announces that he would like to visit the school next week! Hence, he asks the children to make a map of the neighbourhood of the school for him. Of course they will! But how? The group decides to go to the main street of the village, that being the place where St Nicholas always enters the village. From that point they take the quickest route to the school. Along the way the children make pictures and they make notes such as "after the pub to the left" or "about fifty steps further to the right". The next day the teacher gives the children, grouped into sets of three, the pictures and the notes to make a map. However, first of all they have a look at the floor plan of St Nicholas' castle to answer questions like: "How do we draw a street"? or "How do we draw a house"? After that each group starts drawing a map. Teacher Jannie helps the group of Anne, Floor and Lars. They are quite well able to draw the map, but they confront a problem: how does St Nicholas know which building the church is or which is the school? Floor has an idea: "You can write the word on the map". But how to do that in the proper way? Teacher Jannie takes this opportunity to add a new action to this activity. She says: "It's a very good idea to write on the map to make clear which buildings there are. But we can't write the whole words on it, that's true. Is it possible to write parts of the words?" Anne answers that you can write the letter "c" instead of the whole word "church" or the letter "s" instead of the word "school".

The other children understand her and they think it a very good idea! Jannie shows them another map with a legend. Then the children start to make a legend for their own map. They are sure that St Nicholas will find the school with the help of the map with the symbols!

This example shows that confronting a problem stimulates discussion. It also gives the teacher the opportunity to bring in new actions, concepts, and symbols. Pupils appropriate these new actions, concepts and symbols. The children of teacher Jannie frequently use the notions "map" and "legend" in their conversations about their own plans of the village.

So learning mathematics in a developmental way:

- is connected with diverse relevant activities and interesting themes;
- is to be embedded in a play-based curriculum;
- requires communication and cooperation with others, and
- proceeds with the help of a more knowledgeable other, e.g. the teacher.

These four assumptions have consequences for the teacher's activities of designing, planning, guiding and observing of mathematical activities. In the next paragraph I will give examples of these teacher qualities.

Important Qualities Required for Teaching Mathematics in a Developmental Way

In Developmental Education the teacher and the children work with themes that cover a longer period (for example 6 or 7 weeks). Young children are primarily interested in "discovering" their environment and the world. They have questions about their environment and they are eager to find answers to these questions. By bringing actual and interesting contents from the world into the classroom, the teacher creates opportunities for the children to participate in relevant theme-related activity settings. All core activities in Developmental Education, including mathematics, are connected to the ongoing theme. That's the way mathematics is related to the other activities in the classroom. So there is a close relation between the core activities and the contents of the theme of a certain period in the curriculum.

Designing and Planning a Range of Meaningful Mathematical Activities

The teacher prepares the theme period with the help of the so-called book of activities of HOREB (Janssen-Vos and Pompert 2007; see also Chap. 14 of this volume). The book of activities offers teachers starting points and means for designing and planning a range of activities, including mathematical activities.

I will give two examples of this. In a group 1/2 (4–6 year olds) teacher Marjolijn draws up a plan for the theme "The bus". It's a first planning, a framework with the main outlines of the theme. What does the teacher consider and what does this framework look like?

First she considers the meaningfulness of the theme for the children. She believes that the choice of this theme is meaningful for both the children and the teacher. The children will experience it as meaningful because there are many buses and trams driving round in town. She expects that most of the children have experiences with travelling by bus. Some children have told her about a bus ride they have had. Therefore she thinks this theme can make sense for them, because it is a practice in which they want to take part and in which they can adopt a meaningful role. Secondly, she considers the meaningfulness of the theme for herself as a teacher. For the teacher, the theme is meaningful because the roles that the children will play in the theme-related activities require new tools for participation (e.g. new mathematical notions and reading ability). The theme gives plenty of opportunities for other important broad goals for the teacher, like learning to work and play together, being active, and learning to take initiatives. The teacher also looks for occasions for stimulating specific knowledge and skills like vocabulary, and subject matter tools and techniques.

Thirdly, she links the theme with other relevant core activities of the curriculum of Basic Development (see Chap. 4). The core activities are related to the theme and they are important for achieving the teacher's educational goals within the chosen theme. In this first planning she designs the following activities:

- *Play activities:*
  - Role-play: the bus and a bus stop
- *Constructive and expressive activities:*
  - Make a bus
  - Make a bus stop
- *Reading and writing activities:*
  - Stories of your own experiences
  - Route description at the bus stop: names of the streets and the buildings (like the mill and the library)
  - Route description in the bus: pictures and names of the streets and the buildings
- *Mathematical activities:*
  - Make a bus ticket (numbers/numbers sequences/counting)
  - Draw the floor plan of the bus (understanding numbers and their meaning/geometry; spatial orientation)
  - Make a bus stop and the route description (geometry; spatial orientation by mental reasoning/numbers/times of departure)
  - In the role-play activity:

- telling the times of departure
- buying the bus ticket
- reading the route description at the bus stop
- counting the numbers of the bus ticket and stamping the right number

- *Conversational activities:*

  - About your own experiences
  - About the design of the bus
  - About the design of the bus stop
  - About the role-play activities
  - About mathematics and other cultural tools

The teacher decides to begin with some start activities (see Chap. 4 for further explanation) to introduce the theme so that the children get involved in it and the teacher can find out what the children know about the theme and what they would like to know and to do about the theme. After the start activities the teacher adjusts and extends her first planning.

In the second example I will particularly focus on the mathematical activities. In another group, a group 3 (6–7 year olds), teacher Monique draws up a plan for the theme "The post" for about 7 weeks in the months of November and December, the period with the feasts of St Nicholas and Christmas. After considering the meaningfulness of the theme for both the children and herself, teacher Monique links the theme with the relevant core activities. She designs the following mathematical activities:

- Designing and using stamps (numbers/relation weight – distance – value)
- Addressing and delivering the post (numbers/postal codes/drawing a map for it)
- Constructing the post box (measuring) and times of collection (time)
- Selling things in the post office (numbers/practicing addition and subtraction with money)
- Making and using a calendar, counting the days (sequence of numbers/time: days of the week)
- Preparing Christmas dinner (quantities/dividing)

The mathematical activities are functionally related to the other core activities in the classroom and they are formulated as "real world" socio-cultural activities. In advance, the teacher notes (as formulated in brackets above) the mathematical knowledge and skills "embedded" in these activities. The teacher knows that she can relate her intended mathematical goals to the activities. The "real" socio-cultural mathematical activities bridge the mathematical knowledge skills and the meanings of the children.

Furthermore, the teacher has to consider her mathematical meanings and her goals more precisely, to make sure that all relevant mathematical content will be covered over the year. Therefore she uses our 3D model (Fijma 2003b). With the help of this model (see below) she makes an analysis of some mathematical activities focused on three content oriented aspects:

- *Domein* (the Dutch word for: domain): which domain/field of mathematics is involved? In the lower grades: numbers/operations, measuring and geometry.
- *Doel* (the Dutch word for: aim): which aims can be achieved within the planned activity?
- *Didactiek*[2] (the Dutch word for: didactics): which instructional tools are important to guide these activities?

The teacher uses the mathematical text book as a resource instead of a prescriptive curriculum device (Fijma 2000). By the 3D analysis the teacher not only specifies the mathematical knowledge and skills (domain and aim), but also how to guide the activity (didactics).

Teacher Monique makes 3D analyses of two mathematical activities:

1. "selling things in the post office";
2. "addressing and delivering the post/drawing a map for it".

The teacher's 3D analysis of the activity "selling things in the post office" yields different possibilities:

- Domein (domain): numbers
- Doel (aim): numbers up to 20: counting backwards; number sequence (which number before or after?)
- Didactiek (didactics): number line

Or:

- Domein (domain): numbers
- Doel (aim): add up by analogy ($2 + 5 = 7$; $12 + 5 = 17$)
- Didactiek (didactics): money (note of 10 euro) and a "rekenrekje" (an abacus with 5-structure; see Fig. 16.2)

Or:

- Domein (domain): numbers
- Doel (aim): counting money: recognising the coins of 2, 5 and 10 eurocents and 1 or 2 euro; notes of 5 and 10 euro
- Didactiek (didactics): reasoning

Or:

- Domein (domain): numbers
- Doel (aim): counting money: how to pay?
- Didactiek (didactics): making amounts of money in several ways and comparing the several ways: which way do you prefer and why?

The results of the teacher's 3D analysis of the activity "addressing and delivering the post/drawing a map for it":

---

[2]For a proper understanding of this word, see also Chap. 4, note 4.

- Domein (domain): numbers
- Doel (aim): even and odd numbers up to 20
- Didactiek (didactics): number line; counting aloud and still

Or:

- Domein (domain): geometry
- Doel (aim): drawing a map
- Didactiek (didactics): taking a walk in the neighbourhood (making pictures!) and from aerial photographs of the town (Google Earth!) to drawing a map; which signs and symbols? Frequently asking: "Is it right?"

Or:

- Domein (domain): geometry
- Doel (aim): drawing a route on the map
- Didactiek (didactics): using the pictures of the walk with attention to putting action and objects into words; which sign/symbol (arrows)?; attention to "clever" routes (thinking ahead)

Or:

- Domein (domain): measuring
- Doel (aim): telling the time: the hour/the half hour
- Didactiek (didactics): using different clocks (analogous and digital)

The teacher articulates the connections between the "real" socio-cultural activities and the mathematical issues by making the 3D-analyses. By doing this the teacher creates a fruitful starting point for designing a mathematically specific, purposeful range of activities, with "room" for the meanings of the pupils. These 3D-analyses support the teacher in teaching mathematics in a play-based curriculum, and in taking care that all relevant mathematical content will be covered in due course.

Teachers in Developmental Education want to stimulate the broad development of their pupils too. Teaching mathematics means more than just teaching specific mathematical knowledge and skills. That is why they use, within this phase of planning and designing the theme, another instrument of HOREB: the observation model of mathematical activities. This is a tool for the teacher to identify children's developmental needs and to mark out a hypothetical learning trajectory for individual pupils. This observation model guarantees a broad and coherent view of the development of the pupils. It consists of the following aspects with several points of observation:

A. The means and the motives of the pupils

   Possible points of observation: interested in mathematical problems and mathematical activities? Or the need "to be sure", pursuing of certainty?

B. The development of the mathematical activity

Special attention to the mathematical activities of Matz, Sem,
Daan, Naomi, Jay, Tobias, Sean and Lin. I will observe and guide:

- The means and motives: having pleasure in performing
  mathematical activities; pursuing of certainty, the need "to
  be sure"?

- The language-cognitive development: being able to explain
  and clarifying quantitative or spatial problems?

- The specific knowledge and skills: numbers: ordering
  numbers in the number row; counting backwards; counting
  in steps of two; even – uneven numbers.

Fig. 16.1 Example of a teacher's planning in the book of activities

In role-play, in constructive play and in learning activities the teacher observes the mathematical actions within the activities, and how precisely these actions are being performed:

Measuring: e.g. point of observation: comparing indirectly by measuring out (the towers of the castle must be equally high and the pupil measures them with a tape).

Quantifying: e.g. point of observation: structured counting (in the supermarket the pupil counts the eggs by using the five structure of the box with eggs).

Understanding space: e.g. point of observation: constructing or locating objects by using a map.

C. The language-cognitive development in mathematical activities

E.g. point of observation: within solving quantitative or spatial problems reasoning with variables and their relations (three apples are two euros, so if I want four apples it will be more than two euros).

D. The broad development in mathematical activities

E.g. point of observation: reflecting on plans and performances (last time the castle tower wasn't round, but when I use this circle as a floor . . . .)

E. The specific knowledge and skills in mathematical activities

Points of observation of numbers/operations, measuring and geometry. For this aim the teacher has made the 3D analyses.

Teacher Monique uses the observation model for the guidance of a group of pupils during the theme period. She wants to pay special attention to them. She makes a group plan and registers in the book of activities (Fig. 16.1 above; see also Chap. 14 of this volume).

In this phase of planning the theme, the teacher has designed purposefully a number of meaningful mathematical activities. A more detailed planning of the activities will take place during the theme's implementation phase, when the teacher starts the theme period with her group.

Developmentally Guiding the Activities

In Developmental Education the teacher tries to guide the child's mathematical activities in such a way that they get added value for the pupils and are in line with the teacher's intentions.

Every day the teacher plans some guided activities with small groups with the focus on new tool-mediated actions that might be learned (zone of proximal development).

Teacher Monique has started "The post" theme and the pupils are very enthusiastic about it. In the first week they write letters to friends or family, and visit the post office in town. After this visit they make a plan for constructing a post office in the corridor near the classroom. For the delivery of the letters the group wants to draw a correct map of the neighbourhood. But: how to do it?

In the phase of the theme planning the teacher made a 3D analysis of this activity:

- Domein (domain): geometry
- Doel (aim): drawing a map
- Didactiek (didactics): taking a walk in the neighbourhood (making pictures!) and from aerial photographs of the town (Google Earth!) to drawing a map; which signs and symbols? Frequently asking: "Is it right?"

She uses this 3D analysis to make a plan for guiding the activity. Therefore she uses another instrument of HOREB: the logbook. She uses this as a means for short-term (daily) planning.

With the help of this tool, teacher Monique registers in her digital logbook the following planning (see Chap. 14 of this volume for more information about assessment and registration procedures in Developmental Education):

1. activity: drawing a map of the neighbourhood;
2. with: the whole group, but especially guiding: Naomi and Tobias;
3. my role: participating coach;
4. observation points: having pleasure in participating in the activity? Need "to be sure"? Putting the problem into words? Which signs/symbols (to what extent of abstraction)?

Some of these observation points are goals of the group plan she made.

The Progress of the Activity

As already explained, all pupils in this group (grade three, age 6) have experience with drawing maps, because they made floor plans of their constructions in grade two. And they are familiar with the floor plan of their classroom hanging on the wall.

The teacher reminds the children of these experiences and the pupils begin to realise that they need to be able to fly over the neighbourhood in order to get a picture of it "from above". But then, much to the teacher's surprise, one of the pupils says that she once saw her house from above on the computer with her elder brother! And another pupil had the same experience. A little later the whole group looks at their town with Google Earth on the digital board! They look for familiar places, the streets and their own houses and of course they look for the school building. They decide to use these pictures for drawing the map of the neighbourhood.

The pupils work in pairs. They've already noticed that it is a good idea to draw the school building in the middle of the paper. Drawing the map is not so easy. Some pairs try to draw the school building "realistically". The teacher points to the pictures on Google Earth and asks questions like: "How does the school look from above? How important is it to draw details?"

When the pupils are busy drawing in pairs, the teacher goes to Naomi and Tobias. They are working seriously together. They have already discussed what to do and how to do it. Tobias has drawn the school building as two rectangles and that's correct. Now they want to draw the routes from the school building to their own houses. They look closely at the pictures on the digital board and Tobias starts drawing. Naomi controls this very precisely: "Stop Tobias, this way, you have to make a curve." Tobias takes Naomi's comments seriously and continues by drawing more precisely. Teacher Monique compliments them on their thinking and drawing. When Tobias has finished drawing his street, Naomi also takes a pencil and they both draw the houses along the street. Tobias looks at the pictures on the digital board and he draws the houses as small rectangles, which corresponds with the pictures. Naomi draws a cross for each house . . . Teacher Monique says: "Ay, you are drawing the same houses in a different way, I see! Tell me!?" Tobias explains that the houses in the pictures on the digital board look like small rectangles. He points this out and Naomi understands him. She says she has drawn crosses because she has seen a cross on a treasure map, and a cross is the place where the treasure has been hidden. Teacher Monique says: "You're right, on a treasure map a cross is often drawn to mark the place where you have to go to. So it's possible to draw a cross on our map to mark the place the post man has to go to! But where has the post man to go to?" Tobias: "To my house!" The teacher asks Naomi: "How are you going to continue?" Naomi says that it will be difficult for the post man to know which house he has to go if she continues drawing it in this way. She adds that it is also nicer to draw a rectangle because a rectangle looks more like a house. The teacher says: "Okay, you are going to continue drawing houses as small rectangles, but which rectangle is the house of Tobias? Can one of you point it out on the map?" Tobias says: "I live in the middle of the street on this side." Naomi nods, draws a cross in the rectangle and says to Tobias: "You can also write your name in it." Tobias thinks this is a good idea! Then teacher Monique says: "The post man wants to be sure that he puts the letter or card in the right post box. Yet, he must know one more thing." Tobias and Naomi look to her with questioning glances. The teacher says: "On the card is written the name and the address." Tobias calls out: "The number of our house, of course, number twelve." The teacher says: "Okay!" and Naomi nods.

After the activity the teacher reflects on the activity in her logbook. The logbook is an important tool for the teacher. It supports the teacher's observations of children's activities, which is necessary for planning new steps in children's course of development in close harmony with their actual level of development.

The teacher considers:

- the progress of the activity;
- the meaning the activity has for the pupils;
- the observations she planned which are indicative for possible proximal developments.

Teacher Monique registers the observations in her digital logbook and writes about the goals of the group plan she made. She writes about each pupil:

Naomi:
> Naomi works seriously with Tobias to draw a map of the neighbourhood. She wants to do it precisely ("Stop Tobias, you have to make a curve." And later: "You can also write your name in it."). She can tell why she wants to draw each house: otherwise you don't know how to find the right house.

Tobias:
> Tobias works seriously with Naomi to draw a map of the neighbourhood. He accepts directions from her. He wants to do it as well as possible. He draws rectangles as symbols for the school building and the houses. He "reads" the pictures on the digital board well: [his house is] … "in the middle of the street on this side".

The Group Plan for the Post Office

The teacher also uses the mathematical activities in the post office to stimulate children's development purposefully. E.g. the teacher's planning in the logbook on the 18th of November:

1. activity: selling things and sorting the post cards
2. with: Sem and Matz
3. my role: first taking the role of a customer and after that coaching at sorting the cards
4. observation points: having pleasure in participating the activity? Need "to be sure"? Insight into number line/number sequence? Counting in steps of two (even – uneven)?

After the activity the teacher reflects on the development of the pupils and she writes in the logbook:

Sem:
> Sem operated the till. He did it with pleasure, but he found it difficult to add up the amounts. He needed my support with the abacus: reading the outcome. He also helped Matz writing the receipt. He listened with full attention to counting in steps of two by Matz. Sem counted aloud with him now and then.

Matz:
> Matz sold things with a lot of pleasure and he tried to do it as well as possible. He adds up well with the abacus. Some sums he knows by heart: $3 + 3, 4 + 4$.

Fig. 16.2 "Rekenrekje"

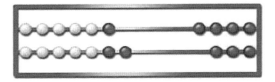

Sorting the post cards he counted well in steps of two. The even numbers were no problem. He hesitated at some uneven numbers between 10 and 20.

In Developmental Education guiding the activities through communication in small groups constitutes the essence of teaching mathematics. In this way the teacher also deals with heterogeneity in the group, with the differences between the pupils (Fijma 2003a). The teacher supports the pupils in their needs and in their actions within the activity. She gears her own actions towards the needs and actions of the pupils. Hence in the context of the meaningful activity the pupil "borrows" the support of the teacher. Teachers' goal-oriented interactions with the pupils are regulated by her planning/intentions and by the observations made during the activity. In this way, she brings cultural value (meaning) and personal value (sense) together in the pupils' tool-mediated actions.

The teacher also connects whole group instructions to the meaningful mathematical activities. E.g., she connects adding up by analogy ($2 + 5 = 7$; $12 + 5 = 17$) to the activity "selling things in the post office". See also the previously described examples of 3D analyses.

She starts her instruction by letting two pupils sell things in the post office. All the pupils add up the prices of the things with a "rekenrekje" (an abacus with 5-structure; see Fig. 16.2).

The teacher can make clear, with the use of this abacus with 5-structure, the analogy of $2 + 5 = 7$ and $12 + 5 = 17$. After making a few examples with the whole group, she gives the pupils a sheet with some sums. The pupils are going to do the sums and the teacher is going to help the pupils who need special attention.

Actively Observing Intensive Interactions of and with Children

In the digital version of HOREB the reflections on the development of the pupils are automatically transported into the *children's diaries*. In this HOREB instrument the teacher categorises the data that show the children's developmental steps. This enables the teacher to evaluate the developmental progress the children make (see also Chap. 14 for further explanation). Careful observation of pupils' needs, interests and abilities is an essential condition for productively guiding pupils' mathematical development. Developmental Education provides teachers with tools that support their planning and observations. The teachers will learn to write their observations "to the point". This starts already with the goal-oriented planning in the logbook. The observation points of the HOREB observation model, completed with the 3D analyses, give direction to the daily planning in the logbook. The HOREB observation model is broad and complete. It covers all the aspects of mathematical development.

In the course of the theme period the teacher collects important observations which show development. Below are a few other examples of reflections on children's development from guided activities in the post office. The examples concern the pupils to whom special attention was paid.

Daan:
    Daan works seriously and is really involved in the post office. He wants to be sure that he works correctly (he controls the sorted post cards a second time). He determines the sequence of the post cards with the help of the list of addresses.
Naomi:
    Naomi likes sorting the post cards and letters. She determines the sequence by comparing it with the list. She sorts quickly and correctly.
Jay:
    Jay works seriously and is very involved, although at first he wasn't eager to play in the post office. Jay divides the post cards and letters in even and uneven numbers by looking at the list and the number line. After that he determines the sequence independently and systematically.
Lin:
    Lin needs support with sorting the post cards and letters: sequencing the even numbers. She enjoys playing in the post office.

Conclusion

Our classroom work on mathematics education has produced a number of important insights. Most importantly, pupils need teachers who work systematically and are activity-oriented from a theoretical frame that also involves the meanings of the pupils in the designing and planning of mathematical education. Learning mathematics is connected with the pupil's personal interests and motives, and aims to provide pupils with the (communicative) tools, skills and understandings to take part in cultural activities where mathematical issues are involved. In order to achieve this, the teacher gears her intentions and goals towards the meanings of the pupils. Teacher Monique, for example, gives up the plan to make a walk through the neighbourhood when she learns that the pupils already have experiences with Google Earth. Later she makes the walk to post the post cards using the route-map. That is very important because we want the pupils to be optimally involved in the activities of the group. In our experience this produces better results through stimulating pupils' broad mathematical development. Concerning cognitive mathematical knowledge and skills the pupils score as good as or even better than the national norm group (Suhre 2001; Edelenbos 2003; van Oers 2010).

On the basis of the goal-oriented planning in the logbook with the help of the HOREB observation model, the teacher is able to guide the pupils in a responsive and interactive way. (See the examples of teacher Jannie and teacher Monique in this chapter.) A spatial or quantitative problem is the starting point for teaching mathematics by mathematising. In the interaction the teacher balances the actual qualities (actions and language) with the developmental perspectives of the pupils. The pupils need to argue and discuss a lot with each other and with the teacher in order to integrate the new actions and language. The teacher helps the pupils in weaving new concepts into existing knowledge. In this way the pupils learn to communicate about the numerical and spatial aspects of cultural reality with the help of mathematical tools. They learn mathematics by mathematising.

References

Burton, L. (2003). Children's mathematical narratives as learning stories. In B. van Oers (Ed.), *Narratives of childhood* (pp. 51–67). Amsterdam: VU Press.

Dematons, C. (2007). *Sinterklaas* [St Nicholas]. Rotterdam: Lemniscaat.

Edelenbos, P. (2003). *Realisatie en effecten ontwikkelingsgericht reken-wiskunde onderwijs* [Realisation and effects of Developmental mathematical education]. Groningen: GION, Rijksuniversiteit Groningen.

Elkonin, D. B. (1972). Toward the problem of stages in the mental development of the child. *Soviet Psychology, 10*(3), 225–251.

Fijma, N. (2000). *The curriculum for mathematics in a heterogeneous group: Towards a developmental strategy*. Paper presented at the 10th conference of the European Early Childhood Education Research Association in London, England.

Fijma, N. (2003a). Mathematics learning in a play-based curriculum. How to deal with heterogeneity? In B. van Oers (Ed.), *Narratives of childhood* (pp. 146–163). Amsterdam: VU Press.

Fijma, N. (2003b). Vele rijsjes maken een bezem [many twigs make a broom]. *Zone. Tijdschrift voor Ontwikkelingsgericht Onderwijs* [Magazine for Developmental Education], *2*(1), 7–10.

Fijma, N., & Vink, H. (1998). *Op jou kan ik rekenen* [I can count on you]. Assen: Van Gorcum.

Janssen-Vos, F., & Pompert, B. (2007). *Handelingsgericht Observeren, Registreren en Evalueren van Basisontwikkeling* [Activity-oriented observation, registration and evaluation of basic development]. Assen: van Gorcum.

Suhre, C. (2001). *Praktijkbrochure ontwikkelingsgericht reken-wiskunde onderwijs* [Practical brochure Developmental Mathematics Education]. Groningen: GION, Rijksuniversiteit Groningen.

van Oers, B. (1996a). Are you sure? The promotion of mathematical thinking in the play activities of young children. *European Early Childhood Education Research Journal, 4*(1), 71–89.

van Oers, B. (1996b). Learning mathematics as a meaningful activity. In L. Steffe, P. Nesher, P. Cobb, G. Goldin, & B. Greer (Eds.), *Theories of mathematical learning* (pp. 91–115). Hillsdale: Erlbaum.

van Oers, B. (2002). Teachers' epistemology and the monitoring of mathematical thinking in early years classrooms. *European Early Childhood Education Research Journal, 10*(2), 19–30.

van Oers, B. (2010). The emergence of mathematical thinking in the context of play. *Educational Studies in Mathematics, 74*(1), 23–37. doi:10.1007/s10649-009-9225-x.

van Oers, B. (2012). How to promote young children's mathematical thinking? *Mediterranean Journal for Research in Mathematics Education, 11*(1–2).

Chapter 17
Developmental Education Schools as Learning Organisations

Hans Bakker

Introduction

This chapter clarifies the concept of "learning organisation" in relation to the Development Education movement in the Netherlands. I would like to connect this concept to the implementation of Developmental Education in the school as an organisation. "Developmental Education" (henceforth DE) is a leading concept in this book. It is an approach based on Vygotskij's Cultural-historical theory of human development. This theory is also fundamental to the present chapter, and for this reason I approach the learning organisation and the introduction of DE from a Cultural-historical paradigm. Proceeding thus, I have come to my own description of a learning organisation. The transition from a traditional organisation to a learning organisation requires gaining insight into possible obstructions that may impede growth towards a learning organisation and – consequently – hinder the implementation of DE. Some conditions are described that may prevent Developmental Education schools from getting stuck in their institutional development and – consequently – not being able to provide conditions that may optimise pupils' and teachers' learning and development. The chapter deliberately focuses on the organisational level of the school as an institute, in order to emphasise the institutional embeddedness of young children's classrooms within school institutions and teams.

H. Bakker, Ph.D. (✉)
Christian University of Professional Studies, Ede (CHE), Ede, The Netherlands
e-mail: jjbakker@che.nl

B. van Oers (ed.), *Developmental Education for Young Children*, International
Perspectives on Early Childhood Education and Development 7,
DOI 10.1007/978-94-007-4617-6_17,
© Springer Science+Business Media Dordrecht 2012

A Bit of History

Throughout the world we see institutions with an explicit commitment to becoming so-called "learning organisations". According to the scientific literature, the concept of a learning organisation was introduced in 1963 (Bomers 1989). Due to the fact that learning organisations are approached from differing perspectives, there is no comprehensive theory regarding them.

The endeavour to transform organisations into "learning organisations" originated in the business world. The reason for striving to create a learning organisation is based on the assumption that it will strengthen institutions in their struggles to cope with ever changing technologies and market relationships. Such organisations want to build an environment in which learning plays a key role. These businesses regard learning as an integral part of working and professional practice for all employees at any organisational level. Modern companies incorporate learning into their core business in order to ensure a rapid and effective absorption of new knowledge within the organisation and to provide a constant striving in perfecting products, services and processes. Japanese companies jolted Western companies into action through their success in the late 1980s and early 1990s. The Japanese not only managed to be faster and more customer-oriented in their production, but they were also better able to innovate their businesses. Nonaka and Takeuchi (1995) illustrate how these companies create their innovation dynamic. In their preface they claim that companies owe their success to three factors: competence, expertise and organisational knowledge creation. With the latter, the authors refer to the company's ability (as a whole) to generate knowledge, and allow it to permeate the organisation and finally express it in products, services and systems. Companies became increasingly aware of the necessity to continually renew their production process. The market demands increasing quantities and faster delivery. Among the companies that had experienced impediments to success, their inability to learn was a common denominator. It appears that companies capable of increasing their ability to learn continuously, are most likely to survive. However, there is more: another aspect that is important to companies that may be characterised as learning organisations is the ability to link individual personal development to the performance and results of the organisation as a whole.

Can schools be learning organisations? There is a risk of comparing schools without reservation to businesses. A school organisation is not a business. It is a non-profit organisation with a social function that transcends profit organisations. There is, however, a trend, as witnessed during the 1990s, that schools have increasingly begun to resemble "regular" companies. An example of this is the introduction of the internationally recognisable approach to funding, which is known as "lump sum financing". This is a payment system for schools that is based on the policy to provide schools with a single large government payment that can be used by schools to finance their education. Other examples in which company characteristics are apparent are: personnel policy, increased competitiveness between schools, accountability, expressing quality of education through results and formulation of strategic policy. A school that focuses on the enhancement of its learning ability (constantly acquiring new knowledge, expertise and skills) for successfully responding to changing circumstances may be called a "learning organisation". A key component in the concept of a school as a learning organisation is its team, composed of people and their associated competencies (i.e. the group of developing teachers).

Teachers' learning in a school for Developmental Education should always be aimed at assisting children to reach their potential for meaningful learning, in order to achieve optimum development. (See also Chap. 4 in this volume). Developmental Education schools that are trying to transform into learning organisations should always keep their pedagogical mission in mind.

The School as an Activity System

To depict the development of schools that implemented the educational concept of Developmental Education in their organisation, I sought an organisational model from the cultural-historical paradigm. I conceive of schools as cultural institutes and – in keeping with Engeström (1987) – as activity systems. The cultural-historical activity theory takes a historically evolving activity system as a unit of analysis for the understanding of developing institutions. This approach is in line with the views presented by Nonaka and Takeuchi (1995). Engeström expanded Vygotskij's model which consisted of a single triangle (the upper Subject/Object/Tools triangle in Fig. 17.1; see also Vygotsky 1978, Chap. 3). The expansion occurred downward so as to say more about the institutionalised context of human action (Engeström 1987; Daniels 2001, p. 89). I have shown the original activity system in Fig. 17.1, as designed by Engeström (1987, p. 78).

Let me first explain the six components of the activity system model illustrated above:

   I. *Division of labour*: refers to the division of tasks, authorisation, and responsibilities, between participants and shows who does what within the activity system. Division of labour can be regarded as the autonomisation of (sub)operations into activity systems and subsystems. Thus, learning activities are incorporated into activity systems, where learning is the central motive.

  II. *Object*: the action object is the activity system's motive. In pursuing the object, subjects' actions lead to products. The subjects strive for the optimal realisation of the object and this is termed the *motive*. Product and motive are linked, as are object and motive – each of which is shared by members within the system.

 III. *Tools*: refers to the used cultural artefacts, tools such as machinery or equipment, but also knowledge, diagnostic instruments, and discourse techniques. Conceptual artefacts, such as school-plans, vision and mission documents, models, methodologies, and scientific theories, as well as material artefacts such as physical lay-out and other necessary preconditions for providing meaningful education are also included.

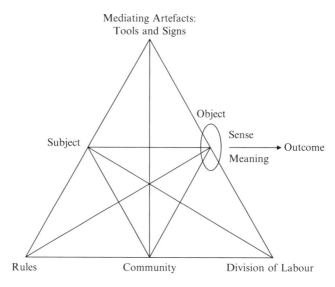

Fig. 17.1 Engeström's activity system triangle

IV. *Subject*: the worker or team of workers. These agents may be regarded as acting subjects with specific characteristics and qualifications.

V. *Rules*: conventions and agreements that are centred around the transformation process taking place within the activity system.

VI. *Community*: refers to all participants in an activity system sharing the same object and values. It is a community within which the activities of the system take place.

The triangle presented contains more than just the six points that are visible. I will explain various concepts introduced above in greater detail with regard to schools as cultural institutions. The concepts are common to the activity theory ideas. The major outcome in the present case of learning organisations is the improved practice which is a result of the transformational process of the subject/object line. I wish to state explicitly that an outcome as a result of actions can never be an endpoint in the transfer process of external processes to processes at a mental level. A developmental process has been instigated and continues to shape and enrich the internal level (Leont'ev 1980, pp. 332, 333).

The Historicity of the Organisation

Communication and interaction with others in an organisational environment influences and shapes the cognitive system of its members. The cognitive system interacts with the environment and – in turn – exerts an influence on members who continuously adapt to the system (Maturana 1997). Viewed from a cognitive perspective, human behaviour can be considered as a process, influenced by frames of reference called schemata (Fiske and Taylor 1991). These constitute conceptual frames that are usually called mental models (Kess 1992). Mental models guide our actual behaviour and are constructed in our memory, based on interactions with others:

> The language we use serves as an indicator in the construction of mental models. Words and phrases, but also other ways of constructing meaning are "small signals" that recall the construction of such mental models. In conversation we actively construct meaning in our memory in the form of a mental model in our memory. Constructing mental models in memory is a constructive and dynamic process: we continually derive new meanings that are then included in the reproduction of a situation (Werkman 2006, p. 196).

While the mental model is supplemented with information from the outside world, it also affects how we view the outside world. "Mental models simplify reality, colour perception, and frequently go beyond the information available, thus creating potential for various distortions. This may lead to stereotyping that consequently determines how we relate to others" (Werkman 2006, p. 197). We share and create our experiences in interaction with others, and this leads to the establishment of routines.

Daily routines and rituals give rise to the creation of frameworks that determine our thought processes, actions and choices. The environment or organisational context is affiliated to our own actions, and it reflects us and our intentions. In this way, the social environment imposes restrictions, and we restrict our own actions and intentions (Weick 1995, p. 122).

Organisations and people in organisations are not isolated entities but social realities that are continually shaped in relational processes in historically evolved cultural contexts. All those involved need each other to add meaning to their reality. They develop meaning through interaction with each other, and this meaning in organisations is often culture-specific (Wierdsma 1999).

In discussing organisational historicity it has become clear that part of our behaviour is influenced by experiences from the past that we may not actually be aware of. This subconscious behaviour is deeply embedded in human behaviour (Engeström 1990). It forms the basis of our actions and our decision-making (Stacey 1996). Thought and action are therefore not merely the product of subjectively perceived reality. We might describe reality as inter-subjective, and as a social or constructive process that is brought about by the actors, each using their frame of reference and group consensus. Communication influences both the group of people who interact and the psychological states of individuals in the group, and is – viewed from an activity theory perspective – "multi-voiced" and "multi-layered" in nature (also see Engeström 1990).

Cognition and social interaction are inextricably linked:

> People add meaning to interaction processes, and meanings add focus to action and create a context through the common experiences that people share. Context is thus created through interaction and constitutes the frame of reference from which people understand reality. We can understand interactional processes and add novel meaning to thoughts and actions – and

the altogether complex nature of processes of change – by paying attention to the contexts as created during the interaction process, and the inter-subjective meanings attached to them (Werkman 2006, p. 215).

Meanings are institutionalised and objectified through rules, procedures and agreements as time progresses, but many people will fail to recollect where and why these meanings came into being. They are seldom questioned and thus become an objectively experienced reality. This relates to historical patterns in organisational development; patterns that arose from organisational members' pre-programmed mental models.

I will assume that schools may be perceived as living systems (see also for instance Pascale et al. 2000, p. 6). Schools develop and grow, and they may be said to have a life cycle. In this view, there is little rational planning to be done. A school development process with its various phases and transitions will also go through developmental crises. An activity system takes shape and changes over a long period of time. Its current problems and potential for change can only be understood against the background of local activity and the activity system's history (Engeström 1987, 1999, 2001). The historicity of the activity system context is one of the principles underlying the framework from which activity theory observes a work area.

It goes without saying that historicity is intrinsically related to cultural development. Culture is largely hidden beneath the surface yet it determines what is (made) visible.

The metaphor of culture as an iceberg is also used by Galenkamp and Vollenhoven (2003). According to them, culture develops across time, and hidden motives, emotions and subconscious beliefs are part of that culture. Trompenaars and Hampden-Turner (2006) also point to the impact of culture on organisations. They state (p. 6) that, "culture is the way in which people solve problems" and that (p. 24) "culture directs our actions". As the culture evolves over time, so does structure as it is directly related to culture. In keeping with Mentink (1997), I distinguish three cultural phases, namely mythical culture, ontological culture and functional culture. Each phase has a negative counterpart listed in respective order: magic culture, substantialist culture and operationalist culture. Six culture categories may therefore be distinguished in organisational growth. If an organisation finds itself in a negative dimension, it will have to shift to a positive counterpart as various individuals and stakeholders, both inside and outside the organisation, will protest against the current state of affairs. "Discontent and necessity are thus important stimuli to shift to another, positive phase" (Van Leeuwen et al. 1997, p. 58, see also Van Leeuwen 1996). This statement is readily connected to observations of van Oers (2009), Meijers and Wardekker (2001) and Engeström (2001); namely that organisational growth goes through the following in the given order: "discontinuity and crises are an integral part to development", "reaching boundary limits in development", and "critical instances as double-bind situations". Trompenaars & Hampden-Turner state that "cultures vary in solutions to common problems and dilemmas" (2006, p. 26). According to them the developmental history of organisational culture determines how it copes with dilemmas. This brings us to the examination of learning disorders in organisational development.

Organisational Learning Disorders in the Organisation of the School

The key lesson management literature authors report when discussing organisational change is that it does not work according to strictly defined patterns. Growth always goes hand in hand with resistance. When you weed a garden, weeds may come back. In stating this, the authors do not mask their own inability, but their conclusion is simply that fundamental change always takes longer than predicted. The factor time appears to be a major stumbling block. Organic growth cannot be planned or placed on a calendar, and neither will behavioural change be measured in time. Reflection appears to be important, as do long-term goals. These authors generally conclude that there are barriers within organisations that disrupt and delay growth. Numerous authors describe the obstacles that prevent organisations from flourishing (Ansoff and McDonnell 1990; Argyris 1990; Engeström 1987; Garvin 1993; Huffman and Hipp 2003; Senge et al. 2000; Snyder and Cummings 1998; Wenger 1998). Engeström regards learning disorders as contradictions, but they do not always hinder learning. Furthermore, barriers are there to be conquered; they contribute to development. In his model concerning expansive learning, Engeström describes critical moments at system level as "double bind" situations. The very existence of the concept of the learning organisation seems to imply that organisations generally do not learn or that they experience barriers to learning. The term "learning disability" clearly needs to be made operational as it has multiple interpretations in educational research. Most of the time, "learning disorders" refers to processes at micro-level in children (e.g. ADHD, PDD-NOS, NLD, etc.). In this chapter, however, I follow Snyder and Cummings (1998) who point to disorders at organisational level, such as OLDs: Organisational Learning Disorders. They claim that organisations may also show an autism spectrum disorder. Various studies have been carried out regarding OLDs, but these have not established a clear link to the underlying characteristics of a learning organisation. All innovative endeavours are slowed down by various internal obstructions, as has become apparent from the innovation literature (Fullan 2003).

Changes within and between the activity system components will lead to tensions, problems and even contradictions. This occurs when available methods fail and there are no new methods available. Changes in the labour system are described in Engeström (1987) in terms of a model, as a cycle of evolving transformations. The notion of tensions, dilemmas and contradictions as learning disorders on the road to learning new things can lead to renewal, and is not unique to activity theory. Pascale et al. (2000) also claim that living systems do not follow a linear path.

In the wake of the above described organisational theories, we need to conceive of schools as historical organisations. Conceiving of schools as historical organisations gives a better understanding of their current status. Due to different, and often incompatible, influences and interests, most schools have developed into hybrid systems in the course of their development. As a result, they are often internally contradictory as well.

Translation of Engeström's Model to Developmental Education Schools as Learning Organisations

Translating Engeström's model to primary schools that are transforming into schools for Developmental Education, I propose the following interpretations:

I. *Division of Labour* can be identified as "Division of Roles": The roles within which individuals carry out their activities within the school context.

II. *Object*: The purpose of innovation is the introduction of DE in the learning primary school. The school's practice is the object that needs to be changed towards DE. That is to say, that teachers develop a DE-style of teaching as described in the present book. This concerns the activities of all individuals involved in the transition from a "method-bound" school to a DE-bound approach as the result of changed practice. *I will regard "outcome" as the result of innovation processes in an evolving activity system.*

III. *Tools* are described as "Resources": There are tools at meso- and micro-level. Meso-level tools are used by the management to implement DE in the school as a learning organisation through learning by teachers. The micro-level tools serve to ensure DE implementation for children at classroom level. Peer coaching and consultation are methodologies deployed at meso-level to provide teacher support for professionalisation in the field of DE. At the micro-level, thematic working can be used as a spearhead to allow DE to engage with the activity system. Teaching through theme-based activities is an integrated form of interdisciplinary and meaningful education which may be used as part of a holistic view of child education. The resources used for DE serve to support the transition. Opinion leaders too often provide a fitting direction for development, but should rather take into account that teachers in their learning processes attribute personal meanings and interpretations to the directions imposed.

IV. *Subject*: Explanation of this component should be interpreted in a broad sense. I regard the organisation (school) as a living entity, and for this reason I also position schools as a living system under the subject heading. I regard "subject" as being the group of DE schools with their concomitant members: teams, individual teachers, coaches and school managers. Hence, *"subject" also represents "LEARNING ORGANISATION" in this case.*

V. *Rules* are described as "Field and Rules". "Rules" are set by the school management in the activity system (in consultation with employees through middle-up-down management). They facilitate, set boundaries and support team members. I regard "Field and Rules" as the area and the regulations within which individuals can carry out their activities. This involves shaping the agreement system in the school through interaction between leaders and other system members.

VI. *Community* is termed "Communities of Practice": The organised group of teachers is the context for teachers' training and learning. Teacher activities are to be viewed here from the perspective of collaboratively learning teachers.

Translating this to the transformation of DE routines, i.e. how staff members deal with syllabi, learning targets, methods and how content is provided. Mediating processes take place through collaboration in the Communities of Practice. For example, Engeström (1987) describes the horizontal interaction between teachers in a team and the interaction between implicit and explicit knowledge. Relationships and the interactions between individual members are deliberately put in plural form. There are multiple communities within a single community of practice: between teachers, between early grade and upper grade teachers, between teachers and management, between teachers and parents, between teachers and children, between teachers, management and inspection, etc.

If I were to formulate a definition of a learning organisation from the activity theory perspective and base on the description in the previous section, it would be worded as follows:

A learning organisation is an organisation (as an organism) in the form of an activity system, that deliberately targets being an evolving expansive learning culture, where cooperative learning (Community of Practice) and learning capabilities (driven by an inquisitive attitude in a transformational process) of individuals, groups and the organisation as a whole (Subject) are interconnected, so that continuous (qualitative) change takes place (cognitive, affective and conative) through social interaction at all three levels (individual learning, collaborative learning and organisational learning) in the direction of jointly established (activity oriented) and vision-based output (Object, Product), resulting in sustainable quality improvement of activities across the activity system, where system components (in addition to the above-mentioned Subject, Object and CoP: Tools, Rules and Division of Labour) are aligned.

The activity theory perspective, in which the collaborative dimension of learning takes centre stage – as outlined here – fits the concept of DE. Hence, all teachers' learning in Developmental Education schools should directly or indirectly be aimed at strengthening the following conditions in the classrooms:

1. pupils learn to take part in meaningful social-cultural activities through continuous and purposeful interactions with each other and with adults;
2. the format of the activity includes cultural rules that are meaningful to the pupils, thus stimulating pupil involvement, lending pupils freedom to choose activities, tools, roles and goals. This ensures that the learner can always create his/her own version of social-cultural practice.

Both points refer to the school micro-situation, but may apply equally to the meso-level in schools as learning organisations. This means that the view of learning presented in the definition (see above) may become visible in DE-schools as: expansive learning culture, learning from each other, social interaction and shared vision, improved activities, and matching educational components. This will yield a learning school as a balanced activity system. Combining the DE principles and the concept of "learning organisation", I conclude that DE schools should advertise their learning organisation objectives.

Requirements for Developmental Education Schools as Learning Organisations

Having established that DE schools should advertise their learning organisation objectives, I can now establish the requirements for development into genuine learning organisations. I will formulate ten conditions in Table 17.1 below. These conditions are the result of PhD research concerning the implementation of DE in the learning primary school (Bakker in preparation). Four components from the activity theory by Engeström (see Fig. 17.1) have been used by way of illustration. When referring to *institutionalisation,* I view the entire DE implementation in a school organisation. *Resources* refer to the type of support that is required to enable implementation at teacher level. *Field and Rules* refers to what a school leader should provide in terms of conditions and interventions to help shape implementation, and *roles* involve the competencies required in teachers to ensure adequate DE implementation.

Barriers and Elimination of Barriers

The obstacles observed in this study are manifest at four distinct levels. The results are exhaustively described in this section, with each key item marked in underlined italics. The different organisational components are marked in *italic script*.

Organisational Level

In relation to the organisation of the school, it is observed that the *overloaded programme* forms an obstacle from the teacher's perspective. The DE philosophy puts pressure on execution of the educational programme in primary education. Everyday practice in schools which are in the early phase of DE implementation requires teachers to work through the "old" curriculum within DE. People are unaware of the fact that DE needs to be linked to working through a curriculum. This requires further development of vision (see also for example Chap. 13 in this volume). Teachers perceive a curriculum as providing a foothold for offering pupils all the content that is required. Most teachers have to learn under guidance of an expert coach how *to let go of curricular content* from a textbook, so as to be able to bring out the best in children through DE.

Place and time are specified as conditions for development and implementation. Logistics in spatial form helps to maintain an overview to allow for organising. Adequate storage spaces are required to store materials from earlier themes, and to have space in – and outside – the classroom to enable children to work individually

Table 17.1 The conditions linked to the activity system components

Components activity system	Conditions
Institutionalisation	Vision regarding DE is a prerequisite to embedding DE, but it is not the only requirement. The vision should be a directive for all members involved in the school and classroom.
	Formalising agreements is key in innovations, and is therefore of importance in implementation of DE. Syllabi will have to be firmly established in a teachers' memory, so that it provides direction for children and the course of innovation when teachers extend beyond their comfort-zone (school method).
	Schools need to develop the reflective abilities of all those involved in the transition process to shift from content oriented education to DE.
Resources	The implementation of DE requires help from colleagues and other parties such as coaches or colleagues who provide inter-collegial support or educational assistants from outside the school organisation. Both internal or external support is clearly required to ensure a smooth transition for teachers.
Field and rules	A requirement is a strong school leader who uses middle-up-down management, and who shows transformational leadership in the organisation's culture facet and educational leadership in the organisation's structural facet.
	Aside from empathically oriented transformational leadership, educationalist leadership is required to maintain a balance between structure and culture. An inquisitive attitude in a school leader is highly recommended to model learning processes in the learning activity system.
	Ensuring long-term human development is a point to be taken into consideration. Teachers need to be challenged by managers, particularly at the intellectual level, and they also need to be confronted with their own actions.
Roles	Teachers need to develop DE specific competencies while learning to move away from content oriented education in a transition toward DE where education may take place independently from content offered through traditional methods.
	DE schools need an integrated DE approach in working with special needs pupils. Consequently, they have to appoint a team member in the role of expert in this area who can support the teachers in their catering for special needs persons (internal coach).
	DE schools need to develop their own DE-concept oriented registration system to allow for monitoring and registration of pupil progress.

or together. The factor of time to facilitate individual teachers' development must be taken into account. Development will stagnate if sufficient time is not available. Teachers need to be given time to implement small developmental steps into their routine actions and to practice them for further fine-tuning. Teachers will then gain ownership of what they have learned. Teachers indicate that a lot of time is lost in consultation and meetings. Attending meetings occurs at the expense of actually working on preparation for themes and such like. However, these consultations are required due to the fact that micro-level actions need to be provided with input, even though it is not perceived by teachers in this way. Through interviewing a large number of teachers at different schools I discovered that a particular school might use "obstructions" as an area of development, while another has not yet taken that step, and so remains impeded by the obstruction. As mentioned earlier, obstructions are there to be overcome as they contribute to continued development. Schools do not always regard this as such, however.

Team Level

The following obstacles may be noted at *team* level: an island-culture needs to change to develop joint vision and unity in a professional learning culture. If a team does not form a single coherent unit, this will hamper or halt development of vision. To implement change, a specific leadership type called *shared leadership* is required to provide schools with a positive impulse.

Class Level

The following obstacles may be noted at *class* level: The teacher needs specific skills and competencies to shape content and group format according to the DE-concept. Higher-order thinking skills and reflection on personal actions are required to progress with DE. Teaching with an open door, inviting colleagues to find out where development is currently taking place, are prerequisites for the development toward DE. Reflection is very important as DE (being a pedagogic and didactic concept) calls for teacher competences in personal pedagogy and didactics. It is generally found that all schools (some more than others) see teacher development as an obstacle. I have found that some schools turn teacher development into a priority to support teachers. Schools that have formulated a policy and linked this to various instruments (video material and manuals) to ensure DE implementation, are generally successful. When schools employ internal coaches to support teachers in their development, this provides an impulse toward teacher professionalisation and – in turn – makes for successful DE implementation. Teachers who are "do-ers" generally show less developed higher-thinking skill, and this may hamper personal and professional development. Too many "do-ers" in a team may form an obstruction to implementing change; thinkers (not "do-ers") are capable of transferring tacit knowledge to the explicit domain.

A large number of teachers are unable to provide pupil guidance at an appropriate level. Children with behavioural disorders, or those with an autistic spectrum disorder, need structure. Working in an unrestricted area where children are allowed to develop using their own initiatives causes problems for children as described above.

The concept does work if the environment is structured and children are coached according to their capabilities and competencies. Children with a social *stigma* or a so-called *"backpack"*[1] *(special educational needs children; at-risk children)* receive guidance using a special care-plan. DE can be used to offer children structured content. Schools may choose to adapt to child-level, but there are schools that select care-plans that do not follow the DE concept (group care-plans conflict with DE principles). Some teachers work through their content-based curriculum and add DE as an occasional extra. They will generally use the curriculum and its differentiation tools to cater for different pupils. When using HOREB (see Chaps. 4 and 14) as a means for observation, there is more sensitive connection with pupils from a DE perspective. In working with DE, teachers find out that they need fewer special care-plans since the concept enables an ongoing sensitive connection with all children (see Chap. 10 of this volume for further examples of how special educational needs children are addressed in DE).

External Factors Level

There are potential _external_ obstructions to be listed as well. Dealing with *parents* is one of them. Parents have their own *perceptions* of school results and *expectations* of the attainment of the highest possible standards, which should facilitate their child's future and guarantee that he/she will do well at college and university. Parents may ask difficult questions or their reactions may reveal their suspicion that their child's result is below par. Parental attitude is a cause for concern in schools. The obstruction is not only caused by parents, but also by schools that are unable to cope with parents, thus turning parents into a problem (see also Chap. 11 for further elaboration of the school-parent partnership in DE-schools).

The inspectorate is to be listed as a potential external obstruction too, as it places top-down demands on educational *results*. The same applies here as in the previous section: this issue could become an obstruction if schools fail to cope with it. There are school leaders who regard inspection as a challenge by showing that they meet quality standards using their own resources and not those supplied by the inspectorate. The compulsory standardised *pupil-monitoring-system* does create issues for most DE schools; being held accountable for test results by the inspectorate causes schools to opt for the standard monitoring system. It is shown that there are two types of schools in this respect: schools that use the standard instrument to show their results, and schools that develop their own way of showing results, thus showing their pro-active attitude.

Teacher training institutes do not always provide graduate pupils with the tools required for DE in primary education. The connection between theory and practice

---

[1]"Backpack" (in Dutch: Rugzakje) is a provision of the government that supplies extra financial support for the assistance of individual pupils with special needs in the classroom.

is not always consistent across the syllabus. Graduate pupils may have heard of the concept, but may be unable to view DE from a conceptual stance relating to paradigm development.

School Leadership

Field and Rules provide a significant impetus in guiding the transition towards DE schools. Leadership always takes a key position in this process.

In *shared leadership*, leaders know that they should delegate parts of the implementation process when they are unable to take full responsibility for the activity system's functioning, due to school size and the amount of bureaucratic work involved. Internal coaches, unit leaders and mentors are appointed to maintain contact with the everyday classrooms, and to ensure school- and individual teacher development. School leaders need to be able to delegate and to realise this kind of distributed responsibility, but he/she needs to have a detailed knowledge of DE; both practical and theoretical knowledge are required as the school leader needs to guide implementation. This will only work if a school leader knows the concept inside-out.

Confrontation with obstacles is a desirable intervention to stimulate the development of individuals and of the entire organisation. Resistance is something to be conquered. Confrontation and guidance should, in some cases, be used more frequently. This mechanism is used to show people their own developmental progress.

Tension between leadership and management is felt by both teachers and leaders. Leadership represents "culture" and management represents "structure". Some are pro-active in selecting a role, and will lead using the middle-up-down principle. Others do not know how to handle this and sense external pressure. This tension is common to most schools. There are schools that do not adequately cope with the culture side of the organisation, which relates to human development. As a result, new political or bureaucratic demands are imposed on teachers, which are to be adopted mechanically. Finally this leads to a lack of professionalisation in teachers which – in turn – results in the inability of a school to become a learning organisation. Successful implementation of DE requires commitments at all levels of the system.

Transformational leadership comes into view when listing the characteristics that people look for in leaders. Characteristics for DE school leaders are: positive attitude, leading through coaching, encouraging interaction, nourishing the community feeling and thinking, investing in people through empathy, attending to individuals, connecting via zones of proximal development, creating trust, facilitating, promoting bottom-up thought processes, possessing adequate knowledge of the DE concept and its implementation, being alert and sensitive to varying developmental rates. The typology of transformational leadership in education has been introduced by Leithwood and his staff (Leithwood et al. 1996) and was introduced for general leadership by Bass (Bass 1985; Bass and Avolio 1994). This leadership perspective assumes that leaders are directed toward involvement, motivation, and capacities of individuals in the organisation. Transformational leadership is aimed at increasing the capacity for change and innovation in a school organisation. Teachers and school leaders state that leaders do inspire confidence, delegate responsibilities, provide clarity when needed and leave room for teachers' personal freedom in working as a team. Formalising agreements is an important issue. Syllabi need to be anchored in teachers' long-term memories, to ensure that when content-based education is exchanged for the syllabi there is sufficient guidance for children and for the renewal in general. *Internal coaching* is regarded as the core of the transformation process. Structure (at both micro- and meso-levels) is important in the organisational domain to aid planning, and in the implementation process cycle. *Formalisation* is an indispensable tool for anchoring the internalisation process. Schools use different tools to formalise manuals, handbooks and other such documents. Spearheads for the improvement of education in DE are selected from various disciplines, with language as the most basic discipline. At teacher level, learning to let go, promoting language development across the curriculum, and acquiring the ability to use the observation manual (HOREB) properly are clearly spearheads for development that need to be supported by a leader. Fear of failure can be overcome, and this supports self-efficacy.

Conclusion

Promoting meaningful learning among pupils and optimising their developmental potential requires ongoing reflection on the conditions of both pupil development, teacher professionalisation, and the school leadership. This requires careful guidance of the teachers and the team from the beginning of the innovation process (see Chap. 12 of this volume).

Developmental Education demands unremitting reflection on the "social development situation". This has implications pertaining to school organisation. The main conditions that need to be in place for schools to enable them to be learning organisations and to avoid "organisational learning disorders" are as follows: (i) gaining insight into teacher talents and skills, and to adjust their duties and role to a place in the organisation where their competencies are fully exploited, (ii) providing teacher support so that they can be coached to carry out their tasks and actions to a sufficient degree to enable them to serve the organisation and the pupils in the school to the best of their ability, (iii) a school leader who combines educational leadership with transformational leadership to lead the school as an organisation and to encourage individuals to get the best out of themselves – gaining positive energy from self-efficacy. Aside from self-efficacy, "collective-efficacy" is important to enable a community (CoP) to pursue a goal and to support each other to serve pupils and the organisation as a whole.

References

Ansoff, H. I., & McDonnell, E. J. (1990). *Implanting strategic management*. Hemel Hempstead: Prentice Hall International.

Argyris, C. (1990). *Overcoming organisational defenses: Facilitating organisational learning.* Boston: Allyn Bacon.

Bakker, J. J. (in prep.). *Expansive learning of a school organisation. The implementation of developmental education in the learning school organisation.* Dissertation, Van Gorcum, Assen.

Bass, B. M. (1985). *Leadership and performance beyond expectations.* New York: Free Press.

Bass, B. M., & Avolio, B. J. (Eds.). (1994). *Improving organisational effectiveness through transformational leadership.* Thousand Oaks/London/New Delhi: Sage.

Bomers, G. B. J. (1989). *De lerende organisatie* [The learning organisation]. Nijenrode: Universiteit voor Bedrijfskunde (University of Management).

Daniels, H. (2001). *Vygotsky and pedagogy.* New York/London: Routledge Falmer.

Engeström, Y. (1987). *Learning by expanding: An activity theoretical approach to developmental research.* Helsinki: Orienta-Konsultit Oy.

Engeström, Y. (1990). *Learning, working and imagining. Twelve studies in activity theory.* Helsinki: Orienta-Konsultit.

Engeström, Y. (1999). Learning by expanding: Ten years after. In Y. Engeström (Ed.), *Learning by expanding* (pp. 1–10). Marburg: BdWi-Verlag.

Engeström, Y. (2001). Expansive learning at work: Toward an activity theoretical reconceptualisation. *Journal of Education and Work, 14*(1), 133–156.

Fiske, S. T., & Taylor, S. E. (1991). *Social cognition.* New York: McGraw-Hill.

Fullan, M. (2003). *Change forces with a vengeance.* New York: RoutledgeFalmer.

Galenkamp, H., & Vollenhoven, M. (2003). *Als scholen een gezicht krijgen* [When schools get a face]. Amersfoort: CPS.

Garvin, D. A. (1993, July–August). Building a learning organisation. *Harvard Business Review, 71*(4), 78–91.

Huffman, J. B., & Hipp, K. K. (2003). *Reculturing schools as professional learning communities.* Lanham: The Scarecrow Press.

Kess, J. F. (1992). *Psycholinguistics: Psychology, linguistics and the study of natural language.* Amsterdam: John Benjamins.

Leithwood, K., Tomlinson, D., & Genge, M. (1996). Transformational school leadership. In K. Leithwood, J. Chapman, D. Corson, Ph Hallinger, & A. Hart (Eds.), *International handbook of educational leadership and administration* (Vol. II, pp. 785–840). Dordrecht: Kluwer Academic.

Leont'ev, A. N. (1980). Activiteit als psychologisch probleem [Activity as a psychological problem]. *Pedagogische Sudiën, 57,* 324–343. Translated from Russian by B. van Oers. Groningen: Wolters-Noordhoff.

Maturana, H. (1997). *Objectivity: A compelling argument.* Providencia, Santiago, Chili: Dolmen Ediciones.

Meijers, F. J. M., & Wardekker, W. L. (2001). Ontwikkelen van een arbeidsidentiteit [Development of a work-identity]. In J. Kessels & R. Poell (Red.), *Human resource development: Organiseren van het leren* (pp. 301–319). Alphen aan den Rijn: Samsom.

Mentink, H. B. J. (1997). Verschijningsvormen van organisatieculturen (Forms of appearance of organisational cultures). In O. C. van Leeuwen, R. H. I. van Schoubroeck, & R. van Breemen (Eds.), *Management en informatie, de kunst van het kiezen* [Managament and information, the art of selection] (p. 59). Alphen aan den Rijn/Diegem: Samsom.

Nonaka, I., & Takeuchi, H. (1995). *The knowledge-creating company. How Japanese companies create the dynamics of innovation.* New York/Oxford: Oxford University Press.

Pascale, R., Millemann, M., & Gioja, L. (2000). *Surfing the edge of chaos.* New York: Crown Business Publishing.

Senge, P., Kleiner, A., Roberts, C., Ross, R., Roth, G., & Smith, B. J. (2000). *De dans der verandering. Nieuwe uitdagingen voor de lerende organisatie* [The dance of change. The challenges of sustaining momentum in learning organisations]. Schoonhoven: Academic Service.

Snyder, W. M., & Cummings, G. (1998). Organisation learning disorders: Conceptual model and intervention hypotheses. *Human Relations, 51*(7), 873–895.

Stacey, R. D. (1996). *Strategic management and organisational dynamics*. London: Pittman.

Trompenaars, F., & Hampden-Turner, C. (2006). *Riding the waves of culture, understanding cultural diversity in business*. London: Nicholas Brealey.

van Leeuwen, O. C. (1996). *Managementinformatie voor periodieke besluitvorming: Tollen of stilstaan?* [Management information for periodical decision-making]. Alphen aan den Rijn: Samsom BedrijfsInformatie.

van Leeuwen, O. C., van Schoubroeck, R. H. I., & van Breemen, R. (1997). *Management en informatie. De kunst van het kiezen* [Management and information. The art of select]. Alphen aan den Rijn: Samsom.

van Oers, B. (2009). *Ontwikkelingsgericht werken in de bovenbouw van de basisschool, een theoretische verkenning met het oog op de praktijk* [Developmental education in the higher grades of primary school, a theoretical exploration in view of practice]. Alkmaar/Den Bosch: De Activiteit.

Vygotsky, L. S. (1978). *Mind in society: The development of higher psychological processes*. Cambridge, MA: Harvard University Press.

Weick, K. E. (1995). *Sense making in Organisations*. London: Sage.

Wenger, E. (1998). *Communities of practice: Learning, meaning and identity*. Cambridge: Cambridge University Press.

Werkman, R. A. (2006). *Werelden van verschil: hoe actoren in organisaties vraagstukken in veranderingsprocessen hanteren en creëren* [Worlds of difference: How actors in organisations problems handle and create in processes of change]. Dissertation, Optima Grafische Communicatie, Rotterdam.

Wierdsma, A. F. M. (1999). *Co-creatie van verandering* [Co-Creation of Change]. Delft: Eburon.

Chapter 18
Conclusion: Actual and Future Consequences of Implementing and Researching Developmental Education

Bert van Oers

Using Vygotskij in Education

Studying Vygotskij's ideas from his earlier work such as "The Psychology of Art" to his later work ("Thinking and Speech") is a fascinating experience of immersion in a world of ideas. The evolution of some of these ideas can be followed throughout his work (like the notion of 'zone of proximal development', or 'sign'); others remain notions expressed in common language not yet transformed into academic concepts (like activity, leading activity, play). It was the work of his colleagues and followers to develop these ideas further into a coherent theory of human development. Leont'ev, for example, elaborated the notion of activity (dejatel'nost') and leading activity (veduščaja dejatel'nost') into an activity theory; El'konin has developed the notion of play and leading activity into a theory of ontogenetic development; Božovic worked on the notions of personality and the social situation of development; Zaporožec contributed significantly to the elaboration of the theories of movement and perception, and so on. The evolution of Vygotskij's ideas has been described in a number of accomplished works (Kozulin 1990; van der Veer and Valsiner 1991; Wertsch 1985; see for a brief historical summary regarding early childhood education: Veraksa and van Oers 2011). Diverse readings of Vygotskij still exist (see for example van Oers 2011).

Many researchers since Vygotskij's day have tried to contribute to the mission of understanding human development as a cultural-historical process embedded in socio-cultural activities and driven by interpersonal interactions focused on the negotiation and appropriation of cultural tools. Without doubt Vygotskij's mission was the perfection of human practice for the benefit of humanity. In his view culture

B. van Oers, Ph.D. (✉)
Department Theory and Research in Education, Faculty of Psychology and Education,
VU University Amsterdam, Amsterdam, The Netherlands
e-mail: bert.van.oers@vu.nl

B. van Oers (ed.), *Developmental Education for Young Children*, International
Perspectives on Early Childhood Education and Development 7,
DOI 10.1007/978-94-007-4617-6_18,
© Springer Science+Business Media Dordrecht 2012

couldn't be transmitted to new generations in any fixed and clear-cut way. Education should help young children in learning to live their lives. Life, in Vygotskij's view (see Vygotsky 1997, p. 346) is basically an endeavour of creation, and education should aim to help pupils become autonomous and creative agents in cultural practices. Therefore he also refused to accept the idea that instructional theories should determine educational practices.

As said, many researchers and educationalists have made serious efforts to elaborate Vygotskij's cultural-historical approach. They have articulated many of Vygotskij's concepts in slightly different ways, which has resulted in different readings of Vygotskij (see for example Cazden 1996; van der Veer 2008). Many "neo-Vygotskian" approaches have appeared on the international academic forum (see for example Daniels 2008).

Vygotskij's cultural-historical approach to human development has also attracted attention in the world of early childhood education, resulting in different approaches to educational practices for young children (see for example Bodrova and Leong 2007; Dolya 2010; Fleer 2010; Tuna and Hayden 2010).

Developmental Education as presented in this book is one of them. Developmental Education has translated Vygotskij's mission to deliberately promote young children's broad development into an approach that emphasises the importance of cultural learning in ways that authentically make sense to the children, as this improves their abilities to participate in a wide range of cultural practices. Developmental Education primarily aims at broad development of children's agency, and at facilitating children's appropriation of a wide range of cultural tools in different curricular areas (literacy, mathematics, art, technology, moral thinking etc.). Children's and teachers' potential for collaboratively creating and improving cultural tools and meanings is a core issue in the Developmental Education approach. Playfully formatted activity is taken as a context for this type of constructive learning. The previous chapters have presented ample examples of how this is realised in everyday practices.

The distinctive characteristics of the Developmental Education approach can be summarised in two ways. Firstly, Developmental Education for young children is seen as an approach to children's meaningful learning that helps them in living their current lives and participating in a range of cultural practices. Additionally, the Developmental Education approach for young children at the same time also strives to lay *a firm foundation for children's future learning and participation in cultural practices*. Hence, the approach called "Basic Development" (which is the young children version of Developmental Education) explicitly tries to *bring the children's future into the present* (to borrow Mike Cole's expression) and makes them familiar with cultural tools (like academic concepts, thinking strategies, or norms) which will help them to cope with future (learning) challenges. Therefore the play-based curriculum is not only seen as a cultural space in the early years classrooms, but essentially continues into the higher grades of primary school. The activity format in the higher grades of primary schools entails more and more complex (conceptual, moral and technical) *rules*; it starts out from meaningful problems and the questions of the children themselves in different subject matter areas, guaranteeing optimal conditions for high *involvement* of the pupils, and finally allows pupils some freedom in exploring meanings and constructing new tools, inventing new goals etc. The play-based curriculum that starts out in the early years continues throughout the whole duration of primary school. A second distinctive characteristic of the Developmental Education approach as described in this book is, that it is conceived as a collective philosophy to be adopted by teams of teachers and entire schools, rather than an instructional procedure for individual teachers working alone in their classrooms. Some of the consequences of this approach for the innovation of schools will be further described below.

Consequences of Developmental Education for Classroom Innovation

A fundamental assumption behind Developmental Education relates to Vygotskij's claim that theory and practice are intrinsically related. Theory can only be developed *as* a tool for the understanding and development of practice, and as such it is always a part of practice itself (see Chaiklin 2011a, b). Workers with the Developmental Education approach (teachers, educational innovators, researchers) put this starting point into practice and collaboratively developed ways for bridging the old theory-practice gap. This point of view had several consequences:

(a) Redefining Schools

One of the consequences of the close interrelatedness of the theory and practice of Developmental Education is that the institute of school must be redefined in essential ways. Becoming aware that any practice implies (implicit) theory, while any theory implies conceptions of "good practice" too, unavoidably must lead to the conclusion that the classical idea of school innovation as an enterprise of constructing new practices for pupils' learning must be rejected. Innovation encompasses both the evolving practices and the elaboration of the teachers' theories. Hence, schools shouldn't be seen anymore as places for learning of pupils, but as *cultural spaces for learning of both pupils and teachers*! In our experience, this redefinition of schools is actually quite an important assignment for all stakeholders, including the principals, parents, innovators, researchers, the inspectorate and policy makers. Furthermore, for the pupils and their parents the culture of the classroom must also be redefined, from the traditional view of a process of culture transmission into a conception of classrooms as communities of playful inquiry and learning. The success of the implementation of Developmental Education in schools strongly depends on the extent that we succeed in realising this redefinition for all stakeholders. The preceding chapters give numerous examples of how we have addressed this issue (see for example Chap. 11).

(b) Intensified Focus on Teacher Learning

One of the ways of helping teachers to redefine their responsibilities for their pupils' development can be seen in the strong emphasis on, and careful guidance of, the implementation of Developmental Education in schools. This is a process that takes years, and since the early 1980s successful strategies for teacher guidance have been developed that integrate theory and practice. This whole process consists of at least three components:

- *Thematising:* the process of thematising is an important starting point for pupils' meaningful learning, as described in several of the previous chapters. Those chapters give a lot of examples of the stages in which schematising should be accomplished in classrooms (e.g. Chap. 4). On the whole, it always involves transformations of themes into playful activities/practices, including roles that employ specific tools. Schematically:

> **Theme→Activity/Practice → Formatting as play → Identifying relevant roles → Deciding on the tools to use**

  For the implementation of Developmental Education it is necessary that teachers learn to use this strategy and implement it in their classrooms in systematic steps. A number of the previous chapters have described the stages in the implementation of this strategy in their classrooms. In the guidance of the teachers' learning the dynamics are similar to those that constitute children's learning and teaching (negotiation of meaning, zone of proximal development, appropriating relevant tools etc.). (See especially the chapters in Part II.)
- *Promoting learning in the context of playful activities:* Teachers often have to redefine their notions of play and learning. Conceiving of play as a specifically formatted activity changes the position of the teacher/adult with respect to play and integrates learning/teaching as an aspect of play. A fundamental requirement of Developmental Education is that teachers accept their role as participants in their pupils' play and learn how to participate without destroying the fundamentals of the play format. The Developmental Education approach has constructed over the years, in close collaboration with teachers, teacher trainers, curriculum counsellors and researchers, different tools that may help teachers to play their part in pupils' learning and development. Particularly the notion of *didactic impulses* is crucial here, as well as many tools for planning new steps in pupils' learning trajectories in different curricular domains. Numerous examples can be found in the previous chapters (see especially those in Part III).
- *Mastering new ways of assessment:* in a play-based curriculum it is important to monitor children's development in detailed ways, especially in ways that reveal pupils' actual level of development, but also their zone of proximal development in a specific task. That is why much has been invested in the development of strategies for Dynamic Assessment. This is not yet a finished task, but

important steps have been made (see Chaps. 6 and 7), and new research is underway. Teachers in Developmental Education classrooms are aware that they should follow their pupils' development as closely as possible. That is why an assessment tool has been developed (named HOREB; see for example Chap. 14) that can be used on a day-to-day basis as a tool for the teacher for the registration, evaluation and planning of learning processes tailored to the pupils' interests and developmental potential. In our work on the implementation of Developmental Education we have discovered that mastery of HOREB and of forms of dynamic assessment is essential for the success of Developmental Education. Much effort is made to assist teachers in mastering this method of assessment.

(c) A New Paradigm of Academic Research

Another consequence of attempts to implement Developmental Education in everyday classroom practices consists in the re-conceptualisation of research. The unification of theory and practice as envisioned in the Developmental Education movement has far-reaching consequences for the conception of academic research as well. Although researchers involved in our research programme at the VU University are also involved in theoretical studies, the core of the research programme is not Vygotskij's theory by itself, but consistently conceptualised classroom practices. In the theory-driven reflection on Developmental Education practices, multidisciplinary approaches are combined, studying psychological, pedagogical, sociological, subject matter, historical, epistemological and moral-ethical dimensions in close combination with each other. Research questions can emerge both from theoretical analyses and from practical needs. In both cases, however, questions are always translated into both theoretical and practical issues. Methodologies range from design research, case studies, observational studies, ethnographic research, surveys, quasi-experimental research, etc. Depending on the nature of the research questions the data-gathering and analysis can be quantitative, qualitative or a mixture of both. The preferred design is always negotiated with the participating schools. A particular complexity with this research approach is the necessary redefinition of the notion of "objectivity" (see for example Wardekker 2000). Traditionally, objectivity is defined in terms of distance of theory from practical concerns. In our approach we have reconceptualised objectivity in terms of inter-subjectivity that includes the practitioners' point of view and concerns.

(d) Building a Multidisciplinary Network

The accomplishment of our ambitious plan to innovate early childhood education along the lines of a Vygotskian view of human development required bringing together different disciplines (those of teacher, innovator, teacher trainer, and researcher). Without the help of many stakeholders that share the same basic ideas on human development, it is impossible to render our attempts at innovation successful. A powerful characteristic of the Developmental Education Movement in the Netherlands is its extensive network community that has been built up over the past three decades. This network facilitates the chain of knowledge production in essential ways. The Developmental Education Network is facilitated by a Developmental Education Association (www.ogo-academie.nl) that unites all stakeholders, such as schools for primary education, teacher trainers, a school innovation and counselling institute "De Activiteit" and researchers. The Developmental Education Association also issues a journal ("Zone") and organises a bi-annual conference which bring research, practice and policy together. Finally a research group at the VU University Amsterdam is involved in the network as a research partner. Through the support of this whole encompassing network, the Developmental Education community can continue to undertake some of the necessary small-scale research and obtain objective evidence for the effectiveness of the DE-approach (see for further descriptions of the network organisation van Oers 2009). The nation-wide implementation of Developmental Education in the Netherlands is one of the most important achievements of this community. It must be added, however, that only a small percentage of the 8,000 Dutch schools has decided to adopt the Developmental Education approach. For Basic Development in the first grades of primary school (4–8 year-olds) this is estimated at 25 %; with regard to the adoption of Developmental Education as a concept for the whole school the number is far less (5–10 %).

The Future of Developmental Education

As will be clear by now, Developmental Education not only entails the optimisation of classroom settings, but also the responsibility for ongoing improvement of the conditions for learning of both pupils and teachers. This is an unending quest. New societal demands, ongoing research, and practical attempts to improve classroom practices result in an ever-evolving understanding of Developmental Education, both in practice and in theory. As a result we always have to innovate educational practices for (young) children. Essentially, the project is never finished. Two assignments for the future following from the chapters in this book will be briefly discussed:

(a) The practices described in the preceding chapters need further empirical evidence, not only for reasons of theory corroboration and for answering the societal demands of evidence-based teaching, but also for ethical reasons with respect to pupils and parents. A lot of empirical evidence is already produced (see for example van Oers 2010a, b; van Oers and Duijkers 2012; many more examples by other researchers can be given), but there is still the need for more detailed, stronger evidence of the value of this approach for all children and teachers.

(b) Developmental Education for young children claims to optimise young children's opportunities in future learning as well. The extension of the approach into the higher grades of primary schools is underway and intensive work is being undertaken by many teachers, curriculum developers, and researchers to implement Developmental Education in these grades, including the promotion of autonomous and critical inquisitive thinking of pupils in all subject matter domains (mathematics, literacy, history, music etc.). The play format is now extended to the playful imitation of inquiry as a way of learning. For now we assume that the quality of pupils' development under the conditions of their education in the early years is a fruitful basis for pupils' progress into an inquiry-based curriculum, and for finally becoming autonomous and well-informed critical participants in cultural practices.

References

Bodrova, E., & Leong, D. J. (2007). *Tools of the mind. The Vygotskian approach to early childhood education*. Upper Saddle River: Pearson Merril Prentice Hall.

Cazden, C. B. (1996). Selective traditions: Readings of Vygotsky in writing pedagogy. In D. Hicks (Ed.), *Discourse, learning and schooling* (pp. 165–187). Cambridge: Cambridge University Press.

Chaiklin, S. (2011a). The role of *practice* in cultural-historical science. In M. Kontopodis, C. Wulf, & B. Fichtner (Eds.), *Children, development and education. Cultural, historical and anthropological perspectives* (pp. 227–246). Dordrecht: Springer.

Chaiklin, S. (2011b). Social scientific research and societal practice: Action research and cultural-historical research in methodological light from Kurt Lewin and Lev S. Vygotsky. *Mind, Culture and Activity, 18*(2), 129–147.

Daniels, H. (2008). *Vygotsky and research*. London: Routledge.

Dolya, G. (2010). *Vygotsky in action in the early years. The "Key to Learning" curriculum*. New York: Routledge.

Fleer, M. (2010). *Early learning and development. Cultural-historical concepts of play*. Cambridge: Cambridge University Press.

Kozulin, A. (1990). *Vygotsky's psychology. A biography of ideas*. Brighton: HarvesterWheatsheaf.

Tuna, A., & Hayden, J. (Eds.). (2010). *Early childhood programs as the doorway to social cohesion. Application of Vygotsky's ideas from an East-West perspective*. Cambridge: Cambridge Scholar Publishing.

van der Veer, R. (2008). Multiple readings of Vygotsky. In B. van Oers, W. Wardekker, E. Elbers, & R. van der Veer (Eds.), *The transformation of learning. Advances in cultural-historical activity theory*. Cambridge: Cambridge University Press.

van der Veer, R., & Valsiner, J. (1991). *Understanding Vygotsky. A quest for synthesis*. Oxford: Blackwell.

van Oers, B. (2009). Developmental education: improving participation in cultural practices. In M. Fleer, M. Hedegaard, & J. Tudge (Eds.), *Childhood studies and the impact of globalization: Policies and practices at global and local levels – World Yearbook of Education 2009* (pp. 293–317). New York: Routledge.

van Oers, B. (2010a). Children's enculturation through play. In L. Brooker & S. Edwards (Eds.), *Engaging play* (pp. 195–209). Maidenhead: McGraw Hill.

van Oers, B. (2010b). The emergence of mathematical thinking in the context of play. *Educational Studies in Mathematics, 74*(1), 23–37.

van Oers, B. (2011). Where is the child? Controversy in the Neo-Vygotskian approach to child development. *Mind, Culture, and Activity, 18*, 84–88.

van Oers, B., & Duijkers, D. (2012). Teaching in a play-based curriculum: Theory, practice and evidence of Developmental Education for young children. *Journal of Curriculum Studies, 44*(1), 1–24.

Veraksa, N., & van Oers, B. (2011). Early childhood Education from a Russian perspective. Editorial to the special issue. *International Journal of Early Years Education, 19*(1), 5–18.

Vygotsky, L. S. (1997). *Educational psychology*. Boca Raton: St Lucie Press.

Wardekker, W. L. (2000). Criteria for the quality of inquiry. *Mind, Culture, and Activity, 7*(4), 259–272.

Wertsch, J. (1985). *Vygotsky and the social formation of mind*. New York: Oxford University Press.

Index

Printed by Printforce, the Netherlands

Critical Care Focus

Critical Care Focus series

Also available:

H F Galley (ed) Critical Care Focus 1: *Renal Failure,* 1999.

H F Galley (ed) Critical Care Focus 2: *Respiratory Failure,* 1999.